The Public Library of Nashville and Davidson County

STRANGE AND SECRET PEOPLES

STRANGE AND SECRET PEOPLES

Fairies and Victorian Consciousness

Carole G. Silver

New York   Oxford

OXFORD UNIVERSITY PRESS

1999

Oxford University Press

Oxford   New York
Athens   Auckland   Bangkok   Bogotá   Buenos Aires   Calcutta
Cape Town   Chennai   Dar es Salaam   Delhi   Florence   Hong Kong   Istanbul
Karachi   Kuala Lumpur   Madrid   Melbourne   Mexico City   Mumbai
Nairobi   Paris   São Paulo   Singapore   Taipei   Tokyo   Toronto   Warsaw

and associated companies in
Berlin   Ibadan

Published by Oxford University Press, Inc.
198 Madison Avenue, New York, New York 10016

Oxford is a registered trademark of Oxford University Press

Library of Congress Cataloging-in-Publication Data
Silver, Carole G.
Strange and secret peoples :
fairies and Victorian consciousness /
Carole G. Silver.
p.   cm.
Includes bibliographical references and index.
ISBN 0-19-512199-6
I. Fairies.   2. Folklore—Great Britain.   3. Great Britain—
Social conditions—19th century.   I. Title.
GR141.S55   1998
398.21—dc21   98-10318

1 3 5 7 9 8 6 4 2

Printed in the United States of America
on acid-free paper

TO
CARL RAY WOODRING

ACKNOWLEDGMENTS

THE GENESIS OF THIS BOOK WAS A statement made by my nephew, then six years old, who announced that his recently deceased grandmother could be found "among the fairies." His remark led me to think briefly about the cultural confusion between the angels and the tribes of elfin and, at length, about how frequently the latter found their way into the Victorian and early-twentieth-century literature I taught and wrote about. The actual research and writing of *Strange and Secret Peoples* was begun some twelve years ago; it could not have been carried out without the aid of numerous friends and colleagues and of libraries and librarians on three continents.

I am forever indebted to the British Library and to the wonderful, eccentric collection of books on the occult at the Harry Price Library in the tower of London University's Senate Building. My debts to the Library of the (British) Folklore Society at University College, London, and to the Columbia University Libraries are almost as great, and I have also been graciously aided by the staffs of the New York Public Library, the Bobst Library of New York University, the Library of the New York Academy of Medicine, the Special Collections Library of the American Museum of Natural History, the Pierpont Morgan Library, the Henry E. Huntington Library, the Irish National Library in Dublin, the Durban Municipal Library, and the libraries of the University of the Wittswatersrand in South Africa—as well as the Heidi Steinberg library of my own institution, Yeshiva University.

The pictures constitute a second story and, although I could utilize only a small number of the images I found, I must acknowledge the numerous curators who pulled out their fairy paintings, drawings, pottery, and decorated tiles and let me look at their notes. The people at the Victoria and Albert Museum, the Tate Gallery, and the Maas Gallery in London were especially helpful. I had great fun examining the fairy paintings at the Fitzwilliam Museum of Cambridge University, the National Galleries of Scotland in Edinburgh, and the Glasgow Art Gallery at Kelvingrove, as well as at the museums in Manchester, Birmingham, and Liverpool. I am indebted to my curatorial buddies, Katharine Lochnan of the Art Gallery of Ontario, Peter Cormack of the William Morris Gallery, and Susan Casteras formerly of the Mellon Centre at Yale, for their counsel on how to find and whom to talk to about materials.

Then, too, I cannot sufficiently thank my friends and fellow Victorianists for letting me "try out" materials through papers at seminars and conferences and articles in journals. An early version of parts of the introduction and first chapter was published by Adrienne Munich in *Browning Institute Studies* 14 (1986), and an equally early version of the third chapter, "East of the Sun," was published in *Woman and Nation*, edited by Nina Auerbach, a special issue of *Tulsa Studies in Women's Literature* in Fall 1987. My fellow participants in the CUNY Graduate Center Victorian Seminar, in particular Rachel Brownstein, Anne Humpherys, Gerhard Joseph, Norman Kelvin, John Maynard, Reneé Overholser, Jeffrey Spear, and Herbert Sussman, have patiently listened to a work in progress and offered helpful suggestions and wise comments.

From the beginning, other friends have been willing to hear my tales of the fairies, help me find images of them, and push me to focus my ideas about them. At various stages, sections and drafts of this project have been read by Zelda Boyd, Laurel Hatvary, Norman Levy, Sally Mitchell, Adrienne Munich, Judith Neaman, Ellen Schrecker, and Carl Woodring.

Institutional help has been equally important; a fellowship provided by the National Endowment for the Humanities in 1986–87, when this book was in its inchoate beginnings, gave me the psychological as well as financial support necessary to begin a journey into uncharted waters. Yeshiva University has been most generous and I am especially indebted to Dr. Karen Bacon, Dean of Stern College for Women, for her endless assistance whether in the form of a student research assistant, a travel grant, or aid with the funds for an index. I cannot overlook the whole-hearted support of this project by Oxford University Press in the United States. I am grateful for the time and effort spent on the book by Susan Barba, and, above all, by E. Susan Chang, my intelligent and enthusiastic editor. My deepest gratitude, however, must be reserved for two people: first, for Carl Woodring who, as my Ph.D. advisor many years ago, taught me to "connect," and who has remained an invaluable friend and resource to this day and, second, for Norman Levy—South African activist, historian, and husband—whose sympathetic reading of my work and measureless enrichment of my life transcend acknowledgment.

New York
February 1998

C.G.S.

CONTENTS

LIST OF
ILLUSTRATIONS

XIII

There is a secret Common-Wealth of Elves, Fauns, and Fairies, living beneath the earth [of Scotland]. . . . They are distributed in Tribes and Orders; and have children, nurses, marriages, deaths and burials, in appearance even as we. . . .

—The Reverend Robert Kirk,
Minister of Aberfoyle,
Scotland, 1691

Just near to Senne, are found to this day a strange and separate people of Mongol type . . . one of those "fragments of forgotten peoples" of the "sunset bound of Lyonesse" of whom Tennyson speaks.

—Henry Jenner,
Local Secretary for Cornwall of
the Society of Antiquaries,
Cornwall, 1910

STRANGE AND SECRET PEOPLES

INTRODUCTION

GREETINGS FROM
ANOTHER WORLD
Romantic Rediscoveries

I N A LETTER, QUOTED BY JONATHAN COTT in *Beyond the Looking Glass*, his friend, David Dalton remarked on "how elemental the Victorians were, how intact that cord was that tied them to savage Celtic tradition, almost like an underground railway transporting treasures from the incredible depths of the past to the very door of the crystal palace" (Acknowledgements).

This book is about that cord or, more accurately, the web that connected the Victorians to a vast network of traditions—Celtic, Norse, and native—and enabled what Dalton perhaps hyperbolically considers "the most repressed society ever" to ventilate its obsessions and anxieties. At its center are the elfin peoples, for the cultural preoccupation with the secret kingdom of the fairies is a hallmark of the era.

That the Victorians were utterly fascinated by the fairies is demonstrated by the art, drama, and literature they created and admired. Their abiding interest shows in the numerous, uniquely British fairy paintings that flourished between the 1830s and the 1870s—pictures in part inspired by nationalism and Shakespeare, in part as protest against the strictly useful and material, but in either case, as attempts to reconnect the actual and the occult. (When fairy painting lost its glamour, the impulse that had

3

spawned it issued in the fairy illustrations of Dulac and Rackham and in the photographing of the fairies themselves.)

The same preoccupation with the elfin peoples is manifested in the constant staging, throughout the era, of spectacular productions of Shakespeare's fairy plays, *A Midsummer Night's Dream* and *The Tempest*,[1] as well as in repeated performances of romantic fairy ballets (including *La Sylphide* and *Giselle*), operas, and children's plays and pantomines, some derived from the Bard, others from actual folklore or from literary fairy tales—and all immensely popular. As this enthusiasm for the fairies swept all branches of the arts, their images appeared on the wallpapers in Victorian bedrooms and nurseries (as, for example, in the designs of Walter Crane) and even on the vases of sitting rooms.[2] The Victorians' enthrallment is vividly revealed in the fairy tales and fantasies, written for both children and adults, that surface to create the "Golden Age of Children's Literature" and to begin the passion of the twentieth century for fantasies for grownups. That authors as various as Dickens and George Eliot, as diverse as Thomas Carlyle and Oscar Wilde, participated in the exploration of the elfin world says much about its power and centrality.

But the fascination with the fairies manifests itself in other ways, as well. It is evidenced in the society's concern with the "occult beings" found at seances; with the spirits, poltergeists, and elementals of Spiritualist, Rosicrucian, and Theosophical belief; and the attempts to connect these creatures to the elfin species known to folklore. Yet, above all, the enchantment that the fairies wrought shows in the flood of information on their habits and lifestyles, the materials collected, analyzed, published, and made famous by the British folklorists. For the study of the fairies appealed to those in the new disciplines emerging as the "social sciences," to a rising group of folklore theorists determined to explain and to preserve England's rapidly vanishing past, to cultural anthropologists, anxious to connect the local to the meaningful and universal and to explore the evolution of peoples and societies, and even to archaeologists, digging for the origins of beliefs. The theories that folklorists (supported by the social sciences) postulated to rationalize the irrational, to explain the supernatural and belief in it simultaneously explain the culture itself—exposing fears and fantasies close to the Victorian unconscious. Looking at the ways Victorians looked at fairies provides an insight into the underlying attitudes of a society.

Thus, this book is a study in cultural history, an attempt to recontextualize a Victorian concern and hence recapture a legacy that we in the twentieth century have lost. As such it proposes and investigates new areas for study. Few scholars have been aware of the importance of fairy lore, though Michael Booth in *Victorian Spectacular Theatre* astutely comments that "the acceptance and rapid growth of fairyland as fit subject matter for literature, painting and the stage from the 1820s to the 1840s and its survival at least until the First World War is one of the most remarkable phenomena of nineteenth-century culture" (p. 36). No one has examined this phenomenon in detail.

This book is also an archaeology of a culture—that is, an examination of layers of meaning, of the ways in which Victorian folklorists and theorists built upon traditional and inherited materials and, through selection and revision, raised a superstructure that was then further developed and elaborated by Victorian painters, writers, and essayists. My emphasis is on how pervasively the fairies and their lore infiltrated and transformed mainstream Victorian culture, on what the fairy presence hints at or signifies. Sometimes the influence is overt; more often it is subtle, a matter of allusion or metonymy or encoding. There is a valuable subtext, for example, beneath Mary Garth's telling of "Rumpelstiltskin" at Mr. Vincy's New Year's party in George Eliot's *Middlemarch* (1871–72). For, while the story of the evil dwarf was first translated from the Grimms' *Kinder- und Hausmärchen* by Edgar Taylor in 1823, and had by the new year of 1832 become quite popular in England (and thus accessible to the children of Middlemarch),[3] significant issues relating to the tale were not discussed in popular magazines and journals until the early 1870s. Only then did folklorists begin hypothesizing about such issues as the power of the name in primitive thought and, most directly relevant to the novel's plot, about supernatural pledges and the sacrifice of the first-born child. Rosamond Vincy, sitting placidly in the room where Mary tells the tale, is clearly connected by her "netting" to the foolish spinning-maiden of the tale while her willful miscarriage—the "sacrifice" of what would have been her first-born child, is mentioned right before the tale is told.

George Eliot's allusion suggests that fairy lore and fairy faith penetrated even the so-called realist tradition. Comments made by those less committed to realism are even more revelatory of the cultural beliefs experienced by the Victorians and either buried or forgotten in our era. Andrew Lang, the folklorist and author, creator of a long series of colored "Fairy Books" —Blue, Green, Red, Yellow—(some thirteen of which were published between 1889 and 1910), remarked that "the children to whom and for whom they [fairy tales] were told represent the young age of man" (*Blue Fairy Book*, p. xii). Almost offhandedly, he evidenced a Victorian attitude toward childhood, fairy lore, and prehistory that we have, for the most part, overlooked. Not only was he seeing such lore as "the uncontaminated record of our cultural infancy" (p. xii) and creating an analogy between children and "primitive" peoples, but he was assuming that, through the lore, the child had direct access to the prehistoric past—that childhood actually provided entry to a primitive or lost state and could safely restore this world to adults. Just as Lang connected children to the "savages" newly discovered by explorers and travelers, so others connected various groups of supernaturals to the plant and animal species of the biological world and to the tribes and races of Victorian ethnology.

Such connections are meaningful—linkages between ideas like that of the reality of supernatural "changelings" substituted for human children and the actual, but unspoken belief that incestuous or "unnatural" unions could breed such monsters—confluences established between the keeping of a supernatural bride by taking and hiding her tail, cap, or plumage and the belief of Victorian marriage historians that, in "primitive" marriage rites, the male partner often took an article of dress from the female as a pledge or symbol of his marital power (see, for example, Westermarck 2: 526). Whether these ethnological statements (and, more generally, the assumptions of Victorian anthropology) are true or false is not the question; they were believed and accepted and are, thus, part of the ethos of the age.

A few caveats must be noted. Although its subject is, in large part, the uses of folklore in nineteenth-century Britain, this is not a book primarily about Victorian children's literature or the fairy tales so popular in the period. While such literature serves as an excellent reflector of the dominant ideas, values, and fantasies of an era, and I have mentioned and used some of the works of the Golden Age of Children's Literature, I have focused on other, often less well-known materials for adults. Because these are sometimes rare or difficult to locate, I have found it necessary at moments to summarize plot and discuss narrative structure more than I might otherwise do. Moreover (last of the caveats) this book is not a complete study of all aspects of Victorian fairylore. Instead, I have selected segments to examine in detail, culling fragments that enthralled the Victorians and especially interested me. Thus, I have explored questions of the development of interest in the fairy world, looked at issues of origin and of belief, and examined changelings, dwarfs and midgets, fairy-brides, the slaugh, and other representations of evil rather than such topics as the proliferation of "flower fairies."

Although this is not a chronological study, I think it necessary to begin with the English romantics. Because of their nationalism, because of their search for a new and different past, because of their antipathy to arid rationality, they revived the interest in the fairy world and lore. Thus, I start with an overview of their attitudes toward and contributions to the study of the kingdoms of elfin—a survey without which it would be difficult to evaluate Victorian contributions. The main part of my book, however, is not shaped as a survey. Instead I examine a number of themes that preoccupied the British in the period from the 1840s to the early 1920s, thus creating a series of studies in fairy lore. Although I do indicate when motifs or attitudes become especially prominent (and this is often between 1880 and 1910), my emphasis is less on the development of an idea than upon its continuity and its variations.

After a look at the romantics, I move to a more specific exploration of theories the Victorians postulated about the genesis of and thus the nature and behavior of the fairy tribes. The same passion for origins that propelled

George Eliot's Casaubon to seek the key to all mythologies and, more profitably, that impelled Charles Darwin to search for the primeval sources of human nature, led folklorists and occultists to quest for answers about the origins of the fairies. Logically, the issue of genesis involved questions of belief and actuality. Did the fairies exist? How did belief in them originate? From the 1840s to the 1920s various explanations of fairy origin and nature jockeyed for preeminence. Throughout the whole period, there were those who believed in the existence of fairies on the basis of experiential evidence: they had seen or interacted with supernatural creatures, and they offered memorates (personal accounts of experiences with the supernatural) providing records of their experiences. Others provided explanations that I have grouped together as "religious views" or "scientific views." Religious explanations, whether Christian, pagan, or occultist, assumed that fairies were spiritual beings and had not originated on this earth. Whether they were the fallen angels of the folk and the orthodox, the elementals of the Theosophists and the occultists, the "survivals" of the old gods or the spirits of the dead that many of the mainstream folklore theorists thought them, fairies (though not necessarily believed *in*) were linked to belief. Scientific explanations were equally varied, ranging from the linguistic analysis stemming from Max Müller and the solar mythologists through occultist doctrines of separate evolution.

After 1859 and Darwin, explanations of origin changed. Theories of cultural evolution, championed by Victorian anthropologists and anthropological folklorists, explained that paralleling biology, cultures themselves were evolutionary processes. Fairies had actually originated in "savage" societies and the lore about them was a reflection—sometimes accurate, sometimes distorted—of savage ideas and customs. Aided by the new science of archaeology, euhemerism (the belief that myths and folk beliefs arise from actual historical persons or events) became a major explanation of fairy origins—raising issues related to Victorian ideas of race and empire. Were the originals of the fairies a lowly, perhaps aboriginal British tribe or were they a superior group who brought magical knowledge to those they invaded? The new euhemerism climaxed in the 1890s in David MacRitchie's once famous, now discredited "pygmy theory" of fairy origins. By the turn of the century, however, Darwin reinterpreted (or misinterpreted) gave rise to the idea of fairies as invisible life-forms, not yet understood, that had developed on a separate branch of the evolutionary tree—but that would soon be classified and verified by scientific means.

Science and pseudo-science play significant roles in the succeeding chapter on changelings. It deals with a once widespread but now forgotten Victorian preoccupation: the idea found in folklore collections, newspapers, and journals, as well as in fiction, that a loved one, usually a child or young woman, might be supernaturally abducted and, in some cases, replaced by an inferior and monstrous substitute. What such changelings were, in popular, medical, and social terms; how they were depicted, treated, and exorcised; and how folklore theorists explained their origins and the survival of belief in their existence constitute a study of Victorian power relations—of attitudes toward inferiors and "others."

What is surprising is the way in which "changelingism"—a folklore belief—melded with assumptions about evolution, race, and class to create a fantasy image that both displaced and conveyed the anxiety of educated middle-class Victorians. Significantly, the figure of the changeling, reconstructed, came to represent to the middle class the possibility of the loss of security, of power, and of hope for the future.

The figure of the swan maiden or fairy bride, explored in chapter 3, encodes a different cultural message. Tales of supernatural brides and the ways in which they were interpreted constitute a sociocultural history of Victorian attitudes toward women and marriage. In a period of debates on the origins of matrimony, on women's right to property and to divorce, an era of the discussion of gender power relations, swan-maiden tales raised questions about female power and sexuality as well as about female superiority, equality, or inferiority. They also made disturbing comments about parental responsibility for and power over the children of the union. Suggesting the otherness of women, the analysis of these tales raised questions about female bestiality. Were women originally animals needing control, as some said, or so highly evolved—like Sue Bridehead in Thomas Hardy's *Jude the Obscure*—that they had outgrown sex and even maternity? What disturbed the folklorists most, however, was the issue of divorce or freedom implied by the tales. When, they queried, did women have the right to leave their mates? What about the children? Was deserting them "unnatural"? Rendering fairy brides and tales of them acceptable became a Victorian preoccupation. Whether the process involved mythifying them as ancestral figures or subduing and muting them (like the "Little Mermaid"), these supernatural rebels were assimilated into the culture of their era. While images of the fairy bride suggested women's desire for autonomy and equality in marriage, they also encapsulated men's fantasies about capture and power, hence appealing to the culture at large.

Dwarfs and pygmies, on the other hand, haunted Victorian imaginations in far harsher ways. Chapter 4, "Little Goblin Men," discusses racial myths and mythic races as it explores the conflation of natural and supernatural dwarfs, their equation with elementals and goblins, and ultimately their identification with malice and evil. It emphasizes how the "discovery" of the African Pygmies in the 1870s led to the racializing and remythifying of dwarfs in general and to the creation of new and frightening monsters for Victorian fantasy and fiction. What I find particularly interesting is that the significant change in the status of dwarfs was caused not only by overt racism (it was not merely that the Pygmies were black that made them so frightening) but also by a more subtle, covert idea of inferiority. Pygmies and dwarfs were dangerous because they were "Turanians"—survivals of a race earlier than *Homo sapiens* that had dropped out of the grand march of evolution. Thus, as crude, primitive anthropoids such creatures epitomized social and anthropological fears of regression and reversion.

"The Faces of Evil," chapter 5, suggests how other species of fairies became further embodiments of evil and generators of cultural anxiety. The host, horde, or slaugh—a faceless and featureless mob that rides the wind or leads mortals astray or takes them "away" by abducting bodies or souls—is the folkloric equivalent of the demos. Not unlike the little goblin men, the elfin hordes are perceived as forces of anarchic barbarism, harassing, invading, and destroying the civilized world. Some are identified with unruly or destructive forces of nature; some are viewed as combatants in a constant struggle with others of nature's offspring and with each other; still others are perceived as the supernatural "nuisances" of Victorian seances and occult phenomena. Still other elfin species were connected to the coming of death, to the guardianship of the dead, and most frighteningly, to the possibility of their resurrection. Here, in the varied forms of the banshee, the bean-nigh, the glaistig, and the lhiannon-shee, individual female fairies were connected with death, witchcraft, vampirism, and parasitism. Not surprisingly, when evil was endowed with features its face was frequently female. Moreover, behind the projection onto the fairies of fears of the mob or of "free" and sexually destructive women lay the culture's concern about failing institutional restraints—for example, about such factors as the weakening of the patriarchal and hierarchical underpinnings of the church.

A final chapter, "Farewell to the Fairies," bids the elfin tribes adieu, while it explores the reasons for their apparent vanishing. Perhaps paradoxically, I argue that the industrialization and urbanization of the modern age were less damaging to the fairies than their very popularity—that their excessive and trivialized representation in literature designed for the nursery, coupled with the vast publicity attendant on the Cottingley fairy photographs, forced them back underground. Closing with the idea that the elfin peoples have merely metamophosed once again, I suggest that their farewell is perpetual—that their departure is an integral part of the construct of their existence.

The Romantics and the Fairies

In different forms, the fairies have always been among us. They have inhabited the British Isles for at least fifteen hundred years; though sometimes forced underground, they have always reemerged. It was with their resurfacing at the end of the eighteenth century, in part through the offices of the poets and antiquaries among the English romantics, that the systematic, analytical study of their types, traits, and origins really began. For it is in English romanticism, in the attitudes of its adherents to the elfin peoples and their worlds, that the roots of the Victorian fairy fascination lie.

Impelled in part by political and nationalistic concerns, the English romantics began to explore their own supernatural heritage. Perhaps they felt the need to find rich fairy lore to compete with that of France and, later, Germany. French tales, both traditional and literary (especially those of Perrault and Madame D'Aulnoy), dominated England, while both the Märchen and the research of the Brothers Grimm were universally admired. There was a sense that fairies — utilized by Chaucer and redesigned by Shakespeare — were part of England's precious heritage. Nostalgia for a fading British past was yet another factor. Many agreed with the poet-folklorist James Hogg that the fairies were leaving England. The nation was growing too industrial and technological, too urban and material for their health and welfare. It became important to locate the fairies and chronicle their acts before they departed forever.

Themselves influenced by the ballad revival of the eighteenth century, especially by Bishop Percy's *Reliques of Ancient English Poetry* (1765), and by such works as William Collins's "Ode on the Popular Superstitions of the Highlands of Scotland," the romantics began to explore the closely related genres of folk tale, local legend, and fairy memorate. Their legacy to the Victorians was a rich one, including the "fairy" poetry of Coleridge, Southey, Keats, and Shelley; that of lesser lights like Tom Moore and Thomas Hood; and the now forgotten work of James Hogg, "The Ettrick Shepherd," as well as the supernatural fiction of Hogg, Sir Walter Scott, Allan Cunningham, and others.[4] In another discipline, again connected to English nationalism, romantic painters, particularly Henry Fuseli and William Blake, created fairy paintings that were to be important visual sources of the Victorian genre. But the most significant single element of the romantic legacy to the Victorians was the beginning of "fairy scholarship," especially the major studies produced by Scott. Along with the two great early nineteenth-century collectors of folklore, Thomas Crofton Croker (the author of the first collection of folk tales in the British Isles gathered through fieldwork) and Thomas Keightley (one of the early and important comparativist collectors), Scott and his friends — Robert Southey, Allan Cunningham, and James Hogg — collected and examined primary materials for a British fairyland. As these romantic antiquaries speculated about the possible origins of belief, described and classified preternatural creatures, and collected lore about them, they began to delineate the shapes of future research.

Because of both his fame and his personal force, Scott became a central figure in the collection and utilization of fairy lore. He had believed in fairies as a child and seems never to have entirely lost his faith in "second sight" — both the ability to foretell the future and the power to see "things invisible to mortal sight" including fairies. But his adult view of the "good neighbours," shaped by the French and Scottish Enlightenments, was increasingly rationalistic. Yet he repeatedly returned to fairy lore, utilizing it, alluding to it, and explaining it. His major prose essays on the fairy world—the essay "On the Fairies of Popular Superstition," in *Minstrelsy of the Scottish Border* (1802–3) and *Letters on Demonology and Witchcraft* (1830)—reveal an intense fascination with the same aspects of fairy lore: the sources of the elfin peoples, the beliefs in changelings and fairy abductions, the connections between fairies and witches, and the use of euphemisms as safeguards against fairy malice. Legalistic and logical in his investigations of the reality of preternatural creatures, Scott could never quite deny the "abstract possibility" that such phenomena as "apparitions" existed, "for these," he noted, "must be admitted by everyone who believes in a Deity" (*Letters*, p. 116). And, though he tended to dismiss fairies as originating in the misperceptions of simple folk, he could not altogether deny the possibility of their existence either. As Coleman Parsons indicates, Scott's "receptivity was crossed by doubt and his scepticism by glimmering conviction" (p. 9).

Scott's changing opinions on fairy origins influenced the views of his contemporaries. In 1803, he had speculated that the fairies were essentially fictional creatures, derived from Gothic tribal traditions of elves, to which had been added Eastern influences, chivalric tales, classical myths, Christian beliefs, and finally, the imaginative visions of the Elizabethan poets and playwrights (*Minstrelsy*, p. 306). By the time he wrote *Letters on Demonology*, he had become convinced that a residue of real occurences formed the basis of the belief in fairies. An early historical realist or euhemerist, he thought the prototypes of the fairies were duergars, or dwarfs—distorted images of the early Lapps, Letts, and Finns, peoples who had inspired superstitious fears in the hearts of those who encountered them. He had probably derived this idea from Paul Henri Mallet's extremely popular book, *Northern Antiquities* (trans. 1770), specifically from the author's suggestion that the "Laplanders, who are still as famous for their magic, as remarkable for the lowness of their stature; pacific even to a degree of cowardice, but of a mechanic industry which formerly must have appeared very considerable" (Mallet 2:42) were the originals of the mythic dwarfs.[5] But unlike Mallet, Scott believed that these figures had been fused in the popular mind with the more attractive and social Celtic fairies (derived mainly from Irish myth) to form the modern species (*Letters*, p. 103).

Moreover, Scott's theories about the origins and nature of the fairies permeated his fictions and thus gained wider currency through the enormous popularity of his poems and novels. He makes Fenella in *Peveril of the Peak* (1822) a fairy changeling, marked by a composite of traits from a variety of supernatural creatures; Norna's dwarf, Nick Strumpfer or Pacolet, in *The Pirate* (1822) is turned into an almost parodic semisupernatural duergar, a mute hideous, demonic creature.[6] His most famous preternatural characters, the White Lady of Avenel in *The Monastery* (1820) and Elshie, the reclusive dwarf of the brief romance, *The Black Dwarf* (1816), reveal the breadth and bias of his studies. The White Lady is a sort of supernatural polyglot, part elemental—that is, a spirit of one of the four elements as described by Paracelsus—she is "of the race of Ariel" and thus a sylph. But, inspired by Baron Friedrich de la Motte Fouqué's *Undine*, Scott also depicts her as an undine or water nymph; she is also part banshee, part brownie, and part kelpie. Speaking only in verse or through gesture, she gnomically defines herself, revealing how much Scott knows of the traditions of fairy lore. She is

> Something betwixt heaven and hell,
> Something that neither stood nor fell,
> . . . .
> Neither substance quite, nor shadow,
> Haunting lonely moor and meadow. . .
> Aping in fantastic fashion
> Every change of human passion, . . . (p. 97)

In these apparently simple lines, Scott encapsulates much traditional belief, materials he and his contemporaries have already uncovered. The White Lady hints at both her nature and her origins in depicting herself as "betwixt heaven and hell," since folk belief identifies the fairies with the angels of Lucifer's rebellion who either chose to remain uncommitted to God or Satan or who, though ejected from heaven, had not yet reached hell when its gates were locked. Her description of herself as something between substance and shadow, as barely visible or only indirectly perceivable ("A form that men spy/With . . . half-shut eye"[p. 73]) echoes repeated accounts of how fairies are usually seen by humans—in dream, daydream or trance, or out of the corner of an eye. But most significant is the comment on her emotional nature. She "apes" rather than "feels" human passion. Her actions, Scott tells his readers, are guided not by "feeling or reasoning" but by "temporary benevolence or caprice" (p. xiv). The capriciousness she manifests is one of the essential traits of fairy being, and the White Lady prefigures in large part the ambiguous female fairies with whom the Victorians will be so fascinated.

Elshie, the Black Dwarf of Scott's novel of 1816, is an even more complex and successful fusion of natural and supernatural traits. Though defined as human, his characteristics include those of malicious earth spirits, Germanic duergars, and those associated euhemeristically with the undersized Lapps or aboriginal British. But his portrait is significant for an additional reason; it becomes a case study in the making of euhemerism. As Scott explains in his preface, the fictional character is based on David Ritchie, a seriously deformed dwarf Scott had met in 1797 and who had retreated to the wilderness and built a small fortress-house there. Superstitious—to the point of keeping an elf-stone and planting rowan trees (safeguards against fairies and witches) around the place where he wished to be buried—

Ritchie was thought of as "uncanny" by the local villagers. Commenting on Davie's encouragement of the belief in his supernatural traits, Scott noted that it empowered the dwarf and "power was what David Ritchie desired to possess" (p. 187). Explaining that "the author has invested . . . him with some qualities which made him appear, in the eyes of the vulgar, a man possessed of supernatural power" (p. 185), Scott euhemeristically magnifies these preternatural traits. His Elshie has the gift of "second sight," the skill in healing, the vast amounts of gold (explained only at the end of the book), and above all the irritability and craftiness of the traditional duergar or supernatural dwarf. He uses the power that comes from people's believing him supernatural to impress and subordinate all around him. He creates illusion, selecting a place thought haunted for his dwelling, letting people believe that he has built his house of massive stones unassisted by others, refusing to explain how, though ostensibly poor, he has huge sums of money to dispense. His ability to accurately foretell the future through his "second sight" is never rationalized, nor is the efficacy of his cursing ever explained. Although he turns out to be a fairy godfather in goblin's clothing, responsible for the "happy ending" of the romance, his portrait maintains its strange waver between the natural and supernatural. By the end of the romance he has been simultaneously humanized and elevated into a folklore fairy.

When Elshie (finally revealed as Sir Edward Mauley) vanishes at the end of the tale, readers are not told "the place to which . . . [he] had finally retired, or the manner of his death, or the place of his burial" (p. 382). Simultaneously, his sudden disappearance leads some ordinary folk among the novel's characters to maintain that he has been taken away by the Devil, while others are sure that his disappearance is only temporary and that he may be seen (like the Heathcliff of Emily Brontë's later *Wuthering Heights*) among the hills. As time passes, Scott tells us, and the villagers retain "according to custom, a more vivid recollection of his wild and desperate language, than of the benevolent tendency of most of his actions, he is usually identified with the malignant demon called the Man of the Moors"(p. 383). Thus fairies are made, and "the evils most dreaded and deprecated by the inhabitants of that pastoral country are ascribed to the agency of the BLACK DWARF" (p. 383). But the *either/or* of Davie's existence and nature remains and Scott's Todorovian wavering between natural and supernatural impulses and explanations is one important romantic attitude. Moreover, Scott's work is significant both because he makes his natural/supernatural creatures and their actions palatable to a large, middle-class audience and because he espouses and promotes euhemeristic explanations of the origin and nature of the elfin people.

Several of Scott's fellow collectors of lore were almost as important in their contributions to fairy lore but somewhat less hesitant in their belief than he. Allan Cunningham, friend and admirer of Scott and Hogg, remarked in 1828 that he had only recently lost his fairy faith. He, too, had once believed and now lamented, "would to God I could do so still! for the woodland and the moor have lost for me a great portion of their romance, since my faith in their [the fairies'] existence has departed" (qtd. in Parsons, p. 8). Yet, it was Cunningham who popularized the anecdote about William Blake's attending a fairy funeral and who perpetrated one of the major romantic works of fake lore, the *Remains of Nithsdale and Galloway Song* (1810). Like Thomas Chatterton, he persuaded a publisher, in this case the engraver Robert Cromek, to print works he described as "old songs," traditional folk ballads, but which were really his own modern poems.[7]

Cunningham's own tales, printed as *Traditional Tales of the English and Scottish Peasantry* (1822), though ostensibly based on folklore, are almost as fake as the *Remains*. Written in what Richard Dorson calls a "windy, wordy, artificial style," they are clearly "Literary Tales Faintly Suggested by Oral Traditions of the Scottish Peasantry" (*British Folklorists*, p. 122). Yet, they, too, introduce what will become important themes for the Victorians. "The Haunted Ships," for example, is an embellished version of a convincing account of a fairy abduction, first told by Cunningham in his appendix to the *Remains*. Another tale, "Elphin Irving, The Fairies' Cupbearer," has a poignancy all its own. Really a version of the ballad of Tamlane, this tale of the elfin kidnapping of a handsome young man and of his twin sister's failed attempt to rescue him derives its force both from the cultural fascination with the kidnap motif and from the author's reasoned hesitation between natural and supernatural explanations of events.

However, Cunningham's most important contributions to fairy lore and to the later compilers of it were neither his poems nor his tales but the appendices and notes he provided for the *Remains*. A long comment on the nature of brownies, and his most important appendix, "The Character of the Scottish Lowland Fairies, From the Popular Belief of Nithsdale and Galloway," are collections of fresh and colorful lore. Less sceptical than Scott, Cunningham still half-believes in fairy existence. Moreover, he attempts to incorporate folklore into orthodox religious belief. He suggests, for example, that brownies were created "to relieve mankind under the drudgery of original sin" and that this is the reason that they are thus "forbidden to accept of wages or bribes" (p. 265). Like Scott in the *Minstrelsy*, he traces fairy origins to the Peris of the Arabs and Persians, later blended with gothic mythology. Like Scott, too, he goes on to describe the elfin peoples, elaborating on their appearance, their habits, their haunts, and their activities; he tells tales of fairy abductions, banquets, changelings, midwives, and, most interestingly, of the "Fairy Rade" (or "Raid"). He, too, appears to feel that fairy faith is good for ordinary, rural people; he seems pleased that belief "still lingers in those remote regions of simplicity and primitive ignorance, where the torch of science has not yet reached, or sheds doubtful and uncertain light" (p. 294). Yet, perhaps to align himself with science and her light, he indicates his suspicion that fairies — unlike brownies? — are mainly the products of human imagination. They have "a vein of earthly grossness, which marks them Beings created by human invention" (p. 300), he suggests. Yet, again wavering between his rational and emotional responses, he ends his appendix with a lovely "Farewell to the Fairies," one which notes that since fairies cannot live on "land once ripped by the plowshare or the sward once passed over by the scythe . . . the quick progress of Lowland agriculture will completely overthrow their empire" (pp. 309–10). Even now, he mourns, only a "few solitary and dejected fugitives" remain (p. 310).

For Cunningham's friend and more famous contemporary James Hogg, "The Ettrick Shepherd," the issues were similar although the tendency to believe was stronger. A working shepherd for part of his life, Hogg was in touch with the living fairy faith of his part of Scotland. As E. A. Waite (himself a brilliant scholar of the occult) described Hogg at the end of the nineteenth century, he was one "for whom the doctrine of spiritual essences was still true, for whom those elemental intelligences 'Which have their haunts in dale and piny mountain,' . . . still survived in the 'faith of reason'"(Intro, p. xxxiii). Hogg's stance is exemplified by one of the characters he creates, Old Barnaby, the shepherd-hero of "The Wool Gatherer." Explaining that he and other intelligent local people do not believe in frivolous fairies, in "fantastic bogles an' spirits," Barnaby adds, "but we believe in a' the apparitions that warn o' death, that save life, an' that discover guilt" (Hogg 1:70). Hogg comes by his beliefs partially through descent, for in another essay, called "Odd Characters," he tells of his ancestor, William Laidlawe, known as Will o' Phaup, a shepherd who was "the last man of this wild region, who heard, saw, and conversed with the fairies; and that not once or twice, but at sundry times and seasons" (1:409). Hogg tells the incidents passed down to him without comment, yet they reverberate with his belief.

Hogg's literary tales of the supernatural have the same aura of conviction and authenticity; they are studies in character and psychology that clearly influenced such Victorians as Charles Dickens and Sheridan LeFanu. "The Brownie of the Black Haggs" is a brilliant study of a woman's love and hatred, desire for and disgust with her grotesque preternatural servant. No one quite knows what the servant Merodach is, though readers learn that he "was a boy in form, and an antediluvian in feature" (1:330), that he works harder than others, is preternaturally strong, and lives entirely on bread and milk. (All are the prime traits of the folklore brownie.) But Hogg neither affirms nor denies Merodach's supernatural nature; instead, he shows us another form of enchantment, as Lady Wheelhope, not knowing what she feels, torments and abuses Merodach, even trying to poison him (he retaliates by killing her dog). She goes mad, murders her own son, and obsessed with Merodach, flees to follow him into poverty and wandering.

Hogg leaves open the question of whether it is fairy enthrallment or the human enchantment of passion that makes her follow Merodach like a dog even when he beats and rejects her. The relationship ends only when Merodach vanishes and Lady Wheelhope's battered body is found in a ditch.

"Mary Burnet," Hogg's tale of a fairy abduction, is equally mysterious, yet vivid and plausible in its treatment of guilt and retribution. When Mary's would-be seducer, John Allanson, prays to the fairies to make Mary come to an assignation, they apparently grant his wish. But who, as both readers and characters ask, is the "real" Mary, the maiden who flees John and drowns or the woman who is found weeping in her parents' house but disappears the next day? Allanson's punishment is both poetically just and psychologically valid. As he becomes an increasingly obsessed Don Juan, and goes to the annual market-fair to hire a pretty servant as a mistress, he discovers that every woman he desires (and each wears green, the fairy color) is named "Mary Burnet," while each insists that her "wages must be in kind." He meets his death, appropriately enough, through a great lady, dressed in green and gold, who seductively invites him to visit her at her mansion. The mansion is an artifact of fairy "glamour" or illusion and where the great house seems to stand is "a tremendous gulf, fifty fathoms deep, and a dark stream foaming and boiling below" (1:348). The fairies have enforced the moral law and Mary's wages have been paid in kind, for John Allanson's body lies floating in the stream. (In the second movement of the tale, an anticlimax for most readers, Mary briefly reappears to display her young sons, the offspring of her union with a fairy prince or lord, to their mortal grandparents before returning to the fairy realm forever.)

Though different in tone, "Kilmeny," Hogg's most famous fairy poem is, like "Mary Burnet," an account of a fairy abduction. Like Mary, Kilmeny returns briefly to this world after a seven-year absence. But the fairies' motivation here is less ambiguous. Because Kilmeny is "pure as pure could be" (2:32), they have taken her to a subterranean paradise to protect her "frae the snares of men,/That sin or death she never may ken" (2:33). Temporarily leaving a fairy realm the poem describes in detail, she has come back to give the mortal world a message of morality and hope: to tell humanity that "kindred spirits" watch over them and "grieve" for their guilt (2:34), to lead women, in emulation of herself, to sexual chastity, to tell Scotland of its future and, above all, to speak of the joys that are waiting beyond this life. After a month and a day on earth in which she creates prelapsarian peace and harmony in the natural world, she returns to the glen and the greenwood tree where she had first disappeared and again vanishes.

Hogg's long note to the popular poem was as important as the piece itself, for it detailed "modern incidents of a similar nature" (2:32n) with singular conviction. Such tales as that of seven-year-old Jane Brown who vanished from her father's side, but was restored after days of absence when the congregants of all the neighboring churches prayed for her simultaneously, reverberate throughout the entire nineteenth century.[8] But "Kilmeny" was most attractive to its first audience, as well as to the Victorians, because of its fusion of the romantic and the religious. Christianized and idealized, Kilmeny is a second Virgin Mary, "a sinless virgin, free of stain" (2:33) and a Miltonic Eve before the Fall, whose perfect beauty is without pride, passion, or even "the soft desire of maiden's een" (2:35). Her return "to the world of thought again" (2:35) suggested a hope for the existence of a paradisical otherworld, and the possibility of living contact with it. Hogg's attempt, whether conscious or unconscious, to reconcile two beliefs, the abiding fairy faith of the peasantry and the more orthodox Christian faith of the establishment, was deeply appealing to the Victorians. While his moralized, pietized, and idealized fairies may sometimes seem inauthentic and sentimental (as in "Kilmeny"), his attempt at fusing separate supernatural beliefs in hopes of keeping them alive and mutually suportive was to be endlesssly repeated.

While Hogg occasionally moralized the fairies, others, including Coleridge and Keats, popularized their darker aspects. In their quest for possibilities that a dominant rationalism would otherwise hide, they too turned to the world of Faerie. The Geraldine of "Christabel," for example, manifests Coleridge's considerable knowledge of numerous fairy traditions. Whether she is a vampire, a lamia, or simply an unlabeled preternatural creature, Geraldine bears all the traits of an authentically evil female fairy. Appearing at night, wearing white (often a fairy color in Scotland), she cannot cross a threshold gate "that was *ironed* within and without" (my italics; Part I: l.127), for fairies cannot bear iron. Thus, she must be carried in. Her presence makes the mastiff howl (dogs ostensibly both see and fear fairies) and the dying fire springs up at her approach. She enchants, as fairies do, through the power of her eye and her touch, is threatened and weakened by Christian symbols (the lamp with angels on it), and is heartened by wildflower wine. Her imperfections, according to a cancelled stanza, her bosom and side "lean and old and foul of hue," are not solely the property of witches; such fairies as the Danish *hulde* (who are hollow in the back) share defects that mark them as nonhuman. Yet her moral nature remains capricious and unknowable; there are hints that she pities and suffers, suggestions that she does not will the evil she causes, that she is the product of a different order, functioning upon the basis of a separate law.

The Belle Dame sans Merci of Keats's poem is the same sort of ambiguous figure, and the problem of crossing the boundary, of loving a being of another order, is at the heart of the poem. The ballad far transcends its most obvious source, "Sir Thomas Rhymer," in characterizing its fairy *femme fatale*. Yet in her use of "glamour," her beauty, her enchantment of the knight through song, her alien language and her habitation of "an elfin grot," La Belle Dame is also very much a creature of tradition. The Knight's doom, awaking on the cold hill's side, dead-alive in spirit and body, is the usual fate of the folklore figures who have dared to enter and been expelled from the fairy kingdom. In poetry, painting, and fiction, the Victorians were to endlessly reiterate both the figures and the problem of Keats's poem.

Thus, the best-known romantic poets and novelists outlined many of the figures and themes that would be of great interest to their Victorian successors. They began the search for the realm of Faerie as part of their quest for alternative, autonomous worlds. They began to probe the relations, usually tragic, between fairies and mortals. They began to explore the problems of fairy morality, to examine random cruelty and benevolence, to investigate caprice. Their work sometimes reflected the "religious view" of the fairy world; they sometimes believed in at least the possibility of the truth of fairy existence and even, with Hogg, in its reality. They established one major theory of fairy origins, the euhemerist view, and reflected upon others. In a sense, they delineated the subjects of Victorian investigation; their fascination with fairy abductions and changelings and with dwarfs and hobgoblins would be intensified as would their interest in the ambiguous female fairy and preternatural *femme fatale*.[9]

Romantic literary fairy tales, the *Kunstmärchen* of the Germans and their imitators, also excited interest and were to cast long shadows over their later Victorian imitators. These literary fairy tales that experimented and expanded upon folk materials, using folk motifs, figures, and plots for their own esthetic and philosophical purposes, were to be enormously influential. Baron de la Motte Fouqué's *Undine*, the story of an elemental water spirit and her gaining of a soul through her marriage with a Christian knight, would have a major impact on the Victorians. Published in 1811, translated soon after, Undine was repeatedly painted, first by Fuseli, to whom she represented the fluctuating moods and fairylike spirit of young girls—a sort of mirror image of the fairy courtesan—and later by Maclise and Watts; the figure found her way into fairy plays, ballets, and even an opera by E. T. A. Hoffmann. The Pre-Raphaelite circle (especially William Morris and Edward Burne-Jones) would find her fascinating and the more conventional Victorians would find the romance's blend of the exotic and pious moving and edifying. The transformation through which a capricious water sprite is tamed by love and gains a Christian spirit both epitomizes German romanticism and becomes a model for Victorian moralized fairy tales. Undine's "desire to rise to higher things" (p. 106), her movement from siren to angel, and her learning of patience, forbearance, and self-sacrifice, made her an ideal fairy heroine, a prototype of the fairy-bride morally superior to the mortals around her. Wieland's *Oberon*, translated as early as 1805, had only slightly lesser impact. This verse play based on the romance of Huon of Bordeaux and centering on his and his beloved's perfect fidelity, sponsored and tested by the fairies, spawned Fuseli's illustrations (to the Sotheby edition of 1795), other fairy plays, ballets, and Weber's opera.[10] As the century progressed, the richly suggestive tales of the German romantics, those of Tieck, Hoffmann, and Novalis, would be translated, adding their occult, mystical, and metaphysical treatment of folk motifs to the English repertoire.[11]

Romantic ballet, briefly flowering in England in the 1830s and '40s and then fading away, brought glittering visual images of the fairy world before a large audience. Stressing romantic supernatural themes, it featured a principle character, fairy or spirit, who became involved with a mortal in a relationship impossible to fulfill in this world. Beginning as early as 1812, with *Zelis*, a "fairy ballet" about a princess and her protecting sylph, its most popular manifestation was *La Sylphide*; based on a story by Charles Nodier called *Trilby*, it is the tale of a sylph who falls in love with a mortal Scotsman. First performed in London in 1832, it became enormously popular when danced by Pauline DeVernay in 1836. Her performance moved Thackeray to raptures and another ecstatic critic to exclaim: "She danced like a fairy, the incorporation of a zephyr and died as a sylph should die, her tiny wings dropping from their place and her whole frame not struggling but fainting into death" (Guest, p. 73). The rage for "fairy ballets" led to treatments of *Giselle*, *Le Lac des Feés*, *Sire Huon* (from *Oberon*, 1834) and even a *Miranda* (1838) with the character from Shakespeare's *Tempest* transmuted into a nymph. *Ondine* and *Eoline*—the latter a tale of a half-dryad, half-mortal destroyed by a gnome, jealous of her betrothal to a mortal—joined the ranks of popular ballets rendering magical visual images of supernatural creatures.

Painting the Imagined

In yet another sphere, that of fairy painting, the romantics once more laid the groundwork for their Victorian descendants. Again the choice of subject was influenced to some degree by political and nationalistic motives, as the English searched for a heroic past and looked for events from their history and legend suitable for visual depiction. Fairy painting began in earnest at the end of the eighteenth century, drawing at first primarily on Shakespeare and later expanding to incorporate a growing body of fairy literature and scholarship.[12] In effect, the evolution of fairy images provides a significant commentary on changing tastes and attitudes throughout the nineteenth century.

The first major impetus for fairy painting came from the Boydell Shakespeare venture. While its avowed aim was to found a British School of history painting with Shakespeare as an ideal, patriotic fount of subjects, its actual practice resulted in a plethora of fairy paintings based on two great sources, *A Midsummer Night's Dream* and *The Tempest*. Even those painters who did not contribute to the Boydell Shakespeare Gallery (a collection of large oil paintings on Shakespearean subjects that opened in 1789) or to the Boydell Shakespeare edition (filled with engravings of smaller oil paintings) began to think about Shakespearean fantasy as subject matter. Sir George Romney and Sir Joshua Reynolds—among the "greats" commissioned by Boydell—both painted portraits of Puck; in *Titania, Puck and the Changeling*, Romney made his Titania a portrait of Emma Hamilton;[13] in a painting drawn from the *Tempest, Prospero and Miranda*, he filled the sky above

the shipwreck with Ariel-like sylphs. Reynold's pointed-eared and impish Puck was a great popular success. Fashionable painters like John Stothard and Francis Danby produced additional Shakespearean fairy paintings; Danby's shadowy *Scene from A Midsummer Night's Dream* of 1832 would become a Victorian favorite. Minor figures like Henry Thomson, who painted a *Titania* in 1810, and Joseph Severn, most famous as a friend of Keats, who painted several versions of Ariel riding a bat through the darkened heavens, tried their hands at the genre. Even talented amateurs like Amelia Jane or "Emily" Murray of the Isle of Man, whose "Fairy Bower" (c. 1818–1829)— charming watercolors of fairies in empire dress perched on shells, birds, or flowers—was only published in 1985, were clearly effected by the vogue for painting supernatural figures.

For Henry Fuseli the vogue for fairy painting came as a major opportunity. For William Blake, not included among the painters asked to contribute to the Boydell Gallery (or even commissioned to engrave the paintings selected), it nonetheless served as a spur to the imagination. He promptly retaliated against his exclusion by producing his own scene from *A Midsummer Night's Dream*. Both Fuseli and Blake—especially the former— were important influences on the Victorian fairy painters, creating the exciting new fusion of classical and folkloric forms and motifs they would utilize. Blake's visionary perception of fairies was less imitable than Fuseli's more tangible representation of occult phenomena, but it, too, had an impact.

Fuseli was not, like Blake, an entire believer in the reality of the preternatural, but he was endlessly fascinated by it. He even contributed an anecdote supporting fairy existence to the third volume of Thomas Crofton Croker's *Fairy Legends*; it was an account of a elfin figure in military dress seen by people in a coach as it ran beside the road some three miles from London. Like Blake, Fuseli transformed the fairies into symbols of his psyche; however, his symbolism was more accessible than Blake's and his popularity guaranteed that the educated public would attempt to understand it. His impact on Victorian painters such as Daniel Maclise and Joseph Noel Paton is obvious, but in subtler ways, he also touches others ranging from John Anster Fitzgerald to Aubrey Beardsley.

Always interested in literary works, Fuseli created fairy paintings derived from them throughout his career. In addition to the paintings from Shakespeare, a second large group stem from Milton (Fuseli attempted to create a Milton Gallery parallel to Boydell's Shakespeare Gallery), and there are numerous pictures derived from Spenser's *Faerie Queene*, Pope's "Rape of the Lock," and from the two popular fairy romances, de la Motte Foqué's *Undine* and Wieland's *Oberon*. A last group of paintings, to which his famous *Nightmare* belongs, are folkloric in inspiration and conjoin Fuseli's private mythology with traditional folklore subjects. These, especially, reflect his own obsessions; they are filled with both grotesques and fairy *femmes fatale*.

Indeed, Fuseli is one of the first English painters to "recognize the enormous visual potential of English folk superstition" (Tate, p. 12). He seems to have painted fairies whenever and wherever he could, inserting them into scenes from Shakespeare even when his source did not require them.[14] Fuseli's two most famous fairy paintings based on Shakespeare, *Titania and Bottom* and *Titania's Awakening* (c. 1785 – 90) far transcend the mere transcription of Shakespeare's metaphors or allusions.[15]

Both paintings, executed for Boydell's Shakespeare Gallery, are set in landscapes so dark as to be nearly invisible. Each swarms with fairies of all types and sizes. Not only does Fuseli meld the grotesque and the erotic but he also fuses the classically derived Shakespearean fairies with those more directly drawn from English folklore. Touched by nationalist impulses and, perhaps, by commercial considerations, he converts classical demiurges into British folklore figures. In *Titania and Bottom*, a graceful fairy queen, posed like a classical goddess, calls on her fairies, some dressed in contemporary fashions, to attend Bottom. In addition to Pease-blossom, Mustard-seed,

I.1. Henry Fuseli, *Titania and Bottom*, oil, (c. 1780 – 90). Tate Gallery, London/Art Resource, New York.

and Cobweb, the painting depicts a hooded witch or nighthag holding a hideous waxen male changeling. Next to her (in the right foreground), an elegant full-size fairy courtesan leads a tiny wizened old man on a leash. Some identify her with Nimue, the medieval fay who enchanted Merlin and the tiny figure with the wizard, literally reduced and stripped of power.[16] Strange, hybrid child-size fairies cluster on the left—one has the head of a butterfly; near her, a grotesque figure in a headdress holds an infant monster over her shoulder, a creature whose limbs end in a bestial red vein–covered tail and whose microcephalic head is too small for its body. Another creature, whose face is averted, holds the hand of a lovely but seemingly waxen or lifeless little girl. Meanwhile, tiny but well-formed fairies mysteriously cavort at the edges of the painting; one tiny figure on the left is about to attack something invisible, another is ready to enter the calyz of a flower on the right.

Fuseli's companion piece, *Titania's Awakening*, is equally replete with both conventionally graceful "good" fairies—who look as if they had stepped out of a romantic ballet or one of the elaborate, richly staged early-nineteenth-century productions of Shakespeare's play—and Fuseli's own inventions, evil fairies and monsters who torment Bottom in sleep. An incubus riding a nightmare gallops over Bottom's head; three witchlike, erotic courtesan

I.2. Henry Fuseli, *Titania's Awakening*, oil (c. 1785–90). Kunstmuseum Winterthur, Switzerland.

fairies simper and leer at the sleeper; one (like the standard icon of Lust or Milton's Sin) suckles a monster with an animal-like head, while a young girl leaning at the nursing mother's knee hides her face but reveals her reptilian tail and a mishapen monster child crawls under the hem of the mother's gown. The actions the painting depicts are darkly mischievous and perversely erotic; the work's sinister effect is intensified by both the darkness of the background and the suggestions of the symbolism and illogic of dream.[17]

The same qualities are evident in the many Fuseli paintings based on other literary sources that incorporate fairies.[18] Here, too, fairy painting may free Fuseli—as it does in the Shakespeare pictures—to play with size and space, but it is equally important in freeing his vivid and sinister imagination. That imagination functions as freely in transforming his sources as it does in creating them. In all the groups, certain figures recur: Queen Mab, the grotesque misshapen bringer of disturbing dreams, sometimes with her famous ape-faced incubus, the figure of *The Nightmare*, grotesque changelings or monster-hybrids, erotic "courtesan" fairies. The figures Fuseli adds to *Belinda's Awakening* (c. 1780–90), for example, have little to do with Alexander Pope's account of the event in Canto One of "The Rape of the Lock," though some literal details from the poem are faithfully tran-

I.3. Henry Fuseli, *Dream of Belinda* (from Alexander Pope's, "The Rape of the Lock"), oil (c. 1780–90). Courtesy of the Vancouver Art Gallery, Canada, photo: Robert Keziere.

I.4. Henry Fuseli, "Seated Woman, with Switch" or "Courtesan with Naked Breast . . . behind Her to the Left a Small Crouching Fairy," pen and ink over pencil (c. 1800–5). Kunsthaus Zürich, Switzerland, Copyright 1998 by Kunsthaus Zürich. All rights reserved.

scribed. Here Mab and Titania-Diana (her descent from the classical goddess is suggested by the crescent moon in her hair), Fuseli's rulers of bad and good dreams, are brought in to join the elementals derived from Paracelsus and Rosicrucian thought. Over Mab hovers a mischievous Puck. In yet another blending of preternatural figures, the sylph Ariel (an elemental whose home is air) and the attendant nymph bringing Belinda's dressing table (here depicted as a a spirit, perhaps based on a misreading of

Pope's euphemism for Belinda's maid) are joined by a strange version of "Shock." This is no ordinary lap dog, for the creature under the sheet that waits to awake Belinda (who seems dead) has a paw like a human hand. The witty spirit of Pope has vanished in a painting that, even to the phallic couch leg and two ugly mating butterflies, suggests both perverse passion and death because of it.[19]

The same fusion of varied sources all working toward a "grotesquerie of the erotic" informs such paintings as *The Shepherd's Dream* (1793) from Book I of Milton's *Paradise Lost*, where Fuseli introduces a naked fairy combing her hair — a seducer and stripper of men derived from Shropshire folklore — (Tate, p. 87) to reinforce the theme of the danger of erotic dreams already indicated by the presence of Mab and her incubus in the painting. The more private paintings, those less obviously based on external literary sources, again use fairies of classical, folkloric, and alchemical derivation and of all shapes and sizes as symbols of passion and terror.[20] Perhaps the most revolutionary is a simple pen-and-ink sketch of Mrs. Fuseli as a courtesan (one of the painter's fantasies). Called *Courtesan with Naked Breast . . . in front of a Fire, Holding a Switch; behind her to the left a Small Crouching Fairy* (1800 – 6), it suggests the perverse sensibility and the sado-masochistic impulses that Fuseli's fairies come to symbolize. For, as erotic fantasies invade reality, Mrs. Fuseli is depicted as a dominatrix about to punish her male victim while her small familiar (seated in the same position as she) gleefully watches.

William Blake, who greatly admired Fuseli, also incorporated fairies into his private symbolism, though he made his views about their reality public. His account of witnessing a fairy funeral (an unusual one, since most believe that fairies do not die) was quoted by Allan Cunningham in the *Lives of the Eminent British Painters*. Blake was reputed to have asked a lady sitting with him if she had ever seen a fairy's funeral; when she responded in the negative, he told of his experience:

> I was walking alone in my garden; there was great stillness among the branches and flowers, and more than common sweetness in the air; I heard a low and pleasant sound, and I knew not whence it came. At last, I saw the broad leaf of a flower move, and underneath I saw a procession of creatures, of the size and colour of green and grey grasshoppers, bearing a body laid out on a rose leaf, which they buried with songs and then disappeared." (qtd. in Gilchrist I: 159)

In both poems and paintings,[21] Blake associates fairies with "natural" and "creative" joys; they are part of his strategy for "turning the Heathen Gods back into the Fairies of Albion" (Frye, p. 132). The nationalist impulse was just as alive in Blake as in his contemporaries. Not only were the fairies associated with the battle against the age of reason and its offspring, neoclassicism but they had been used by the English writers he revered, Ossian and Chatterton, as well as by his favorites, Milton and Spenser. Moreover, he thought of the elfin peoples as anticlassical, as true British antiquities, as "originals" rather than codified deities—all elements that greatly enhanced their appeal.

Though fairies participate in a number of Blake paintings and etchings, their most significant appearances are in the Shakespearean *Oberon, Titania and Puck with Fairies Dancing* (1785) and the Miltonic *The Goblin* (c. 1816).[22] To Blake, Shakespeare's fairies are "the rulers of the vegetable world" (Adlard, p. 79), and they appear as such in his vision of the reconciliation of Oberon and Titania. All are full-sized figures, placed in a starlit, pastoral arcadia. Calmly and contentedly, Blake's Oberon and Titania half embrace, as they watch Puck, with a pair of castenets, provide the rhythm for a ritual circle dance performed around a fairy ring by four fairies. Oberon and Titania wear the garb of the ancient Britons, while the fairies wear the flowing transparent draperies associated with classical nymphs. This discrepancy in costume is part of the very point, for the world of the once classical nature sprites is in the process of being made English. Oberon bears a phallic flower as a scepter, in token of his "naturally based sovereignty" (Adlard, p. 82), and the spirits have added nonclassical headdresses to their classical draperies. One wears butterfly wings on her head, another a cap made from the petals of a giant flower, the others, garlands of large leaves. Puck himself is girdled with ivy and wears leaves in his hair, another association with fertility. The fairy ring, the ivy, the flowers, and the embrace of the fairy queen and king all suggest the traditional associations of fairies, sexuality, and the fertile earth.

I.5. William Blake, *Oberon, Titania and Puck with Fairies Dancing*, watercolor and pencil (c. 1785). Tate Gallery, London/Art Resource, New York.

While the fairies of *Oberon* are akin to the graceful elementals, of whom Blake would know from his studies of Paracelsus and Rosicrucianism, the fairies of Milton's "L'Allegro" (*The Goblin*) are those of English folk tradition. Blake's manuscript notes for the picture serve as a gloss upon it (and explain some of its features, since he misquotes Milton's lines slightly):

> The Goblin crop full flings out of doors from his Laborious task dropping his Flail & Cream bowl, yawning & stretching vanishes into the Sky. in which is seen Queen Mab Eating the Junkets. The Sports of the Fairies are seen thro the Cottage where "She" lays in Bed "pinched & pulld" by Fairies as they dance on the Bed the Cieling [sic]& the Floor & a Ghost pulls the Bed Clothes at her Feet. "He" is seen following the Friars Lantern towards the Convent. (Blake, p. 664)

I.6. William Blake, *The Goblin*, plate 5 from Blake's edition of John Milton's *L'Allegro*, pen and watercolor (c. 1816–20). Courtesy of the Pierpont Morgan Library, New York.

Significantly, here, the fairies are English spirits, ranging from tiny to huge and from grotesque to lovely. Blake's gigantic lubber fiend is almost an illustration of his statement in the Descriptive Catalogue that "A Spirit and a Vision are not . . . a cloudy vapour or a nothing; they are organized and minutely articulated beyond all that the mortal and perishing nature can produce" (Blake, p. 532). The tiny fairies pinching and pulling the bedridden woman are frankly sadistic; the combination of ghosts, monsters, apparitions, and a courtly sky queen being served by an attendant fay suggest the richness of Blake's vision of the folk imagination. Blake, like Fuseli, recognizes that the sports of the fairies are usually cruel; the sinister nature of some of the images suggests Blake's recognition of the dark side of the fairy tradition.

The eroticism and cruelty with which Fuseli and sometimes Blake invest their fairies, their images of elfin realms touched by tension and strife, were to be reutilized by such superficially "wholesome" Victorian fairy painters as Richard "Dicky" Doyle and Sir Joseph Noel Paton. The Victorians were to increase the number and variety of figures from folklore, so that they formed more than a "picturesque addition" (Philpotts, *Fairy Paintings*, p. 8) to mainstream Shakespearean (and Miltonic) fairy images. They were, as well, to add the full visionary landscape that links Victorian fairy painting with the romantic landscape tradition.[23] Moreover, their visual recreations of fairyland would be enriched by their more abundant knowledge of folklore scholarship and by the theorizing of their contemporaries. Fuseli and Blake had laid the foundations upon which the later fairy painters were to build their palaces.

Romantic Fairy Scholarship

Despite the rich literary, cultural, and visual contributions to fairy lore that I have described above, the romantics' most significant legacy to the Victorians probably lay in their collection and analysis of primary materials. In 1825, a book entitled *Fairy legends and traditions of the South of Ireland* appeared anonymously and was so popular that its author, Thomas Crofton Croker, was asked to add additional materials to it. Two further volumes — the third dealing with English and Welsh materials — appeared in 1828, and the volumes were frequently republished throughout the Victorian period, rendered even more popular by their illustrations, the work of William Henry Brooke, Daniel Maclise, and, later, George Cruikshank. Croker, cited in Richard Dorson's history of folklore study as the first deliberate field collector of lore in Great Britain, was significant in other ways, as well. He insisted that the fairy faith was still alive, at least in Ireland, and to support this view, he printed (in the preface to the second volume) current accounts of the effects of such belief, ranging from a newspaper story of changeling torture to an account of a murder ostensibly committed by the fairies. His third volume concentrated on English fairy lore, which he believed to be on the point of vanishing. But this volume was even more important for Croker's translation and transmission of Jacob and Wilhelm Grimm's long essay, "On the Nature of the Elves." The Grimms' essay argued that fairy lore was a complete and connected whole, part of an Aryan mythic system that, until the advent of Christianity, had dominated all of Europe (Croker 3:54). Croker agreed; the result was the introduction into Great Britain of a comparative and linguistic approach to fairy life and lore.

Stimulated by Croker, Thomas Keightley, one of the contributors to his first volume, produced another work central to Victorian fairy lore. *The Fairy Mythology* of 1828, revised and expanded in 1850 and newly prefaced in 1860, was also immensely popular among Victorian folklorists and literary figures alike. For Keightley produced what Richard Dorson calls one of the "most mature English studies on comparative folklore in the first half of the century" (*British Folklorists*, p. 52) and also turned his material, without unduly falsifying it, into entertaining narrative. By the time of his 1850 edition, he had thoroughly absorbed the Grimms' *Teutonic Mythology*, as well as their essay on the elves. Thus he, too, took fairy lore seriously, seeking to prove that the fairy faith descended from primitive Gothic and Teutonic religions and that it had spread to the Celts and others. It was probably his lively and exotic tales (he even included Finnish, African, and Jewish lore) and the imaginative Cruikshank frontispiece that made the book so popular, but his work, particularly his comparative method, was important to later, major folklorists.

Among "the literary folklorists" (*British Folklorists*, p. 91), as Richard Dorson calls them, Robert Southey holds a place perhaps second only to Scott, though he never produced a single popular volume of lore. Another friend of Scott's, as well as an acquaintance of Croker's, he was most famous for reproducing and popularizing the nursery tale of "The Three Bears." But his poems on fairy subjects, including the Wordsworthian "Fountain of the Fairies" and such supernatural ballads as "The Witch," were highly esteemed in their day. He suspended his own judgment on the reality of supernatural creatures, though as he suggests in reference to one anecdote he evaluated, he was "not a disbeliever in these things. . . . I lean to belief myself" (qtd. in Dorson, *British Folklorists*, p. 93). His theory of fairy origins, however, linked him to a popular late-eighteenth and early-nineteenth-century euhemeristic "Druid theory." Quoting at length from a Dr. Cririe, who had written specifically of the Scottish fairies, Southey suggested the widespread applicability of the view that the elfin peoples were derived from the Druids. He argued that it was the Druids who, fleeing their conquerors and hiding in underground dwellings topped by artificial mounds, had given rise to a set of traits later ascribed to the fairies. A declining people, the Druids borrowed food from ordinary peasants and abducted women and children to swell their thinning ranks, often returning them years later (pp. 280–81).

Yet Southey's greatest contribution to the development of English fairy lore may have been his encouragement and support of Anna Eliza Bray. Suggesting that she catch, before they vanished, the folk traditions and pixie legends of Devonshire and Cornwall, he asked her to write the book he might have written, had circumstances permitted. Following Southey's advice and defending herself from her neighbors among "the upper and more educated classes [who] hold such stories as unworthy of notice; . . . and would laugh at me for having taken the trouble to collect and repeat them" (*The Tamar and the Tavy,* 1:192), Bray enlisted a young village woman to help with "field work" and to disarm the fearful or superstitious local folk. Thus, she became one of the first female collectors of and commentators on fairy lore, an ancestress of the many illustrious Victorian female folklorists. By 1836, Bray had compiled a three-volume work and given it an imposing title: *A Description of the Part of Devonshire Bordering on the Tamar and the Tavy; its Natural History, Manners, Customs, Superstitions, Scenery, Antiquities, Biography of Eminent Persons, etc. in a Series of Letters to Robert Southey, Esq.*

The Tamar and the Tavy established the pixies as a significant form of fairy life and made their images vivid to the nineteenth-century imagination. Although Anna Bray did not favor any single theory of pixie origins, she remarked upon the relations between the words *pygmy* and *pixie* and was persuaded that the old idea of supernatural dwarfs, or duergar, lay beyond both terms. She commented as well on the "religious view" of pixie origins, an almost universal belief among her peasant informants that pixies were actual creatures: the reembodied souls of infants who had died unbaptized (1:172).

Although Mrs. Bray expressed no opinion of her own on the question of fairy existence, she probably did accept at least the possibility of such life; as the wife of the vicar of Tavistock, she would not have doubted the power of the Creator to manifest himself in any way he chose. It was, of course, the radicals and "free thinkers" who doubted the reality of the elfin peoples.

Thus, among the writers of this period who expressed their opinions on the reality of fairies, it is Leigh Hunt who is most skeptical. His thoroughly rationalist and materialist view permeates the series of articles he produced on "Fairies" (in *Leigh Hunt's London Journal* of 1834). After describing fairy types and behavior he notes, for example, that "all without exception are thieves, and fond of power. In other words, they are like the human beings that invented them" (1 Oct.: 209). Concerned mainly with two issues, the question of fairy size and the question of the connections between fairies and the Devil, he stops to make a euhemeristic historical point. Quoting extensively from Mallet's *Northern Antiquities,* he argues that English and Teutonic and Scandinavian fairies are small because of the small size of their originals, the Lapps. His argument against the actual presence of the elfin tribes is a rational and "scientific" one:

We are among the number of those who . . . do yet believe that fairies have actually been seen; but then it was by people whose perceptions were disturbed. It is observable that ordinary seers have been the old, the diseased, or the intoxicated. (15 Oct.: 232)

The fairies, says Hunt, are the creatures of our disordered imaginations. But just as partial belief in the possibility of fairy life may be seen as patriotic, so Hunt's underlying objections may be viewed as political. He argues that belief in fairies is dangerous and destructive; it has caused delirium and serious illness in individuals; it has kept the folk frightened and base. Unlike Scott and Hogg, who see the fairy faith as an alternative to or amelioration of the hegemony of official, orthodox Christianity, Hunt sees it as an unpleasant opiate of the people. Hunt's was a minority view; it is worth noting, however, that even in attacking the fairies he registers his fascination with them.

Thus, by the mid-1830s, the debate over the actuality and value of the elfin peoples had started and the basic historical, empirical, religious, and linguistic approaches to fairy lore were in place. The procedures developed by the Brothers Grimm and transmitted by their English apostles — linguistic analysis, categorization, systematization — had begun to turn the quest for fairies into science. The belief that fairy lore was not just "superstition" but also the detritus of a once vital Aryan religion, a faith that had been shared by the Angles, Jutes, and Saxons from whom most English felt they had derived their significant traits, increasingly incited British patriotic fervor — and made the elfin peoples suitable for serious study.

The romantics had hatched the fairies and the reasons for the cultural fascination with them were to remain and, indeed, intensify throughout the century. The reaction against utilitarianism, the celebration of the possibility of magic in a world of facts, would increase. The attempt to capture a national heritage and reveal its unique greatness would wax as Britain increasingly ruled both the waves and the marketplace. As the shift from the rural to the urban world intensified, the retention and celebration of traditional rural lore and custom would seem to be increasingly important, at least to middle-class and aristocratic collectors. To the rural laboring classes, fairy lore and the belief in it would become (in some cases and places) a sort of secret learning, a knowledge they controlled and did not have to share with class, governmental, or religious oppressors.

Moreover, the periods of spiritual doubt and duress during the Victorian era, the crises in religion, and the tensions between religious and scientific truths would lead to the postulation and assertion of faith in other worlds. Aided, but not caused, by Spiritualism, which would become a force in England by the mid-1850s, reinforced by Theosophy, which was to trigger the occultism of the 1880s and '90s, fairy beliefs would proliferate and expand. As the known, especially within the world of nature, became either too mundane or, because of Darwinian thought, too unpleasant, the preoccupation with the fairies would increase.

Yet what truly altered the face of fairy lore was the emergence of the "new" Victorian social sciences—anthropology, ethnology, and archaeology—and the impact they had on the increasingly scientifically oriented study of folklore. Ironically, the study of fairies was really rendered possible and made respectable by the rise of Darwinism in the 1860s. As Darwinian thought lengthened the past of humankind and hypothesized stages along the way, as theories of social, cultural, and spiritual evolution proliferated, as debates on origin intensified, they added new dimensions to the exploration of the fairy world.

Thus, the Victorians—wavering between a somewhat outmoded but not abandoned belief in such creatures as fairies and an enlightened skepticism—attempted to use the sciences, especially the new social sciences they were developing, to heal the breach. Folklorists and occultists alike used the methods and language of the sciences for both description and verification. As new personal and psychological attitudes toward belief emerged, scientific techniques were utilized to support or to disprove ideas about the preternatural—concepts that had formerly been held to lie outside the possibility of proof. In effect, the Victorian passion for scientific investigation in a world that might be emptying itself of "others" amply nurtured and nourished the fairies the romantics had hatched.

O N E

ON THE ORIGINS
OF FAIRIES

IN 1846, WILLIAM JOHN THOMS, who contributed the term *folklore* to the English language, commented in *The Athenaeum* that "belief in fairies is by no means extinct in England" (Merton, p. 55).[1] Thoms was not alone in his opinion; he was merely echoing and endorsing the words of others such as Thomas Keightley, the author of *The Fairy Mythology*. For believers were not limited to gypsies, fisherfolk, rural cottagers, country parsons, and Irish mystics. Antiquarians of the romantic era had begun the quest for fairies, and throughout Victoria's reign advocates of fairy existence and investigators of elfin origins included numerous scientists, social scientists, historians, theologians, artists, and writers. By the 1880s such leading folklorists as Sabine Baring-Gould, Andrew Lang, Joseph Jacobs, and Sir John Rhys were examining oral testimony on the nature and the customs of the "little folk" and the historical and archaeological remains left by them. At the beginning of the twentieth century, eminent authors, among them Sir Arthur Conan Doyle and Arthur Machen, swelled the ranks of those who held the fairy faith and publicized their findings. In a remarkable "trickle up" of folk belief, a surprisingly large number of educated Victorians and Edwardians speculated at length on whether fairies did exist or had at least once existed.

For the Irish, especially those involved in the Celtic revival, belief in fairies was almost a political and cultural necessity. Thus, William Butler Yeats reported endlessly on his interactions with the sidhe (Irish fairies) and wrote repeatedly of their nature and behavior. His colleagues Æ (George Russell) and William Sharp/Fiona Macleod proudly enumerated their fairy hunts and sightings, and the great Irish Victorian folklorists—Patrick Kennedy, Lady Wilde, and Lady Gregory—overtly or covertly acknowledged their beliefs. Even those not totally or personally convinced, like Douglas Hyde, remarked that the fairy faith was alive and well in Ireland.[2]

Irish interest in what was perceived as a national and ethnic inheritance —one the English could not expropriate—is not surprising, but English fascination with the fairies is more complex in origin. Celtic influences within the British Isles were a major factor, for there were rich Anglo-Celtic enclaves in Cornwall, Wales, the Isle of Man, and the Scottish Highlands and islands. Political and nationalist impulses contributed as well. As collectors and writers began to perceive the fragmentation of their societies, local traditions that had always been taken for granted aquired new significance as lifelines to the origins of the race. Nostalgia for a fading British past was another related element. Many agreed with the geologist and folklorist Hugh Miller (*The Old Red Sandstone*, pp. 222 – 23) and the novelist Charlotte Brontë (*Shirley*, p. 576) that the fairies were leaving England. The nation was growing too industrial and technological, too urban and material for their health and welfare. It was important to locate the elfin peoples and to chronicle their acts before they departed forever.

Perhaps ironically, however, it was the Victorian concern with origins, a concern aided and abetted by developments in the sciences and social sciences, that promoted the serious study of supernatural creatures. The same habit of mind that made George Eliot's Casaubon seek a "Key to All Mythologies," and impelled her Lydgate to search for the primitive tissue underlying all life, sent folklorists and anthropologists in quest of explanations for the origin of the fairies—and for the origins of belief in them. Some of those explanations were religious, some scientific, some historical; they ranged from the Theosophical belief in the existence of elementals (the spirits of the four elements) to the argument for a worldwide, prehistoric dwarf population. But all shared a common assumption that the truth of fairy existence could and would be discovered—and by some sort of scientific or verifiable means.

Only a relatively small group of questers was satisfied with purely experiential evidence, with saying "I believe in fairies because I have seen them." Lafcadio Hearn, the Japanologist, was more Celtic than Saxon when he commented that he had faith in "ghosts and goblins, because . . . [he] saw them, both by day and night" (Temple, p. 30). Richard Dadd, the fairy painter, seems to have encountered them at least once, when they modeled for his Bedlam masterpiece of "Fays, gnomes, and elves, and suchlike" (qtd. in Allderidge, *Late Richard Dadd*, p. 128), *The Fairy Feller's Master-Stroke* (1855–64). He stated that he had gazed at his canvas, his mind blank, until shapes literally took form within the cloudy underpaint that covered it (Allderidge, pp. 125–26). But his contemporaries could dismiss his testimony as that of a madman; the same was true of Charles Doyle, brother of the more famous fairy painter Richard and father of Arthur Conan Doyle; he sketched his fairies (according to his notebooks) just as he saw them. Sane and rational W. Graham Robertson—artist, playwright, and theatrical designer—would give no grounds for his belief. Instead, in his memoir, *Time Remembered* (published in America as *Life Was Worth Living* [n.d.]), he recounted an incident that had changed his life. In what he afterward viewed as a "dangerous experiment," he had created a pageant to be held at twilight in a local wood thought to be "fairy haunted." "Perhaps," he remarked, "as a result of meddling with things and beings better left alone, luck seemed to desert me and grey days in plenty set in." Punished by the offended elves with illness and depression, he expressed his belief that fairies, "whoever they may be . . . still allow themselves to be glimpsed rarely, and by few, in the woodland of our rapidly disappearing countryside" (pp. 313–14). Maurice Hewlett, best known for his historical romances and travel books, was another who ostensibly glimpsed members of the elfin races; his *The Lore of Proserpine* (1913) is a full-length memorate (or ostensibly "believed" report of personal experience) of his and others' interactions with supernatural creatures. However, he repeatedly refused to comment on the reasons for his own belief. Robert Louis Stevenson, equally rational, was also mysterious about the extent and nature of his fairy faith. Like all children, he remarked, he had believed in youth in the actuality of the elfin world: "No child but must remember laying his head in the grass, staring into the infinitesimal forest and seeing it grow populous with fairy armies" (*Essays*, pp. 452–53). In adulthood, he suggested, the "little people" came only in dreams; then, however, they suggested ideas for his tales and novels. In "A Chapter on Dreams," he noted that many details of *Dr. Jekyll and Mr. Hyde* had been dictated to him, while asleep, by the brownies (pp. 247–48).

Other eminent Victorian investigators had, like Sir Walter Scott before them, believed in fairies in their childhoods. Andrew Lang had dug for "fairy gold" (Green, p. 9). Sabine Baring-Gould—the distinguished minister, medievalist, and folklorist—had witnessed "a crowd of little imps or dwarfs surrounding the carriage" in which he and his parents traveled to Montpellier. He indicated, as well, that both his wife (in her adolescence) and his young son had seen creatures they identified as elves or gnomes.[3]

If some people, including Baring-Gould, later ascribed the etiology of such visions to sunstroke or hallucinations caused by heat, or to nurses' tales and unconscious memories of the illustrations in their childrens' books (*Book of Folk-Lore*, p. 200), others, who retained their faith as adults, often sought to buttress their arguments with tangible proof. Some were content to argue by "authority," contending that additional and reliable witnesses had reported the same or similar experiences. Others pointed to the evidence provided by physical phenomena and artifacts or tokens. Rural folk still collected elf-shots or fairy bolts (prehistoric flint shards or arrows), as well as fairy pipes (small pipes often found near prehistoric monuments), but so, too, did folklorists. Fairy rings were located and examined, though most scientists believed that they had been produced by fungi rather than by fairy feet. The pages of *Notes and Queries* and of *Folk-Lore* were dotted with accounts of elfin sightings and activities around standing stones.[4] The Rollright Stones, near Oxford, for example, were thought to be raised by the Druids and later occupied by supernatural creatures. They were visited by many who hoped to see the fairies—"little folk like girls to look at"—dance around them (Evans, p. 22).

Evidences of fairy existence were also to be found in such popular examples of fairy workmanship as the metal cauldron at Fresham, Surrey (a large vessel "borrowed" from the fairies and never returned), the famous "fairy flag" of the MacLeods of Skye, and the equally famous "fairy banner" of the Scottish MacDonalds—presented to the clans by various fairies. Most popular of all was the "Luck of Edenhall," enshrined in the great mansion of the Musgrave family near Penrith in the Lake Country. An enameled glass vase (now in the Victoria and Albert Museum) supposedly crafted by the fairies, it was said to have been stolen from them by a retainer of the Musgrave family. The oracular fairies had predicted: "If that glass shall break or fall/Farewell the luck of Edenhall," but the house and its "luck" remained intact (and much commented upon) throughout the era.[5]

A larger and more significant group of Victorian questers incorporated personal experience and physical evidence into a framework of belief. They based their fairy faith on theological or philosophical premises. These "religious views," as I have chosen to call them, might be grounded on Christian, occultist, or pagan assumptions and adopt widely varied colorations, but all were based on the premise that fairies were actual spiritual beings or, at the very least, that they had originated in realms beyond the material. The most basic form of the "religious view," one long held by many of the folk, was that the elfin peoples were the fallen angels. All over England, Ireland, Scotland, and Wales, folklorists found local people who believed that the fairies were the uncommitted angels or those trapped on earth during Lucifer's fall. Equally widespread was the view that the fairies were the souls of the dead who were not good enough for salvation or evil enough for damnation; the semireligious notion that the fairies were the spirits of unbaptized children was also widespread and popular. Only slightly less prevalent was the idea that they were spirits of "special" categories of the dead, those awaiting reincarnation, or those killed before their time, or those from long-dead, pagan, or extinct races.

1.1 "The Luck of Edenhall" beaker of enamelled and gilt glass (Syrian, mid-thirteenth century). Courtesy of the Victoria and Albert Picture Library.

They Are Spirit: Religious Views

The more orthodox segment among those who held "religious views" drew strength from the biblical text: "And other sheep have I that are not of this fold" (John 10:16). Both clergy and laypeople read in this passage the implication that there had been a separate creation of the inhabitants of fairyland. Martin Luther could be called to witness; he had believed in the existence of supernatural creatures and insisted on the reality of changelings (see chapter 2). Thomas Lake Harris, the mystic, poet, and religious leader, had incorporated fairies into his system of belief. John Henry, Cardinal Newman, did not exclude them from his. At least one Scottish Protestant minister thought, as he told W. Y. Evans-Wentz, that fairies were still extant, though only visible to those in a state of mystical ecstasy (p. 91). Evans-Wentz himself believed fairies to be analogous to

Christ in their ability to become invisible—as He had done at His Ascension and Transfiguration (p. 93).

Victorian Spiritualists, Rosicrucians, and Theosophists grounded their faith on their sectarian theologies, although they generally insisted that their evidence was scientific. Early Spiritualists, who often perceived their movement as simply adding another dimension to already firm Christian beliefs—as offering evidences of immortality through contact with the departed—were not initially much concerned with fairies. They regarded them mainly as nuisances who interfered with seances and were responsible for the poltergeist phenomenon—that is, the moving or throwing of objects at seances or in "haunted" houses. They agreed, however, with the Theosophists that the elfin peoples were really the "elementals"; "subhuman Nature-Spirits of pygmy stature" (Evans-Wentz, p. 241) first described by medieval alchemists and mystics.

The association of the elements with guardian or governing spirits was probably first made by the third-century Neoplatonists, but the first full acount of them was in the work of Paracelsus, the fifteenth-century alchemist and mystic. He detailed the nature and power of the inhabitants of the four elements: the sylphs of air, the salamanders of fire, the undines or nymphs of water, and the gnomes of earth. His elementals occupied a position between humans and pure spirits, though they lived exclusively in one of the four elements. Made of flesh and blood, they ate and slept and procreated like humans do. But unlike mortals, they were long-lived, capable of superhuman speed and movement, and without immortal souls. The elementals gripped the Victorian imagination. Integrated with the fairies of folk literature and belief, they were first rendered important by Rosicrucian or pseudo-Rosicrucian groups and individuals, and later—slightly transmuted—by Theosophists and other occultists. In their earliest manifestations in the period, they appear as the figures in the various plays and ballets derived from *Undine* and as the undiscovered but "scientifically possible" forces in the fiction and, perhaps, the belief of Sir Edward Bulwer-Lytton; they play important roles in his *Zanoni* (1845) and *A Strange Story* (1862). In their later manifestations, they are staples of Victorian occultist thought, and they are systematized, classified, and rendered scientific.

When, in the late 1870s, the impact of Theosophy and the doctrines of its foundress, Madame Helena Blavatsky, began to be felt in England, the elementals came of age. In *Isis Unveiled* (1877), H.B., as she was called, stressed the reality of their existence:

> Under the general designation of fairies and fays, these spirits of the elements appear in the myth, fable, tradition, or poetry of all nations, ancient and modern. Their names are legion—peris, devs, djins, sylvans, satyrs, fauns, elves, dwarfs, trolls, norns, nisses, kobolds, brownies, and many more. They have been seen, feared, blessed, banned, and invoked in every quarter of the globe and in every age. (1:xxix)

Noting that they were often present at seances and manifested themselves in various psychic phenomena, she indicated that they were worthy objects of speculation and study.

Her disciples were quick to take her at her word. Charles W. Leadbeater (later self-appointed bishop of his own church) explained, in *The Astral Plane* (1895) that fairies were the inhabitants of one of the seven subdivisions of the astral plane. Most were nature spirits, creatures who could change their shapes at will but did have "favorite forms" (pp. 54–55). These, like their human counterparts, were evolving to a higher plane and would ultimately become "devas" (the equivalent of angels) or local village or wood deities. There were, however, also "artificial" elementals; beings, often ugly and dangerous, created as "thought-forms" by human beings (p. 56). Though not visible to ordinary sight, these monsters were real enough to the clairvoyants who saw them or the people they attacked.

Others added to the classification and definition of various orders of elementals. Anna Kingsford, both seeress and medical doctor, insisted that "a distinction . . . be made between astral and elemental spirits and *qenii loci*." Elementals, in her sense of the term, "are more material than any of the others, and have an independent existence" (qtd. in Maitland 1:412), while it is really the *qenii loci* who "are the spirits of forests, mountains, cataracts, rivers, and all unfrequented places. These are the dryads, kelpies, fairies, and elves" (1:412). Herbert Arnold, writing an article called "The Elementals" for *The Occult Review* (vol. 18:1913), further distinguished and subcategorized his invisible subjects. One class of elementals "composed of semi-intelligent entities" was destined to evolve into human beings (p. 209). Another class was composed of "nature-spirits," each confined to its own element. These were the elementals of Paracelsus and the fairies of medieval (and modern) tradition. Still others, Arnold believed, were responsible for the "noises, movement of tables, disturbances, raps" (p. 210), childish or foolish answers to questions at seances, and for the so-called poltergeist phenomenon.

Franz Hartmann, in his article "Some Remarks about the Spirits of Nature" written for the same periodical (vol. 14:1911), argued that elementals were the cause of "otherwise unaccountable incendiarisms and conflagrations"(p. 28). He believed them partially responsible not only for unexplained fires and volcanic eruptions but also for human pyromania—they either compelled the weak-minded to set fires or gave them the psychic ability to will them. A medical doctor, Hartmann insisted that the real powers of elementals were psychological. In effect, elemental fairies shaped our temperaments: "the spirits of nature have their dwellings within us as well as outside of us, and no man is perfectly master over himself unless he thoroughly knows his own nature and its inhabitants" (p. 29).

Hartmann's occult psychology was echoed by others who argued, as he did, that since we are all possessed, we must learn to know those who possess us. Nature, as William Butler Yeats suggested in *Mythologies*, was full of invisible peoples reacting to and interacting with us.

"Occultist" or "mystical" folklorists like Yeats and Evans-Wentz (both of whom were believers) sought to philosophically reconcile the elementals and the supernatural creatures of folklore. They inquired, through informants, about traits common to both popular fairies and elemental spirits, and they sought to locate the ways in which the various orders of beings had merged. Æ (George William Russell) believed, for example, that the lower orders of the sidhe were the elementals seen by the medieval mystics. Evans-Wentz argued that the Druids were the common source of both varieties of invisible creature. Modern fairy faith was shaped by the ancient Celtic religion, which, along with magic that involved the elementals, was known to the Druids and passed on by them. The gnomes described by Paracelsus were the same as the pixies, corrigans, leprechauns, and other elves who lived in rocks or caves or in the earth. Sylphs were to be equated wth the ordinary Celtic fairies, not the graceful "gentry" sidhe, but the pygmy-size apparitions that appeared to ordinary country folk (Evans-Wentz, pp. 256–57). Henry Jenner, writing on the fairy faith in Cornwall, simply argued that folklore came first and the elementals second:

> The subdivisions and elaborations . . . by Paracelsus, the Rosicrucians, and the modern theosophists are no doubt amplifications of that popular belief in the existence of a race, neither divine nor human, but very like to human beings, who existed on a 'plane' different from that of humans, though occupying the same space which . . . resembles the theory of these mystics in its main outlines, and was probably what suggested it to them. (qtd. in Evans-Wentz, p. 168)

While many modern folklorists would agree with Jenner's theory of etiology, few would argue, as he does, that elves and elementals actually exist.

Occultists often Platonized the fays as well, asserting that they were the preexistent Forms of human beings who "enter the . . . plane of life by submitting to the natural process of birth in a physical body" (Evans-Wentz, p. 383). Platonic, too, was the occultist notion that fairies were the spirits of the recent dead, awaiting incarnation in new bodies or transportation to new astral planes. Debate even raged about the normal residence of the elemental spirits. Was it the "astral plane"? Was it the "Summerland" of the Spiritualists — the place to which those who had recently "passed over" were relegated? Or was it something else, perhaps even a sort of Purgatory or, more optimistically, a chamber of rebirth? All in all, for the group of religious faithful (and both Spiritualists and Theosophists were among them), fairies provided an imaginative alternative or at least a supplement to Christianity, offering a promise of immortal life in a creed not yet outworn. In effect, all who asserted that fairies were actual rather than imaginary did so with a sense that their reality was a protest against sterile rationality, evidence that the material and utilitarian were not sole rulers of the world. For occultists, at least, the bonds that linked nature and man were not completely broken; the universe was still alive; "for the whole of the universe is a manifestation of life and consciousness expressed in innumerable different forms" (Hartmann, p. 30). Perhaps this element explains why so "scientific" a folklorist as J. F. Campbell of Islay (who carefully documented the place, date, and time at which he heard the lore collected for his *Popular Tales of the West Highlands*) supposedly subscribed to a belief in the existence of the elfin peoples. According to a deposition made by his assistant, Michael Buchanan, and printed by Evans-Wentz, Campbell was convinced that fairies were "spirits appearing to the naked eye of the spectator as . . . men and women, except that they were smaller in stature." To which Buchanan added, in terms reminiscent of the Nicene Creed: "And I also believe in the existence of the fairies . . . and accept the modern and ancient traditions respecting . . . [their] ways and customs" (Evans-Wentz, pp. 114–15).

However, with the possible exception of Campbell and the occult folklorists, most Victorian scholars who held one of the "religious views" did not participate in the fairy faith; instead, they studied religious belief. They saw the elfin peoples not as actual beings but as folk memories of ancient faiths, "survivals" of decayed pagan gods or local English deities. Croker and Keightley had found in the characters and actions of the "little folk" the remnants of an ancient Aryan religious system (see Keightley, p. 512) similar if not identical to that mentioned by the Brothers Grimm in their essay "On the Nature of the Elves." Wirt Sikes, the American consul to Wales, whose *British Goblins* was a popular book of the 1880s, favored the theory that the belief in fairies was one of the "relics of the ancient mythology" (p. 1) as did Patrick Kennedy (p. 81), the Irish folklorist revered by Yeats. The theorists and investigators connected with the burgeoning Folk-Lore Society were more specific. Edwin Sidney Hartland, the prolific anthropological folklorist, believed that at least some of the fays were the vestiges of ancient goddess worship, survivals from the era of the mother right. He contended that other preternatural creatures derived from the rituals of "stone age worship" (*Science of Fairy Tales*, pp. 291, 306). At one point in his illustrious career, Alfred Nutt speculated that belief in fairies originated in ancestor worship; at another point he argued that the fairy faith came from the widespread practice of worshipping local agricultural deities (*The Voyage of Bran* 2:231).

Others argued for the identity of fairies and the dead; some of the elfin peoples were clearly the souls of the departed, and fairyland itself could be seen as a sort of Hades. Folklorists like Yearsley, writing soon after the turn of the century, argued that not only were the places of the dead and fairyland often indistinguishable—both were subterranean—but also the rituals for dealing with both groups and the prohibitions governing such relations were identical. For example, one could summon both fairies and the dead by striking the ground; one was forbidden to taste food in either fairyland or Hades. Both worlds were marked by timelessness; both groups lured the living to them and both were placated in the same way, with offerings of food or milk or with gifts. Both fairies and the dead were local, confined to one locality or even to one living group or family, and both presided over fertility. Significantly, the same tales and legends were told of both; interchangeability seemed to some, including Canon J. A. MacCulloch, a sign of identity. Hartland, for instance, noted in *The Science of Fairy Tales* (1891) that no clear-cut distinctions could be made between ghosts and fairies, since they shared the same traits, the same taboos, and the same tales. Even the relatively small size of some fairies became a support for this argument, for souls have traditionally been depicted as smaller than the bodies of the persons they inhabit. The revived interest in lore itself, starting with Scott's republishing and discussion of the Scottish witch trials of the seventeenth century, added further evidence; so many of the accused had reported seeing dead friends and relatives among the fairies. Such popular tales as "The Fairy Dwelling on Selena Moor" also heightened the connection between the fairies and the dead. In this tale from Cornwall, a certain Mr. Noy, who inadvertently stumbles on a fairy realm, is saved from captivity by his former sweetheart, one who had ostensibly died years earlier. Among the fairies, he sees other neighbors who were thought to be dead. The same tale was told of a young farmer, Richard Vingoe, and, in other variations, of people all over England.[6]

Other proofs were brought to support the theory. Many folklorists noted that Gwyn ap Nudd, the ruler of the "fair folk" of Wales, was also the Lord of the Dead; others that the slaugh, or Host of the Air, were the dead in some parts of the British Isles and the fairy horde in others. A number commented on how frequently fairies were seen in graveyards or rising from cemetary grounds. Still others, including Andrew Lang, used as support the thesis of Reverend Robert Kirk's famous *Secret Common-Wealth of Elves, Fauns, and Fairies* (c. 1690), a document largely rediscovered and often utilized in the Victorian era. (Sir Walter Scott, in "On the Fairies of Popular Superstition," had earlier pointed out the importance of *The Secret Commonwealth*, with its guide to and geography of fairyland.) Lang found himself in agreement with Kirk. "There are excellent proofs," he noted, "that fairyland was a kind of Hades, or home of the dead" (Introduction, p. xxxiv).

The places with which fairies were most identified, their mainly interior and subterranean habitations, were the strongest and most widely cited evidences of their similarity to or identity with the souls of the dead. The ancient mounds, burrows, and tumuli, in which they often lived (as well as their nocturnal habits) suggested the realms of death. In the seventeenth century, Reginald Scot had informed his readers that English "Faeries— do principally inhabit the Mountains, and Caverns of the Earth" (qtd. in Briggs, *Dictionary*, p. 348) and the strong tradition, itself based on numerous medieval sources, survived. The fairies were, as Kipling's Puck calls them, the "People of the Hill"—and they lived not *on* the hill but *in* it. To Thomas Keightley, England and Lowland Scotland shared the same tradition— fairies lived in the hills; the Highland variety also lived in hillocks or in masses of rock. One branch of the Irish fairies, the sidhe—who were thought to take their names from the mounds or *sidhe* in which they dwelt—lived in these mounds, or raths, or forts. (The forts were the remains of prehistoric fortifications.) Other sites were added by other commentators and included the ideas that fairies could be found beneath ancient castles (Lowland Scotland), under ruined Pictish towers or beehive houses (Highlands and Ireland), and within mountain caves. The Victorians seemed to have emphasized the idea of a world within the earth—in part because it was an area that remained to be investigated, in part because it was a realm that the emerging science of archaeology was exploring. Subterranean habitations emphasized, as well, the interiority of the fairy realm. Yet they almost always implied connections between the fairies and the dead. For some, fairyland became the place where these souls waited, in Christian terms, for the Last Judgment and, in pagan terms, for rebirth or an end to things.

They Are Matter: Scientific Views

All of these "religious views" were merely second to a cluster of opinions that may be termed "scientific views." Whether their approaches were mythological-linguistic, comparative-anthropological, or euhemerist, all who accepted versions of the scientific view shared the conviction that fairies or their prototypes had, in some sense, originated on this earth. From the mid-1850s till the outbreak of the First World War, the various scientific theories jockeyed for position, rising and falling in popularity as new evidence flowed in. For some among the scientifically oriented scholars, the truth of fairy existence filled the void left by a dying Bible; for others, the ability to weigh the evidence for and against fairy existence was a proof of the validity of the new scientific disciplines at which they labored.

For the mythological-linguistic "school" associated with Max Müller, the answer to the question of the actuality of the fairies lay in language. Though the main emphasis of the "school" was on the gods, specifically the Sun God, from whom, Müller contended, almost all myth was derived, its proponents applied its principles to the study of fairy lore. From about 1856, the date of Müller's significant essay on "Comparative Mythology," to the mid-1880s, when the theory became suspect, the celestial mythologists had considerable impact. While they agreed on the basic premise that the central figures in Greek and Roman mythology and in the fairy tales descended from them reflected heavenly phenomena, they argued about which natural phenomenon was paramount. Was it the sun, as Müller said, or the lightning, as Walter K. Kelly insisted? Were clouds or thunder, stars or the moon the source of such concepts as supernatural dwarfs? Since myth, they believed, came from a "disease of language," a condition in which a later group of people misunderstood the language or metaphoric usage of an earlier group (in the most famous instance, the classical Greek gods were revealed by Müller as verbal misapprehensions of ancient Sancrit names), the barbarous features of fairy lore were now explained as poetic, metaphoric phrases from early human mythopoeic thinking. Since myth really derived from a sort of "creative forgetting," the celestial mythologists attempted to unravel the verbal confusions that had led to a belief in fairies. Müller emphasized the Greek gods and their derivation from the mother of the Indo-European languages, Sanscrit, but George W. Cox, his disciple, explained to the British public the meaning of folklore as early man's view of the conflict between night and day or wind and calm. As he argued in *An Introduction to the Comparative Science of Mythology and Folklore* (1881), folklore and myth "embody the whole thought of primitive man on the vast range of physical phenomena" (p. 13). Fairies are only secondary in Cox's allegorical schemata, but he indicates that, for example, "the fairy queens who tempt Tannhäuser and True Thomas to their caves" (p. 156n) are really figures for "the beauty of the night, cloudless and still" (p. 156). In Cox's view, most fairies are to be associated with the stars; their origins are to be found in stellar phenomena. But a rival to the mythological-linguists in the form of a far more significant set of scientific theories claimed the foreground after 1859 and the publication of Charles Darwin's *On the Origin of Species*. Darwin's theory of biological evolution was quickly appropriated by anthropologists and resulted in a parallel theory of cultural evolution.[7] By the 1870s, an important group of anthropological or ethnological folklorists (whom I have called the comparative-anthropological group) had come into being, inspired by the the work of the "godfather" of comparative anthropology, Sir Edward Burnet Tylor. For these folklore scholars, the savage elements in folk tales and customs were again (as with the celestial mythologists) the attempt of primitive peoples to interpret the basic, universal situations of life, but they were not always mistakes or distortions. In *Primitive Culture* (1871), Tylor proposed two ideas important to the study of fairy lore: the doctrine of survivals and the theory of animism. What degree of historical truth, if any, does folk and fairy lore contain, Tylor inquired? What is its basis? Were similarities in lore the results of diffusion or the separate inventions of groups, tribes, or races? At first, there was no conflict with Müller's celestial theories for Tylor, believing that people uniformly ascended the ladder of cultural evolution, simply noted that the savages, whose customs he analyzed, preceded Müller's early Indo-European-speaking Aryans. Tylor was sophisticated in suggesting a broad spectrum of answers: he believed, for instance, that *some*, though not all, fairies clearly derived from animistic perceptions of nature, for, according to the doctrine of animism, primeval humans personified nature and perceived it as living. Moreover, as primitive peoples composed myths animating nature, so contemporary peasants preserved folklore—the remnants or "survivals" of prehistoric animistic beliefs and primitive myths. Indirectly, Tylor made the study of fairies quite important to the study of comparative anthropology. Not only did the doctrine of "survivals" make the more pejorative idea of "superstitions" seem condescending and outmoded but also the seemingly irrational beliefs and practices of the rural peasantry became significant and valuable. They were "scientific evidence," the fragments of ancient "less evolved" human culture; they both illustrated the past history of the human race and confirmed the theory of man's development. There was, Tylor argued, a clear continuity between the savage and the peasant and Tylor's equation of the two inspired folklorists to examine the culture of the folk and to trace its likeness to the behavior of savage tribes. Equally important, Tylor, like most Victorian social scientists, assumed a simplified, linear, Darwinian progress; human development was upwards; human beings work out the beast, evolving from savagery through barbarism to civilization. Thus, it was of major importance to trace the relics of savagery and barbarism still surviving among civilized peoples.[8]

Tylor's theories attracted such luminaries of anthropology and folklore study as James Anson Farrer and Andrew Lang. Farrer and Lang did further anthropological spadework, comparing the beliefs and practices of non-European primitive peoples with similar accounts imbedded in European folklore. Their theories were most fully and coherently elaborated by Canon J. A. MacCulloch in *The Childhood of Fiction* (1905). To MacCulloch the originals of the fairies were the ancient and modern "savages," and folk tales were direct reflections of savage ideas, beliefs, and customs. The lives of fairy-tale kings, he argued, were exaggerated replications of the simple lives of primitive tribal chieftains: the magic slumbers of sleeping beauties were evidences of an early tribal knowledge of hypnosis. The princess who was ravished by a giant or a fairy was none other than a savage maiden kidnapped in the widespread ritual known as "marriage by capture." Cannibalism as a prominent motif in folklore came from its widespread practice by the savage races; a "superior" tribe that had renounced the custom told tales of those who still practiced it—describing them as goblins, ogres, or witches.

The concept implicit in MacCulloch's book—that fairies and their lore resulted from the clash of cultures or races—had been earlier and more explicitly stated by others, including Alfred C. Haddon, George Laurence Gomme, and John Stuart Stuart-Glennie (Dorson, *British Folklorists*, p. 310). It became a particularly useful concept in an era of imperial expansion.[9] Professor Haddon argued that "fairy-tales point to a clash of races" and could be regarded "as stories told by men of the Iron Age of events which happened to men of the Bronze Age in their conflicts with men of the Neolithic Age" (qtd. in Evans-Wentz, p. 137n). In his brilliant *Ethnology in Folklore* (1892), Gomme, then president of the Folk-Lore Society, argued that folklore often represented the clash of peoples, and that English lore, specifically, spoke of the battles between those of prehistoric non-Aryan stock and the Indo-Europeans who invaded them (p. 19). Much of the inconsistency in folklore could be explained by a difference in point of view, he suggested; the influences on the lore of the conquered race and of the conquering race differed, each group ascribing certain supernatural powers to the other. The nature of given concepts was dictated by whether they were believed and enunciated by the conquerers or the conquered. For example, beliefs about fairies and about witches were very similar, said Gomme. The belief in fairies, however, came from the conquerors; it was a belief about the aborigines from Aryan sources. The belief in witches, on the other hand, came from the conquered aborigines themselves; they believed they had magical powers and tried to spread this belief (in part, to guarantee their survival) among their conquerors. Significantly, Gomme ascribes the cruder and bloodier superstitions to non-Aryans. To Stuart-Glennie, however, the clashes between early peoples were not mere power struggles, but conflicts filled with racial and imperial implications; the importance of the fairies was that they were white. All civilization arose from the "Conflict of Higher and Lower Races"; such tales as "The Swan Maiden" recorded actual events: the rape or forced marriage of white women by black or brown men (see chapter 3). Only the "Higher Races" could create civilizations; the "Lower" at best were the sources of folklore (Dorson, *Peasant Customs* 2:520; 2:323–30).

Few fellow folklorists took up the white man's fantasy quite so overtly and Stuart-Glennie had almost no disciples. However, the racial composition of the fairies, their inferior or superior status, and their place in British history became major issues, especially to those who took the historical-realist or euhemerist position. The euhemerists believed that fairies were derived from an early group of invaders of the British Isles or from the British aborigines themselves. Various forms of euhemerism had been popular at the end of the eighteenth century and the beginning of the nineteenth, when the Reverend Peter Roberts, Dr. Guthrie, and the Dr. Cririe cited by Robert Southey had theorized that the elfin races, with their organized societies and systematized customs, were, in actuality, the Druids hiding underground from Roman and Christian persecutions. Other pre-Victorian antiquarians had speculated that the English fairies were really early Irish invaders; still others, that they were early but unspecified mortals whose actions had been exaggerated in fabulous tales (Sikes, p. 130).

The Druids and the Irish were relegated to minor roles in the Victorian debate on fairies, but the conquered British aborigines gained favor, and with the increasing historicism of the period, euhemerism became a major

Victorian explanation of origin. Campbell of Islay may have privately affirmed that the fays were "spirits"; he publically wrote, however, that they were based on dim memories of the skin-clad warriors who made and shot flint arrowheads (elf-shots) but lost England to the iron-weaponed ancestors of the modern British (1:lxix–lxxx). Although he stressed the heterogeneous nature of their sources, John Rhys agreed that the fairies stemmed, in part, from "an early race of men," "pre-Pictish," the "oldest and lowest" in England (*Celtic Folklore* 2:667). The concept of the fairies as a "superior," civilizing race was even more popular, albeit briefly. In the late eighteenth century, Mallet had hypothesized in *Northern Antiquities* (1770) that the Laplanders (always considered magical) were the original fairies. Sir Walter Scott, also a believer in the Oriental Lapps as one of the sources of the fairies, speculated that they had gained their reputation as supernaturals by foretelling the weather, something they knew from careful observation. Jacob Grimm, ahead of his time, had theorized (in *Teutonic Mythology*) that there was once a widely diffused dwarf population all over northern Europe whose actions had given rise to the many traditions associated with supernatural elfs. Benjamin Thorpe, the Scandinavianist, speculated in the 1830s that the dwarfs of Norse belief were "Oriental Lapps," perceived as magical because, unlike the Norse, they knew the manufacture and use of iron. George Webbe Dasent, Thorpe's colleague in Scandinavian studies, thought that the nomadic Finns and Lapps had been mythically transformed to trolls or enlarged to giants (Dorson, *Peasant Customs* 2:596). In 1881, Karl Blind retransformed the transformation by asserting that the skin-clad Finns who rode the waves in kayaks were the sources of the mermen, mermaids, and selkies (seal people) of Scottish lore (qtd. in MacRitchie, *Testimony*, pp. 1–6). By the time of Frederic T. Hall's *The Pedigree of the Devil* (1883), it was almost taken for granted that dwarfs, trolls, and fairies were folk memories of prehistoric races of small people. It is impossible, says Hall, "not to conclude that the dwarfs and trolls must be identified with primeval races of men of low stature; who covered a large area of the habitable globe, and were gradually driven into mountain fastnesses, swamps, ice-bound tracts, or tractless steppes, before the steady advance of a larger, more powerful, or better armed race of men" (p. 76). To Hall, the early Babylonian or Accadian peoples represented the nucleus of this "Turanian" group (p. 77); to Sabine Baring-Gould, the prehistoric Iberians were at its center. George Laurence Gomme noted (in *English Traditional Lore* [1885]) that not only did the new science of archaeology indicate that fairies had existed, but that they were a small pygmy race; fairy lore preserved traditions of short, dark, early aboriginal peoples who preceded the Aryan occupation of Europe (p. vi).

Building on the work of all who came before him, David MacRitchie popularized what came to be known as the "pygmy theory" in his important and controversial book, *The Testimony of Tradition* (1890). His argument was reiterated and further elaborated in *Fians, Fairies and Picts* (1893). Buttressing his case with philological, topographical, traditional, and historical proofs, MacRitchie correlated fairy lore with the archeological remains of underground abodes as evidence for the existence of an ancient, dwarflike non-Aryan race in England. The idea was not new, but the development of archaeology as a science and the increased exploration of prehistoric sites gave MacRitchie's new euhemerism a force beyond the theoretical. A sort of Victorian Thor Hyerdahl, he crawled through and diagrammed mounds and tunnels to prove the validity of his assertions.

The heart of MacRitchie's argument was that the Finno-Ugrian or Mongol peoples (including the Lapps) were also the Fians (the race preceding the Scots) and the Picts of Irish and Scottish history, and that they had coexisted with the other inhabitants of England until at least the eleventh century. Skilled in medicine, magic, and masonry, they inhabited concealed underground earth houses—later known as fairy hills or fairy forts—and sophisticated chambered mounds like Maes-Howe in the Orkneys or New Grange and the other mounds at Boyne. The fires that shone at night through the tops of their underground dwellings were responsible for the persistent legends, found all over England, of "fairy lights." Their "clever" women gained the love of Irish chieftains, married them, and became, in legend, the powerful Irish fairies known as sidhe. MacRitchie even explained why fairies favored the color green: it was the hunting color worn by the tiny Lapps.

While some of the comparative-anthropological authorities on fairy lore, including Andrew Lang, Alfred Nutt, and Edwin Sidney Hartland, took issue with MacRitchie, others, equally respected, flocked to his cause. Elizabeth Andrews tried to do for Ireland, especially Ulster, what MacRitchie had done for Scotland. In *Ulster Folklore*, published in 1913 but based on earlier articles and lectures, she argued that dwarfs living in Ireland had built the souterrains (caves with underground structures built of rough stones without mortar and roofed with large, flat slabs) found throughout the country. Evidences of a dwarf race were not solely archaeological, however; the tales of gorgachs (brownie-like creatures), of Pechts or Picts, of the sidhe, and of the so-called short Danes who invaded Ireland were also derived from memories of this "Turanian" race. All, she believed, "represent primitive races of mankind and . . . in the stories of women, children and men being carried off, we have a record of warfare, when stealthy raids were made and captives brought to the dark souterrain" (p. vi). Short, strong, and with skills in music and other arts, these "fairy" peoples, once all over Europe, were pushed back and ended up in Lapland where their descendents may still be found (p. 45). Andrews, like MacRitchie, thought that pygmies had survived into the historical period. A ballad like "The Wee Wee Man," with its description of a short, sturdy little creature, was evidence of their existence.[10] Although not quite so enthusiastic about the "pygmy theory," Sir John Rhys remarked that when fairyland is shorn of its glamour, it reveals "a swarthy population of short stumpy men occupying the most inaccessible districts of our country" (*Celtic Folklore* 2:668–69). Joseph Jacobs—Andrew Lang's rival as a collector and editor of fairy tales for children (his *English Fairy Tales* and *Celtic Fairy Tales* are still to be found in many children's libraries)—used MacRitchie's theories to explain what lay behind such places as the "Dark Tower" (a fairy mound) in "Childe Rowland" (see *English Fairy Tales*, pp. 260–64). The Reverend Gath Whitley considered piskey dwarfs, that is pixies, the earliest Neolithic inhabitants of Cornwall and described them as small hunters who, like bushmen, danced and sang to the light of the moon (qtd. in Andrews, p. 101). Henry Jenner, local secretary for the Society of Antiquaries in Cornwall, was certain that "a strange and separate people of Mongol type" were still extant and dwelling in the Cornish wilds. This "little 'stuggy' dark folk," once thought to be composed of witches and wizards, were really the descendants of the Pictish tribes; (qtd. in Evans-Wentz, pp. 166–67); thus had the Picts become the pixies.

Sabine Baring-Gould's quibbles with MacRitchie's theories were over how far south in England the Finno-Ugrians had come and whether they had been entire tribes or gypsylike itinerants. In an article on "Pixies and Brownies," reprinted in *A Book of Folk-Lore* (1913), he concluded that yet another group of pygmies, who had lived in caves or earthen huts but had not built in stone (and hence, in folklore were shown as emerging from mounds or caverns), were the sources of the knockers and pixies of Devon and Cornwall. It was, he thought, Oriental Lapps who taught the Norse mining and metal working, for iron fabrication, he believed, was not native to northern and eastern Europe. His "fairies" were dwarfs or pygmies, "not found in large numbers nor forming big colonies, but vagrant and dispersed," practicing crafts and migrating like gypsies. "Shy, living a different life than those for whom they worked" (p. 216), they gave rise to tales. There might, he argued, have been different groups of them with different skills; some were miners, some smiths, some mere laborers on farms. From these "people of foreign race, misunderstood, looked on with superstitious fears, whose very ways encouraged mistrust" (p. 224), came the tales of dwarfs (if they were smiths) or brownies (if farm laborers). Baring-Gould thought that an archaeological excavation near Padstow in Cornwall had yielded their prehistoric necropolis, located on a site the local people long considered "fairy haunted." But the most conclusive skeletal remains of these small dolichocephalic (long-headed), non-Aryan, "intrusive people" had been destroyed (pp. 227–28) not by the superstitious country folk but by the bourgeois tourists trampling on the site in their quest for the English past.

When the remains of neolithic Swiss dwarfs were found at Schweizerbild near Schaffhausen around 1893, the "pygmy school" thought it had found conclusive physical evidence. MacRitchie had not found dwarf skeletons in his chambered mounds, but here they were, clear physical evidence of an early dwarf creation as well as an explanation of the origin of the fairies. Additional dwarf skeletons found at Spy in Belgium seemed to further validate the "pygmy theory." Professor Fraipoint, the expert examining the skeletons at Spy, identified them as those of very early peoples. To him they looked analogous to modern Laplanders; they were very short, he concluded, with "voluminous heads, massive bodies, short arms and bent legs. They led a sedentary life, frequented caves, manufactured flint implements . . . and were contemporary with the Mammoth" (qtd. in Andrews, pp. 129–30).

The euhemerist case did not depend solely on the findings of archaeologists. After the 1870s, the African Pygmies discovered by George Schweinfurth became the living physical support for the "pygmy theory" of fairy origins and the most likely and visible proof of the prehistoric existence of fairies. When, in the course of colonial expansion, British explorations located dwarflike and Pygmy peoples where they had not been previously known to exist—in the Congo and the Uganda borderlands, and ostensibly near Mount Atlas, in Morocco—MacRitchie's theories seemed incontrovertible. The findings of archaeology, prehistory, ethnology, and of recent explorations—when added to the quasi-Darwinian theory of cultural evolution—seemed, by the turn of this century, to make the origin of the fairies a simple matter: they were Pygmy peoples who had once inhabited the entire world. For Colonel R. G. Haliburton, "little dark-complexioned smiths and magicians" (closely resembling the Akka dwarfs of Morocco he believed he had discovered) were responsible for the Scottish belief in brownies and the Welsh memory of Merlin's band of dwarf smiths (*Dwarf Survivals and Traditions*, p. 76 [1895]). According to the anonymous reviewer of a book called *Prehistoric Man and Beast*, they might even have been the builders of Stonehenge. "Certain analogies," he argued, "lend weight to the idea that possibly Stonehenge was erected by the dwarfs or fairies, who . . . are shown to have been a real people" (qtd. in Haliburton, *Race of Pygmies*, p. 305).

His was a minority view. For most folklorists and anthropologists the fact that the Pygmy descendants of the fairies were black, yellow, and red—clearly "less evolved" than British Victorians—rendered them definitely incapable of monument building and distinctly inferior. Thus, as the discovery of the Pygmies rendered the fairies actual, it caused them to lose much of their stature and "superiority" (see chapter 4). The fairies were racialized, and dwarfs, in particular, became new figures for powerful though bestial evil.

As Real as X-Rays: Psychic Evolution

At the same time as the new euhemerists were actualizing and demytholo-gizing the elfin world, yet another group was insisting on its reality while further idealizing it. As the Victorian scholarly community replicated that pattern of folklore in which the more fantastic the tale, the more solid the material proof surrounding it, other "realist" but nonhistorical and nonan-thropological approaches gained adherents. In a fascinating fusion of the scientific and religious views of fairy origins, occultists, Spiritualists, and Theosophists argued for the actuality of fairies on scientific grounds. From the faith in science came the certitude that new, perfected sciences and parasciences could prove that fairies did exist. By 1909, Sophia Morrison, folklorist and secretary of the Manx Language Society, could assert:

> There is nothing supernatural [about the fairies] . . . what used to be so
> called is something that we do not understand at present. . . . Our fore-
> fathers would have thought the X-rays, and wireless telegraphy . . . "su-
> pernatural." (qtd. in Evans-Wentz, p. 119)

From popularizations of Darwin's theories and vitalistic views of evolu-tion came the widespread notion that fairies were life-forms developed on a separate branch of evolution. Though he did not speak specifically of fays or gnomes, Alfred Russell Wallace had suggested that there were "preter-human discarnate beings" who shared the world with man (Oppenheim, p. 326). Spiritualists, Theosophists, and Victorian occultists, eager to escape the depressing implications of Darwinist materialism, were in agreement with him. Emma Hardinge-Britten, for example, writing on "Nature Spir-its and Elementals" in the Spiritualist journal *Light* (3 Dec. 1881), uttered what amounted to a call to action: how, she asked, since Darwin's proofs have been accepted, "can the Spiritualist be content to supplement Dar-win's merely materialistic footprint and utterly ignore the existence of Spiritual realms of being as the *antecedents* of matter?" In search of a ladder of descent parallel to Darwin's, she finds that there are "*embryonic* states for the soul, as well as for the body . . . realms of gestation for Spiritual, as well as for material, forms." The rungs of the spirit ladder of evolution are filled with sub- and superhuman spirits, fairies among them; there are "many grades of the scale of being" (p. 382). Evans-Wentz, the occult folklorist, thought the fairies "a distinct race between our own and that of spirits" and concluded his impressive research into Celtic fairy faith with a "logical and scientific" argument for psychic evolution (pp. 47, 479).

Theosophists were particularly enamoured of the "separate evolution" idea and rapidly incorporated it into their beliefs. Analogies between mate-rial and spiritual evolution literally pepper Madame Blavatsky's *Isis Unveiled* (1877). Darwin's descent of species, for example, is compared to that of the ancient Neoplatonists, while elementals are like "Mr. Darwin's missing link between the ape and man" (1:285). Her disciples became engrossed in determining the position and function of nature spirits in the spiritual ladder of evolution. Fairies seen and described by occultists, usually through clairvoyance, were defined as powers of nature—little sprites who aided in the growth of trees, flowers, and even vegetables. Occultists like Charles W. Leadbeater, who considered the elfin tribes "an evolution apart" (*Hidden Side*, p. 84), were quick to articulate and systematize the evolutionary relations of fairies and mortals. Devoting an entire chapter of *The Hidden Side of Things* (1913) to fairy evolution, Leadbeater described nature spirits, including gnomes, fairies, undines, sylphs, and elementals, as the *aboriginal* peoples: "the original inhabitants of the country, driven away from some parts of it by the invasion of man" (p. 84). As humans derived from mammals, so some of the elfin tribes evolved from grasses and cereals, others from reptiles and birds, and still others from sea flora and fauna. Paralleling the upward spiritual evolution of man (from an ordinary half-evolved state through stages as "Advanced Man," "Disciple," and finally "Adept"), fairies also evolve, becoming sylphs, devas (or angels), and ultimately higher angels. Even providing a diagramatic chart, Leadbeater elaborates the complex heirarchical chains of fairy being. One strain of nature spirit, for example, "just touches the vegetable kingdom in the shape of minute fungoid growths, and then passes onward through bacteria . . . through the insects and reptiles up to the beautiful family of the birds, and only after many incarnations among these joins the still more joyous tribe of the fairies." Another "comes up through the vegetable kingdom in the shape of grasses and cereals . . . [and then] turns aside . . . into the animal kingdom and is conducted through the curious communities of the ants and bees, and then through a set of etheric creatures closely corresponding to the latter —those tiny hummingbirdlike nature-spirits which are so continually seen hovering about flowers and plants, and play so large a part in the production of their manifold variations" (p. 90). It is because human beings are only half-evolved themselves, endowed with only crude sensory perceptions, that nature spirits are not visible to them. Only clairvoyants, like Leadbeater himself, are capable of seeing them.

Like a biologist, botanist, or ethnologist, Leadbeater continues his unnatural natural history by assuring his readers that, although fairies may assume almost any size, shape, and color they choose, they do have distinct genera and species types—definite "natural" forms and colors of their own. Here, the language of anthropology joins the language of biology in a "scientific" explanation of the invisible. Diverse elfin races populate different countries or parts of them, Leadbeater notes. Like the "pygmies and ape-like men of the Uganda borderland"[11] and the other "savages" studied by travelers and anthropological folklorists, some elfin tribes are less highly evolved than others. Those who live near the sites of volcanic disturbances are espe-

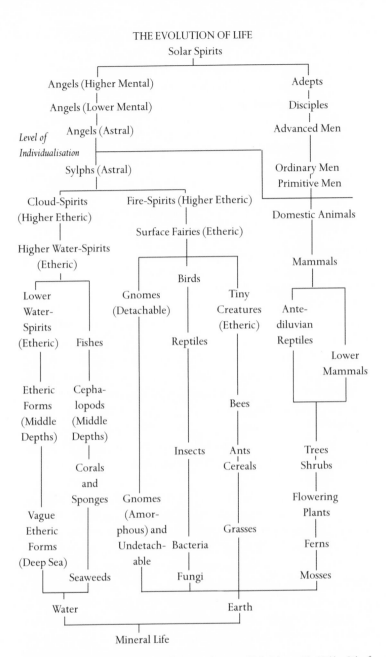

THE EVOLUTION OF LIFE

1.2 Charles W. Leadbeater, chart of "The Evolution of Life," from *The Hidden Side of Things* (1913).

cially primitive, he remarks, intermediate between gnomes and fairies. Like separate species, Leadbeater continues, mountain fairies and plains fairies do not mate or mingle. Even Darwinian natural adaptation plays a role; for example, elfin coloration varies according to habitat. In what sounds like a species report written by a botanist, clairvoyant Leadbeater reports:

> In England the emerald-green kind is probably the commonest, and I have seen it also in the woods of France and Belgium, in far-away Massachusetts, and on the banks of the Niagara river. The vast plains of the Dakotas are inhabited by a black-and-white kind which I have not seen elsewhere, and California rejoices in a lovely white-and gold species which also appears to be unique. (qtd. in Arthur Conan Doyle, *Coming of the Fairies*, p. 134)

Leadbeater pleads for further "scientific" study of nature spirits. "I am not aware that any attempt has yet been made to classify them in scientific fashion. This vast realm of nature still needs its Cuvier or its Linnaeus" (*Hidden Side*, p. 123). He concludes that, like foreign travel or African exploration, the careful examination of the fairy world will broaden human horizons; "the comprehension of a line of evolution so different from our own . . . helps us to recognize that the world does not exist for us alone, and that our point of view is neither the only one nor the most important" (*Hidden Side*, p. 124).

Psychic-evolutionist and "naturalist" approaches such as those of Bishop Leadbeater prepared the way for the acceptance of the Cottingley fairy photographs of 1917 — pictures in which small creatures with bobbed hair and butterfly wings frisked in the midst of nature (see also chapter 6). Supporters of the photographs' validity, including Edward Gardner (secretary of the Theosophical Society) and Sir Arthur Conan Doyle, saw the fairies as forces of nature, seldom visible because they were outside the human color spectrum or on the other side of the "vibration line" (A. C. Doyle, *Coming*, p. 89). Gardner was quite certain of the nature and function of the elfin specimens, which he described in biological terminology: "Allied to the lepidoptera, or butterfly genus . . . rather than to the mammalian line . . . they are as real as we are, and perform functions in connection with plant life of an important . . . character" (pp. 122–23). Although they are not insubstantial, their bodies are made of a matter lighter than gas, and hence, appear invisible to non-clairvoyant mortals. While they may assume human forms, they are really "small, hazy, and somewhat luminous clouds of colour with a brighter spark-like nucleus" (p. 124). Their wings are actually emanations. Like the amobea or protozoa they resemble, they seem to divide by mitosis and, similarly to other lower organisms, they have little or no individuality, consciousness, or language. Gardner provides a mechanistically scientific exposition of their role in the scheme of things:

> The function of the nature spirits of woodland, meadow, and garden . . .
> is to furnish the vital connecting link between the stimulating energy of

the sun and the raw material of the form. That growth of a plant which we regard as the customary and inevitable result of associating the three factors of sun, seed, and soil would never take place if the fairy builders were absent." (qtd. in A. C. Doyle, *Coming*, p. 124)

In Gardner's system, one he finally came to call "devic evolution" (Hodson, p. 50) after the "nature-spirits, devas, fairies or elementals" whose specific role is "the evolution of beautiful and responsive forms," highly specialized fairy groups literally construct and organize the cells of flowers, some working with root development, others specializing in shape and coloration. The beauty and variety of the floral world is not the result of blind "evolutionary processes" but of fairies (A. C. Doyle, *Coming*, p. 129). As Dr. Vanstone (one of Doyle's authorities) commented, in yet another telling analogy, they serve as little "factory hands . . . facilitating the operation of Nature's laws" (p. 98).

Gardner, like Leadbeater, devoted much of his life to the "scientific study" of the invisible world of nature spirits. Always arguing that fairy evolution runs in partnership with human evolution, he increasingly classified elfin species and formalized his system. By his last book, *Fairies*, written in the 1940s, he had repeopled his world, at least, with an enormous, complex "ladder of evolving life rising to the loftiest heights, the whole system composing a sister evolution . . . to the animal and human kingdoms, but all using bodies of a subtler material than the physical" (p. 46).

1.3 "Frances and the Fairies," Cottingley photograph number 1.

Geoffrey Hodson, friend of both Gardner and Doyle, and one of the clairvoyants who "verified" the existence of the Cottingley fairies, also heeded Leadbeater's call for scientific study of the invisible world. He, too, penned an unnatural natural history of nature spirits and devoted much time and energy to these lesser-evolved spiritual species. Like Leadbeater

and Gardner, he assumed a sister system of evolution:

> Just as on the human line of evolution the life works up through the mineral, vegetable, and animal stages, and then moves on into the human kingdom and becomes an *individual human being*, so the stream of nature-spirit life evolves likewise through the mineral and vegetable and on to the animal world, where it is associated with the smaller birds, fishes and insects." (Hodson, p. 83)

In his system, "The lesser fairies . . . are about at the level of our domestic animals," while higher spiritual life "finally passes through these forms to that of the sylph, after which stage it is able to act as an individualized 'angel'" (p. 83). Cultural anthropology merges with Darwinian biology in his examination and classification of species, while the language of ethnology infiltrates his text. Lowly moor gnomes, for example, have a consciousness that is "ultra primitive and very limited. . . . The tribe is animated almost entirely by group consciousness and herd instinct" (pp. 43–44). In contradistinction, flower fairies are sufficiently evolved to be aware of their special work and to actually enjoy it. Hodson clairvoyantly watches biological processes in action as "small sub-microscopic etheric creatures" (p. 15) make a plant bulb grow, absorbing something from the atmosphere, reentering the tissue of the plant, and discharging what they have absorbed. He is even present at the rapid "evolution" of a group of highly imitative Brownies, although he candidly explains that he is unable to ascertain precisely what natural function they fulfill.

Thus, for occultists, at least, Darwin did not empty the world of nature; instead, he peopled it with other if invisible species. The world the occultists created—or perceived—was as richly teeming with life as the visible realm. And they truly believed that the progress of science would reveal the actual existence of the tribes and species they described. Like Schweinfurth's Congo Pygmies, once thought mythical but newly discovered and proved actual, fairies too would be located. Like X-ray beams, they only *seemed* intangible. The supernatural, affirmed occultists, would prove to be the natural not understood.

However, although believers in spiritual evolution insisted on both the actuality and omnipresence of the elfin people, they saw them as small, even microscopic in size, and categorized them as subhuman, lower creatures in traits and functions. Thus, the fairies were further diminished. While the Cottingley pictures and the publicity about them created a temporary fairy fever in the early 1920s, engendering other fairy photographs and inducing reports of sightings in wild New Zealand and remote British

Columbia (in the latter region local elfin colonies were "bright blue" in the hop fields and "silvery green elsewhere"),[12] in the long run they drove the fairies and the serious study of them underground. The more conservative among the folklore scholars shied away from disputation. The Folk-Lore Society, already weakened by internal strife about psychic phenomena, refused to comment on them. Narrowing the great debate on fairy origins and existence to a question of whether specific photographs were fraudulent, proffering pictures that invalidated private or heroic images of spirits, rendering the elfin tribes as psychic insect life, they trivialized and diminished the elfin races almost beyond recognition. When the "little people" next emerged, their origins were different. They were small green creatures from another planet who visit earth in close encounters of a different kind.

But in the interim, from the 1840s till the 1920s, the elfin peoples had a surprisingly large impact on the society that witnessed, studied, painted, dramatized, and wrote about them. The Victorian study of fairy lore acts as an excellent reflector of both the dominant ideas and the concealed anxieties of the era. The specific areas and problems in fairy faith and fairy lore that preoccupied Victorian folklorists and believers are revelations of social and cultural concerns perhaps shown elsewhere, but never in such sharp relief. Concerns about change and growth in children, about the status of women in marriage and divorce, about the discovery of new and alien racial groups, and about the sources of evil, occult and natural, are all revealed in the lore the Victorians chose to emphasize and how they "read" and used it.

T W O

"COME AWAY THOU HUMAN CHILD"
Abductions, Change, and Changelings

WHEN, IN A CLIMATIC MOMENT in Emily Brontë's *Wuthering Heights* (1847), Lockwood is troubled by an apparition of Catherine Earnshaw and hysterically exclaims "she must have been a changeling—wicked little soul" (p. 13), he is expressing a fantastic anxiety peculiar to the period. Similarly, when Edward Rochester, angered at her rejection of his prenuptial caresses, accuses Charlotte Brontë's Jane Eyre of being not *his* Jane but a "changeling," he is attempting to fathom what to him is a strange transformation in personality and behavior. In actuality even more than in fiction, changelings—that is, children perceived as abnormal surreptitiously substituted for normal ones—were very much a part of the Victorian world. An article in the *Daily Telegraph* of 19 May 1884 informed readers that

> Ellen Cushion and Anastatia Rourke were arrested at Clonmel on Saturday charged with cruelly illtreating a child three years old, named Philip Dillon. The prisoners were taken before the Mayor, when evidence was given showing that the neighbours fancied that the boy, who had not the use of his limbs, was a changeling left by the fairies in exchange for the original child. While the mother was absent, the prisoners entered her house and placed the lad naked on a hot shovel under the impression that this would break the charm. The poor little thing

was severely burned, and is in a precarious condition. (qtd. in Hartland, *Science*, pp. 121–22)

For Victorians, on some level at least, the changeling phenomenon was a mysterious and frightening occurrence that could, if successfully probed, provide explanations for sudden death or disappearance, mysterious illness, and eccentric and bizarre behavior. Moreover, the possibility of the existence of actual changelings increasingly came to be located in the nexus of Victorian anxieties about difference, race, and class.

The Victorians seem almost obsessed with the question of changelings. Not only did the concept permeate both their Scandinavian and Celtic folklore inheritance but folklorists also retold hundreds of tales of elfin creatures substituted for human beings—especially children[1]—and newspapers and journals reported the widespread survival of belief in such beings, as well as numerous cases of death or injury caused by the practices used to exorcise them.

While such stories sold collections of folklore and punctuated the pages of Victorian newspapers, novel-reading members of the middle classes pondered the violent passions and demonic energies of fictional changelings such as the "elfish Robert" in Elizabeth Gaskell's tale, "The Doom of the Griffith's," whose "little practical jokes, at first performed in ignorance of the pain he gave, but afterwards proceeding to a malicious pleasure in suffering, really seemed to afford some ground to the superstitious notion of some of the common people that he was a fairy changeling" (p. 69) or "the gypsy brat," Heathcliff, that "imp of Satan" (pp. 17, 19) whose changeling soul tormented both himself and those around him in *Wuthering Heights*. Even Catherine Earnshaw, who was not, as we shall see, a true changeling, came under suspicion. And there were other literary creations, like Dickens's dwarfish Quilp in *The Old Curiosity Shop* (1840), with his large head, yellow skin, high squeaky voice, and joy in malice, or that calculating, ancient-faced "weird changeling to whom years are nothing," the "elfin Smallweed, christened" Bart (p. 329), of *Bleak House* (1853) who bore the identifying marks of this unnatural creature.

Most Victorians knew what an authentic changeling was: a substitute for an infant, child, or adult whom the fairies had abducted. Left in their stead, it was actually a starving imp, an aged, useless member of the elfin tribe, or even an animated log or stump of wood. If the changeling, as was most usual, took the form of a child, the child had an old, distorted face, a small or wizened body, and dark or sallow skin, and was often backward in learning to walk or speak. Some changed children were active though monstrous little beings; others were immobile, doll-like wooden creatures who soon lost all semblance of life, becoming "stocks." But whether child or adult in form, the changeling was a creature noteworthy for its gluttony and peevishness, its lack of heart or soul, and its strange, malicious, or ungovernable spirit.

In earlier days, changelings had been exhibited in street fairs, the equivalents of twentieth-century circus sideshows. Among the monsters and prodigies Henry Morley catalogued in his 1858 *Memoirs of Bartholomew Fair* was one "changeling child" to be seen at "the Black Raven Tavern in West Smithfield." This fairy child was ostensibly "born of Hungarian parents but chang'd in the nursing":

> aged nine years and more, not exceeding a foot and a half high. The legs, thighs, and arms are very small, that they scarce exceed the bigness of a man's thumb, and the face no bigger than the palm of one's hand, and seems so grave and solid as if it were threescore years old. . . . It never speaks. It has no teeth, but it is the most voracious and hungry creature in the world, devouring more victuals than the stoutest man in England. (p. 255)

George Waldron, the great eighteenth-century chronicler of Manx folklore (*The History and Description of the Isle of Man*, 1744), vividly depicted the changeling he had seen in similar terms. An emaciated five- or six-year-old, though with a beautiful face, this child could neither walk, stand, or move: "he never spoke nor cryed . . . and was very seldom seen to smile, but if any one called him a 'fairy-Elf,' he would frown and stare at the person" (p. 57). When the changeling was left alone, neighbors reported, he would laugh uproariously. If left dirty or unkempt, he would be miraculously cleaned in his mother's absence (p. 58).

Still earlier, in the sixteenth century, Martin Luther had encountered and attempted to exorcize a changeling who "did nothing but feed and would eat as much as two clowns or threshers were able to eat" (qtd. in Hartland, *Science*, p. 109). Luther characterized changeling traits as perverse moods, ravenous appetites, filthyness, and a tendency to injure their mothers by literally sucking them dry. Describing a changeling that he had seen at Dessau, he recommended that the child be drowned. To him, such creatures were diabolical in origin, "devil's spawn," and merely masses of flesh devoid of soul (qtd. in MacCulloch, "Changelings" 3:678). Luther made no clear distinction between the incubus and the changeling; both were diabolic, both were to be destroyed.[2]

At the beginning of the Victorian period itself, Thomas Crofton Croker described what came to be perceived as the archetypal fairy changeling in his account of an Irish example, "The Young Piper." Ugly and emaciated, this creature was unable to stand. It was notable for its black, shaggy, matted hair, greenish-yellow skin, hands like "kite's claws" (1:29) and, though less than a year old, a mouth full of great teeth. It was described as screaming or whining constantly, except when fed; then, it had the appetite of a cormorant. The creature did have one great talent in token of its supernatural heritage: it was a brilliant musician. Later in the century, J. G. Campbell identified Highland changelings as recognizable by "large teeth, inordinate appetite . . . and unnatural procosity" (qtd. in Spence, *Fairy Tradition*,

p. 232), while the author of a volume entitled *Welsh Folklore and Folk-Custom*, discussing the numerous changeling tales of the region, observed that "fairy children are small, ugly and old-looking, peevish and frequently preco-cious" (T. Gwynn Jones, p. 68). Sir John Rhys, the eminent Celticist, spoke for all in noting that "when the fairies steal nice, blonde babies, they usually place in their stead their own aged-looking brats with short legs, sallow skins, and squeaky voices" (2:667). Thus, changeling traits, physical ugli-ness — especially large heads and stunted bodies — sallow skin and dark hair, gluttonous appetites, and disruptive behavior were, in effect, codified.

The Victorians were frequently exposed to accounts of the treatment of changelings in the newspapers and journals they perused, in the works of the collectors and theorists of the emerging discipline of folklore, and in the popular and mainstream literature they read. Reports of grotesque be-havior more Dickensian than Dickens — stories of children and, occasion-ally, young women tortured or killed for being changelings — frequently appeared in the press. Closely related accounts of "fairy abductions"— the mysterious disappearances of children and of young men and women — were also considered newsworthy. Well-documented cases attesting to a living belief in changelingism came from all over England and they did not decline as the century progressed.[3]

Many people may have remembered a famous case of 1826—Anne Roche's killing of four-year-old Michael Leahy, a child who could neither stand, walk, or speak. Michael's grandmother had ordered Anne to bathe him three times in the icy waters of a local river in a time-honored ritual for persuading the fairies to reclaim their offspring and restore the mortal they had taken. Swearing that she meant merely to cure Michael, "to put the fairy out" of him, Anne had drowned him. The practice of placing those suspected of being changelings at the intersections of rivers, at the shores of lakes, or at the tideline of the sea (so that the fairies would take their offspring back and restore the human child) continued throughout the era. James Britten reported (in the *Folk-Lore Journal* of 1884) a case of a changeling exorcized in 1869 by being dipped three times in an Irish tarn. As late as 1878, the *Celtic Review* published an account of a woman in Tiree (in the Hebrides) who had left her child on the shore "so it might be taken away by the fairies and her own infant restored" (Sands, p. 253). In this case, the result was not tragic; she had to take the "changeling" back since her own child did not reappear. Such accounts, however, found their way into fiction in tales such as William Sharp/Fiona Macleod's "The Fara Ghael" (1895) or "False Love."

Macleod's story focuses on the results of an ostensibly successful ex-change, effected by a peasant woman of the Scottish Isles who cannot be-lieve that she has borne an imperfect baby. Seven years earlier, she had ex-posed her infant — mute, sickly, and partially paralyzed — at the edge of a tidal beach. The child she returned to find seemed normal and happy, and grew into a beautiful though strangely wild little girl. Only when Morag, as she is called, announces that it is time for her to return to the sea, though she is sad to leave her mortal fosterer, does the mother realize what she has done. Told to return to the pool to reclaim her "true" child, she begins to understand the nature of fairy morality. She had not previously known that "the secret people . . . could have the hardness and coldness to give her again the unsmiling dumb thing she had mothered with so much bitterness of heart" (*Works* 5:133). When the restored human child dies—still unloved—and the mother is forced to recognize that Morag, the object of her "false love" will not return, she drowns herself in the "Pool of the Changeling" (5:134).

Macleod's ironic tale reverses the usual tradition to make its point. Here, the changeling is loved and valued, while the human child is despised and abandoned. Here, too, the fosterer rather than the fostered is false in love. Morag is not blamed for following the laws of her nature and returning to her kind; it is the "mother's" misdirected love and pride that leads to her tragic end. And the tale is cautionary, a warning against the refusal to accept the value of any human being.

In the realm of the factual, the 1840s and '50s provided an interested public with numerous cases of additional rites designed to exorcize changelings. In 1843, John Trevelyan of Penzance was charged with ill-treating his young son. Convinced that the boy was a fairy-changeling, he had first exposed him, placing him outside on a tree for several hours at Christmas time. Later, he had ordered servants to beat, kick, and starve the child, again hoping to make the fairies reclaim their offspring and restore his human son. In Wick, in 1845, a suspected female changeling was subjected to an ordeal by fire. Placed in a basket filled with wood shavings, she was suspended over a kitchen hearth until the shavings ignited. Another common test for changelings was practiced in Wales in 1857; it proved fatal. Changelings supposedly vanished if bathed in or fed solutions of foxglove, and a child immersed in a digitalis bath was killed by the treatment. Another child met its end in the same way in County Donegal in the 1870s, and a third in the 1890s, though temporarily rescued by a doctor, was soon after killed by its parents who believed it still "in the fairies."

Fairy abductions and changeling incidents took on still more sensational dimensions in several other cases reported in the 1880s and 1890s. In the "West Ham Disappearances" of the early 1880s, a number of young girls vanished from the London slums. One of them, Eliza Carter, returned briefly before her final disappearance to tell her schools friends that "They" (the fairies) had kidnapped her and now forbade her to go home.[4]

And little Philip Dillon—the child mentioned early in this chapter—was not the only alleged changeling exorcized in the vicinity of Clonmel, Ireland. In the most widely reported incident of the 1890s, a young married woman, Bridget Cleary, was tortured and killed because her husband, her neighbors, and six members of her family thought her a fairy substitute for the actual Bridget.

The case, called "The Tipperary Horror" (or, misleadingly, "The Witch-Burning at Clonmel"),[5] reveals how prevalent the belief in the existence of changelings still was. Michael Cleary, a cooper, and his twenty-six-year-old wife Bridget lived with her father, Patrick Boland, in a sparsely populated area in Ballyvadlea, some fifteen miles north of Clonmel. Neither extremely poor nor totally uneducated, they lived in a "tidy" new laborer's cottage, where Bridget Cleary supplemented the family income by selling eggs and making dresses; they even had money enough to consult the local doctor when she developed a "nervous condition." When Bridget mysteriously disappeared in March 1895, rumors — that she had been abducted by the fairies of Kylegranagh Hill and that her husband and other members of her family had exorcized and killed the changeling left in her place — reached the ears of local officals who began to investigate. Michael Cleary, Patrick Boland (Bridget's father), Patrick, James, and Michael Kennedy, her cousins, Mary Kennedy, her aunt, as well as two neighbors, John Dunne and William Ahearne, were arrested and charged with "having assaulted and illtreated her [on March 14, 1894] and caused her actual bodily harm" ("South Tipperary Horror," 26 March 1895, p. 3). Her badly burned body was found on 22 March in a shallow grave by a dike a quarter of a mile from her home; two more men, William Kennedy, another cousin, and Denis Ganey, the local "fairy doctor," were also charged; the charge was changed to "wilful murder" and the sensational trial — reported all over the British Isles — began.

Through the testimony of the chief witnesses for the crown, two other neighbors of the Clearys, the horrible story emerged. Bridget had been suffering from some form of mental illness, and when the services of a local priest and local doctor proved ineffectual, a frustrated Michael Cleary turned to other means. Convinced that his wife had been exchanged for a fairy woman, he sought the advice of Denis Ganey, a "fairy doctor," who prescribed folk medicine for her. (Ganey was acquitted and it is not possible to ascertain whether he prescribed the exorcism that killed her.) On the first night of the ritual, Bridget, held down by her cousins, was forced to swallow a concoction of milk and herbs while a more odious mixture of water, urine, and hen's excrement was repeatedly sprinkled on her body. After threats, physical abuse, and repeated questioning, she was, at the suggestion of John Dunne, held over the kitchen hearth fire to drive the fairy out of her. Clearly, her family and friends agreed, at least initially, with Michael's diagnosis of her condition, for they were willing to help exorcize her. However, when the fire did not drive out the changeling, all — except Michael — believed that the person with them was actually Bridget. Michael, however, claimed, "it was not my wife, she was too fine to be my wife, she was two inches taller than my wife" ("Tipperary Horror," 30 March 1895, p. 5).

On the following night, Michael, with family members and friends again present, attempted another round of interrogation. When Bridget began to argue, telling her husband "your mother used to go with the fairies, and this is why you think I am going with them" (thus accusing his mother of unchastity), he became furious ("Extraordinary Case," 27 March 1895, p. 5). As his rage increased, he threatened his wife with a blazing brand from the fire. Finally, he poured the oil from a lamp over her prone body and ignited it. Still persuaded that he was burning a fairy, he told the horrified witnesses that they would soon "see her go up the chimney."[6] Not convinced of his error, he later asked to borrow a revolver (and did borrow a large knife) and went to await Bridget at the fairy hill. The authentic Mrs. Cleary was to reappear, riding a gray horse, when the imposter had been exorcized. Cleary was said to have waited for three nights.

The charge of willful murder was dropped in favor of manslaughter, for it was clear, as *The Cork Examiner* commented, that Bridget Cleary was not deliberately murdered, but "killed in the belief that an evil fairy had taken possession of her" ("Tipperary Horror," 28 March 1895, p. 5). All the accused were found guilty and sentenced to prison, while Michael Cleary received twenty years at hard labor.

The reasons behind an incident such as the murder of Bridget Cleary may be impossible to condone, but they are not difficult to understand. A number of people, mainly the poor and unlettered, believed their loved ones—either adults or children—had been transformed into alien and frightening beings. Unconsciously externalizing a felt evil, they sought to determine its source and, if possible, to exorcize it. If someone became a changeling, it was not neglect, disease, or a taint in the blood line that was responsible. And if the affected creature died, either naturally or as a result of changeling tests, it had not been meant to live. Besides, the real person had been taken by the fairies. She or he was elsewhere.

The mildest of the changeling tests or exorcisms practiced during the period probably received no publicity, for it merely involved tricking the changeling into betraying its nonhuman nature by doing something preposterous before its eyes, such as making porridge, beer, or ale in an egg shell. Equally harmless was having a changed person touched or sprinkled with holy water by a priest or minister. Prompt baptism was considered an excellent preventive to the exchange of an infant, but should such a substitution occur, there were always fairy doctors. The largest part of their business was the treatment of changelings; W. R. LeFanu reported (in 1893) on his own witnessing of one such doctor's treatment of a case. The changeling, one Jimmy Tucker, the eight-year-old son of a local laborer, was placed on a bed, his feet on a bolster and his head at the foot, while a dish of salt with two rushes across it was laid on his chest. The doctor's role was to coax, trick, or force the creature to speak (the same procedure followed in the Bridget Cleary case). Once it spoke, it would declare what it wanted, leave, and restore the mortal child. Tucker did indeed speak, but he and his parents believed thereafter that he had been "away" with the fairies and was never quite the same again (pp. 39–40).

But the underlying principle in the reclamation of a victim, especially a child, was far more dangerous, since it was to "expose the changeling to peril of life." As one Victorian folklorist noted, the assumption was that "rather than see their own offspring suffer, the fairies would come to its rescue and bring back the human babe" (MacCulloch, *Childhood of Fiction*, p. 102). Leaving the child outdoors was a simple and effective method, and hills, especially those ostensibly inhabited by fairies, were favorite places for such expulsions. Victorian folklorists recounted numerous cases of the practice. One told of a man who had a sickly child he thought a changeling, who exposed it on a knoll, the scene of fairy revels, and in the morning found it dead. Another, of one Mary Findlay, who was the last person laid down at the Lykar Cairn because she was believed to be an elfin changeling (Rust, qtd. in MacCulloch, *Childhood*, pp. 103–4). In this form of exorcism, one placed the afflicted at the cairn after sunset and left it there all night. Meanwhile, relatives chanted incantations, brought food for an offering, and watched from a distance. If the offering disappeared by morning, that meant the fairies were appeased and the human had been restored.

However, if such rites were not effective, if the afflicted was not retransformed, fairy doctors and others would have resorted to even more severe measures. They might have flogged the victim, thrown bits or hunks of iron at it, exposed it on a shovel in a dung heap, abandoned it in a ditch or on a grave, or branded it with fire. Only when such methods, including the "shovelling" (placing the suspect on a hot shovel or over a hearth fire with instructions to "go up the chimney") detailed earlier, resulted in the victim's severe injury or death, did they become news items or materials for fiction.[7]

Significantly, most of the incidents recorded involved the victimization of either children or women—that is, of those who were perceived as dependent or subordinate. Episodes like those detailed above suggest a widespread if horrifying pattern of how a society deals with an unacceptable transformation, especially in persons viewed as relatively powerless. The belief in supernatural etiology and intervention permits the more dominant group—here adults—to reject an imperfect infant ("It's the fairies' child, not ours") and allows as well for denial ("We didn't do anything; it was born normal"). In this total inversion of Freud's family romance— that is, the child's belief that her or his true parents are other and superior to the putative parents—the attitudes of the dominant figures, with their components of anger and guilt, can be expressed in a socially sanctioned way by rituals of exorcism (Eberly, p. 232) or expulsion. But they can also lead to infanticide, "pardonable" since unintentional ("We had to get the fairies out of it"), or (as in the case of Bridget Cleary) to murder, with the charge reduced to manslaughter, again because the intentions were curative.[8]

Power, in the form of social dominance, also plays a considerable role in explaining the interest of sceptical, educated, middle-class Victorians in reading about these brutal incidents. While reports of changed infants and fairy abductions did engage Victorian cultural preoccupations with children, innocence, and death, they did not, at first, disturb preexistent bourgeois economic, social, and religious prejudices. If anything, they bolstered feelings of superiority. Changeling episodes usually occurred in rural areas and among poor or working-class Roman Catholic and Celtic rather than Saxon peoples; such groups were expected to believe in elves and exorcism. Not Anglo-Saxons inherently superior to all others in character and morality, they were by weak by nature with an innate tendency to selfishness and ignorance. They were, as Sir Charles Wentworth Dilke put it, among "the cheap races" along with Chinese, Malays, and Indians (MacDougall, p. 99). Moreover, children born to "the alien Jew . . . [or] the Irish Roman Catholic," as Dr. F. W. Mott asserted, bore a "neopathetic taint" in the first place (qtd. in Showalter, p. 110). They, and others like them, might be the products of disreputable mothers or even of incestuous unions; unnatural fruits of unnatural behavior (as Edward Westermarck said some "savage" peoples believed, 2:174–75). The barbarous tests to which members of "inferior" groups subjected children were really proof of how backward and primitive they themselves still were— evidences of their kinship to savage tribes and even to lower primates. By the last third of the century, however, the middle class no longer felt itself quite so secure.

Meanwhile, throughout the period, popular writers ranging from W. Harrison Ainsworth to Arthur Machen derived sensational materials from and capitalized on the horrors attendant upon such creatures and incidents.[9] Changelings entered children's literature in such folklorically accurate tales as Juliana Horatia Ewing's, "Amelia and the Dwarfs" (1870). There, when "naughty," self-assertive Amelia is kidnapped, she is replaced by a wooden stock. She returns, triumphant over the sadistic dwarfs, but "socialized" in Victorian terms, just at the moment when her replacement "a fairy imp, and a very ugly one, covered with hair" (Auerbach and Knoepflmacher, p. 125) is about to die. George MacDonald dealt with the fairies' abduction of two children in "Cross Purposes" (1867; rpt. in *Gifts of Child Christ*) and with the goblins' stealing of the princess in *The Princess and the Goblin* (1872); Walter de la Mare described the kidnapping of a little girl in his fairy play for children, *Crossings* (1921). So popular was the motif that Kipling's Puck, in *Rewards and Fairies* (1906), feels called upon to defend the English supernaturals against accusations of child stealing and substitution: "'All that talk of changelings is people's excuse for their own neglect. Never believe 'em'"(p. 7),[10] Puck tells his audience. However, when Una protests that people in the enlightened early twentieth century no longer behave that way, Puck corrects her:

> "Whip, or neglect children? Umm! Some folks and some fields never alter. But the People of the Hills didn't work any changeling tricks. They'd tiptoe in and whisper and weave round the cradle-babe in the chimney-corner—a fag-end of a charm here, or half a spell there— . . . but when the babe's mind came to bud out afterwards, it would act differently from other people in its station. That's no advantage to man or maid. So I wouldn't allow it with my folk's babies here."(p. 8)

He then tells Dan and Una the story called "Cold Iron," the tale of an unwanted slave-child taken and raised by the fairies, who intend him for power, wealth, and glory but who becomes instead a universal servant, a sort of yeoman-Christ.

Numerous and popular Victorian poems including Samuel Lover's "The Fairy Boy" and Dr. Anster's "The Fairy Child," lamented in verse the plight of the mother, often Irish, bereft of her beautiful infant and forced, as in Anster's lyric, to raise the "weakling" (Duffy, p. 49) left instead.[11] Yeats's "Stolen Child" ("Come Away Thou Human Child," 1888), though less usual in dwelling on the fairies' seduction rather than the mother's lament, is simply one example of a sizable poetic subgenre.[12] So, too, is James Stephens's "Fairy Boy" (Duffy, p. 53), which shares with Yeats's poem the idea that the child, in being "taken," will miss the woes of the mortal world more than its pleasures.

The motif permeates Victorian fiction, as well. Sheridan LeFanu used his knowledge of fairy lore to write a frightening tale of the abduction of a little boy—"The Child That Went With The Fairies" (1870)—while Walter Besant treated the material within the realist tradition in *The Changeling* (1893). Changeling figures abound in the works of the Brontës, Dickens, Elizabeth Gaskell, Arthur Machen, and J. M. Barrie, while Maurice Hewlett went so far as to "document" a case of the fairy kidnapping of a child in his pseudo-realist collection of essays, *The Lore of Proserpine* (1913).[13]

For many, however, Sir Joseph Noel Paton's famous painting *The Fairy Raid* (1867) visually encapsulated the popular lore about changelings and abductions. Although Fuseli had earlier treated the subject (in *The Changeling. Abduction by Moonlight*), his focus on the hideous substituted elf-monster and the theatrically horrified mother might have been too overtly unpleasant for Victorian tastes. Paton's picture, completed in 1867,[14] at first seems visually harmless as it illustrates the following verse (probably by the painter himself):

> Fast, fast, through the greenwood speeding
> Out in the moonlight bright,
> Her faery raid she is leading,
> This dainty queen so light,
> And the baby heir of acres wide

She is carrying away to fairyland.
A changeling is left by the nurse's side
And he in the young heir's place shall stand.

The picture is replete with particularized images of many denizens of fairyland, suggesting the increased influence of folklore studies. Dwarfs of various types, a Teutonic metalworker, a Cornish kobold, a red cap, and clusters of tiny elves line the route of the Fairy Queen's progress. A dryad watches the procession from her tree. The procession itself, fairy ladies and knights, a Puck, and smaller attendant goblins and elves—including a jester with an animal face—wends its way toward a clearing in the woods marked by a few standing megaliths, reminders of the connection between the fairies and prehistoric and druidic peoples.

The pictured scene is less innocent than it first appears; like Paton's poem, it implies a darker subtext. While the large fairies are the conventionally beautiful and artistocratic denizens of medieval romance, their smaller attendants are the grotesque creatures more often associated with folklore. The muted horror of the scene is suggested by a fairy knight, in

2.1 Henry Fuseli, *The Changeling*, pencil and watercolor (1780). Kunsthaus Zürich, Switzerland, Copyright 1998 by Kunsthaus Zurich. All rights reserved.

the right foreground, who is about to plunge his lance into something that looks like a monster-maiden holding a lantern (perhaps a will-o'-wisp). There are strange, black-hooded creatures in a pit who struggle to climb out of it. The black horses ridden by several of the fairies are clearly demonic "devils' mounts."

Even more telling is the depiction of the stolen child. Thumb in its mouth, it stares blankly out of the painting while its royal abductress — intent on the handsome fairy knight beside her — ignores it. Three pretty blond children, whose comparatively large size identifies them as human, appear to be dancing in a circle as they stroll beside the fairies on horseback. The little girl looks wistfully at the baby. The sinister implications of the painting emerge only when one notices that the children wear slender chains around their ankles. They, too, are captives of the raid; monitored by a tiny elf who stands between their legs, they are also viewed with sublime indifference by the fairies who have stolen them. In effect, the ostensibly "pretty" picture is actually of slaves and the slavers who have captured them. In both composition and subject, *The Fairy Raid* is a study of a sort of Roman "triumph" and its victims.

In focusing on the little captives, Paton suggests how intense a cultural anxiety child abduction had come to be, as well as how integrally if imaginatively connected it was to the changeling phenomenon. The possibility that an otherworldly (or primitive) order still lurked at the edges of civilization and took children or young women for evil or unnatural purposes simultaneously titillated his audience and increased its anxiety. This possibility is at

2.2 Sir Joseph Noel Paton, *The Fairy Raid: Carrying off a Changeling, Midsummer Eve*, oil (1867). Courtesy of Glasgow Art Gallery and Museum, Kelvingrove.

play in Sheridan LeFanu's tale of Northumberland, "Laura Silver Bell" (1872), with its depiction of an innocent (but unbaptised) young woman first enchanted, then seduced and mistreated by a malignant, black-clad fairy "lord" and finally forced to give birth to a demonic imp. It generates the terror in works of fantasy like Arthur Machen's "The Shining Pyramid" and John Buchan's "The Watcher By the Threshold"—both tales of young women abducted as sacrificial victims by aboriginal fairy creatures.

In both fantasy and reality the cultural anxiety was increased by the near impossibility of rescue. "All the young are in danger [from fairy kidnapping]," warned William Butler Yeats (*Unpublished Prose* 2:76) and folklorists who studied Irish, Welsh, Scottish, Manx,[15] and English materials heartily agreed, cataloguing innumerable accounts of those abducted and the efforts, usually vain, to rescue them (see chapter 5). If a changeling were substituted for the kidnap victim, the problems of the substitute's anarchic and inhuman nature had to be considered, but there was still hope that the process might be reversed. Babies were almost never returned, though there was some possibility that adults might be restored (as in the ballad and tale of "Tamlane" or in Childe Rowland's rescue of Burd Ellen kidnapped by the Elf King). Even if those stolen were returned, however, they were never the same again. Like J. M. Barrie's Mary Rose, in the play named after her, there was always something "different" about them.[16] But when no substitute was provided, the implications were that the victim was gone forever.

Interestingly, as the century moved on, the fear of losing a child to alien powers seems to have spread from rural folk and the unlettered working classes to the more affluent. As the concern about the stability and security of the family grew—in response to an increasingly uncertain outside world—and as children themselves became more important, in part because of a decreased birth rate, the fear increasingly affected the Victorian middle class. For members of the middle class, the feared abductors might sometimes be nurses or gypsies rather than denizens of the elfin world, but the implications were similar. Mr. Dombey's selfish fear of Paul's being kidnapped by a nurse or the Tullivers' belief that little Maggie has been stolen by the gypsies (in Eliot's *Mill on the Floss*, 1859) seem to be fictional reflections of actual anxieties. There was the possibility that beings of another order— and baby nurses were often Irish and almost always working class, while gypsies were perceived as total aliens and only questionably members of the human race—might steal their hope, their future, their identity.

In effect, the abduction of a helpless child, the sudden vanishing of a young life struck special chords of pathos and terror in the Victorian heart, regardless of its social class. Such emotions lie behind Maurice Hewlett's "Beckwith's Case," a supposedly true account of the fairy kidnapping of the middle-class narrator's little daughter.

In an essay possibly intended as a hoax (and published as part of *The Lore of Proserpine*), Hewlett offers an account of the supposedly verifiable experiences of one Stephen Mortimer Beckwith of Wishford, Wiltshire, a clerk at the Wilts and Dorset Bank in Salisbury. To authenticate his narrative, Hewlett tells readers that the complete story, as told by the Reverend Richard Walsh, Congregationalist minister, at the meeting of the South Wilts Folk-lore society and Field Club at Amesbury in June 1892, "may be found in the published transactions of that body" (p. 159). Beckwith's tale of his rescue and lodging of a fairy and of her subsequent abduction of his four-year-old daughter, Flossie, is filled with undramatic, realistic detail. Cycling home in the late evening in November 1887, he (or rather, one of his dogs) encountered a wounded female fairy some three feet, five inches in height (a note gives us her exact measurements). Visible to him and his dogs, though not to either Mrs. Beckwith or the local constable, the fairy he calls Thumbeline is confined in his dog kennel. Wayward, charming, full of motion and passion, she subjugates first the dogs, than Beckwith, and finally his only child. Communicating without words, for though she sings like "the wind in the telegraph wire" (p. 144), she does not speak, she entices the little girl to leave her home and family. And, on 13 May 1888, Florrie vanished.

Beckwith had left his daughter, his greyhound, and Thumbeline (now let out of her cage) in a water meadow near his house, and had watched, charmed, while the fairy wove a wreath of flowers with which to crown the little girl. A few hours later, he is told by his frantic wife that both his dog and his child have disappeared. A thorough police search of the area revealed no trace of them, nor did notices in local and London newspapers or further, wider investigations result in any leads. At last, the stricken Beckwith told of the full story of Thumbeline to a sceptical minister and to a police officer. But all was in vain. "We found no trace of our dear one, and never have to this day" (p. 158), Beckwith concludes. Unable to bear his guilt about his negligence or his memories of the place of abduction, Beckwith leaves England forever.

By situating this incident in suburban England, placing at its center the family of an ordinary, respectable bank clerk, and insisting that his tale is *true*, Hewlett both plays to and testifies to the increasing fear among the educated middle classes of the abduction of children. The lost child itself assumes symbolic significance as it becomes a sort of paradigm for Victorian concerns with both the loss of innocence and the loss of self. The leaving of a substitute, however, epitomizes still further anxieties. As the Victorians remythified the folkloric construct, changelings came to suggest the frightening replacements that might follow such losses—the monstrous forms that might replace one's offspring, that might result from the loss of self and innocence. The nature of the replacements and the reasons for such substitutions became the almost obsessive subject of folklorists' discussions.

Changelings in Folklore and Medical Theory

Not unexpectedly, the folklorists' analyses of the changeling phenomenon —the theories they formulated to explain changelings, and the"enlightened" and scientific hypotheses they created—reinforced and intensified the subtle prejudices of their society. Almost every major folklorist writing in Great Britain between the 1860s and the first decade of the twentieth century discussed changelings. While all noted that the belief in their existence was worldwide, most commented on the local extent and "survival" of such belief and focused specifically on the etiology of the phenomenon in the British Isles. They were especially preoccupied with two related issues: the historical or mythical origins of the belief in changelings, and the persistent survival of that belief as exemplified in those people still identified as "living" changelings, their physical appearance, and mental characteristics.

Only a few British folklorists were not primarily interested in explaining the presence of living changelings. Instead they saw the general belief as stemming from an ancient practice of abducting children, or from corrupted memories of an equally ancient rebirth doctrine, or from folk memories of a once widespread ritual of infant sacrifice.

The Brothers Grimm had remarked that fairies stole human offspring to improve their breed. Victorian euhemerists richly elaborated upon this idea. They assumed that changelings—though not parented by fairies— had actually existed. According to their "kidnap theory," primitive, dwarfish English aborigines or prehistoric settlers had stolen healthy Celtic or Saxon babies and attractive young girls to increase their dwindling, malnourished population. Thus arose tales of fairy abductions. Sometimes these peoples had substituted their own sick infants for the conquerors' healthy ones, creating the belief in changelings. Arthur Machen summarized this view in stating that "much in the old legends may be explained by a reference to . . . [a] primitive race. The stories of changelings and captive women, become clear on the supposition that the 'fairies' [that is, "a short, non-Aryan race"] occasionally raided the houses of the invaders" (*Dreads and Drolls*, p. 23). Sir John Rhys argued that modern Welsh changelings (some of whom he had seen) were, in actuality, "representatives of the . . . aboriginal stock" extreme specimens "of a dark-complexioned," "long-skulled" type of Welshman (2:667). Whether the early inhabitants who gave rise to this changeling belief were Rhys's aboriginal Welsh (related to the Basques), Sabine Baring-Gould's pre-Celtic Iberian Pygmies, or David MacRitchies's early Mongols, the hypothesis was essentially the same.

Victorian occultists, on the other hand, favored "possession" and reincarnation theories. Many, including W. Y. Evans-Wentz, thought of such children as "taken over" in the same way that a medium might be overcome by her spirit control at a seance.[17] But Evans-Wentz, like others, does not rule out the possibilities of demonic possession, nor does he deny the "Soul Wandering Theory"—that is, the belief that changelings are "children, whose souls are absent from the body due to a spirit or ghost interference" (p. 248). Still other believers in the occult thought that changelings might be the souls of the dead returned to inhabit the bodies of mortal children. Their old faces and wizened forms were indications of the fact that they were reincarnations, that such changed children were really "old souls," a premise still accepted by occultists today.

Most interestingly, however, Victorian anthropological folklorists saw the changeling belief as a "survival" of ancient sacrifical rites.[18] Alfred Nutt developed a complex and ingenious theory about the changeling lore of Ireland. Unlike death itself, Nutt argued, the fairy does not take without giving something in turn. He "acts upon the principle of a life for a life; true, the exchange he makes with the mortal is an unfair one for the latter, who receives a worn-out peevish, ailing existence in return for the new and vigorous one of which he has been robbed" (*Voyage of Bran* 2:229). Moreover, the Irish fairies, Nutt explains, were "the ancient lords of life and increase . . . the powers to whom man looked for the periodical outburst of new life, and whom he strengthened in their task by sacrifice" (2:229). To these fertility deities the ancient Irish had offered unblemished infants, rejecting the weak and unattractive as inappropriate victims. Hence, when the practice died out, the folk gradually evolved the myth that the fairies had carried off healthy infants and left, in exchange, sickly ones.

Why the fairies took infants and children was also subject to considerable discussion. Not all agreed with the most popular theory that it was to improve the elfin breed, though many noted that female fays appeared to have difficulty bearing children. Some, including Hugh Miller, Lady Wilde, and many collectors of Scottish lore reported the folk belief that human infants were used as substitutes for fairy offspring in the elfin annual or septannual sacrifice or tithe to the devil. Another motive for abducting children, especially boys, in Scotland, was said to be the belief that a champion of mortal strength but fairy indoctrination would one day emerge to lead the forces of Elfland against human beings (Aitken, p. 4). Yeats, Lady Gregory, and others argued that fairies needed mortals for their physical strength. As one of Yeats's informants told him, the sidhe were shadows and spirits who could not move objects. "But they have power over mankind, and they can bring them away to do their work" (*Unpublished Prose* 2:268). Some even argued that, since the salvation of fairies was questionable, they needed mortals to be with them at the Day of Judgment. Canon J. A. MacCulloch indicates how frequently this case was made in stating that fairies stole human beings "to share in the spiritual benefits of the religion from which . . . [they] are supposedly excluded" (*Encyclopedia of Religion and Ethics* 3:679).[19]

But most folklorists coupled their theories about the origins of the changeling belief with statements about the reality of "changelingism" as the product of disease or heredity, as the result of abnormal physical or mental development. Twentieth-century folklore and medical theory largely identifies changelings as folk explanations of disabled children with congenital diseases. The Victorian medical establishment also recognized some so-called changelings as victims of disease, though it could not determine the specific, often hereditary illnesses from which they suffered. Children with spina bifida, cystic fibrosis, cerebral palsy, and physical malformations that prevent digestion (and thus induce the ravenous hunger, insatiable appetite, and inability to thrive characteristic of changelingism) were probably not diagnosable. Metabolic disorders such as PKU (phenylketonuria), common among those of English and Irish stock, in which "normal looking," light-skinned and fair-haired, blue-eyed children become hyperactive, irritable, retarded, and palsied (because they cannot metabolize certain amino acids), were entirely unidentified. So, too, was progeria (a sort of premature aging syndrome that might serve as an explanation for other cases) and homocystinuria, which produces retardation and long, thin spider limbs. In a recent article, Susan Schoon Eberly describes dozens of diseases (many of which produce physical symptoms similar or identical to each other) that result in what uninformed people would consider the traits of changelings. (In addition to the conditions already mentioned, she discusses William's syndrome (also called "Elfin facies"), which results in pretty, though retarded children like Waldron's changeling, and Hurler's and Hunter's syndromes, which result in what was formerly called "gargoylism"—that is, apparently "normal" babies suddenly becoming hairy, ugly, sallow, and retarded (p. 237ff). Eberly notes that "stocklike" changelings may be explained by the presence of infantile paralysis or other paralyzing diseases, while the changeling's traditional love of dancing may be a fanciful rendering of the impact of cerebral palsy. Less obviously, she observes that many of the congenital disorders that created changelings hinder normal sexual development so that children afflicted either do not mature or else mature abnormally early; this, she argues, may be the basis of the myth of fairy barrenness and the rationale for the well-known elfin practice of stealing human babies (p. 238). Interestingly, too, Eberly comments on the recurrent idea in folklore that male children are more often "taken" than female ones, saying that statistically boys are more prone to be born with congenital disorders than are girls (p. 235).[20] Another recent study sees the changelings of folklore as models for infants and children described in twentieth-century medical literature as suffering from "failure to thrive" (Munro, p. 258). This parental (especially maternal) deprivation results in offspring who, without physical cause, seem unable to develop. Marked by listlessness, immobility, and emaciation, such infants often die; if they do survive, it is as "psychosocial dwarves, with voracious and strange appetites, hyperactivity and disturbed interper-

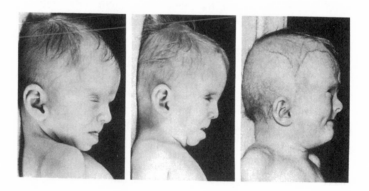

2.3 Medical photographs of infants suffering from progeria who might have been perceived as changelings. From "An Unidentified Neonatal Progeroid Syndrome: Follow up Report," H.–R. Wiedemann, from *European Journal of Pediatrics* 130, 1 (1979). Permission kindly granted by Springer-Verlag, New York; photograph, courtesy of the New York Academy of Medicine.

sonal relationships" (p. 277). Irritable and apparently retarded in speech and intellectual development, they are often scapegoated and abused; nonetheless, they improve when they are removed from the unhappy home or general environment.[21]

While the Victorian folklore collectors and theorists did not possess these sophisticated medical and psychological hypotheses or the means of supporting them, they did seek to explain the connections between changelingism and disease. Sir William Wilde, eye surgeon, medical commissioner for the Irish census, folklorist, and father of Oscar Wilde, believed that changelings were really people suffering from marasmus, or wasting disorder. Writing in 1854, he attacked "the many superstitious notions entertained by the peasantry respecting their supposed 'fairy stricken' children" as well as "the cruel endeavours to cure children and young persons of such maladies generally attempted by quacks and those termed 'fairy men' and 'fairy women'" (fairy doctors; Wilde's "Census of Ireland Report, 1854," qtd. in Eberley, p. 237). Robert Hunt, the author of a frequently reprinted collection of tales called *Popular Romances of the West of England* (1860), reported on his examination of several allegedly "changed" children. "In every case," he argued, they were "sad examples of the influence of mesenteric disease" (p. 85), that is, disease of the intestinal membrane. He commented that the children's distorted faces, "wasted frames," and "abdominal enlargement" gave "the sufferer" "a most *unnatural* appearance" (p. 85; my italics), thus leading to the local people's belief that these victims were changelings. Other collectors and theorists were just as convinced that what the folk called changelings were produced by forms of consumption, of "atrophy," or of rickets.[22] Sir Walter Scott, and the many who subscribed to his theories, believed consumption in its various forms was responsible for the appearance of changelingism. Thomas Macaulay, the historian, thought that in the past, at least, it was smallpox that had "turned the babe into a changeling at which the mother shuddered" (4:530).

This view of changelingism as caused by physical disease spread into literature, but almost always with undertones of supernatural influence or intervention. Paul Dombey in Dickens's *Dombey and Son* (1848) is partially depicted as a victim of a "wasting disease," though he is also marked by disquieting preternatural traits. Born with the "old, old face" (p. 151) and the melancholy temperament of the changed child, he becomes increasingly changelinglike as, called by the voices in the sea, he moves toward death. With his large head and increasingly fragile body (he is unable to walk), he is shown wasting away both literally and metaphorically. He suffers from the cold, figuratively from the lack of normal childhood identity and experience, and he is always seeking warmth, repeatedly warming his hands before the fire "like an old man or a young goblin" (p. 126). Yet his character has supernatural overtones; he is depicted as resembling Mrs. Pipchin's familiar, as having expressions of "slyness" (the changeling's "cunning") cross his face (p. 125), and, above all, as looking and talking

> like one of those terrible little Beings in the Fairy Tales, who, at a hundred and fifty or two hundred years of age, fantastically represent the children for whom they have been substituted. (p. 123)

2.4 Phiz [Hablot K. Browne], "Paul and Mrs. Pipchin," illustration for Charles Dickens, *Dombey and Son* (1848).

Although his father fears his being "changed" by a nurse rather than a fairy, in what Gerhard Joseph argues is the middle-class version of the changeling myth, Paul has in effect already been changed. He is not his father's son in character or attribute. By nature he is a being of another order who must leave—as most changelings did—this mortal realm.

All Dickens's changelings, whatever their moral nature, bear the traditional aged faces and undersized bodies of the folklore type. All combine the literal or physical and metaphorical or supernatural qualities of the changeling and all seem incapable of change or development.[23] Both Quilp in *The Old Curiosity Shop* (1840) and the Smallweed twins in *Bleak House* (1853) are immediately identifiable as changeling figures by their physical abnormalities. Quilp is the earliest and, perhaps for that reason, the most overtly preternatural of them. Though seen only as an adult (his childhood remains shrouded in mystery) and as a demonic Beast to Nell's Beauty, he is more derived from folklore figures than from theories about them, although he is akin to Luther's demonic changelings.

Dickens's first description of Quilp elaborates his physical characteristics:

> His black eyes were restless, sly, and cunning; his mouth and chin, bristly with the stubble of a coarse hard beard; and his complexion was one of the kind which never looks clean or wholesome. But what added most to the grotesque expression of his face was a ghastly smile . . . which had no relation to mirth. (p. 65)

Quilp's sallowness, grotesque smile, meaningless, inappropriate laughter, screaming, and stamping link him to the folklore type as does his "extraordinary greediness" (p. 86) about food. He has a ravenous appetite that makes him devour boiled eggs with their shells intact and prawns without removing their heads or tails.

While Quilp's parentage remains unspecified, Dickens repeatedly describes him as an "evil spirit" (pp. 159, 239), an "imp" (p. 69), a "goblin" (p. 81) and even a nightmare—clearly with Fuseli's incubus in mind. When, because of his uncanny ability to drink scalding liquids, Dick calls him a "salamander," he does not merely allude to the lizard that can supposedly withstand fire, but to the dangerous elemental salamanders (from Paracelsus and the Rosicrucians) who inhabit fire. Dickens never again created such a

2.5 Phiz [Hablot K. Browne], "Quilp at the Window," illustration for Charles Dickens, *The Old Curiosity Shop* (1841).

hybrid-changeling figure (his source here may have been the supernatural tales of Bulwer-Lytton), and his later changelings, though grotesque, are perceived as more inherently human than Quilp ever becomes.

Bart Smallweed of *Bleak House*, for example, has the same aged face and unchanging character as Quilp, although his physical abnormality lies in his being a midget rather than an achondroplastic (large-headed, short-limbed) dwarf (see chapter 5). Referring to Bart as "a weird changeling, to whom years are nothing" (p. 329), Dickens proceeds to describe his changeling nature and to connect him with the animal kingdom rather than the human one:

> He stands precociously possessed of centuries of owlish wisdom. . . . He has an old, old eye, has Smallweed: and he drinks and smokes, in a monkeyish way; and his neck is stiff in his collar; and he is never to be taken in; and he knows all about it, whatever it is. (p. 329)

Depicted as a "fossil imp" (p. 329) in token of his unalterable nature and appearance, he has both the cunning and the voracious appetite of the folklore changeling, using his "elfin power" (p. 330) to order and consume enormous quantities of food—without paying for it. Despite his appetite, however, he is thin, sallow, and wizened like his twin, Judy. She shares both his preternatural and bestial traits and we are told that, even as a child, she seldom played with others. "She seemed like an animal of another species," Dickens reports, "and there was instinctive repugnance on both sides" (p. 344). Both young adults (they are fifteen) are changelings in part, Dickens implies, because they have never been permitted to "thrive," to be children or to be human. Coming from a family that has denied them love, deprived them of amusement, levity, fancy, and imagination, even bred them without "story-books, fairy tales, fictions and fable" (p. 342), they have grown up bearing a "likeness to old monkeys with something depressing on their minds" (p. 342). Bart and Judy are ambiguous creatures, marked as "other" by Dickens's continual emphasis on their simian characteristics. They are creatures of the borderland, a different and lower order. Like Barrie's Peter Pan, himself a sort of hybrid changeling, they are "Betwixt-and-Between" (*Little White Bird*, p. 136).[24]

Even when changelings are most sympathetically depicted, as in Paul Dombey or Dinah Muloch Craik's Olive Rothesay (in the novel *Olive* of 1850), or later, in the persona of Charlotte Mew's famous poem, "The Changeling" (written in 1915), they are still perceived as outsiders and aliens, threatening the established order and social norms by their very difference. Suggesting an almost innate Victorian fear of the "other," they are generally doomed to a borderland existence.

The tormented child of Mew's "The Changeling" (1916), for example, is another "Betwixt-and-Between," neither fully human nor entirely supernatural, and hence without a place or function in this world. Marked by a "queer brown face" (a sign of his heredity?) in a pink and white Anglo-Saxon world, he sees himself as his parents do—"Never . . . but half . . . [their] child" (p. 69). Summoned by the fairies, who offer him only the chill and darkness of a wild land beyond the warmth of home, he, unlike Peter Pan, struggles to stay human. He even prays, but a conventional God "Has nothing to do with us fairy people" (p. 70). His questioning of his nature and predicament,

> Why did They bring me here to make me
>   Not quite bad and not quite good,
> Why, unless They're wicked, do
>   They want, in spite, to take me
> Back to their wet, wild wood? (p. 70)

is never answered. Instead, moving beyond the human to the fairy world, the changeling receives an intimation of his bleak future:

> I shall grow up, but never grow old,
> I shall always, always be very cold,
>   I shall never come back again! (p. 71)

Even creatures as sensitive as Mew's could be seen as warnings that nature was filled with modes of being that were not human modes, with forces that were usually indifferent, often hostile and sinister, sometimes truly evil.

For the most part, both in fiction and in life, the psychologically alienated and the physically handicapped were conflated. Those with deformed limbs, cerebral palsy, or what we now recognize as infantile paralysis were most rapidly categorized as changelings, as were those suffering from mental retardation or illness. Their condition became an unconscious excuse for their rejection. When beautiful, petite Sybilla Rothesay, herself described as "quite a little fairy" (p. 8), bears an ugly brown child in Dinah Muloch Craik's *Olive*, she is persuaded it is a changeling. "Take her away; she is *not* my sweet angel-baby," she screams to the Scottish nurse Elspie (p. 18), despising and ignoring her deformed offspring. The child, Olive, is described as follows:

> By her stature she might have been two years old, but her face was like that of a child of ten or twelve—so thoughtful, so grave. Her limbs were small and wasted, but exquisitely delicate. The same might be said of her features; which, though thin, and wearing a look of premature age, together with that quiet, earnest melancholy cast peculiar to deformity, were yet regular, almost pretty. Her head was well-shaped, and from it fell a quantity of amber-coloured hair—pale "lint-white locks," which, with the almost colourless transparency of her complexion, gave a spectral air to her whole appearance. She looked less like a child than a woman dwarfed into childhood; the sort of being renowned in elfin legends, as springing up on a lonely moor, or appearing by a cradle-side; supernatural, yet fraught with a nameless beauty. (p. 28)

Olive's "defect" or "imperfection" is "an elevation of the shoulders, short-ening the neck, and giving the appearance of a perpetual stoop" (p. 28), which when combined with her tiny stature and her "uncanny smile" (p. 33) render her unloved and an inadvertent cause of alienation between her parents. Yet, in Craik's sentimental revision of *Jane Eyre*, Olive's sensitiv-ity, creativity (she is an artist), and virtue ultimately triumph. Rescued by a fairy godmother in the form of Miss Van Brugh, the spinster sister of a fa-mous painter, she helps support her helpless, widowed mother. Through her meek, gentle sweetness and her "true womanly nature" (she triumphs by goodness and self-sacrifice), she wins the heart and hand of her Rochester, a tormented, unbelieving minister, Harold Gwynne. Her human spirit tri-umphs over her changeling body, and, ironically, it is because she is "other," *not* considered a normal human female that she can achieve: to the painter, she is worth training because her deformities exempt her from a life of flirtation and marriage; to Gwynne, she can become a friend because he cannot see her in sexual or matrimonial terms. Craik is unusual in her sympathy for Olive's "otherness," but here too suggestions of supernatural origin and intervention endow the changeling figure with traits beyond the "real."

An even larger number of experts and authors perceived so-called changelings less sympathetically as hydrocephalics, cretins, or mentally re-tarded creatures — the "innocents" and "naturals" of Victorian nomencla-ture. Ella Leather suggested (in discussing the ample changeling tales gleaned in Herefordshire) that the belief in changelings was an attempt to account for cases of cretinism, noting that "in this disease, supposed to be caused by the absence of an internal secretion of the thyroid gland, devel-opment is completely arrested" (p. 46n). But, she added, almost any men-tally abnormal child might be held to be a changeling. By the 1870s, after evolutionary thought had begun to permeate folklore theory, medicine, and anthropology, Victorian intellectuals saw even "normal" children as primitive or undeveloped adults. The concept of recapitulation — the idea that the child evolves as the race evolves — created a cultural parallel be-tween the two. Children (like savage peoples) were supposed to develop; the changeling was the child or individual who would not or could not do so. Hence, like the lunatic, it was a throwback to earlier stages of human development. The idea that the retarded were changelings was current throughout the British Isles. One commentator noted that all over Ireland "as a general rule an innocent is supposed to be a fairy or changeling," adding that "this is often believed by educated people" ("Notes on Irish Folk-Lore," p. 114).

Some folklorists even thought so-called changelings were victims of Down's syndrome rather than of cretinism. For Dr. John Langdon Haydon Down had, in 1866, argued that white Caucasian idiots (who reminded him of "normal" African, Malay, American Indian, and oriental peoples) repre-

sented arrested development and owed their appearance and mental defi-
ciency to a retention of traits that would be considered normal in adults of
"lower races." According to Down's racist classification of idiots, those afflicted with "Mongolian idiocy" were evolutionary throwbacks to a less
evolved oriental race. "A very large number of congenital idiots," he remarked, "are typical Mongols" (qtd. in Gould, *Panda's Thumb*, p. 137). Although the central and defining traits of children with Down's syndrome
are not actually suggestive of an oriental appearance, Dr. Down focused on
the fact that some of his "Mongolian idiots" did have a slightly yellowish
cast to their skin (possibly the effect of infantile jaundice) and that some
did have the small epicanthic fold on the eyelid characteristic of oriental
eyes. Moreover, he pointed to the behavior of these afflicted children as oriental in nature. "They have considerable power of imitation, even bordering on being mimics" (qtd. in Gould, p. 137)—a sign of their innate oriental
facility for imitative copying rather than for Caucasian innovative and creative learning.[25] It is probable that a larger number of Victorian folklorists
would have adopted this theory were it not that Down's syndrome is often
visible at or right after birth; in a sense, the victim of this malady is not radically "changed."

However, as "idiots" (in Victorian nomenclature those unable to master
even spoken language) or as "imbeciles" (those who could speak but not
write) or as the generally "feeble-minded," changelings were closely linked
in Victorian medical theory to the animal world. They were borderline creations, a species midway between humans and the brutes. After Darwin
they became, of course, prime examples of reversion or arrested development. As Dr. Henry Maudsley stated in a passage quoted by Darwin in *The
Expression of the Emotions in Man and Animals* (1872):

> every human brain passes, in the course of its development, through
> the same stages as those occuring in the lower vertebrate animals, and
> as the brain of an idiot is in an arrested condition . . . "it will manifest its
> most primitive functions, and no higher functions." (p. 244)

Changelings thus became examples of how phylogeny recapitulated ontogeny: their howls, snarls, grimaces, inability to use language, and destructive actions revealed their kinship with the lower vertebrates.[26]

The literary depiction of changelings was influenced by these evolution-
ist scientific and medical theories and, as Victorian reconstructions of the
folklore type proliferated, some fictional changelings bore the marks of
various mental disabilities or abnormalities, while still adhering in other
traits to the traditional folklore descriptions of the preternatural substitute. Others were depicted as victims of their heredity, occasionally even as
Darwinian throwbacks like John Rhys's sallow and long-headed representatives of "aboriginal" Welsh stock. The "evil" in Humphrey Woodroffe, the
"changeling" in Walter Besant's realist novel *The Changeling* (1893), is presum-

ably, though not actually, owing to the vicious traits he has inherited from his birth-father. Purchased from a starving woman by his society "mother" when her own infant dies, Woodroffe grows up to be a scoundrel: cold and insolent, selfish and unprincipled, and prone to all the fashionable evils. Yet he has been correctly, strictly, and virtuously raised. As one character remarks, "how strong must be the force of hereditary vice when it breaks out after such an education" (p. 88). Although only metaphorically a "changed child" in this study of nature versus nurture, he is nonetheless endowed with the traits of the folklore changeling. Repeatedly described as heartless and soulless, he is a peevish, irascible creature, notable for his gluttony. Utterly dedicated to sensuality, he is marked by his "selfish pleasure in . . . food above the delights of society and conversation" (p. 135).[27]

Humphrey is atypical in being handsome. Usually it was the ugly physical appearance and unpleasant characteristics of changelings that aroused in folklorists and writers alike a set of associations situated between illness, bestiality, and savagery—that caused their depiction as monsters. The adolescent Nial in William Sharp/Fiona Macleod's *The Mountain Lovers* (1895) is depicted as a large-headed, misshapen dwarf, probably cretinous, as are the "creatures" in the Walter de la Mare story named after them. Moreover, Nial, de la Mare's "creatures" and Jervase Cradock, in Arthur Machen's "Novel of the Black Seal" are all portrayed as mentally retarded and as working class in origin.

Nial, for example, is thought by himself and the others in his community to be a changeling and hence "without a soul." Described as a "wild, rude, misshapen creature who looks subhuman, with his over-large and heavy head" (p. 233), he too has the "worn, fantastic face" of the folklore changeling. Like Dickens's Quilp he is a large-headed, small, somewhat humpbacked dwarf, but though capable of rage and savagery, he is not essentially demonic. Instead, he is what the Victorian medical establishment termed "feeble-minded." While local people superstitiously believe him in league with the fairies and spirits, he believes himself the child of a cailleach (a sort of Scottish fairy *femme fatale*) and a mortal shepherd. In his simplicity, Nial spends much of his time looking for his soul and the rest of it loving Oona, a fairylike child so sensitive to nature she is almost an element in it. Though ostensibly sympathetic to him, Macleod repeatedly connects Nial to the subhuman. Describing him mumbling gutturally, climbing trees and swinging on branches, the author links him to the simian and the savage (the two terms become almost synonymous in the Victorian mind). Nial's destiny is to be totally alienated from humankind. After the tragedy that forms the main part of the tale, he is forced into life as a wild man. He literally returns to an earlier phase of civilization, one for which he feels better suited. No one but Oona ever sees him again; local people hear, from time to time, "the chanting of a gaunt, dwarfed, misshapen figure that moved like a drifting shadow from pine-glade to pine-glade" (p. 397).

The creatures of Walter de la Mare's tale (of 1923) are actually retarded cretins, strange racial hybrids, though the people in their world perceive them as changelings. "Children in face and gesture and effect," they are actually adolescents. Their coarse dark hair, deep-set eyes, large heads sunk between their shoulders, and simple-minded behavior—they are "naturals" (p. 433)—links them to traditional changelings. De la Mare's description, however, is telling; clearly influenced by evolutionary and ethnological theories, he sees them as the products of racial mixing: "they were ungainly, their features peculiarly irregular, as if two races from the ends of the earth had in them intermingled their blood and strangeness; as if, rather, animal and angel had connived in their creation" (p. 430). Like many of the changelings described by folklorists, they are largely deficient in most areas but have one great gift; supernaturally beautiful voices—as "haunting, penetrating, pining, as the voice of the nix or siren" (p. 430). Tended by a hermitlike farmer, the creatures dwell in a world separate from others, like early man, in a magic garden of prelapsarian innocence. The offspring of mysterious parents, they are seen, in a sense, as preterhuman forbears, earlier innocent but crude and imperfect models for civilized people.

Even the liberal de la Mare suggests his belief that part of the monstrosity of his creature-changelings comes from the strange racial mixture that renders them "Betwixt-and-Between," from their status as lower-class half-breeds and throwbacks. By the end of the century, ethnological parallels to these biological assumptions could be found in the reports about "savage" peoples discovered or colonialized by missionaries and explorers. Changelings were like these "savages": "low in the scale of humanity" like the Ainos of Japan; ugly and stunted like the "black and yellow dwarfs of the African forest" (MacRitchie, "Hints of Evolution," p. 10); similar in appearance and behavior to the "Pygmies and Ape—like Men of the Uganda Borderland," groups who "even occasionally steal [the] children" (Johnston, p. 178) of the more highly evolved tribes around them. If changelings survived to maturity, they shared with savages—or so the folklorists implied—a combination of adult passions and childlike minds. In this way, too, they were akin to those modern savages, the poor. For were not the poor closer than those who had "achieved" to mankind's primitive, ignoble roots?

Thus, the final ingredients in the making of the Victorian changeling myth came from the infusion of social Darwinism into folklore study and theory, and from thence into popular fiction and thought. Guided by the cultural anthropologists, especially E. B. Tylor, and by the growing study of ethnology, the folklorists, too, saw evidences of progression and regression in the various racial and social groups that constituted the human species. In both fantasy and reality, changelings were increasingly associated with the Darwinian notion of groups or races that had not ultimately triumphed, particularly with "inferior human experiments" of which only a few examples had "survived."

The popularity of these theories, the extent to which they became a part of assumptions about evolution, race, and class, is suggested by their presence in such works as Mew's and De la Mare's. But the power and pervasiveness of the theories is made even more strikingly apparent through an examination of one fictional hybrid-changeling, Jervase Cradock, a character in Arthur Machen's novel, *The Three Imposters* (1896). At the center of an interpolated novella called "The Novel of the Black Seal," is Professor Gregg, an ethnologist of the euhemerist school, who believes the "stories of mothers who have left a child quietly sleeping . . . and have returned, not to find the plump and rosy little Saxon, but a thin and wizened creature with sallow skin and black piercing eyes, the child of another race" (*Strange World*, p. 300). The professor is in search of the originals of the Welsh fairies, a mysterious and evil "race which had fallen out of the grand march of evolution" (p. 301). Thus, hearing that strange-looking, dark-haired, olive-skinned Jervase is thought to be a changeling, he hires him as a servant. Although the adolescent Jervase is actually a hybrid (his mother is a local working-class woman), he exhibits all the attributes folklorists ascribed to fairy changelings. He is "mentally weak," "a natural . . . who, has fits at times" (pp. 286–87). When he has a seizure, his face swells and blackens, he froths at the lips, and he squeals in a queer, hissing "half-sibilant, half-gutteral" voice" (p. 291), mouthing a jargon a local expert associates with the Welsh fairies.

When the professor, who is convinced that supernatural and magical powers are really "survivals from the depths of being"—that is, reversions to lower evolutionary forms of life (p. 301)—subjects Jervase to "scientific" tests, he discovers a horrible secret. He watches the boy, possessed by his brute nature, literally slither down the ladder of evolution to reveal a hideous reptile within. While the professor goes off to find the "Little People" and does not return, Jervase, feeble-minded and diseased, remains in the mortal world as a changeling proof of evolutionary regression, an example of "Protoplasmic Reversion" (p. 311).

Arthur Machen's Jervase Cradock is just one example of how traditional changelings—figures populating the life and folklore of the rural poor—were appropriated by educated Victorians and reconstructed as frightening and monstrous symbols of "otherness." Overtly or covertly, they were increasingly perceived by folklorists, by educated readers, and by authors obsessed with them as diseased and animalistic, as evolutionary "throwbacks" or species hybrids and as creatures of savage and inferior ethnic or racial stock. In this way, these creatures crystallized the cultural angst about the fact that evolution could and often did suggest not only progress but also reversion; they revealed the widespread fear of "reeling back into the beast." Moreover, their presence often implied a closely related panic about neighboring and subject peoples. Changelings became, in this sense, sociocultural signs for British racism and xenophobia. They were not unlike those less evolved groups in the process of being "civilized" by the empire. They were especially prevalent among the Irish—whom most English saw as another superstitious, primitive, and backward race. They resembled popular steotypes of "alien Jews" and other ethnic or racial "inferiors" with their sallow skins, dark beady eyes, large-nosed and emaciated faces, and diabolic "cunning." Then, too, the fact that the reports of these abnormal creatures came mostly from the working classes could imply the inherent monstrousness of the poor or at least the horror of life among them.

As the products of every sort of underclass, changelings thus came to represent the horrible possibilities of the behavior of such classes, focusing bourgeois terror on the threat posed by their existence. To a middle-class Victorian public, "the child that went with the fairies" became a paradigm of themselves. Like little Billy of Sheridan LeFanu's tale, they were attractive, charming, innocent, and good. Like Billy's mother, they had done everything possible to ward off evil from their environment. But tricked and menaced by outsiders, they might be snatched away, deprived of their familiar world, shorn of their power, and finally condemned to starve. The image of the fabulous monster that might replace them—an alien and bestial changeling—was a reflection of their submerged but omnipresent fear.

T H R E E

"EAST OF THE SUN AND WEST OF THE MOON"
Victorians and Fairy Brides

WHILE MOST VICTORIAN FOLKLORISTS agreed that fairies were of both sexes, they were particularly drawn to the females of the elfin species. What is more surprising, at first glance, is their special interest in *married* fairy women—those wedded to mortal men. These fairy brides or swan maidens, as they were often called, were figures derived primarily from English and continental folklore rather than from romance or literary fairy tale (though they had been incorporated into these genres). Repeatedly analyzed in the works of the numerous amateur and professional folklorists who collected, chronicled, and studied materials about them, their personalities and behavior were endlessly fascinating to the Victorians. Moreover, it is not coincidental that the Victorian preoccupation with fairy brides reached its zenith in the 1880s and '90s, when the debates on other issues pertaining to women—their right to keep their property in marriage and their right to separate from abusive mates (or even to divorce them)—were also escalating. The figure of the supernatural wife and the discussion of her rights and duties thus came to occupy an important and controversial place in the Victorian imagination.

At the beginning of the period, collectors made available many tales that indicated the nature and power of female fairies, especially in their relations with mortal men. As early as 1828, Thomas Keightley, whose book, *The Fairy Mythology*, was reprinted frequently thoughout the period, retold the tales of fairy brides, ranging from the French "Legend of Melusina" (a famous medieval lamia or serpent-woman) through the Shetland tale of "The Mermaid Wife" to the Welsh account of "The Spirit of the Van" (called by others "The Lady of the Van Pool"). Thomas Crofton Croker, to whose work Keightley contributed, had already popularized the tale of "The Lady of Gollerus" in his *Fairy Legends and Traditions of the South of Ireland*. By the late 1850s, Scandinavian accounts of swan maidens were widely known in England through such popular works as Benjamin Thorpe's *Yule-Tide Stories* (1853) and George Webbe Dasent's *Popular Tales from the Norse* (1859). Sabine Baring-Gould's *Curious Myths of the Middle Ages* (1866–68) retold, in a chapter on swan maidens, tales of the fairy bride ranging from the Sanscrit to the Irish. Baring-Gould isolated the major motifs (or "story radicals" as he called them) of the stories, and, by suggesting that the maidens were embodiments of the "fleecy clouds, supposed in the ages of man's simplicity to be celestial swans" (p. 578), connected them all to the theories of the solar mythologists.

Romantic ballets like *La Sylphide*, with its *corps de ballet* in swan-white romantic tarlatans, and its tale of a sylph, beloved and inadvertently killed by her mortal Scottish lover, and later works such as Tchaikovsky's *Swan Lake* of 1877 (based on a Russian fairy-bride tale), brought before the public eye yet other versions of the story.[1] The Odette of Tchaikovsky's *Swan Lake*— the powerful, demonic side of her nature severed and displaced onto Odile, the daughter of the evil sorcerer (though both roles are usually played by the same dancer)[2]—has since become one of the best known representations of the swan-maiden figure, while the image of an ethereal ballerina in a white tutu and a headdress of swan's plumage—gracefully bending and swaying in imitation of a swan—has become a cultural icon in the Western world. But in the 1890s, Odette had many, equally popular sisters. The author of a popular *Introduction to Folk-Lore* could confidently assume that at least "some of the many European versions of the swan-skin story are probably familiar to all" (Cox, p. 121).[3]

However, whether the fairy bride's skin was that of a swan, a seal, or a fish, her story was basically the same: in a land east of the sun and west of the moon, or under the sea, or beneath the earth, dwelt a beautiful woman who was either nonhuman or enchanted. She might be under some kind of mysterious spell that made her change her shape to that of a bird or beast; she might be a creature devoid of a soul. She often had the power to change size or shape, become invisible, cast illusions or "glamour," see visions, and foretell the future. A natural aristocrat, she lived by her own code, valuing courtesy, deference, and independence.

Sometimes, one of these creatures of more than human beauty, power, and stature was captured by a mortal and hence forced to become a fairy bride. In the most popular European account of this occurrence, the fairy was depicted as a swan maiden. Spied upon while bathing or dancing with her sisters, the maiden would find her plumage stolen. Unable to flee, she would be forced to accept the embraces of her captor. But whether the animal disguise was that of a swan, dove, partridge, or other bird, whether the fairy appeared as a seal, a mermaid, or a lamia, her fate was essentially the same. Deprived of her own magic realm, she was obliged to lead a different and less glorious existence in the world of mortals. Yet even in captivity, she strove to keep her separateness and power. Though, in general, she was a tractable wife, often excelling in the menial domestic tasks in which she spent her days, she prohibited her husband from certain speech or action and retained the right to leave him—with or without the offspring of the union—if he violated the prohibitions.

As one Victorian folklorist, Charlotte Burne, reports:

> Melusina forbids her husband to visit her on Saturday. . . . The Lady of Little Van Lake vanishes on receiving the last of "three causeless blows," and the many other Gwragedd Annwn, or Ladies of the Lake, whom bold Welshmen are reported to have captured, must never be touched with cold iron, either by accident or design. (p. 61)

But in all cases, if the fairy bride could regain the garment that had led to her capture she was again free to return to her own world and did so without guilt or second thoughts. Seldom did her mortal husband win her back, though sometimes she was thought to see or aid her children by him.[4]

Even even before the Folk-Lore Society was a historical reality, the fairy bride and the folkloric tales that enshrined her had entered nineteenth-century literature. With Goethe's new Melusina,[5] Friedrich de la Motte Fouqué's Undine, and Keats's Lamia among her literary progenitors, she made her way into the poetry, romance, and novels of the Victorian period. Victorians were enchanted by literary, visual, and terpsichorean versions of the tale of Fouqué's *Undine*, the beautiful nymph or water sprite who gained a soul and a husband but sacrificed her life to do so. The story was popular not only with the Pre-Raphaelites and other painters and poets but also as a play and ballet. The ballet *Ondine*, introduced in 1843 by Penot, captivated London for eight years, while the figure of Undine (perhaps best known to our century by the Arthur Rackham illustrations) was painted by Maclise and Watts, as by Fuseli before them. Hans Christian Andersen immortalized her—though in muted and mutilated form—as "The Little Mermaid" of 1837, and his tale was translated into English and into instant fame in 1846. Moreover, many Victorians knew such literary inversions of the folk material as Matthew Arnold's "Forsaken Merman" (based on the Danish ballad, "Agnes and the Merman"), though they probably had little sympathy for the mermaid who had deserted her children and "left lonely

3.1 Arthur Rackham, illustration for Baron de la Motte Fouqué, *Undine* (1909). "Soon she was lost to sight in the Danube."

forever a king of the sea" in exchange for a mortal husband. And by the late 1860s, with growing interest in tales of the Highlands and Islands, many knew the various versions of the tales of the selkies, the seal women captured by and wed to sailors and fishermen of the Orkneys and outer isles.

Thus, throughout the period, fairy brides led at least three connected lives—one in folklore itself, another in literature and the arts, and a third in the theoretical studies produced by a burgeoning group of folklorists. By the 1880s and thereafter Victorian folklorists focused their concern on the marriage relations of fairies and mortal men found in the swan maiden tales and on the social and cultural explanations of these phenomena. That the 1880s should be especially fascinated with the marriage of fairies is not, as I have said above, surprising: this was the era of a debate on the origins of matrimony, as well as on the Married Women's Property Acts, the decade of the "New Woman," of the rise of the "marriage question" and the fall of Parnell (the Irish leader who lost all influence after being named corespondent in a divorce suit), and of the arrival on English soil of Ibsen's controversial Nora, the "elf" who promised to "dance in the moonlight" (*A Doll's House*, p. 748) for her husband.[6] Educated Victorians were aware, even if half-consciously, that swan-maiden tales embodied comments on the matrimonial conflicts between men and women, that they spoke, however indirectly, of gender power relations.

Although swan maiden tales offered new perspectives on the questions of marriage, they also presented some of the same issues that were plaguing those who read them: the condition of women in marriage, their lack of freedom and autonomy, the imbalance of power between the sexes, the nature of female sexuality and of maternality, and the right of females to leave their mates and their children. The folklorists' responses to the tales, the theories they formulated to explain them, are even more telling than the tales themselves. In effect, they constitute a sociocultural history of the spectrum of Victorian attitudes toward women and marriage. As the folklorists first accumulated and then deflected or rationalized questions of female power and sexuality and of the rights of females to divorce (all questions implicit in the tales), they exposed some of England's underlying assumptions about gender, race, and social evolution.

Significantly, folklorists ignored part of the material available to them. Only a few argued that all fairies were female or that they existed as a separate, somewhat Amazonian community of women, although the folk traditions on which to base such speculations—Celtic materials including Conla's voyage to a fairyland entirely composed of women and the rule of Irish fairy kingdoms by queens instead of kings—were widely known. The traits that female fairies shared with the mythical Amazons were equally evident; both groups were nonmonogomous, nonmaternal, outdoor creatures who favored hunting, riding, and wandering where and when they would. But the kinship between fairies and Amazons was deemphasized, and the more militant aspects of elfin nature and behavior were carefully neutralized. When a society of solely female fairy power was postulated, it was dismissed, even by the eminent folklore theorist who propounded it, as the result of confusion in the "primitive" mind (Rhys, *Celtic Folklore* 2:662). In the literary world, it formed the stuff of comedy. In William Schwenck Gilbert's *Iolanthe* (1882), a subversive cabal of Peris yields to the love of Peers, while their proud Fairy Queen must solicit the hand of a lowly but manly sentry. It was still possible to dismiss or defuse through laughter the idea of female power and separation latent in Gilbert's folklore sources.

Even without the specter of Amazonism, folklorists found the subject of fairy brides wed to mortal men disturbing. Many of them simply noted the profusion of tales, remarking, for example, that "the marriage of an Elf-maid and a mortal is one of the commonest themes of legend" (Burne, p. 61); they retold those stories they thought most colorful or most indigenous to their area, and commented on the existence of parallels.[7] For swan-maiden tales, as a genre, were dangerous. They suggested the possibility of the superiority or, at least, the equality of women, thus overturning the prevailing hierarchy of gender. They suggested, as well, the symbolic "otherness" of women, their alien and "natural" characteristics; their inability to fit with comfort in a "normal" patriarchal world. Consciously or unconsciously, Victorian male folklorists rewrote seditious tales by reinterpretating them.

Swan-Maiden Marriage: Theories and Fictions

How a given folklorist viewed female fairies depended, in the first place, upon his overall view of fairy origins.[8] Most of those interested in the questions of marriage and superiority were euhemerist (historicist-naturalist) or comparativist-anthropological folklorists; both groups agreed that there was a substrate of historical evidence beneath the fiction of fairy existence, that fairies were derived from actual, prehistoric peoples, and that, as comparativists argued, traces of belief remained as "survivals" in the primitive cultures known to the nineteenth century.

How a given folklorist saw fairy brides in particular depended, in the second place, on his view of the development of marriage. After 1860, most Victorian folklorists were social Darwinists, intent on tracing the precise evolution of societies and institutions. They placed such institutions as marriage, its stages of development carefully distinguished and categorized, within an evolutionary scheme of progressive development or regressive decay.

Most believed that Victorian marriage—monogamous, patriarchal, yet not (by the 1880s) excluding the "legitimate" claims of women for consideration—stood at the pinnacle of evolution. This form of wedlock was a triumph of cultural order over natural chaos. Toward the end of the nineteenth century, social anthropologists reevaluated the family and the sexual roles within it.[9] Folklorists immediately applied the findings of the anthropologists to materials enshrined in folk tales. The more liberal among them tended to follow the theories of J. J. Bachofen in *Das Mütterrecht* (1861) or the similar hypothoses engendered by Lewis Hunt Morgan in *Ancient Society* (1877) and reutilized by Frederick Engels in *The Origin of the Family* (1884). Both Bachofen and Morgan argued that monogamous marriage was not a fact of nature but a product of evolution. Bachofen believed that the earliest societies were promiscuous and exploitative of women and that, following an Amazonian revolt, women seized power, established a matriarchal society, and forced marriage and monogamy on men. Later, however, a second revolution replaced female fertility with male intellect; patriarchal marriage represented the final phase of social evolution. While Morgan's developmental scheme was more complex, he too believed in an early period of "primitive promiscuity" and that an era of female social and marital power—a gyneocracy—had once existed but had yielded to patriarchal unions. His vision was of a future age of equality between the sexes.[10]

Other social anthropologists provided folklore theorists with more conservative views of the history of marriage. John McLennan, in *Primitive Marriage* (1865), insisted that cultures evolved through a period of group marriage ("polyandry") in which descent was reckoned through the female line. This period of matrilineality (rather than of actual female power) occurred because wives were held in common; hence, the sole way of determining the child's lineage was through the mother. Fascinated by the custom called "marriage by capture," McLennan believed that it had been a nearly universal practice and had created modern wedlock. A man who captured his wife, he argued, held and valued her as individual property; thus, patriarchal succession followed.[11] Sir John Lubbock, the archaeologist and prehistorian, refined McLennan's theory. He, too, did not believe that a period of matriarchy had ever really existed—since women were incapable of such self-assertion—but he did accept the concept of matrilineality, caused, he thought, by savages' indifference to their offspring. For him, too, marriage by capture was a source of modern wedlock, for the captor was proud of his conquest and such pride was at the root of a man's love for his wife.[12] Herbert Spencer, in *Principles of Sociology* (1876), capped these theories by asserting that patriarchal and monogamous marriages were the results of natural selection, the institutions that evolution and civilization ordained.[13]

These anthropological theories were of immediate consequence to folklorists since they seemed to shed light on the relative independence or preeminence of the fairy brides depicted in swan-maiden tales. The tales themselves were often seen as relics or folk memories of a prehistoric period of matriarchy or of matrilineality; the relatively high position of women within them was a sign of how ancient such tales were. Most ancient of all—preserved and transmitted mainly through Irish materials—were the tales of truly independent powerful fairy queens who simply seduced, consorted with, and abandoned mortal heroes at will. Next in age were the swan-maiden tales, perhaps relics of savage exogamous marriage, in which captive brides resided, if only temporarily, in a male tribal world.[14] But how were folklorists to deal with the culturally sensitive questions that remained—those of female superiority, female sexuality, and the female right to leave her mate and even her children by him?

Of the three major issues, Victorian folklorists could most easily handle that of female superiority or equality. While they might find the idea unpleasant to contemplate and difficult to accept, it was, at least, suitable for public discussion. In some few cases, they accepted the possibility that women, under some conditions, might be the superiors of men, but they considered this phenomenon culturally irrelevant and historically obsolete. In other cases, they neutralized the concept still further; they saw an era of female rule as a relic of savagery, a vestige of a way of life so primitive that it was best forgotten. Such anthropologically based theories are perhaps behind William Morris's fictional treatment of an early society in *The Wood Beyond the World* (1894). The Maid, the beloved of the hero, Golden Walter, is asked to be queen among the People of the Bear, who have evolved to what Morgan and Engels would label "middle savagery" (Engels, p. 88). They are a people without the knowledge of iron weapons, who dress in the skins of beasts, practice human sacrifice, and worship an Ancient Mother of tribes for whose incarnation they take the Maid. Only such a primitive group would see their god as female or seek a woman as ruler, the text implies; Walter, in contrast, becomes king of the more highly evolved, civilized land of Stark Wall.

Still other folklore theorists and those who utilized their ideas diminished the idea of female rule in a different way; they explored the negative characteristics of the men to whom women could be superior. The clearly bestial and inferior savage males over whom Ayesha rules in H. Rider Haggard's *She* (1887) are perfect—though again fictional—examples of this doctrine. The explicit and predictable racism of Haggard's romance veils a subtler hierarchical structure; not only is a white woman seen as superior to a black man, but the society in which a woman rules is primitive enough to be a matriarchy in which women select and rule their husbands—that is, until they are beaten or killed by them.

Even those who valued the idea of a period of matriarchy qualified their notions of female power. Charles de Kay, for example, writing on "Women in Early Ireland" in *The Century* (1889), explained that the great power ascribed to the Irish sidhe (fairies) and banshees (tutelary fairies who warn of impending death or disaster) resulted from the high status women held in ancient Ireland. De Kay believed that during an early period of colonization women had led the primitive swarms that invaded Ireland; thus, they had been euhemerized into the great Irish war goddesses. In later, though pre-Christian eras, women had been teachers, lawyers, military tacticians, physicians, and poets and had possessed the rights of inheritance and divorce. When, still later, the groups that had empowered women fell, their "clever" females obtained "power over the chiefs of invading and conquering hoards and became legend as supernatural Sidhes" (p. 437). But the early Irish goddesses and sidhes (and, by implication, the women from whom they were derived) were tainted by promiscuity. In the name of a higher morality, de Kay believed, Christianity opposed the worship of such supernatural beings and disempowered Irish women.

De Kay's simple equation between actual female superiority and powerful female fairies attracted other theorists, including David MacRitchie, England's most famous euhemerist. Citing de Kay's work in his own important book, *The Testimony of Tradition* (1890), MacRitchie agreed that the idea of fairy brides originated in folk memories of actual and forceful women. He was most interested in the seal maidens or selkies of Scotland and the Shetland Islands. MacRitchie argued that these figures were probably Finnish or Lappish females who, because of their sealskin clothing and kayaks, had been misidentified as selkies or as mermaids. Captured by Shetlanders and coastal Scots and intermarried with them, making excellent housekeepers and mothers (though, MacRitchie notes, they would promptly leave if they regained their seal skins; p. 4), these women had given rise to numerous regional tales of fairy brides. Yet while de Kay's animal brides were pretty Finnish girls with white skins and long golden braids, MacRitchie's were dark, squat mongols. Their intelligence, however, compensated for their lack of beauty. One of the few Victorian folklorists to conceive of alien women as superior in knowledge to their captors, MacRitchie speculated that fairy brides were the civilizers of the early Gaels, teaching them such arts as healing. Their reign had been superseded, however, and they had been absorbed into the later patriarchal order.

But the majority of folklorists considered swan maidens and female rule the products of far earlier epochs; female superiority or even power was, to them, a vestige of barbarism. On the basis of the prohibitions in many swan-maiden tales against striking the fairy wife with iron, Edwin Sidney Hartland argued in *The Science of Fairy Tales* (1891) that the stories were "survivals" from the late Stone Age, generated before the common use of iron (p. 307). For John Rhys, the period in which women had sovereignty was so early in the history of civilization that their rule was meaningless. His female fairies stem from a period "so low in the scale of civilization" (2:662) that it failed to understand the male role in conception. This "primitive society where matriarchal ideas rule and where paternity is not reckoned" (2:661) was composed of small, poor, ignorant peoples—in Rhys's analogy, comparable to the aborigines of central Australia—easily conquered by the next wave of superior and patriarchal tribes.

Although he, too, placed female power in the remote past, John Stuart Stuart-Glennie made the strongest, most complex case for the superiority of fairy brides; unfortunately, his argument was part of a blatantly racist theory of culture. According to Stuart-Glennie, civilization arose from the clash and later the mingling of the "Higher White Races" with the "Lower Coloured Races" (Dorson, *Peasant Customs* 2:519). His "Archaian White Races," as he called them, migrated all over the early globe (suspiciously like British colonialists), coming into contact and conflict with brown, black, and yellow tribes who were often puny or dwarflike in appearance and frequently savage in behavior. At times, the Archaians gave some of their women in marriage to the men of these lower races. In these unions, women conferred the blessings of culture on their mates and kept their personal power. Hence, matriarchy was born and its characteristics preserved in folklore.

In his controversial essays "The Origin of Matriarchy" and "Incidents of Swan-Maiden Marriage" (1891), Stuart-Glennie made much of the high level of civilization that accompanied the metamorphosis of Archaian women into swan maidens. Yet, he too qualified the idea of female power, for he linked what he described as "matriarchal societies" solely to marriages between civilized white females and savage nonwhite males. In these matriarchal unions, as he depicted them, the mother or wife is supreme, while the father is secondary or insignificant. Most important, the groom must submit to a series of prohibitions that the bride imposes and that are, at bottom, symbols of her power and his obedience. Under this code, any infringement by the groom will lead to the dissolution of the marriage and the departure of the bride.

As a result of these practices, according to Stuart-Glennie, there were vast numbers of stories, worldwide in distribution, about "that Marriage, universal in Folk-Poesy, in which the maiden is represented as of a higher race than, or at least different race from her suitor, and particularly as wearing clothes, and often . . . a feather dress" (Dorson, *Peasant Customs* 2:523). Stuart-Glennie's swan maidens are Victorian beauties, tall, fair and golden haired; they use artifacts—combs and mirrors—to enhance their appearance. Unlike their brown or yellow spouses, they wear clothing—to the Victorians, the very symbol of civilization. Superior in power and knowledge to their consorts, they are regarded by them as supernatural beings. Even their consent to cohabit is purposive; it is a tactic used to subdue, civilize, and educate their savage mates.

Perhaps the most culturally revealing element in the responses to Stuart-Glennie's argument—an argument his contemporaries heatedly discussed—is that, while his racism was not criticized or even questioned, his theory was dismissed on the grounds that he overestimated the abilities of women. While a few folklorists, among them Andrew Lang, simply poked fun at those "who believe in the white Archaian races who gave their rosy daughters and with them laws, to black, brown, and yellow peoples" (Introduction, *International Folk-Lore Congress*, p. 3), most others were deeply distressed at the implications of female assertiveness and ability presupposed by Stuart-Glennie's hypothesis. George Laurence Gomme, the ethnological folklorist, said that although he could believe that there had been a matriarchate somewhere in the history of marriage, the idea of swan maidens was just as likely to have come from "women of a conquered race," feared because they worshiped deities alien to their masters. He postulated that these subject females would "use that fear . . . to establish a place of power that left a mark on the history of marriage" (qtd. in Dorson, *Peasant Customs* 2:544). In effect, Gomme suggested that the notion of female rule and power was the women's phantasmatic strategem, used to intimidate their male captors. Other folklorists, while not denying the possibility of Stuart-Glennie's matriarchate or swan-maiden hypotheses, stressed that times had changed and cultures had evolved. Alfred Nutt, the distinguished Celticist, remarked (no doubt with Africa and India in mind) that "when of late higher races have come in contact with lower ones, marriage between women of the former and men of the latter has seldom obtained." Moreover, as he candidly admitted (expressing the view held covertly by most of his contemporaries), he could not conceive of a society based on "the supremacy of woman" (Dorson, *Peasant Customs* 2:547). For all these commentators, the idea that culturally superior women might transmit the arts, myths, and traditions of a high civilization was essentially untenable.[15] The presence, in their own era, of a woman on the throne of England seemed not to undermine their argument at all. Perhaps in their eyes, Victoria was an entirely domesticated "fairy queen"—a docile wife and mother rather than a forceful potentate.

For most Victorian writers of fiction, as well, the idea of a superior woman in a position of sole power was abhorrent; principles of social evolution dictated that she could only create a barbaric and distorted society. Like the world of She-Who-Must-Be-Obeyed, depicted in Haggard's *She*, it would be an ambiguous, morally peculiar society, a dead world (here symbolized by the mummies of Kôr) that would crumble when penetrated by enlightened men. Or like the world created by Lilith in George MacDonald's romance of 1895, it would be a society based on primitive violence and evil. Lilith's kingdom, Bulika, is a kingdom of death, "older than this world" (p. 253), as she herself is. As the fairy bride turned demon wife (she is both the first wife of Adam and the spouse of the "Great Shadow," (Satan; p. 253), she is depicted as the inventor of mining and commerce, as well as the traditional demon who destroys and feeds on the blood of the newborn. A realm of death—she has literally stolen and locked up the "water of life" (p. 254)—is all she can create. In the same way, her parasitic sexuality—she is a vampire who metamorphoses into the animal forms of a cat, a leopard, a bat, a snake, and a white leech—is seen as a sign of her savage, bestial nature. An "animal bride," she has not yet evolved into a "true" female.

Seal brides, in particular, could be conceived of as more animal than human as in many of the selkie folktales including "The Goodman of Wastness" (1903) or as in Fiona Macleod/ William Sharp's story ostensibly based on Hebrides folklore, "The Judgment o' God" (in *The Sin Eater* of 1895), in which poor mad Murdoch's seal wife is truly a female seal.[16] At the end of this version of the tale, a naked and insane Murdoch seeks to join the great she-seal he loves. According to the fellow residents of his small fishing village who saw "the dark beast o' the sea creep onto the rock beside Murdoch, an' lie down beside him, and let him clasp an' kiss it" (p. 91), such contact causes Murdoch himself to regress back into an animal. As he joins his mate in slaughtering and eating his faithful collie, he falls into the ocean. The watchers, hearing the barking cry of his seal wife, believe him transformed into another great sea beast.

As Barbara Leavy has noticed in her recent book, *In Search of the Swan Maiden*,[17] animal bride and animal groom tales often take different turns in folklore. While the male monster is revealed as a prince, the female beauty is—as in Macleod's redaction—often exposed as a monster (p. 121). Even the delicately beautiful swan maiden who does not metamorphose can be seen as an embodiment of the animal side of human nature. Not purely human, not purely animal, she can be perceived as monstrous and frightening because she is able to call up forces civilized women have repressed and can no longer call on. Her tie to nature gives her power, and it is necessary to confine and domesticate her to female space to subdue her force.

Victorian folklorists (and Victorian writers of fiction) had an even greater problem with the question of the sexuality of fairy brides than with that of their superiority. The folklorists, in general, assumed that women were closer to "nature," less rational and more instinctual, hence more prone to regress into the beast within. Fairy brides were, to many, embodiments of that very tendency.

To those who traced the genesis of these beings to "savage" women in primitive cultures, swan maidens were, as a matter of course, highly sexed. Indeed, most folklorists believed that "women among rude tribes" were "usually depraved" (McLennan, qtd. in Stocking, p. 202). The very words *primitive* and *savage* connoted the opposite of "womanly," for they conjured up images of overt bestiality and blatant sexuality.

In indicating that the original swan maidens were actually animals and that tales about them described the union of a man with the animal totem of his clan, Edwin Sidney Hartland perhaps inadvertently strengthened the connection between fairy brides and bestiality. In Hartland's implicitly evolutionary scheme of progression, men first worshiped (and perhaps consorted with) animals, then, in a slightly higher phase of civilization, with women who represented or were akin to these beasts. Swan maidens, for all their charm, were therefore closer to "the brute creation" (*Science*, p. 298) than to more highly evolved masculine qualities of intellect and reason.[18] De Kay's belief that Christianity was needed to create morally superior, if socially and legally inferior, Irish women was based on a similar premise. To help the Celtic race evolve, it was necessary to tame the unbridled passion of its women.

While the resolutely colonial minds of some theorists perceived females, like "natives," as needing control, another point of view assumed that highly evolved women were barely sexual at all. Thus, whenever fairy brides were the "civilizers" of other groups or races, as in the hypotheses of MacRitchie and Stuart-Glennie, they were not seen as libidinous or sexually active. Stuart-Glennie, for example, implied that his Archaian white women consented to intercourse with their colored consorts only to improve the racial stock of their host group. Unlike the ardent, sometimes fickle swan maidens of folklore, the Archaians resembled their Victorian counterparts in viewing sexual relations as a duty and a sacrifice.

Thomas Hardy's Sue Bridehead in *Jude the Obscure* (1895), for example, is a brilliant fusion of the ancient "superior" (and thus sexually evolved) fairy bride and the "New Woman." She is the offspring of both folklore and folklore theory, for Hardy, steeped in the lore of his native Dorset, was also clearly acquainted (through his friendships with William Barnes, the poet and expert on local lore, and Edward Clodd, then president of the Folk-Lore Society) with the theories of contemporary folklorists. He knew the debate about the nature and historical reality of matriarchy well enough to insert a brief but telling comment about it in a conversation between Phillotson, the husband Sue wishes to leave, and his friend Gillingham (pp. 183–84).[19] Moreover, Jude has been "charmed by [Sue] . . . as if she were some fairy." As Arabella shrewdly comments:

> See how he looks round at her, and lets his eyes rest on her. I am inclined to think that she don't care for him quite so much as he does for her. She's not a particular warm-hearted creature to my thinking, though she cares for him pretty middling much—as much as she's able to. (p. 231)

When Jude, less "charmed" and more frustrated, bitterly reproaches Sue by saying: "You are, upon the whole, a sort of fay or sprite—not a woman" (p. 280), he reveals his problem with her alien nature. Yet Sue can no more be blamed than Jude, for this "spirit," this "disembodied creature," this "tantalizing phantom—hardly flesh at all"—depicted as so insubstantial that she can nearly pass through Jude's enfolding arms (p. 194)—has been utterly etherealized and idealized, by both Jude and his creator. Yet Sue remains a folkloric swan maiden in both her traits and actions. She is acknowledged as superior to Phillotson and to Jude himself in her knowledge and in her power. Moreover, her restlessness, rebelliousness, and pagan spirit—the last encapsulated in her purchase of totemic gods, the statuettes of Venus and Apollo that decorate her room[20]—expose the fairy bride within. Literally and metaphorically married "by capture" to Phillotson, she flees her husband when, violating her prohibition, he enters her bedroom. The nature of Sue's distaste for Phillotson and affection for Jude again suggests the influence of folklore theorists, for she is so highly evolved that sexual desire has been partially bred out of her. Not naturally maternal, Sue is uncomfortable and disenchanted as a mother. Ironically, it is the changeling Father Time's killing of the children whom she has borne but cannot love that pushes her into a state of death-in-life. In leaving Jude, renouncing what the world calls "immorality" and entering a second marriage with Phillotson, she condemns herself to the worst fate of all for an alien creature—humanity. While Jude may die, her fate is to live on, relinquishing her swan skin forever.

By depicting fairy brides either as idealized and etherealized beyond the realm of physical desire or as depraved and degraded, akin to female savages, folklorists and novelists acquainted with their work attempted to bring folk accounts of female sexuality within the realm of Victorian comprehension. Writers using folklore themes, perhaps without the full knowledge of specific theories, had done the same. Fairy brides like William Morris's swan maiden in "The Land East of the Sun and West of the Moon" (a tale in *The Earthly Paradise* of 1868–70), or like Ibsen's Nora in *A Doll's House* (1879), were identified in animal images and linked to the animal world; Nora has the "innocent" sexuality of a lark and other birds, as well as the less acceptable passions of a squirrel and the more destructive powers of the tarantula (symbolized by her dance). She is identified as swanlike through her physical grace in dancing and through Torwald's achingly lecherous description of her "wonderfully curving neck" (Fjelde trans., p. 101). It is worth noting, as well, that like the traditional swan maidens on whom she is based, she is transformed when her dancing dress, the costume she is to wear to the masquerade, is found by her maid. Although it is only late in the play (Act 3) that she realizes that she, like other fairy brides, has been a captive wife, when she has a chance to escape, she takes it. Even her leaving her children behind links her to swan-maiden tales, for that is their characteristic behavior. Other fairy brides like Ellida, Ibsen's mermaid in "The Lady From the Sea" (1888), are sexually frozen or, like Hardy's Sue Bridehead, have almost evolved beyond the calls of fleshly passion.

Making the subject of divorce respectable was by far the most ticklish issue.[21] That swan maidens often left their mates for the breaking of a prohibition was so outside the pale of convention that most folklore theorists simply ignored the act. Though ordinary people, the "folk" of folklore, had for centuries dealt with marital disharmony or abuse by "informal divorce," consisting of desertion, elopement, or wife sale, such arrangements were seldom publicly discussed, though sensational incidents did appear in the press. Collectors of lore in the earlier part of the century had dealt with the problem of divorce by avoiding it, and it is clear that such rewriters as Croker felt they had to rationalize the female fairy's "unnatural" behavior. Croker's Merrow (an Irish mermaid), captured by one Dick Fitzgerald (to whom the author directs his sympathy), is an ideal housekeeper, wife, and mother—until she finds her mermaid's cap and hence may leave her spouse. Building in a dramatic crisis, Croker shows her yearning to see her mer-parents again, weeping over her need to choose, and turning back to kiss her children and instruct her oldest daughter. Dick, we are told, is faithful till death, persuaded that his fairy bride has been kept from rejoining him by force; "for . . . she surely would not of herself give up her husband and her children" (1:247). It is a sentiment with which the redactor clearly agrees.

Even when discussions about the Divorce Law of 1857 and the Maintenance of Wives acts of 1878 and 1886 made the issues of wife beating and of the interpretations of matrimonial cruelty highly public, folklorists chose not to highlight the presence of these materials in fairy-bride tales.[22] Theorists like Hartland—taking an evolutionary approach to the tales—suggested that as civilization advanced and marriage became more highly regarded, the reasons for separation would become more cogent and complex (*Science*, p. 320). But, despite the fact that a number of the tales he analyzed depicted the wife as being taunted or beaten or struck with iron, he chose only to speculate that "homesickness" might be a cause of the wife's desertion. In general, when folklorists of the 1880s and '90s did discuss the issue, they either condemned the wife for deserting her family or speculated disapprovingly on its consequences. Perhaps this is not surprising when we remember that as late as 1832, Bacon's *Abridgement of the Law*, a standard text of the period, stated "that the husband hath by law the power and dominion over the wife and may beat her" though it added "not in a violent or cruel manner" (Stone, p. 389). Only Yearsley, at the turn of the century, suggested that the fairy bride's return to her home, with or without her spouse, was a folk memory of early matrilocal societies—that is, of cultures in which the child was raised by the mother's tribe and in her dwelling. In effect, he argued, such a fairy bride was following the informal divorce procedures of her own primitive world.

To Hartland, who devoted two long chapters in *The Science of Fairy Tales* to classifying and analyzing six types of swan-maiden stories, the fate of the children was an important consideration. Since he believed in an era of matrilineality, he could accept and rationalize the tales in which the fairy bride left her husband but took the children with her or returned to visit them. Such stories reflected "an early period of civilization [when] kinship is reckoned exclusively through the mother" (p. 288); hence the children were *hers* and her culture permitted her to dispose of them as she thought best.

But Hartland was disturbed by fairy brides who, like Ibsen's Nora, chose to leave their offspring behind. Victorian society agreed with him. When, for instance, the Lady of the Van Pool (in a well-known Welsh version of the tale) was struck by her husband three times without cause (in violation of the prohibition upon which the union was based) and left him and their offspring, Hartland condemned her behavior. Discussing the incident, he argued that, since she had legal recourse, the Lady should "not object to the chastisement which the laws of Wales allow a husband to bestow" (wife

103

"East of the Sun and West of the Moon"

beating was permitted for several "just" causes); she should instead collect a fine to compensate her for the "disgrace" (*Science*, p. 311). In Hartland's eyes, the Lady's choice of abandoning her children and deserting, rather than legally suing the mate who beat her, "transfers the hearer's sympathy from the wife to the husband" (*Science*, p. 321).

Joseph Jacobs, the editor of English folk tales for children, echoed Hartland's views. He, too, believed that the "eerie wife," in separating from her mate and leaving her offspring, forfeited the audience's respect; her behavior reinforced the listeners' sympathy with the husband. "Is he not," asked Jacobs, to be "regarded as the superior of the fickle, mysterious maid that leaves him for the break of a taboo?" (Dorson, *Peasant Customs* 2:548–49). No one seems to have noticed that the lack of ambivalence expressed by the fairy bride about leaving her mortal mate constituted a distinct criticism of the romantic view of love and marriage. Moreover, although neither Hartland nor Jacobs ever directly verbalized his assumptions about divorce, Hartland hinted at what most folklorists thought when he contrasted the looseness of the marriage bond among "savages" with the "recent . . . sanctity of the marriage tie" (*Science*, p. 320). Clearly, free and easy separation was associated with primitive societies and savage eras. Complex and difficult divorce, on the other hand, was the hallmark of a highly evolved culture. Such assumptions held even by ostensibly "liberal" folklorists may help explain why, despite discussion and agitation, the reform of divorce laws was such a slow and lengthy process in England.[23]

The fairy wife's "unnatural" desertion of her children raised additional and still more ticklish questions. A woman's rebellion against her domestic role might be imaginable, for folktales presented that role as dreary, sometimes as close to slavery. Croker's tale depicted the mermaid wife as a virtual servant to her husband. Another tale described even more brutal spousal behavior to the fairy bride it depicted. In this version, a young man gets a mermaid's pouch "by fair means or foul" and forcibly makes her his "bride and bondswoman" (1:165). He is not kind to or considerate of her; and coarsened by her drudgery, she loses her beauty. Yet when, after continual mistreatment, she finally flees, she is still viewed as a misguided runaway wife.

It was almost inconceivable to the Victorian imagination that a woman, even a fairy, would find child care onerous; that a female would sacrifice a child to her own search for self-satisfaction was perceived as abnormal. Even traditionally fickle and destructive mermaids were depicted as "good mothers" in the visual iconography of the period. Pictures such as Burne-Jones's *Mermaid* (1882), a study of a Madonnalike mer-mother holding her chubby baby, and Herbert Draper's *Water Baby* (1890), a rather sensuous image of a young sea-woman gazing at the sleeping infant cradled in a giant oyster shell, reassured their viewers that females of all species had innate tendencies toward maternity. Behavior like that of Nora or of Croker's perse-

3.2 Herbert Draper, *Water Baby* ("A Good Mer-Mother"), oil (1890). City of Manchester Art Galleries.

cuted mermaid raised questions about how "natural" the maternal instinct was and how "unnatural" the flight from motherhood and child care might be. Such behavior, folklorists agreed (when they discussed it) could only be described as antisocial and destructive. Again, it was linked to a more barbarous era and to the behavior of savages.

The Fairy Bride Subdued

By diminishing the claims to superiority of the fairy bride, neutralizing her sexuality and limiting, denying or refusing to discuss her right to divorce, Victorian folklorists rendered her acceptable to themselves and their society. Moreover, they attempted to further reduce the threat she represented by domesticating her and taming her powers. Thus, they stressed her role as the ancestress or tutelary deity of a line or family. The Lady of the Van Pool, Hartland's "unnatural" wife and mother, is perceived as important because she produced a line of famous Welsh physicians (the Physicians of Myddfai), imparting to them her fairy skills in healing.[24] Melusina, in earlier tradition an evil or ambiguous lamia, was transformed into a sympathetic mother-wife. A beautiful undine (water spirit) who, once a week, assumed a serpent form, Melusina left the Count of Lusignan and all their children when the count entered her chamber on a prohibited day. As folklorists reiterated her story, they emphasized the importance of her children (the Counts of Lusignan) and of her banshee-like visitations to predict the destinies of her descendants and of the kings of France. They rationalized the count's behavior in breaking the prohibition; all the children, they noted, were strange or deformed; for the sake of his dynasty, he had to know the reason why.[25]

By the turn of the century, the Melusina figure had been transformed into the entirely sympathetic fairy, Oriana, of Vernon Lee's short story, "Prince Alberic and the Snake Lady." Lee makes clear that even Oriana's lamia nature is not a punishment for sin. The inscription on her fairy sepulcher reads: "Here is imprisoned the Fairy Oriana, most miserable of all fairies, condemned for no fault, but by envious powers, to a dreadful fate" (i.e., metamorphosis into a green snake; p. 51). Mother, tutor, and ultimately ideal mistress to a neglected prince, she is cut to pieces—in her animal form—when the prince refuses to desert her and marry a mortal. An embodiment of beauty, truth, and tender erotic love, Oriana is destroyed by the bigotry and corruption of a decadent society.

Only a few fictional swan-maiden figures escaped the Victorian tendency to subdue and mute them. The strange, "unChristian" Jane Eyre of Charlotte Brontë's novel of 1847 is a fairy bride *manqué*; she needed only to have married Edward Rochester *before* she left him to have been a full-fledged swan maiden. However Brontë knew the tale, whether from Keightley's *Fairy Mythology*, from an oral source (such as the family's old servant, Tabby), or from her favorite *Arabian Nights* (where it is the tale of "Hasan of Bassorah"), she endowed Jane, "half fairy, half imp" (p. 11) with the traits and acts of the folklore swan maiden. Rochester half-mockingly recognizes Jane's preternatural quality from the beginning, commenting:

No wonder you have rather the look of another world. I marvelled where you had got that sort of face. When you came upon me in Hay Lane last night, I thought unaccountably of fairy tales, and had half a mind to demand whether you witched my horse. I am not sure yet. (p. 107)

He repeatedly, though teasingly, calls her an "elf" or "sprite," labels the thought that permeates her watercolors "elfish" (p. 111), and requests that, "fairy" as she is, she make him handsome (p. 215).

Betrothed to Rochester on Midsummer Eve, the night of fairy power and love, Jane's role is to transport him to a remote, enchanted fairyland. As he tells his ward, Adele:

It [Jane] was a fairy, and come from Elf-Land, it said; and its errand was to make me happy; I must go with it out of the common world to a lonely place—such as the moon, for instance—and it nodded its head toward her horn, rising over Hay-hill; it told me of the alabaster cave and silver vale where we might live. I said I should like to go; but reminded it . . . that I had no wings to fly. (p. 235)

But Jane, a fairy drawn from folklore, not the consciously literary *conte de feé* mixed with mythology that Rochester invents, leaves him when he breaks a prohibition. She both declares and proves herself morally (as well as intellectually) superior to her lover and to Blanche Ingram, the mortal woman who wishes to marry him. In Jane Eyre's otherness and force—as well as the name that links her to the sylphs or spirits of the air—in her strong sexual and spiritual passions, she manifests the nature of a formidable fairy bride not yet become a wife.

But Jane Eyre is one of the few, and even she is partially subdued in the end. As many critics have noted, Hans Christian Andersen's method of treating folklore materials (his work first appeared in English in 1846) was an important influence on other writers; his christianizing, domesticating, and softening of them had widespread impact. His "Little Mermaid," for instance, is an example of this tendency, as he deprives the traditional fairy bride of her potent nature and makes her a model of renunciation and self-sacrifice. His version, enormously popular in the period—and in our own—takes the folktale of the water sprite or nixie, earlier utilized by Baron de la Motte Fouqué in *Undine*, and turns the originally proud, noble, and pagan character into a self-abnegating, humble female. Unlike Fouqué who, as Jack Zipes comments (*Fairy Tales*, p. 84), punishes the upper-class knight for forgetting his Christian manners, Andersen focuses on the suffering the morally superior but socially inferior preternatural being must undergo to prove her virtue. Young, beautiful, "thoughtful" (p. 58), she leaves her undersea paradise for the sake of a prince who never truly appreciates her. Every step she takes on her unnatural legs is as painful as "though she were walking on sharp knives" (p. 70), thus limiting her independence. She is deprived of speech, rendered mute in order to pay the sea witch, hence she can neither protect nor assert herself. The prince "toys" with her, both telling her of another he loves and almost promising to wed her. Yet, when given the chance to regain her identity and mermaid nature by killing him, the mermaid refuses. Instead of the rightful jealousy or desire for revenge of an Undine, she exhibits the Victorian virtues of humility, subservience, and self-abnegation. Her reward is to be raised from undine to sylph, higher in the order of elementals, almost within reach of a human soul—with which she will be rewarded after three hundred years of good deeds. Perhaps unconsciously, however, Andersen undercut his own fable; it is the prince who appears soulless and the mermaid who is full of feeling and spirit. Yet Andersen's diminishing of the fairy-bride figure, his emphasis upon her pain and suffering, his praise of her acceptance and willingness to submit were to engender other such interpretations of folklore.[26]

Even fairy brides who enjoyed a better fate than that of the little mermaid were robbed of primal traits to render them more subservient and
hence socially acceptable. The swan maiden of folklore dwindles into a
somewhat conventional spouse in William Morris's treatment of the motif,
"The Land East of the Sun and West of the Moon" included in *The Earthly*
Paradise of 1868–70. Morris, the only Victorian to use the tale literally (although Walter Crane did paint the swan maidens), derives its beginning
from Benjamin Thorpe's account in *Yule-Tide Stories* and several of its incidents from other fairy-bride tales, including those in Keightley's *Fairy*
Mythology and, perhaps, Baring-Gould's "Swan Maiden" chapter in *Curious*
Myths of the Middle Ages. Yet, while Morris utilizes the traditional pattern of
events and actions, he softens and subdues the fairy bride, transforming
her into a tender, vulnerable girl who weeps and flees when her swan skin
is stolen. Trembling and naked, she cowers:

> low upon the ground,
> With wild eyes turned to meet her fate,
> E'en as the partridge doth await
> With half-dead breast and broken wing
> The winged death the hawk doth bring.
> (*Collected Works* 5:38)

Though Morris's swan maiden fears rape, she need not, for the mortal
hero, John, kneels down before her and declares his ardent but respectful
passion. Though linked to an animal nature by the bird imagery used to
describe her, she is depicted as blushing rather than bestial. As in Keightley's "Mermaid Wife" tale from the Shetland Islands, the bride's fear and re-
sistance is a source of erotic pleasure to her captor (and to Morris's male
readers). But her marriage by capture yields to a union of love. However, as
a wife superior in wisdom but unwilling to coerce her husband, the fairy
bride lets him leave her fairy world to return to the flawed earth. Tempted
by his brother's wife, mistrustful of his bride's fidelity, John violates the
prohibition when he speaks the fairy's "name unknown to man" (*Collected*
Works 5:86) and summons her to join him. Thus, the swan maiden must
desert her mate, and when he finds her again (east of the sun and west of
the moon), she has become a "sleeping beauty." The ending is Morris's own
invention, and, in his distillation of the tale, the fairy wife waits in a sorrow-
ful and deathlike trance until the hero reawakens her to joy. Significantly,
too, Morris permits the mortal husband to be reunited with his supernatural wife—unusual in folklore, though here the reunion must take place
in a world beyond the ordinary human one.

In part because Morris distanced his tale from its audience (it is told as
the dream of a medieval astrologer-poet who turns its pathos into art) and
centered it firmly on the mortal hero rather than on the swan maiden, his
version was publicly acclaimed and much loved. In depicting the fairy bride
as sexually passive while titillating his readers with the possibility of a rape

scene, in rendering her desertion as an unwilling act—performed in sorrow (she walks off barefoot into the snow) and suffered for by psychic immobility—Morris, temporarily at least, brought the fairy bride within the precincts of respectability.

But one of the most interesting contributions to the literature of the swan-maiden marriage is ostensibly nonfictional. Maurice Hewlett's *Lore of Proserpine* (1913), a work published not as fiction but as truth, insists on the reality of fairies in general and fairy brides in particular.[27] Fairy wives exist (along with other varieties of preternatural life), he tells us, though we do not, for the most part, recognize them. A pantheist, Hewlett believes that fairies, in general, are the "spirit, essence, substance (what you will) of certain sensible things, such as trees, flowers, wind, water, hills, woods, marshes and the like" (p. 160). While their normal appearance is that of these phenomena, at certain times "there is a relation established by which we are able to see them on our own terms" (p. 160). Providing his readers with two examples of differing fairy brides—one an ostensibly "fallen" woman, the other a more traditional folklore figure—he defends both and seeks to explain why they behave as they do. "The Soul at the Window" is one Mrs. Ventris (wind creature?). Drab and slatternly, she is a London prostitute married to a mortal brute. Her fairy self emerges one night as Hewlett sees her fly out the window of her sordid flat in Gaylord's Rents. He again encounters her as she dances with other fairies on the south slope of Parliament Hill in late April. She is now perceived as free and beautiful, erotic in her dancing, a celebrant of spring and life. She is not the shameless hussy some might call her, Hewlett insists: she feels no shame nor should she; she is not to be judged by human laws, for she is "other"—not of the children of Adam and Eve (p. 119).

Mrs. Ventris is the obverse of Mabilla King, the fairy wife in another tale Hewlett insists is true. Noting that he visited the place where the story occurred, Dryhope, near Otterburn and the Scottish border and providing the time of his visit, 1902, he tells of the love of one Andrew King, a shepherd, for his fairy bride.

Andrew, himself the hybrid child of a sailor and a mermaid (we are told that his mother, Miranda, comes from "nowhere" and attracts seabirds to the inland town when her sailor husband brings her home), rescues Mabilla, a dryad, when the birch tree she inhabits falls during a storm. In the traditional mode of the fairy bride, she is forced to wed her captor. Mute, though beautiful, she is hated and taunted by a mortal rival, Bessie Prawle, who believes her to be a witch. When Mabilla is summoned back to her forest by the "King of the Wood," she leaves her husband. But Andrew follows her and again rescues her from death. This time, no longer mute, she offers Andrew her true and lasting love. For Hewlett, Mabilla is an example of the fairy bride tamed and civilized by human love. She chooses to take on permanent human form; her children—and Hewlett insists that he has seen

109

"East of
the Sun
and
West of
the Moon"

them—are entirely mortal, lacking fairy powers. Hewlett's tale, far more traditional than his sketch of the London fairy wife, is punctuated by comments on the nature of fairy women and fairy-mortal marriages. Fairies are other than good or evil, he argues. Highly sexual, free, they are anarchic forces of nature who must not be judged by human norms or laws. They have their own code and it is not, for the most part, one they share with humans. In committing herself to the love of a mortal, Hewlett's Mabilla has made her supreme sacrifice; she has given up the power and freedom of her fairy nature.

When Lord Dunsany created his early twentieth-century version of the swan-maiden tale in *The King of Elfland's Daughter* in 1924, he too softened the figure of the fairy bride. Though his Lirazel, the "daughter" of the title, and mortal Prince Alveric fall in love, she is too "other" in the mortal world to be happy there. Abducted from Elfland and wed to Alveric in a service adapted from the one "used for the wedding of a mermaid that had forsaken the sea" (p. 21), she is forced by an intolerant friar to renounce her elfin home. But, pagan and nature spirit that she is, she cannot learn or accept the conventions of the earth or, in particular, its Christian religion. Like many of the swan maidens of folklore, she behaves inappropriately in earthly terms: she speaks to animals, dances in the road, sings at night, and laughs at funerals. Instead of the cross, she worships the stones around it. Drawn back to Elfland in part by the "homesickness" Hartland described, and in part by her father's power (her husband's neglect and failure to understand her needs is indicated but not explored), she abandons Alvaric and her young son. Alvaric's long and arduous quest for her elfin land and reunion with her ends ambiguously—as do those of most mortal husbands. It is her adult, half-human son, Orion, who succeeds in finding her, and the romance ends with the uncanny absorption and enchantment of the earthly world and its inhabitants, their strange integration into Elfland. Lirazel and Alvaric are reunited not on this earth but in a world beyond the world. (When Dunsany returned to this motif, in "Mrs. Jorkens" [1931], he treated the failed union of mermaid and mortal with comic irony).[28]

Thus, it becomes evident that, at least in idealized and domesticated form, fairy brides had an impact on the world beyond that of folklore theory—in the realm, for example, of popular literature. They impacted on broad, mass culture in other ways as well. Both individuals and families proudly claimed descent from them. Several Irish aristocrats traced their extraordinary good looks to ancestresses who had been the fairy wives of local gentlemen. The Pellings of Wales, who lived near Mount Snowdon, claimed descent from the tylwyth teg as the children of the fairy bride, Penelope (Rhys, *Celtic Folklore* 1:48). Sea-faring families all over the British Isles claimed their ancestors were mermaids; the Gossocks, a Scottish family from Galloway, and the McVeagh's of Sutherland were held to be the fruits of the union of a mermaid and a fisherman. A family on the Scottish western coast were known to neighbors as "Children of the Mermaid" (Benwell and Waugh, pp. 161–62) and the Clan Maclaren argued that it was descended from a mermaid-mortal union. Cornish families also claimed mermaid ancestry, insisting that it was responsible for their "uncanny" powers (Benwell and Waugh, p. 145). So, too, did the O'Flaherty and O'Sullivan families of Kerry and the MacNamaras of Clare (Croker 1:249). Families in the Shetland Islands explained webbed fingers and toes as relics of the marriage of a mermaid and her captor, while the entire MacCodrum clan of the Outer Hebrides, known as "The MacCodrums of the Seals," claimed to be the offspring of a union between a selkie and a fisherman. In this case, the sign of preternatural parentage was not delicate beauty but an hereditary horny growth between the fingers that made MacCodrum hands resemble flippers. In what may have been the culmination of the fascination with the fairy-bride ancestress, the Folk-Lore Society, in 1895, studied magic lantern slides taken of Baubi Urqhart of the Shetland Islands. On the basis of family stories and a seallike appearance, Baubi claimed to be the great-great-granddaughter of a selkie captured by her ancestor.

Selkie, or seal-maiden brides, popular in the folklore of Scotland and Ireland, also made occasional appearances in literature mainly through such writers as William Sharp/Fiona Macleod, who considered themselves folklorists.[29] "The Daughter of the King of the Land of the Waves," printed in both Gaelic and English by Archibald Campbell (in *Waifs and Strays*, pp. 15–17) depicts the capture of a selkie bride by one Red Roderick of the seals, a man of North Uist. Although the bride in this case is not a true selkie but a sea fairy enchanted by an evil fairy stepmother, her tale follows the traditional pattern. Roderick steals her seal skin, has her baptised, and marries her. After a number of years and the birth of three sons, she simply asks him to return her seal skin, remarking that she has never said farewell to the seals with whom she was dancing when captured. Without added drama, he acquiesces; telling him to raise their boys and never to kill a seal (lest it be a relative), she simply leaves him (pp. 15–17). The lack of dramatic heightening and the matter-of-factness of the reportage are evidences of the tale's authenticity. But the informality of the divorce—an echo of the alternative forms of divorce still practiced among rural people in the nineteenth century—is worth noting. This is divorce by mutual consent, often symbolized by jumping over a broomstick or by leaving a room from two different exits or by returning a ring or other token (here, a seal skin).[30]

Sharp/Macleod's *The Sin Eater* (1895) contains several fictionalized tales of the seal people, as well as many references to the MacCodrums of Uist, the offspring of the seal. As Macleod explained, her/his tales were based on Hebrides traditions, but the same superstitions were also to be found on the west coast of Ireland. One tale, "The Dark Nameless One," reminded readers that the brown-skinned, dark-haired, brown-eyed MacCodrum men of

North Uist were always short, supple, and great at fishing like their seal ancestors and that they were reputed to revert to their seal forms at death. For Macleod, at least, the primitive nature of folk material was not entirely eroded. Perhaps because of her/his mystical, occultist bias and unconventional nature, Macleod did not hesitate to deal with bestiality in the source material, to indicate the element of consorting with animals, to suggest that seal brides in the present—as well as the past—were actually female seals.[31]

Mermaid brides, more glamorous than seals, had a special vogue in the period. The fascination with such creatures (already intensified by Andersen in the 1840s) was increased by such songs as "Married to a Mermaid" in the 1860s, and had become almost a literary and a visual cliché by the turn of the century. By "rediscovering" and widely commenting on such folk tales as the "Mermaid of Zennor" (the tale of a Cornwall mermaid who desired, wed, and lured back to the sea the squire's son, a sweet-voiced chorister in the local church), folklorists established the authentically English nature of the motif. It was not just Scandinavian, they argued, but natively English; it had been in Cornwall since the fifteenth century. Ibsen's *Lady From the Sea*, which was to have been called *The Mermaid*, translated into English in 1888 by Eleanor Marx and performed in May 1891, must also have helped the mermaid vogue. In it, Ellida, the fairy wife torn between Wanger, her mortal doctor husband and her supernatural Finnish sailor lover (a sort of fusion of merman and demon), must painfully choose between them. Depicted as a sympathetic (if somewhat strange) woman, she is repeatedly identified with a figure in the artist Ballested's painting, that of a half-dead mermaid who has wandered away from the sea and cannot find her way back. And she is depicted as "other," alienated from ordinary conventional life and superior to it, yet neither frivolous nor overtly rebellious. Mesmerized by the "Stranger" or sailor, haunted by the image of her dead infant (the product of her union with him), she refuses to make love to the husband she says she loves. Passive on the surface, yet strangely intense, she is a peculiar combination of the domesticated woman and the wild spirit. Her dilemma is resolved when she is left free to choose her mate; "Free to choose the unknown—free to reject it" (p. 101). In this version of the fairy-bride tale, it is because Ellida *is* free that she rejects her demon lover and chooses to stay with Wangel, her mortal husband. Yet she is no threat to anyone except herself; she, too, has been subdued and civilized.

On the other hand, Doris Thalestris Waters, the "sea lady" of H. G. Wells's romance, manages to utterly disrupt the society that rescues her. Though an entirely different tone from Ibsen's pervades H. G. Wells's *The Sea Lady: A Tissue of Moonshine*, set in 1898 and published in 1902, it may well be a response to the play's rendition of the fairy bride. Wells's sea lady is no maid, but a fairy *femme fatale*, who has literally stalked handsome Harry Chatteris from the South Seas to Folkstone. She is the sexual animal bride

113

"East of
the Sun
and
West of
the Moon"

3.3 "Married to a Mermaid," sung by Arthur Lloyd (songsheet cover of the 1860s).
Courtesy of Raymond Mander and Joe Mitchenson Theatre Collection, England.

of folklore theorists rendered as an Edwardian sophisticate. Enchanting
and manipulative, she has learned about human life and sentiment from
modern novels and newspapers. She has neither the desire nor the need
for a soul; she simply wants to possess Harry. And, helped by her Mona Lisa
smile and her exquisite beauty—a beauty explicitly linked to that of the
mermaid holding the sailor she has drowned in Edward Burne-Jones's
haunting painting *The Depths of the Sea* (1887)—she woos Harry away from
Adeline Glendower, his "bluestocking" fiancee. What Doris Thalestris Waters offers is passion, freedom, and death. For all the satiric comedy of the
novel, the point represented by its atavistic fairy bride is serious. Hers is the
call of adventurousness, of the "natural," thus, of anarchy, of the lawless

3.4 Sir Edward Burne-Jones, *The Depths of the Sea*, watercolor and gouache (1887). Courtesy of the Fogg Art Museum, Harvard University Art Museums, Bequest of Grenville L. Winthrop.

force of nature. The "Sea Lady" represents "the Great Outside" (p. 236), an escape from duty and convention, and she is dangerously seductive and sexual. In choosing a supernatural wife who will lure him "into the deeps," Harry chooses death. In a mysterious *liebestöd*, on a "night out of fairyland" with "one star shining" (p. 238), he swims out into the sea with her. The only question readers are left with is whether her drowning of him is deliciously erotic or primitively brutal.

Thus, the motif of the fairy bride—first fortified by folk tales and later diffused and rationalized by folklorists' theories—is retransformed in the works of authors as diverse as William Morris, George MacDonald, H. Rider Haggard, Henrick Ibsen, Thomas Hardy, Oscar Wilde, and H. G. Wells. Less expectedly, but perhaps even more significantly, it leaves its traces on novels and in characters that are not ostensibly fantasies; it is found in works of the "realist" tradition by such figures as George Eliot and Edith Wharton.

In calling the fair-haired, blue-eyed Rosamond Vincy of *Middlemarch* (1872) a "nixie" or water spirit, George Eliot shows her acquaintance with the fairy-bride tradition. For Rosamond may well be seen as an undine without a soul, enchanting Lydgate as thoroughly as Sue the bride enthralls Jude. But it is Edith Wharton, in *The Custom of the Country* (1913), who provides one of the subtlest and fullest uses of the motif in the person and story of Undine Spragg. This undine, a daughter of Rosamond Vincy in both appearance and nature, as well as an inversion of Fouqué's figure, is never converted. Undulating, cold, narcissistic, a lover of pearls and of sapphires as blue as the sea, Undine is fairy wife to four husbands. "Divers et ondoyant" (p. 79), she is both beautiful and alien in nature, devoid of heart and soul. Her reddish-gold hair and blue eyes, her gliding movements reveal her fairy self, though her mother nervously denies the significance of her name: "we called her after a hair-waver father put on the market the week she was born. . . . It's from undoolay, you know, the French for crimping" (p. 80).

115

"East of
the Sun
and
West of
the Moon"

The novel is an ironic record of her four failed unions with thoroughly mortal men. "Fiercely independent and yet passionately imitative" (p. 19), she is, at first, unseen in the lake of New York society. Psychically, she is not the child of her phlegmatic parents nor is she of the social world to which she aspires. Marked by her "otherness," she is, with all her faults, mysteriously innocent and appealing. For she lives by her own code and she is, in her way, from a different world. Although already secretly married to the crass Elmer Moffatt, she wins the love of Ralph Marvell, the "good" man of the novel. Extricating herself from her first union by weeping (Elmer has never before seen her cry), she marries a man whose nature is so different from hers that true union is impossible. Ralph is depicted as sensitive and spiritual; yet he is heated by Undine's cool nature—"remote and Ariel-like, suggesting from the first, not so much of the recoil of ignorance as the coolness of the element from which she took her name" (p. 152). As a "sexually evolved" fairy bride, Undine dislikes lovemaking and neither wants nor accepts the son she bears. Like her folklore predecessors she is perfectly content to leave her "elfin child" (p. 514) with its mortal father. In divorcing Ralph, who yearns to make her "feel" and pity, she loses her chance of gaining a soul. When she flees to Paris and embarks on a marriage with Comte Raymond de Chelles—(the ironic pun on *shells* is clearly intentional)—she is punished for her choice. Destroying Ralph, both by demanding for the sake of appearances the son she does not really want and by the revelation that she has been lying about her past, she feels neither guilt nor remorse. But when de Chelles takes her to the family chateau at Saint Desert, she is truly out of her element. Nearly dying in the desert, chained to a husband whom she bores, she now yearns for the newly powerful and successful Elmer. Though she wins Elmer for the second time, finally acquiring the money and property she desires, she is still not content. Her ultimate wish cannot be fulfilled; because she is a divorced woman she cannot be ambassadress to England.

Although Wharton, like George Eliot before her, is critical of the fairy bride she has created, she does not blame her for her nature. Undine is made what she is, Wharton reveals, by society's attitude toward women, marriage, and divorce. Wives, fairy or not, are limited, constrained by social practice, not consulted. The "good" man Ralph looks down upon the bride he has "captured." The "custom of the country"—and the title itself is anthropological—prohibits him from discussing work or the realities of life with her and prevents her from becoming more than "a creature of skin-deep reactions, a mote in the beam of pleasure" (p. 224). (The nonhuman images in which Undine is described are noteworthy.) "We don't teach women to be interested in men's work—we don't take enough interest in *them*" (p. 206), Ralph finally realizes. And, Wharton implies, in not permitting the simple dissolution of foolish or unhappy unions, in making divorce a matter of hypocrisy and subterfuge, society destroys all those involved.

Wharton's Undine Spragg is not by any means the final inversion of the figure of the fairy bride.[32] As embodiments of women's desires for autonomy and equality in marriage (Leavy, p. 240) or for escape from the dailiness of daily life; as reflections of male fantasies of capture and domestic power and male fears of separation from or abandonment by a woman, swan maidens continue to haunt the human imagination. Submerged, anatomized, transformed to fit the eras and societies in which they play their roles, these folklore figures keep their secret lives. Whether they are sentimentalized or vulgarized, idealized or debased, explained away by theorists or retransformed by artists, they survive, mysteriously, both as subversive forces in nineteenth-century and twentieth-century culture and as archetypes of the ancient worlds from which they come.

F O U R

LITTLE GOBLIN MEN

On Dwarfs and Pygmies,
Racial Myths and Mythic Races

Iɴ ᴏɴᴇ ᴏғ ᴛʜᴇ ᴍᴏsᴛ popular poems of the century, "The Fairies,"
William Allingham announced in 1850 that:

> We daren't go a-hunting
> > For fear of little men:
> Wee folk, good folk
> > Trooping all together;
> Green jacket, red cap,
> > And grey-cock's feather!

This fear took on new meaning in the 1870s, when actual races of "little
people" known as Pygmies were discovered, mainly in central Africa. But
even before that time, and throughout the Victorian period, dwarfs—
natural and supernatural—had been conflated with each other and equated
with goblins (a generic name for small, hostile, unattractive, grotesque,
and almost exclusively male supernatural creatures) and thus with malice
and evil. By the end of the century, the dwarf, remythified and racialized,
had become a new variety of monster.

Historically, actual dwarfs already inhabited a borderland between the
natural and the supernatural, and had always been perceived as "freaks" or
"others." Equated with apes as pets and, more important, as degenerate
forms of humanity, they had been the toys of the aristocracy and of roy-

alty. By the middle of the nineteenth century, living dwarfs were generally perceived as falling into two main categories, proportionate and disproportionate. There were midgets (according to the *OED*, the term itself is Victorian, originating in 1865 through analogy to a midge, gnat, or small fly)—a group exemplified by the enormously popular General Tom Thumb—and there were dwarfs (perceived as physically deformed often because of achondroplastic syndrome), usually of normal intelligence but with large heads, short limbs, and sometimes hunched backs. Midgets were often still called "fairies" and sometimes confused in the popular mind with supernatural elves, while dwarfs were often equated with gnomes or hobgoblins, and generally perceived as grotesque or ludicrous. In addition, two other categories of actual "small folk" existed: those known as costovertabral dwarfs, marked by short trunks and normal-sized limbs (their condition often associated with mental retardation or club foot); and microcephalics or "pinheads," not "true" dwarfs but persons retarded in both mental and physical development. All, from midget to pinhead, were essentially considered jokes, tricks or freaks of nature, and called *sports, curiosities,* or *prodigies*; many earned their livelihood by exhibiting themselves as such—in theaters, pantomimes, exhibitions, and circuses.

The entertainment world did not differentiate among them, though several of the most famous figures of the period, Mademoiselle Caroline Crachami, the "Sicilian Fairy," the Dutch Admiral van Tromp, the famous and talented Polish Count Buruwlaski, and General Tom Thumb were midgets. General Tom Thumb performed as *Le Petit Poucet* in Paris and starred as *Hop o' My Thumb* at the Lyceum Theatre in London in 1846. "Tom Thumb Weddings," using midgets, dwarfs, or children, were popular recreations of the actual wedding of General Tom Thumb to Lavinia Warren in 1863 and became a significant Victorian entertainment, at least in America (Stewart, p. 111). The Sicilian Fairy performed even in death, when her tiny skeleton was displayed by the Royal College of Surgeons.

Others were theatrical successes, not for their miniature perfection but for their deformity, and the grotesques among the dwarf population were as popular as its more attractive members. Living dwarfs were often featured in pantomime, and plays were created for them, especially for those who were healthy and intelligent enough to learn their lines. A certain Signor Hervio Nano appeared with Freeman, an American giant, in a play called *The Son of the Desert and the Demon Changeling* (1843); the play's title suggests the dwarf's deformities. One seriously handicapped dwarf built a career on his ability to play a fly. Another, Don Francisco Hidalgo (ostensibly from Madrid and probably achondroplastic) performed the Cluricaine (or Leprechaun) from Croker's Irish fairy lore and also acted in several fairy plays. The wonderful "Dwarf Giantess," Mary Jane Youngman, weighing one hundred eighty-nine pounds but measuring only thirty-five inches, was shown at Leicester Square, while one of Barnum's most popular "freaks" was a legless dwarf named Samuel D. Parks but called "Hop the Frog Boy," after the protagonist of Edgar Allan Poe's tale. Two Bushmen (San people, viewed as dwarfs) were exhibited as "curiosities" at the Egyptian Hall in London; the girl, apparently only eight years old, was no more than thirty-two inches high; her male companion was adult. Wearing the dress of their tribe, dancing, throwing spears, and performing other "exotic" feats (Wood, p. 251), they were seemingly perceived as creatures of another species.

In one of the more sensational episodes of the period, two children, thought to be siblings and billed as "Aztecs," were exhibited in London in the late 1840s. In promoting them, it was argued that they were part of a Lilliputian race in central South America, who had been worshipped as sacred beings by normal-size inhabitants. So important were they that they were shown before the Queen, Prince Albert, and the Royal family at Buckingham Palace. Victorian scientists hotly debated their origins. When they were diagnosed as cretins by some medical experts and merely as ordinary though severely retarded dwarfs by others (they appear to have been microcephalic)—that is, when they were found to be exceptional individuals rather than typical members of a lost race—the scientific world lost interest. Nevertheless, models of them were made for the ethnological department of the Crystal Palace, and their appearance and behavior were clinically described. Though "active and elfin-like in their gambols" (Wood, p. 436), they apparently had little intelligence, little memory, and little language ability. They were marked by exceptionally small heads, and the male's spondaic or one-jointed fingers were considered signs of how primitive a "specimen" he was. Named Maximo and Bartola, no longer considered brother and sister, they were married to each other in 1867 at a great public ceremony—a parodic version of the "Tom Thumb" wedding. The bride's robes were said to have cost some 2,000 pounds sterling.[1]

Thus, like Eskimos, African natives, and South American Indians, dwarfs of all varieties were exhibited to a curious public; physically different from Anglo-Saxons, they both titillated and fed the curiosity of the populace. Moreover, they spoke to the rising philosophical interest in the origin, nature, status, and significance of distant races. For, as the century progressed, living dwarfs came to be considered more than just "freaks of nature"; instead, they were perceived as a separate race, survivors of an aboriginal "Turanian" dwarf population. Additionally, because of new or revivified strands of belief, they received renewed attention through their connections, based on lore rather than reality, with the creatures of folklore and with the elementals, especially the gnomes, made popular by Theosophy and related occultist movements toward the end of the century.

"The natural dwarf" was himself perceived, as one folklorist put it, as "one of the most villainous tricks of ironical or embarrassed Nature" ("Dwarfs and Elves," p. 64) and it is clear that some actual dwarfs, particularly those of the achondroplastic (or large-headed) and costovertabral (or short-trunked) varieties, were the sources of the numerous folk descriptions of solitary nature spirits and goblins so eagerly collected by Victorian commentators. Living dwarfs believed to have supernatural powers had been forced outside rural communities to scavenge for subsistence, and were gradually incorporated into local lore. The boggart (English, North Country), for example, described in folklore as a squat, hairy man, strong and stupid, could well have been based on an actual person or persons. Others, physically or mentally retarded, were metamorphosed in the minds of rural people into the brownies of England, or the urisks of the Highlands, or the fenodyrees of the Isle of Man, or into numerous other humanoid monsters. Sir Walter Scott had depicted one such person afflicted with achondroplastic syndrome, David Ritchie in *The Black Dwarf* (see the introduction to this book). Another, probably a cretin, thought of as a "small hideous dwarf," was transmuted into "the Brown Man of the Muir" (Eberly, p. 243). Leprechauns were related by one commentator to actual living beings—Loughry men, "a race of small hairy people living in the woods" who stole travelers' gold and whose strength and brutality were famous (Lewes, *Queer Side*, p. 81). The Gille Dubh, an historical dwarf who lived on the southern shore of Loch Druing in Scotland, was hunted by a local landowner who, not considering him human, wished to have him mounted as a trophy.[2] Not only ordinary people conflated actual and supernatural dwarfs. Victorian folklorists of the euhemerist school (that is, those who believed that supernatural creatures originated from historical and actual ones) believed that "the ideal [supernatural] dwarf . . . sprang from a real dwarf" ("Dwarfs and Elves," p. 64) and analyzed and cataloged the traits of both the natural and the supernatural varieties, perhaps inadvertently further blurring distinctions between the real and the imaginary.[3] Part of this combining of the natural and the supernatural was inherent in the name *dwarf* itself, for Victorian folklorists were aware that the word was derived from Scandinavian mythology, where it connoted *both* smallness and deformity and was used for both mortals and the goblins who dwelt in the mountains or in the bowels of the earth and were the rulers of metals and mines. As Norse mythology indicates, dwarfs were the oldest of the fairy tribes, emerging after Ymir the Frost Giant's death as maggots feeding on his flesh, which in turn became the earth.

Other folklorists saw supernatural dwarfs as descended from the "dark elves" mentioned in the *Younger Edda*, and remarked upon how distinct they were from the essentially benign "light elves." These dark elves, "blacker than pitch" were the sources of nightmare, the German word for which is *Alp*, derived from *elf*. Here, too, their evil traits were emphasized. Frederick Hall, in *The Pedigree of the Devil* (1883), again linked the modern elves of popular belief to the dwarfs or duergar of the Norse and Teutons. But for Hall, duergar were originally cosmic spirits of nature, specifically those bred from the earth and living within it. People forgot their cosmic origin, he suggested (following Max Müller's "desease of language" thesis), and the originally "mental beings" were anthropomorphized and classed with an actual race of people (Hall, p. 72).[4]

Even when depicted as ostensibly "real" in Victorian fiction, natural dwarfs were regularly endowed with preternatural traits. Dickens's first description of Quilp in *The Old Curiosity Shop* (1840) identifies him as achondroplastic: "so low in stature as to be quite a dwarf, though his head and face were large enough for the body of a giant" (p. 65). Later, he is called "an uglier dwarf than can be seen anywheres for a penny" (p. 95), connecting him to a specimen Dickens viewed at Barnum's American Museum (Fiedler, p. 268). But he is more than just a living "curiosity." Endowed with the characteristics of a folklore changeling (see chapter 2), he also bears the traits of the folkloric supernatural dwarf in his bizarre dancing, and stamping, and in his avarice, cunning, and lechery. So hideous that his wife and mother-in-law doubt "if he were really a human creature" (p. 86), repeatedly described as "goblinlike," or as a "nightmare," he is also connected, at least metaphorically, to other categories of supernatural creatures. Quilp partakes of the nature of the gnome or earth spirit in his malevolence and avarice, and of that of the salamander (the elemental who lives in fire) in his ability to drink boiling liquids. It is no accident that he dies by drowning, his fire literally extinguished by water.

The Marchioness, probably Quilp's "love child," born of his illicit union with Sally Brass (dragon and mermaid), inherits his stature and some of his magical qualities (she is described as "three feet high" and as "appearing mysteriously from under ground"; p. 334). But perhaps because she does not share her father's evil disposition, she is depicted as a proportionate midget. Yet Dickens imbues even the essentially "good" Jenny Wren in *Our Mutual Friend* (1864–65) with some of the characteristics of a grotesque large-headed dwarf as well as those of a preternatural figure. Described as "a child!—a dwarf—a girl—a something—" (p. 227), with the bad back and "queer" legs caused by the syndrome, she is something between a goblin and a fairy. Endowed with exquisite golden hair, "bright grey eyes," and an "elfin chin" (p. 229), she is identified as partially supernatural by her endless chanting and singing (hence the name Jenny Wren), by her magical sewing, and by the power and violence of her fantasies. The grotesque Malay pygmy-dwarf in Harriet Prescott Spofford's "The Amber Gods" (1860) is another such mixed being, far more malevolent in traits and actions. An "Asian imp" who "shouts and screeches, like a thing of the woods" (p. 43), she is brought as a slave to New England. Ugly, perceived as barbaric and essentially nonhuman, believed to be responsible for the sinking of a ship, she ends up as a palace curiosity, a toy servant, in Italy. Her rosary, "her string of amber gods" (p. 44), both helps to bring about the story's tragedy and embodies the magical curse of the primitive and decadent the Malay represents. However, the most powerful conflation of images of natural and supernatural dwarfs is a visual one, exemplified in the figures in Richard Dadd's Bedlam painting of the 1850s and '60s, *The Fairy Feller's Master-Stroke* (1855–64). In this fantasy in paint, Dadd juxtaposes traditional proportionate fairy figures with grotesques, some of whom have the aged faces, disproportionate bodies, and misshapen legs of cretins and of achondroplastic (large-headed) dwarfs. It becomes evident that in visual depictions like Dadd's, in the literary shapes of Quilp, the Marchioness, Jenny Wren, and Spofford's Malay slave, as well as in such other famous examples as Victor Hugo's Quasimodo, the "Hunchback of Notre Dame," and Poe's "Hop-Frog," natural dwarfs were endowed with preternatural traits and powers, blurring the line between the real and the imaginary.[5]

But what, then, were the attributes of the creatures considered supernatural? These had been fully described by Victorian folklorists, displayed in fantasy literature for adults and most strikingly in literature ostensibly

4.1 Phiz [Hablot K. Browne], "Quilp and his Dog," illustration for Charles Dickens, *The Old Curiosity Shop* (1841).

designed for children (and thus reflecting, in simplified form, the dominant ideas and biases of the culture from which they arose). Folklorists and authors alike agreed that supernatural dwarfs were among the least attractive and pleasant of the fairy tribes, though they could on rare occasions be both kind and generous. Keightley described them as hideous: "a repulsive race of beings, of low stature, with short legs and long arms, reaching almost down to the ground when standing upright" (1:114). In the Highlands, they were associated with the "unseelie court," the evil fairies, and all the metamorphoses ascribed to imps and devils were also said to be practiced by them. Frederic Hall depicted them as more grotesque than horrible:

4.2 Richard Dadd, *The Fairy Feller's Master-Stroke*, oil (1855–64). Tate Gallery, London/ Art Resource, New York.

"They are generally low in stature, hump-backed, with long crooked noses and twinkling mischievous eyes" (p. 73). But all agreed with Hall that they were "a very slippery set" (p. 74), prone to movement and grotesque dancing and adept at vanishing. They were creatures of the earth and the dark places, outsiders even in the rich varied fairy community. They were, however, seen as skilled in crafts and metalwork and as generally shrewd and cunning.

A set of physical and psychological traits emerges from various commentators: supernatural dwarfs were prone to evil, like the goblins to whom they were close kin. Notable for their ancient-looking, ugly faces, their hairiness, and their dirty, wizened bodies, they were voracious in their sexual appetites and bestial in their behavior. Yet they were not invulnerable; they might even be captured and held for ransom. Many, like Rumplestiltskin or his English equivalent Tom-Tit-Tot, were thought of as unable to abide the mention of their names. And, in general, they did not engender in humans the respect or even fear that fairies did.

Most significantly, supernatural dwarfs were almost always thought of as male. There were, of course, a few separate female representatives of the species.[6] But, in the main, dwarfs were without women; either solitary or members of male bands or herds, they did not have families or children in the usual way. Found repulsive by both fairy and mortal women, they were often forced to kidnap them as well as children. Often responsible for changelings, they were sometimes themselves the substitutes. Without women, too, their power to reproduce remained mysterious while their motives for stealing women and infants became evident.

The supernatural dwarfs of Juliana Horatia Ewing's children's tale, "Amelia and the Dwarfs" (1870), are evidences of how well known and accepted these stereotypes were. Amelia's creatures are small but not tiny—not much smaller than the eight year old herself. They come out only at night, knowing that: "All under the sun belongs to men,/And all under the moon to the fairies" (Auerbach and Knoepflmacher, p. 113). They are ugly, with grotesque bodies and wizened faces; one is described as "smutty, and old, and weazened," another as "grotesque and grimy" (pp. 121, 119–20). All leer and grimace; they undergo "such horrible contortions as they laughed, that it was hideous to behold" (p. 114). (The original Cruikshank illustrations reveal them as hairy, bearded, hook-nosed, large-headed, and small-bodied creatures; one shown with a violin looks very much like Dicken's Quip (see also figure 4.1). As the tale progresses, we learn that they are long-lived, but, except for Amelia and an old female servant they have previously captured and taken to their subterranean realm, they are without women. Splendid tinkers and craftsmen, they are hard workers and find their only recreation in the grotesque dancing to which they are addicted. Although they are willful and somewhat malicious, their real cruelty does not lie in their physical mistreatment of Amelia (they pinch

AMELIA AND THE DWARFS.

4.3 George Cruikshank, illustration for Juliana Horatia Ewing, "Amelia and the Dwarfs," from *The Brownies and Other Tales* (1870). Courtesy of the New York Public Library.

her funny bone, poke her in the ribs, and tread on her heels). It lies in their intention to keep her with them till she dies; their desire, by implication, is to mate with her. Even in this tale for children, the nature of the menace posed by dwarfs is clear; it is a threat of rape, of being enslaved and used by grotesque, nonhuman beings.[7]

The same threat is implicit in the dwarf so popular among folklorists, Rumplestiltskin and, in his English equivalent, Tom-Tit-Tot. Depicted as large-headed grotesques, they share the threatening and malevolent nature of such typical Grimms fairy-tale creatures as the evil dwarf in "Snow White and Rose Red."[8] In the British folklorist Joseph Jacobs's popular version of the Rumplestiltskin tale, the dwarf demands the queen herself and his desire for a human, whether woman or child, is at best ambiguous. The reader does not know if he he wants the child (or queen) to raise or keep as his own, to rape or marry, to kill or eat. When the Queen utters his name and solves the riddle, he screams, "The devil told you that," indicating his own connection to the diabolic. As he stamps and splits himself in two, like the vicious trolls of Scandinavia, he returns to earth, his element —and also demonstrates the destructive force of his supernatural fury (Thomas, p. 90).

Thus, in folklore, fairy tale, and the literature that derives from them, the supernatural dwarf is shown as standing closer to the demonic than to the fairy folk. Built rather like a compressed giant, he is linked in both appearance and nature to dark elves and other malignant creatures of the goblin world. He is a miniature *trold*, "a word that signified any evil spirit, giant, wicked person, magician or dwarf" (Thomas, p. 88). His domain, as Susan Stewart comments, is that "of the grotesque and the underworld" (p. 111). While his small size may reduce, mitigate, or add comic overtones to his aura of threat, he is always capable of malevolence.

There is threat implicit, too, in the dwarf's kinship to the great supernatural family of goblins. For whether goblins were called bogles (Scottish, North Country, and Lincolnshire) or boggarts (poltergeist-like brownies of the North Country), or brownies, whether they were classed among the trows of the Hebrides (the trolls of Norway reduced in size but not in viciousness), the duergar of Northumberland, the Pucks, Robin Goodfellows, or hobs and lobs of England and the Scottish Lowlands, the bwbach and bwca and coblynau (or kobolds) of Wales, or the leprecauns, cluricanes, far darrigs, and far larrigs of Ireland,[9] they *were* dangerous and frightening. They, too, were categorized as short, stumpy, and disproportioned; as wizened, hairy, and hideous; as large or ugly-footed; as simian; and as tainted with evil. Never were they pink and white; never did they look like Anglo-Saxons.

Again, Dickens had contributed to the depiction of goblin traits and nature early in the period, sketching one variety in "The Story of the Goblins who Stole a Sexton," a tale inserted in *Pickwick Papers* (chapter 29). In this prefiguration of "A Christmas Carol," goblins with small round bodies, long fantastic legs, and sinewy arms (they resemble costrovertabral dwarfs) punish a drunk and sullen sexton, Gabriel Grub. Full of endless movement, they skip and somersault and leap, while beating and kicking Grub. Above all, they grimace and leer maliciously; the goblin king sticks out his tongue in "derision," and grins at Gabriel "with such a grin as only a goblin could call up" (p. 375). Pulling him down through the earth into their subterranean abode, a cavern underneath the graveyard, they educate him through pain. When he awakes transformed the next morning, it is the truth of the pain itself that "assured him that the kicking of the goblins was certainly not ideal" (p. 380), but a reality.

By the mid-1850s and the rise of Spiritualism in England, a further ingredient was added to the supernatural brew, for gnomes—originally among the elementals analyzed and popularized by Paracelsus—also became identified with supernatural dwarfs and goblins. Paracelsus had invented the name *gnome* (probably deriving it from *Gnosis* or *Gnomen*) for the dwarf-like spirits of earth who, in his system, occupied a position between humans and pure spirits. According to him, gnomes, also called pygmies, lived in their own element, the earth. They had bodies, language, and customs, and could eat, sleep, and propagate, but they were without souls, incapable of spiritual development. Usually about a foot and a half tall, they were the least attractive of the elementals and, unless controlled, were usually malevolent to man. Sir Walter Scott had reminded the world of the theory behind the spirits of the elements in his introduction to the *Monastery*. Sir Edward Bulwer-Lytton had utilized them in his *Zanoni* as early as 1842, and had indicated, as well, that he believed them the source of the table rapping at seances. Other occultists agreed that many of the phenomena that interrupted psychic interactions, like the behavior of poltergeists, were best ascribed to elemental gnomes. Believers increasingly reported seeing them: Anna Kingsford, the seer, "beheld a dwarf figure, which she recognized as that of an elemental of the order of the gnomes, or earth-spirits, for it was costumed as a labourer, and carried a long-handled shovel, their distinguishing symbol" (qtd. in Arnold, p. 210). Violet Tweedale, another occultist, wrote of being terrified in a hotel room in Switzerland by a large-headed, vicious elemental gnome. Two daughters of a clergyman reported to the Society for Psychical Research that they had been accompanied by a group of creatures—including dwarfish gnomes—as they walked in a lane near Oxford (*Proceedings* 3:77).

Thus, in the second half of the century (and the trend intensified with the rise of Theosophy or Esoteric Buddhism in the 1870s), elementals, particularly gnomes, were incorporated into the world of folklore creatures. Again, literature quickly manifested the fusion of these two forms of little men, goblins and gnomes, and melded them with the preexistent images of supernatural dwarfs, further accentuating their grotesque nature. The creatures of George MacDonald's *The Princess and the Goblin* (1872) are described as "a strange race of beings, called by some *gnomes*, by some kobolds, by some *goblins*" (p. 8; my italics). Subterraneans, leering creatures of the earth who live in mines and hoard their treasures, they have the large, unwieldy feet of goblins, a trait shared even by the sanitized and moralized Puck of Kipling's *Puck of Pook's Hill* (1906).[10] In MacDonald's tale, a story influenced by evolutionary theory, the dwarf-goblins' soft, distorted, toeless appendages are signs of their degenerated, atavistic bodies as well as of their evil spirits.[11] The goblin merchantmen of Christina Rossetti's "Goblin Market" (1862) are much the same sort of fantastic amalgam. Dwarfs in size, their movements are goblinesque; grotesque and rapid, they hobble and tramp, and race, and whisk and tumble: "Flying, running, leaping,/Puffing and blowing—/Catlike and rat-like" (ll.332–33, 340). They are marked by the characteristic goblin grimace as they are seen "Leering at each other . . . Brother with sly brother" (ll.93–94). When they are vanquished, they behave like elementals. Some "dive into the brook," like water spirits or undines, some ride the gale like sylphs, and others "writhe into the ground" (ll.442–43) like gnomes returning to their element, the earth.

What marks Quilp, Mrs. Ewing's dwarfs, Curdie's goblins, and Rossetti's goblin men as particularly threatening—what all share—is their grotesque materiality, their physical ludicrousness combined with their "primitive" sexuality. Their assaults on women are rapes; perceived as disgusting phallic figures, they suggest the grotesquerie of the erotic. In *The Princess and the Goblin*, they kidnap and abuse the mortal Princess Irene. Knowing that earthly women do not live long underground, they nonetheless plan to forcibly wed her to Harelip, the goblin crown-prince, who is to use this "sun-woman" (MacDonald, p. 162) as he pleases. In "Goblin Market," their torment of Lizzie is characteristically sexual, as is their seductive offer to both sisters of their fairy food (which, if eaten, keeps one in their world). They have already ravished and destroyed Jeanie: "Who for joys brides hope to have/Fell sick and died"(ll.314–15). They attempt to do the same to Lizzie. Their elbowing, jostling, pinching, and clawing amount to near rape, or at least sexual assault. And all are depicted as subhuman; that they are bestial and primitive is suggested by their characteristic hairiness as well as by their explicitly animal features.

Until the last quarter of the century, then, the distinctions between natural and supernatural dwarfs were blurred. Sometimes equated with goblins and gnomes, they usually were seen as freaks of nature, often as grotesque and ludicrous and frequently as prone to evil. But little goblin men came out of the nursery and the rural cottage and into the realm of horror when they were viewed as "real." What made them important as cultural fantasies as well as subjects for literature and art—what made them truly frightening—were three interlinking events that had coalesed by the 1880s: that discovery, mentioned earlier, of large groups of living African Pygmies; their use as support for theories of an original and separate "dwarf creation"; and the acceptance and popularization of ideas of biological, social, and ethnological evolution that linked dwarfs of all kinds to primordial humans, to primitive non-Caucasian races, and to the apes.

Thus, the "rediscovery" of races of black, brown, red, and yellow living Pygmies, coupled with the emergence of the physical anthropology and ethnology springing from Darwinian thought, led—through a sort of "cultural slippage"—to a new amalgam and to a further degradation in status. Instead of dwarfs being *de*mythified, they were *re*mythified. Instead of Pygmies being perceived as natural, they were seen as preternatural. This newly created paradigm of monstrousity suggested the monstrousness of alien and simian races, while dwarf "otherness" was no longer seen primarily as individual abnormality or deformity but as a metonymy for the savage and animal nature of people who were not white. A new racial myth was born.

More Like the Monkeys . . .

In locating the Pygmies of the Ituri forest in 1870, George Schweinfurth, a Russian botanist and traveler, had proved conclusively that they were neither the monkeys nor the mythical beings most Europeans thought them. Pygmies had, indeed, been known in the ancient world. A Pygmy dancer, with the name *Aka* heiroglyphed below it, is inscribed on the frescoes of an Egyptian temple of the fifth dynasty. Homer had alluded to the pygmies and their incessant battle with the cranes (*Iliad*, Bk. 3), and his reference was widely recorded along with the remarks of Herodotus on the "little people" encountered by African explorers (*Histories*, Bk. 2:32, 33 and Bk. 4:43). Even Aristotle, always regarded as a truth-teller, had mentioned pygmies living in caves in upper Egypt. But by the seventeenth century, Europeans had for the most part ceased to believe in their existence. In 1699, the British anatomist Edward Tyson announced in "Orang-Outang or the Anatomy of a Pygmie compared with that of a Monkey, an Ape, and a Man" that he had scientifically proved that the Pygmies of the ancients were really apes (he had, in fact, been given the skeleton of a chimpanzee to dissect)—and had gone on to deride the belief in the existence of racial dwarfs as outmoded superstition. While Tyson was proving pygmies nonexistent, Portuguese slave-traders were glimpsing them, describing them as small manlike creatures with tails (the tails were bark loincloths), and vainly trying to catch them to determine if they were human or simian.[12]

After measuring and describing seven adult Akka Pygmies, Schweinfurth announced his belief that they were a remnant of the aboriginal population of the African continent, now becoming extinct. Later in the 1870s, the Italian explorer Giovanni Miani also saw them; after his death, two young Akkas considered his "belongings" were sent to Italy to be examined by scientists. But it was Henry Morton Stanley of Livingston fame who made the Pygmies front-page news, describing them in his book of 1890, *In Darkest Africa*. As the imperialist adventure intensified in the last decades of the nineteenth century, encounters between Europeans and African Pygmies became more frequent. Pygmies had been heard to speak; they were known to possess weapons; their existence had been reestablished.

But what were they? Were they fully human? How had they originated?

Were they deevolved, degenerate African natives as a minority of scientists believed, Darwininian throwbacks or "missing links"? And how did one describe them physiologically? Were they dwarfs or midgets? Were they to be found all over the world or only in Africa, Asia, and Oceania?

The rediscovery of the African Pygmies fueled the already raging Victorian dispute over origins; to many, they seemed proof of polygenesis—the creation of races as separate and immutable species. Anthropologists divided Pygmies into Negrilloes (Pygmies found in Asia) and Negritoes (African Pygmies) and argued about whether each was a separate race, and which was more primitive.[13] Were the recently extinct Kalangs of Java, "the most ape-like of all human beings" (Leslie, p. 677) members of the true Negritoe race, asked one anthropologist? And were the Bushmen of South Africa, Negrilloes? Although it was commonly assumed that the Bushmen—seen as close kin to the Pygmies—were the lowest in the evolutionary hierarchy of races, Pygmies were ranked only slightly higher. For the most part, anthropologists did not see them as "dwarfed Negros" —that is, as reverted forms of larger African natives—but as among the earliest, hence crudest of the human species, if they were fully human.[14]

Physical anthropologists—who tended to favor polygenesis and to emphasize racial differences—studied Pygmies' physical and mental traits in the context of their evolutionary relationships to the great apes and classified them racially by physical structure and characteristics.[15] Anthropometrists measured their intelligence and potential for civilization by judging hair texture and hairiness, skeletal structure, color, size of skull, weight and convolutions of the brain, and the slope of faces. Craniologists tested intelligence with calipers and tape. They measured the facial angle, and made the prognathous (protruding) jaw and elongated snout signs of lower evolutionary development, with the vertical profile the evidence of civilization. Victorian scientists used the cephalic index—the ratio of skull length to skull breadth—to divide races into dolichocephalic (long-headed) and brachycephalic (round-headed). It was easier, however, to measure heads than to decide on their value, in part because of the differing head shapes of the measurers. Teutonic and Nordic peoples were found to be dolichocephalic while Celts, including the French, tended to be brachycephalic. Many physical anthropologists did, however, tend to connect brachycephalic heads with civilization, arguing that an increase in the width of the head was commensurate with the increase of intelligence. The cephalic index—quickly adapted and utilized by English folklorists—[16] became so much a part of the culture that it could be used in popular fiction. When Sir Arthur Conan Doyle's eccentric but heroic Professor Challenger meets the newspaper man, Malone, in The Lost World (1912), he greets him with "Round-headed . . . Brachycephalic, grey-eyed, black-haired, with a suggestion of the negroid. Celtic, I presume" (p. 26).

Thus, in the interests of science, all parts of the Pygmies' bodies were repeatedly measured while the Pygmies themselves were subjected to a variety of tests, including "intelligence" tests on which they performed poorly. They behaved, said scientists, "in the same way as the mentally deficient person, making many stupid errors and taking an enormous amount of time" (Bradford and Blume, p. 121). They did not excel in physical tests either, doing poorly on "Anthropology Days," a sort of Olympic competition for savage races staged in connection with the 1904 St. Louis World's Fair, although they were said to excite "the greatest race interest of any specimens shown" at the fair itself. Tied to the brain-size theory (that is, that the size and weight of the brain determines intelligence), scientists agreed that the Pygmies' "lack of necessary brain" interfered with the "workings of brawn" (Bradford and Blume, p. 122).

But even more significantly, according to the physical anthropologists, Pygmies exhibited many primate or simian features, in token of their low rank in the human hierarchy. Their skin color varied, causing "problems" in classification. But in the words of the definitive article in the *Encyclopedia Britannica* (1911) by Robert Murray Leslie, all were characterized by their

> long upper lip with the mucous membrane moderately everted, large ape-like mouth, receding chin, pronounced prognathism, abundant fine woolly hair on the body, brachycephalic cranium, proportionately long arms and short legs, and *a general simian appearance.* (p. 678; my italics)

Travelers, whose accounts were the major source of information, also perceived and described the Pygmies as simian; most believed that they represented the "missing links" in the evolutionary chain. The author of an article on "Negro Nileland and Uganda" saw true African Pygmies as having

> considerable prognathism, the upper incisor teeth projecting outwards . . . a nose with a flattened bridge . . . a short feeble neck (the head being somewhat disproportionately large to the body) . . . a protuberant belly, and rather large feet with protuberant heels. . . . The arms are somewhat long in proportion to the body. (p. 33)

The prognathism, large teeth, short neck, and long arms were indicators of the Pygmies' simian nature, while the large, distorted feet implied the goblinesque. In this traveler's eyes, even their temperament was simian: "These pygmies easily fly into violent rages, very much after the style of apes and monkeys," he remarked. Ewart Grogan, chronicling his travels "Through Africa from the Cape to Cairo," found the Pygmies of Albert-Nyanza (one of the groups discussed by Stanley) somewhat higher on the evolutionary ladder than other dwarfed Africans he encountered. "The Pygmies," he said, in a truly backhanded compliment, are "to these ape-like beings as the dog-faced baboons are to the gorillas."[17] Albert Lloyd remarked (*In Dwarf Land and Cannibal Country*, 1899) that, at his first sight of a Congo dwarf, he mistook it for a monkey. Captain Guy Burrows categorized the Pygmies he encountered (in *The Land of the Pygmies*, 1898) as one might describe animals: on the basis of their pelts and coloration:

> One race, somewhat the taller, has a black skin . . . the other, the smaller . . . is reddish-yellow or brownish yellow. The black pygmy's body is covered with a felt-like down of a brownish colour. Amongst all the pygmies the hair of the head is often russet brown instead of black. It is stated that among the yellow dwarfs long beards are quite common. The bodies of the yellow dwarfs are also covered with down. (p. 12)

In a work of fiction derived from anthropological reading, Charles Gilson argued that the Pygmies of the Upper Congo manifested "a very primitive order of intelligence, in physical features bearing a greater resemblance to monkeys than to men" (qtd. in Street, p. 84). He asserted of one Pygmy tribe that their faces were so "hideous and their bodies so covered with hair that they have been frequently taken for a tribe of intelligent chimpanzees . . . while their language is "just about as comprehensible as the jabbering of apes" (Street, p. 85). Like the Bushman described by Bertram Mitford in *The Weird of Deadly Hollow* (1899), the Pygmy was seen as "a shrivelled . . . ape-like dwarf" (p. 187) with long arms and "heavily built hindquarters" who moves with "the quick nervous restlessness of the ape, to which he bore so strong a resemblance" (p. 188). Not perceived as human, he is a "writhing, yelling, monkey-like object" (p. 191).

While physical anthropologists and their adherents argued for the close

4.4 "A Visit from the Dwarfs," frontispiece to A. B. Lloyd, *In Dwarf Land and Cannibal Country* (1900).

relationship between Pygmies and anthropoid apes, Victorian ethnologists insisted on the low evolutionary status of Pygmies on the basis of their childlike characteristics and lack of civilization. Both groups were influenced by the biological axiom that ontology recapitulates phylogeny, a premise almost universally applied in the Victorian social sciences. As in biology, the fetus moves up the evolutionary ladder, so in the history of society, cultures move up a parallel ladder of civilization. However, the idea became prominent that there was, as Paul Broca wrote, an "unequal degree of perfectibility" among races. "Never," said Broca, "has a people with a black skin, wooly hair, and a prognathous face, spontaneously arrived at civilization" (qtd. in Gould, *Mismeasure*, p. 27). One scientist, Carl Voigt, argued that Negros could not mentally evolve beyond puberty because their cranial sutures, like those of anthropoid apes, closed during adolescence, preventing the further development of their brains and mental powers. Another theorist even pushed the analogy back to fetal development. "The negro exhibits permanently the imperfect brow, projecting lower jaw, and slender bent limbs of a Caucasian child some considerable time before the period of its birth," he argued (qtd. in Gould, *Mismeasure*, p. 52). And if the African savage was a perennial child, "the baby of the race" (p. 53), the Pygmy, still lower in the evolutionary chain, was a permanent fetus, a case of arrested development. When dissecting a Bushwoman, anatomists Sir William Flower and James Murie were first struck with the "remarkable agreement between [her proportions] and those of the European child between four and six. It would indeed appear as if the proportions of a child of that age had been permanently retained" (qtd. in Levy, p. 52). Flower amplified his statement in 1880; the Pygmy itself, he said, was best compared to the fetus, as "an infantile, undeveloped, or primitive form of the type from which the African Negroes on the one hand and the Asiatic Melanesians on the other may have sprung"; it was best viewed as "the species which most closely resembles primitive man" (qtd. in Leslie, p. 678).

As enthnologists, following the premises of E. B. Tylor ("The Father of British Anthropology"), sought to determine the value and place of each race in a universal hierarchy, all used the biological analogy. They agreed that Pygmy society represented a cultural stage far below that of European civilization; the only group lower in the human cultural hierarchy were the Bush people, and they were close relatives of the Pygmies if not identical with them. Then, too, the ethnological view of Pygmy behavior and social organization might be best summarized by the dismissive phrase, "Manners beastly, religion, none." John Buchan, in *The African Colony* (1903), argued that the Bushman and "his kinsmen the Pigmies of Central Africa . . . represented a savagery compared with which the Kaffir races are civilized" (p. 6). He found them "true troglodytes" who, without social organization or knowledge of husbandry or stock-keeping, were "scarcely to be distinguished from the beasts . . . [they] hunted" (p. 6). Gilson indicted them for dirtiness, gluttony, jealousy, and vengefulness, and viewed their lack of family affection as the sure sign of their uncivilized nature. The prevailing view, expressed by Captain Guy Burrows, was that the Pygmies' "low state of mental development" as evidenced by their lack of regard for time, and the absence of clothing, records, traditions, family ties, and religion, revealed them as "the closest link with the original Darwinian anthropoid ape extant" (p. 182).

For those using the rhetoric of the three Cs—commerce, culture, and Christianity—to justify imperial claims, it was often convenient to describe the colonized as less or other than human. In one striking manifestation of this view, Ota Benga, an African Pygmy, perceived as alien even among other racial specimens (he was from a tribe different from that of his fellow Pygmies, spoke a distinctive language, and had teeth filed into points), was consigned for several weeks to the Monkey House of the Bronx Zoo. The floor of his cage was artificially strewn with bones to intimate that he was a cannibal, while he was billed as a "missing link" and exhibited with an orangutan. A zoological label identified him as a distinct species of primate:

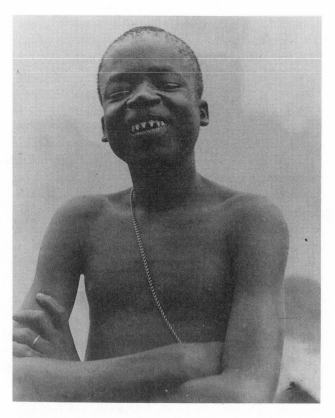

4.5 "Ota Benga," photograph by Jessie Tarbox Beals, from the St. Louis Exposition (1904). Courtesy of Library Services, American Museum of Natural History, New York.

The African Pygmy . . . Height, 4 feet, 11 inches. Weight 103 pounds. Brought from the Kasai River, Congo Free State, South Central Africa, by Dr. Samuel P. Verner. Exhibited each afternoon during September. (Bradford and Blume, p. 181)

After viewing Ota Benga with his orangutan, Dohong, the *New York Times* felt free to comment on their similarity. "One had a good opportunity to study their points of resemblance," remarked a reporter. "Their heads are much alike, and both grin in the same way when pleased" (qtd. in Bradford and Blume, p. 181). Though supernatural powers were not ascribed to Ota Benga, his appearance and habitat did cause women to faint and children to scream in terror; many among those who came to see him viewed him as non- or subhuman.

This example, while distressing, is not entirely surprising. What is initially more difficult to explain—since Victorian photographs and drawings reveal Pygmies as proportionate—is why travelers sometimes described them as deformed, large-headed dwarfs instead of as small people or even midgets. Just as Dr. Downs had taken one feature of those with Downs' syndrome and equated it with traits of the Mongolian race, hence creating "Mongolian idiots" (see chapter 2), so most travelers exaggerated the slightly enlarged heads and the protuberant bellies of some Pygmy groups as signs of deformity and species difference. Stanley is a partial exception: he divided Pygmies into two races: one, "monkey eyed . . . the link

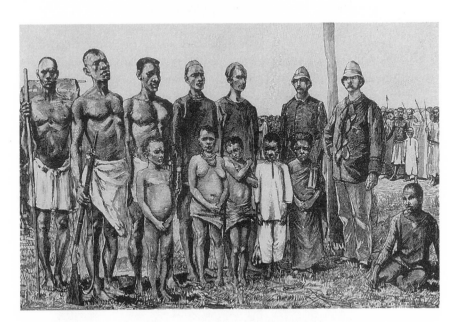

4.6 Henry Morton Stanley, "The Pigmies as Compared with English Officers, Soudanese, and Zanzibaris" (from a photograph by Stanley), for *In Darkest Africa* (1890).

long sought between the average modern humanity and its Darwinian progenitors, and certainly deserving of being classed as an extremely low, degraded, almost a bestial type of a human being" (1:352); the other, red or copper colored, and much more attractive. Burrows also argued for two species, finding the red Akka "not degenerate, as has often been stated, though socially inferior to other tribes" (p. 178), but noting that "the black pygmies . . . are obviously an inferior race, not so well formed nor so intelligent-looking as their ruddy kinsmen" (p. 181). In the eyes of both men, one group resembled black large-headed dwarfs, the other, proportioned midgets.[18]

What becomes clear is that travelers and "scientists" alike were also consciously or unconsciously ascribing to the people they saw the traits of the supernatural creatures in whom they would have insisted they did not believe. All saw the Pygmies' appearance and behavior as analogous to those of supernatural dwarfs, though as lacking the craft skills folklore had bestowed on their Caucasian counterparts. They dealt with the presence of females among the Pygmies (as opposed to their absence among supernatural dwarfs) by seeing Pygmy women, in general, as almost a separate species. Stanley, in particular, waxes ecstatic over the beauty and grace of a tiny Pygmy "handmaiden," and of a handsome captured "Queen of the Dwarfs" (1:345).[19] Others either viewed the women as diminutive and charming or seemed not to notice their existence. Males were differently perceived, repeatedly compared to goblins, gnomes, and brownies. Sir Harry Johnston, in "The Pygmies and Ape-like Men of the Uganda Borderland," remarks that Pygmies remind him "over and over again of the traits attributed to the *brownies and goblins* of our fairy stories" (p. 178; my italics). Illustrating his account with a picture of a Pygmy circle dance reminiscent of the dances performed by dwarfs and goblins, he proceeds to elaborate the similarities. Like brownies and dwarfs these creatures are marked by prankish, mischievous natures, live in caverns and holes, and "have the remarkable power of becoming invisible by adroit hiding" (p. 178). Like them, too, they steal from their neighbors, occasionally taking children and replacing them with Pygmy babies of apelike appearance. Another traveler comments that the behavior of a group of Pygmies is reminiscent "of the descriptions of *gnomes* and elves in European legends" ("Negro Nileland," p. 13). Sidney Hinde describes Pygmies as "small demons" and "gnome-like beings," whose "seemingly magical appearance" and ability to vanish make him "almost doubt their being human" (p. 85). The traits that Pygmies ostensibly shared with supernatural dwarfs and goblins were emphasized; both groups were dirty, hairy, greedy, vindictive, and basely cunning; both groups were marked by gluttony; both stole children; both even shared an immoderate love of dancing.

THE QUEEN OF THE DWARFS

4.7 Henry Morton Stanley, "The Queen of the Dwarfs," from *In Darkest Africa* (1890).

Turanians among Us?

The reason that perceptions of Pygmy "otherness" took the forms they did, of sometimes describing Pygmies as large-headed dwarfs and almost always depicting them as dwarflike quasi-supernatural beings, may lie in the now discredited "Turanian dwarf theory," which seemed to prove polygenesis while supporting prejudice and provoking cultural anxiety. It rendered literal and scientific the Scandinavian mythic belief discussed earlier that dwarfs (including Pygmies) were descended from a race older and other than *Homo sapiens*. Pygmies might be "survivals" of a "dwarf negroid race that at one time existed in northern Europe," said the authoritative 1911 *Britannica*. The African Pygmies were the same as the "dwarf troglodyte races lingering on in the . . . caverns, forests, and mountains of Europe after the invasion of neolithic man," said Sir Harry Johnston (p. 516). Guy Burrows had "no doubt that at one time they flourished on the face of the earth in the flesh, being ultimately killed off to allow the survival of the fittest"

(p. 173). The author of "Negro Nileland" concurs. He supposes "that anciently this dwarfish race [the Pygmies] really did inhabit the greater part of Europe coincidentally with the later-developed types of full-grown humanity, who, before exterminating this . . . little folk, preserved the memory of them in a fantastic form as a fairy race of quasi-supernatural beings" (p. 13).

"Anthropologists of authority" also agreed: some even argued that there had been two dwarf creations, perhaps finding verification in David MacRitchie's "pygmy theory" of fairy origins. For MacRitchie's hypothesis that the fairies of Scotland and Ireland were really non-Aryan, Finno-Ugaric peoples (Finns, Fains, and Picts)—that there had been little, yellow, slant-eyed dwarfs all over northern Europe—now seemed plausible. African Pygmies and "ape-like men" might be survivals from an earlier Paleolithic dwarf population and hence more simian. Better proportioned pygmy races might presumably have evolved in or invaded Europe later, in Neolithic times.

Travelers' information, anthropological data, and archaeological evidences were marshaled to substantiate the Turanian theory. Beginning in 1888, R. G. Haliburton, an armchair explorer, started publishing accounts of "The Dwarfs of Mount Atlas," finding in the Moroccan Akkas, "the missing link," or, at least, an intermediate species between the aboriginal dwarfs he believed had been a first creation and modern *Homo sapiens*. Hailed by some as the most important discovery since Schweinfurth's Congo Pygmies, doubted by others, Haliburton's evidence was widely debated. When some skeptics questioned whether Haliburton's pygmies were actually racial dwarfs or merely cretins, he retorted with conviction "that neither Cretinism nor any other disease can turn ordinary Europeans into pygmies with broad, flat noses, a copper-coloured complexion, and mahogany coloured wool, peculiarities which can only be racial and the results of heredity" (p. 13).

Haliburton suggested, initially, that his Moroccan Akkas and the African Pygmies reported on by Stanley were of the same race, that the essential differences between the groups were only those between civilized people and savages. Later he changed his mind, insisting that it was *his* Moroccan Akkas (copper-colored, flat-nosed, and reddish-haired) who were the sources of the dwarfs of early Europe; it was descent from them that perhaps explained the "negroid" features of the Irish and the red hair of the short Danes.

Haliburton had never actually seen a Turanian dwarf; his evidence came solely from informants. Yet his theory seemed to be supported by archaeological evidence. In 1893, a Professor Kollmann, of Basle, found Neolithic Pygmy skeletons interred with the remains of full-sized Europeans in Switzerland. He believed they represented a distinct species that had coexisted with *Homo sapiens* until they were exterminated. At almost the same time, a Professor Sergi argued that an early migration of African Pygmies to Europe had reached as far north as Moscow; he had found remains of a dwarf race in both Italy and Russia. (He never explained how he knew the bones were negroid.) Other finds were reported in Cornwall, Belgium, France, Sicily, and Sardinia.

Speculations about other branches of a separate, non-Caucasian, simian dwarf species began to surface everywhere. In the later stages of his research, Haliburton sent David MacRitchie to the Pyrennees in search of the Spanish branch of the Moroccan Akka dwarfs. In the dwarfs of the Val de Ribas in Spain, Haliburton argued, one could find other "survivals" of the Turanian race and living evidence of the fact that the species had spread all over Europe. They, too, had negroid traits: copper-colored or yellow skins and wild reddish hair; they walked inclined foreward like the apes; their ancient-looking faces were marked by slanted, Tartar eyes. And their bestiality was demonstrated by their large mouths with "remarkably long and strong" incisors and by "their lips . . . always wet with saliva"(Haliburton, *Race of Pygmies*, p. 79). Cunninghame Graham suggested that there were primordial dwarf tribes waiting to be found in Uruguay and Brazil; plans for the search for a pygmy city in the Andes commenced; small South American Indians, now perceived as dwarfs, were found all over Mexico. Many seemed to have at least half-believed the threat implicit in the theory— that the Turanians had not been "killed off to allow the survival of the fittest" but were still among the living.

Little goblin men, in general, took a new hold on the Victorian imagination. Aubrey Beardsley's creatures, for example, especially the grotesque little monsters of the illustrations for *Salome* (1894–95) are less eccentric and unique when seen as outgrowths of the Turanian theory. At least one of them, the little dwarf-slave on the right in *The Eyes of Herod*, closely resembles an African Pygmy.[20] Fetal, somewhat Africanoid-looking creatures like the figure in *The Kiss of Judas* suggest Beardsley's own imaginative version of ontogeny recapitulating phylogeny. Even Oscar Wilde's sympathetic portrait of a large-headed dwarf in "The Birthday of the Infanta" (1891) seems touched by Haliburton's hypotheses. Though not specifically from the Val de Ribas, the dwarf "had been discovered . . . running wild through the forest . . . in a remote part of the great cork-wood that surrounded the [Spanish] town." Described as "hunch-backed, and crooked-limbed, with huge lolling head and mane of black hair (p. 245), compared to a Barbary ape, he dances wildly and foolishly, "waddling on his crooked legs and wagging his huge mishapen head from side to side" (p. 239). Thus, he reveals his similarity to the missing links that Haliburton and MacRitchie sought.[21] The Ape-Man in H. G. Wells's *The Island of Dr. Moreau* of 1895, literally made from an ape, is vividly depicted as a cross between a "bogle" and a grotesque African Pygmy. His "black face . . . a singularly deformed one," is notable for its bloodshot eyes, large white teeth, and

4.8 Aubrey Beardsley, illustration for Oscar Wilde, *Salome* (1894).

prognathous jaw. Described as "a misshapen man, short, broad, and clumsy, with a crooked back, a hairy neck, and a head sunk between his shoulders" (p. 73), he is the creature the narrator, Prendick, finds most repulsive. Even Tom-Tit-Tot, the English Rumplestiltskin, suddenly becomes a racial monster; in Joseph Jacob's *English Fairy Tales* (1898) he loses his Caucasian traits, becoming "a little black thing . . . a little black impet" (pp. 4–6). Because he lives in a hollow, a subterranean dwelling, Jacobs immediately equates him with MacRitchie's primitive Picts. However, through the song he sings: "I bake, I brew and then a child comes" he is linked to far more savage dwarfs; the song implies that, cannibal-fashion, he will eat his victim (Thomas, p. 90).

As the search for "missing links" intensified—especially after the 1891 discovery of Java Man—dwarf groups and races came to be popular subjects for speculation. Arthur Machen wrote on the Asiki, another group of African dwarfs (inhabiting the French Congo) in "The Little People" (an essay in *Dreads and Drolls*, 1926), again connecting them to the goblins of Europe. Commenting on their resemblance to leprechauns and other treasure guarders, to the sidhe of Ireland and the tylweth teg of Wales, Machen notes "the substratum in both cases is the same: an aboriginal people of small stature overcome and sent into the dark by invaders" (p. 46). In Great Britain, he comments, the dark meant subterranean dwellings under the hills in the wildest and remotest countryside. In Africa, it meant the blackest, thickest forest. Tales of undiscovered humanoid African creatures like the mysterious man-faced monsters called *agogwe* circulated, gripping the imagination of the public. Captain Hichens reported that he had seen these ape-men—little creatures, barely four feet high, who walked on their hind-legs but were covered with russet hair, in Tanganyika (Heuvelmanns, p. 422). He was told—again connecting the ape-men to goblins—that if one put out food for them, these little men, like the brownies of England, would weed and hoe the natives' plots at night.

Bringing the theory uncomfortably close to home, John Beddoe, president of the Anthropological Society of London, found traces of a mongoloid (or Finno-Ugaric) dwarf race in the living peoples of Wales and western England. Atavistic vestiges of their inheritance were their oblique or Chinese eyes, concave or flat noses, and prominent mouths. Beddoe even found a "very ancient" Africanoid type in Ireland[22] (perhaps another explanation of the "negroid" features of Conan Doyle's Irish Malone). Here was further frightening proof that non-Caucasian dwarfs had once possessed the earth.

Euhemerist folklorists had a field day. John Stuart Stuart-Glennie, who argued for an "Archaian White Race" philosophy of history (i.e., that civilization had been created by the subordination of lower by higher races; see chapter 3), made height a criterion for success along with color. He hypothesized that the "Higher White Races (in certain of their tribes, relatively *gigantic*) . . . are to be found as immigrants and colonists all over the world, and in contact and conflict with Lower Coloured and Black Races (in certain of their tribes, relatively *dwarfish*)" (Dorson, *Peasant Customs* 2:518; my italics). Citing physical anthropology and biology as evidence, he argued that "physical features as well as intellectual capacities and moral characteristics have always distinguished Whites from Blacks" (Dorson, *Peasant Customs* 2:532). Because there was an "essential difference between Animal (including primitive Human) Societies and Civilized Societies" (Dorson, *Peasant Customs* 2:521), only the tall Archaian whites could have created cultures; at most, the dwarfish savages made folklore.

But it was again David MacRitchie who, in a paper on "Hints of Evolution in Tradition" (1901), most fully verbalized the connections Victorians were making between the pygmy races, troglodytes, apes, and supernatural creatures. Including the Pygmies among the "certain contemporary races [of whom] it may accurately be said that they are several degrees nearer the brutes than are the members of the great ruling nations," he

noted that "in the past, it must have been a common experience for a nation of conquerors to find itself brought into contact with people who were . . . lower than mere savages. . . . Memories of such a contact must have survived in oral tradition" (p. 1), he insisted. Thus, King Arthur's messenger, described in the Welsh tale of Kilhwch and Olwen as swinging from tree to tree, might well have been a Turanian dwarf (probably of African extraction). Similarly, fenodyrees and brownies—naked, hairy, and deformed—could well be folk recollections of groups closely related to or identical with the African Pygmies. The Swiss dwarfs described by Jacob Grimm as fast-moving, raw-flesh–eating, cave-dwelling savages were clearly analogous to the recently discovered "black and yellow dwarfs of the African forest" (MacRitchie, "Hints," p. 10).[23]

The possibility that the Turanians could still be extant, lurking under the earth and hiding in the dark places of the world, became a major motif in late Victorian works of fantasy. For the dwarf theory contributed not only to the further amalgamation and devaluation of dwarfs, goblins, and pygmies but also to the creation of new monsters for popular art and fiction. The notion that before Dracula in 1897 there are almost no monsters in Victorian fiction is patently incorrect (despite the argument of Thomas Richards in *The Imperial Archive*, p. 45). Dwarfs rendered as simian, alien in race, and preternatural clearly filled the void.

How frightening the new, racialized dwarf monster can be, the cultural anxieties his existence implies, is brilliantly suggested in Robert Louis Stevenson's *The Strange Case of Dr Jeykll and Mr. Hyde* (1886), as well as in Arthur Conan Doyle's *The Sign of Four* (1890). Mr. Hyde, repeatedly equated with non-Caucasians and linked to primitive and alien beings, derives much of his monstrous power from these sources. Depicted as a deformed dwarf, he is twice called a human "Juggernaut" (pp. 337, 343), likening him to the the dark Hindus and their practices, specifically to the followers of Kali— the "Black One"—the Hindu goddess of destruction. "Hardly human! Something troglodytic" (p. 346), his hands are those of a savage: "lean, corded, knuckly, of a *dusky* pallor, and thickly shaded with a swart growth of hair" (p. 391). Not only is his face marked by "black, sneering coolness" (p. 337), in token of his racial analogues, but he has the "extraordinary quickness," and the "odd, light footstep" of the pygmy (pp. 346, 344). He is simian as well, killing with "ape-like fury" (pp. 351–52), jumping "like a monkey" (p. 371), and playing "apelike tricks" (p. 400) upon his other half. His animal snarls, savage laugh, "gnashed . . . teeth" (p. 397) and general "lusting to inflict pain" (p. 398), even the ways in which he maims and kills are signs of his primitive nature. When Hyde comes out of hiding in the subterranean depths of Jeykll, the doctor's fear of "reeling back into the beast" is fully realized. For Hyde is the dark amalgam of the aboriginal pygmy, the primitive anthropoid, and the little goblin man that lurks within.

In Conan Doyle's ostensibly realist detective tale of 1890, *The Sign of Four*, a dwarf-monster from the edges of the world comes back to haunt it at its British center, suggesting the revenge that might be taken by the colonized upon the colonizers. Sir Arthur Conan Doyle's Andaman Islander, a murderous Negrilloe Pygmy brought to England, is at first perceived as "a dark mass, which looked like a Newfoundland dog" but which straightens itself "into a little black man . . . with a great, misshapen head and a shock of tangled, disheveled hair" (pp. 216–17). At the sight of this "unhallowed dwarf," this "savage, distorted creature . . . [whose] face was enough to give a man a sleepless night," whose "features . . . [were] deeply marked with all bestiality and cruelty . . . and . . . [whose] thick lips were writhed back from his teeth, which grinned and chattered . . . with half animal fury" (pp. 217–18), Dr. Watson draws his revolver. The goblin pygmy who has senselessly destroyed a white man is himself destroyed, but the image of his bestial monstrousity lurks throughout the book.

Rudyard Kipling also demonstrates the power and breadth of the Victorian dwarf fantasy when he has Wee Willie Winkie, the protagonist of the ostensibly realist tale of the same name (1889), equate the small "black men" (p. 150), the "Bad Men" (p. 148) of the story (who are actually rebel Afghans) with the vicious goblins of MacDonald's *Curdie* books. Wee Willie's view is not discredited, for Kipling renders the Afghans as monstrous in their decision to kidnap Willie and the Englishwoman he has ridden out to save — as well as in their threat, however comic, to devour the little boy.

Moreover, the danger implicit in this new racialized breed of little goblin men is further intensified when the dwarf is one of many, an unindividualized, featureless member of a horde or tribe. This fear of the nonhuman horde, at least partially generated by the rediscovered Pygmies and the Darwinian implications of the Turanian theory, vividly emerges in the fantasy literature of the 1890s. For in fiction, as in reality, Victorians became increasingly afraid of groups they saw as evolutionary failures or throwbacks. Racial dwarfs like the Pygmies were outcasts from nature, reminders that she could miscarry. Moreover, if human beings were essentially apes of higher development, the possibility existed that something might happen to consign a group or race to less than fully human status. The belief that racial atavism and degeneration were the facts of life, that savages might well become more savage, clearly added to the angst.[24]

Thus, it is no accident that the frightening world of the future in H. G. Wells's *The Time Machine* (1895) is inhabited entirely by fairylike midgets, the Eloi,[25] and monstrous, barbaric dwarfs, the Morlocks. The hideous Morlocks are regressed descendants of the industrial working class—repeatedly described as "ape-like" hairy creatures—"bleached, obscene, nocturnal Thing[s]" (p. 34). They are without pigmentation like the albino pygmies rarely seen but sought by explorers.[26] So simian and bestial are they that the narrator cannot tell if they "ran on all fours, or only with . . . forearms held very low" (p. 34). Like the pygmy goblins that they are, they practice the most primitive of evils, cannibalism.

The bestial African dwarf-monsters of the Tarzan books of Edgar Rice Burroughs are only slightly less degenerated than the Morlocks. The dwarflike men "with great beards that covered their faces and fell upon their hairy breasts" (p. 165) that Tarzan encounters in Opar, the lost city of gold (*Tarzan and the Jewels of Opar*, 1916) are markedly inferior to the great apes Burroughs (like Darwin) prefers to them.[27] With their thick, matted hair, short, crooked legs, long muscular arms, receding foreheads, small, close-set eyes, yellow fangs, and pronounced prognathism, they are Stanley's "monkey-eyed" Pygmies in all essentials but their color, for they are white. Entirely male, a pack of savages who practice human sacrifice, they have, by a genetic accident, inherited the white skins of their captive mothers. In Burrough's version of the racial myth they are—as some said Pygmies were—the products of miscegenation, of mating with the brutes.

But these are only two examples of the hordes of African, Asian, or non-Caucasian dwarfs who surface to threaten and abuse white women, barbarically murder the innocent, and attempt to overrun or to exterminate those higher than themselves in the racial hierarchy. For example, the Huns, one of MacRitchie's Finno-Ugaric peoples (and he reminds his audience that the word *ugaric* is the source of the name *ogre*, for a monstrous cannibal), constitute the cultural menace and become the dwarf-monsters in *The Roots of the Mountains* (1889) by William Morris. Described by early chroniclers as dwarfed, ugly, bandy-legged cannibals with "boar tusks"—which MacRitchie believed were hyperbolic descriptions of their large canine teeth—they battle the noble, far more civilized white Goths in Morris's quasi-historical romance. Taken initially for trolls by the Goths, they are depicted as nonwhites (and called "the Dusky Men"), described as "short of stature, crooked of limb, foul of aspect" (*Collected Works* 15:112), and portrayed as savages devoid of women. Hence, they rape and enslave Gothic women "as their beastly lust bade them" (15:112), valuing them for the whiteness of their skins, but torturing and sacrificing them without mercy.[28] Although they are defeated in the battle on which the romance centers, they do not—history tells us—lose the war.

Jabbering, savage, raw-flesh eating, apelike dark brown dwarfs, one of whom is even called "the missing link," populate another of William Morris's fantasy romances, *The Wood Beyond the World* (1894). One pygmy, monkey-like, gibbers and yells, scuttling along "on all-fours like an evil beast"

(p. 29). Another lurks and watches, "quite unclad, save by his fell of yellowy-brown hair" (pp. 41–42). The most vicious, "dark brown of hue and hideous, with long arms . . . and dog teeth that stuck out like the fangs of a wild beast" (p. 3), has sexually abused and tormented the romance's heroine in ways that she believes would be "unseemly" to discuss (p. 87). All practice primitive magic and appear to have supernatural powers.

The savage little Picts of John Buchan's "No-Man's-Land" in *The Watcher By the Threshold* (1902), are even more threatening specimens of the new, monstrous little goblin men and embodiments of the fears that they provoke. Heavily influenced by MacRitchie's "pygmy theory," Buchan places his Picts—"a horrible primitive survival" (p. 100)—in subterranean caves in the wilds of the Scottish Highlands of his own day. When Graves, the protagonist (and an historian) encounters his first specimen, he is appalled:

> It was little and squat and dark; naked, apparently, but so rough with hair that it wore the appearance of a skin-covered being . . . in its face and eyes there seemed to lurk an elder world of mystery and barbarism, a troll-like life which was too horrible for words. (p. 35)

The Picts' behavior, however, is even more savage than their preterhuman anthropoid appearance. Wantonly murdering those they accidentally encounter, they practice human sacrifice (it is for this purpose that they have kidnapped the sister of a local farmer) as well as rape. Without women, they maintain their race by abducting and then mating with young mortal girls. The tale ends with the call for their extermination, with the warning that they still survive.

It is the more generalized threat, conveyed by Buchan, of the subversion or invasion of the empire by dwarf-monsters of whose existence it is unaware that seems to strike the most fear in the British heart. This is the source of anxiety, for instance, in Sir Arthur Conan Doyle's *The Lost World* (1912). Here, European scientific travelers discover simian, anthropoid dwarfs as well as midget, red South American Indians; the latter are "little clean-limbed red fellows" (p. 159) several notches higher on the racial ladder. Dismissing the speculation that the primitive anthropoid dwarfs are poltergeists or goblins, the party of scientists next identifies them as "the missing link" (p. 134). "Very hairy and deformed" (p. 157) creatures with long arms and rounded backs, "short, bandy legs . . . and heavy bodies" (p. 156), they have faces rendered hideous by small ferocious eyes, flattened noses, curved, sharp canine teeth, and prognathous lower jaws. In all essential features they are like the "inferior" black Akkas and the "ape-like" men so factually described by actual travelers. The savagery of their behavior matches that of their appearance as they torture those they capture, throwing them from cliffs to be impaled on sharpened stakes below. To the English witnesses of a battle between two primordial races, the destruction of most of the anthropoid dwarfs of the lost world promises, though it cannot quite guarantee, that "man was to be supreme and the man-beast to find for ever his allotted place" (p. 177).[29]

Even more frightening, in three of Arthur Machen's horror tales of the 1890s, tribes of aboriginal mongoloid pygmies derived from MacRitchie's theories—"things made in the form of men but stunted like children hideously deformed" (p. 38)—lurk beneath the earth and in the hills of England itself, murdering and raping. In "The Red Hand," a man found slain (by an ancient flint knife) has located the treasure of this ostensibly extinct race. But the protagonist relinquishes the chance to avenge his slaughtered friend and obtain the treasure of the Turanian dwarfs. "The keepers are still there, and I saw them" (p. 191), he announces. Remembering that sometimes the unfit do survive, that "the troglodyte . . . is still lurking about the earth" (p. 164), he will not go to "a place where those who live are a little higher than the beasts" (p. 191). In "The Novel of the Black Seal," Machen presents readers with the retarded hybrid produced by intercourse between a mortal woman and a dwarf-monster, and warns that the professor who has gone in search of the Turanians probably has been killed by them (see chapter 2). Only in "The Shining Pyramid" (1895), one of the most terrifying of all Machen's horror tales, do readers finally glimpse "the faces with . . . almond eyes burning with evil and unspeakable lusts; the ghastly yellow of the mass of naked flesh" (p. 215). Drawn by the disappearance of a young woman in the West Country, spurred on by a set of mysterious clues, including drawings at a child's height of "a Mongolian eye of peculiar almond shape" (p. 205), the protagonists of the tale finally uncover and witness a nightmarish, primitive rite as the dwarf-monsters rise from the bowels of the earth to torture, gang-rape, and ritually sacrifice the woman they have kidnapped.[30]

Thus, little dwarf and goblin men coalesced with actual living "savage" peoples to propogate a new Victorian racial myth. As the empire expanded and awareness of the existence of these peoples grew, with it grew an increasing fear of the primitive they represented. While debate raged about the place of Pygmies and "ape-like men" in creation, actual and supernatural dwarfs lost, in both fiction and the popular mind, their individuality and their "civilized" traits and skills, as well as their traditional foolishness and vulnerability. Instead, they became images of non-Caucasian monsters, hunting in packs and skulking in shadows, threatening to destroy or to subvert the ruling race. Their existence hinted, too, at evolutionary failure, at the fact that the "mistakes" of nature still might be alive—beasts within her bowels, unseen but dangerous to both normal folk and empire.

Through a sort of fusion, then, the traits of African and Asian Pygmies were conflated with those of the dwarfs of Victorian sideshows and the supernatural hobs of folklore and recombined to create figures of preternatural and simian evil. In effect, the Rumpelstiltskins of the world grew fangs, developed the prognathous jaw, and sprouted body hair. Changing their colors—to red, yellow, brown, or black—they took to murder, rape, and cannibalism. As the distorted image of the Pygmy conjoined with a devalued image of the dwarf, post-Darwinian science and belief raised and played on cultural anxieties, confirmed racial prejudice, and fortified the rhetoric and practice of imperialism.

147

Little
Goblin
Men

F I V E

THE FACES OF EVIL
Fairies, Mobs, and Female Cruelty

Unlike the revised or composed fairy tales Victorians read in such profusion, the folklore they gathered was filled with sex and violence. Less expurgated than much Victorian fiction, permitted to be "crude" because authentic, Victorian folklore collections provide a set of insights into the ways in which a culture sought to externalize evil. For the fairies who most frightened the folk and fascinated the collectors were the ones perceived as cruel participants in antisocial acts. Whether they were hordes of "trooping" fairies (as Yeats called them) who traveled the air or misled travelers on the ground or took victims "away," or whether they were solitary and human-size demonic creatures, the figures who most preoccupied the Victorians were those capable of causing discomfort, serious injury, and often death.

Moreover, the sites of much, though not all, fairy evil were the remote Celtic areas, the increasingly diminishing, though still wild regions of Cornwall, Wales, Scotland, and, of course, Ireland. Hence, investigations were suitably distanced for the English Anglo-Saxon folklorists. For the Celtic collectors, on the other hand, even evil could be construed as part of a special and thus precious ethnic and national heritage. But Anglo-Saxon and Celt alike agreed that the slaugh (the host), the sidhe (mainly perceived as female), and many of the other fairies of Ireland and Scotland were neither harmless nor playful—unlike some of the elfin peoples found in other parts of England. Like the Turanian dwarfs—the little goblin men who might still live in the remote wilds of the British Isles—they were very dangerous. While the host or slaugh remained featureless (its power lay in its numbers and effects), the sidhe and their sisters were depicted as tall, often human in size, sometimes beautiful in appearance. Thus, many concluded that when evil had a face (though it was often faceless), if it was not yellow, red, or brown, it was female. Who the evil fairies were, what they did, the nature of the dangers they represented, and their connections to death, witchcraft, and illness is the subject of this chapter.

It had long been held that fairies, at their best, were mischievous and capricious, incapable of such human feelings as compassion. Associated with early periods of history and the behavior of savage or barbarous peoples, they lacked the civilized virtues, behaving like children (the Victorian "little savages") or like the mob. At their worst, they were simultaneously anarchic, spoiling and ruining the products of human culture, and parasitic, living off their hosts while they destroyed them. What made the fairies especially dangerous was their need of human energy and of human beings.[1] Hence, in all sections of the British Isles they were seen as parasites on human substance, as sources of illness, and as abductors and kidnappers, only occasionally returning those they had taken, and then, usually returning them "changed."

Changelings were only one manifestation of their power, and the fairies' general connections with parasitism were even more anxiety provoking, for they suggested evils as subtly amorphous and ambiguous as fairy nature. In the minds of the folk, moreover, fairies were linked to other evils—to disease, to death and the dead, and to witches. And they were all around. The invisible powers crowded the lives of the rural people of Scotland and Ireland. Said Yeats, himself a believer, "the 'gentry' whether in the shape of fairies or demons are always there" (*Unpublished Prose* 1:78).

The Fairy Host as Mob

Bound up with fairy omnipresence and parasitism was their anarchic nature, their power as disruptive forces and the closeness to physical nature that linked them to the bestial and the wild. Unindividualized groups of elves were largely responsible for crude, overt, and often motiveless evil, whether to property or to person. Working in packs, whether they rode the wind as the slaugh, or led travelers astray as bands of pixies did, or simply, blatantly and actively tormented a person for no apparent reason, their actions were brutal. They were a folkloric equivalent to the mob or demos, invading the civilized world from the barbaric wilderness, running amuck, taking or destroying whatever was in their path.

It was perhaps marginally better to be actively attacked than to be covertly diminished, though not according to the many reports of those who believed themselves tormented by evil fairies. Lady Gregory (and Yeats) collected numerous accounts of these in a chapter called "Appearances" in her book *Visions and Beliefs in the West of Ireland* (1920). One of her informants, Old Michael Barrett, for example, was said by local folk to be "tormented" by "Them." "They" sang, played, and screamed all night, only leaving him when he lay dying (p. 203). A letter from an informant, sent by Yeats to Edward Clodd of the Folk-Lore Society, told of a fairy-haunted old woman, a Bible-reading Protestant, living in King's County. Her fairy tormentors cursed and abused her, insulted her family, and struck her with invisible missiles because she would not tell them her name and hence give them power over her (qtd. in Clodd, p. 84). A Suffolk man had his own personal torturer in the form of a fairy or "Pharisee" who would creep under his bed at night and attempt to throw him out of it, while an old female neighbor of his was tortured with equal severity. At night, "she was startled by feeling something pass quietly over her face, and then proceed to hop quickly down her right side" (*County Folk-Lore* 1:122). The occurrence and the noise created by the "Pharisees'" tapping on the wall kept her awake and miserable until she secured a charm against the creatures. Another old woman, living in Lewis, was so seriously molested that she collected every bit of iron she could and suspended it over her cottage door, in hopes of preventing a fairy invasion of her premises. She had made the mistake of talking to "them" when she was a young woman; now they would not leave her alone. They spat on her butter, she insisted, and made the loads she had to carry heavier. She even asked a local man to fire a gun over her shoulder to frighten them away; another man was asked to brandish his razor for the same reason (MacGregor, p. 23).

Moreover, the world of malevolent fairies was all around one; because of the proximity of the parallel world in which the tribes of elfin lived, the threat of incursion was constant. And the immense variety of species added to the dangers of daily life. As well as the more usual fairies of the earth and of the subterranean and watery worlds, there were even wicked tree spirits. The annir-choille, Scottish versions of tree dryads, haunted the woods and snared men. (George MacDonald individualized and utilized their treacherous sister, connecting her to the fairy tree or alder as the Alder-Maid in his early romance, *Phantastes*, 1858.)[2] Ireland was filled, said Diarmod MacManus, a friend of Yeats's, with fairy-haunted or demon trees inhabited by evil spirits. One group of two thorn trees and a boartree, he reports "is guarded by three malevolent demons who, after dark, haunt that stretch of the road" (p. 57). Passersby, he comments, have had their arms grabbed, with marks to show for it, heard inhuman laughs "and even caught glimpses of dim and horribly misshapen figures." Others passing hostile trees have sensed from them "feelings of vicious, bitter evil" (p. 57). Hatred of humans literally emanated from their branches. Yet one could not cut them down, for the penalty for felling fairy trees was often death. Mac-Manus told the tale of the Cottage Hospital of Kiltimagh, never built because its construction would have necessitated the felling of two fairy thorn trees. The man who cut down one had a stroke; other mishaps prevented the felling of the other tree. Belief in the existence of fairy-haunted trees was so strong that in about 1850 a Galloway roadman refused to obey the Scottish County Council's order to widen the highway at a certain point by cutting down an ancient thorn tree reputed to be fairy property. The tree remained, though it stood in the middle of the road impeding traffic for the next seventy years. It was a testament to the belief in and fear of fairy vengeance (Aitken, p. 121).

Among the milder but most prevalent of the faceless fairies' evil acts was the prank of leading travelers and wanderers astray. Tales of being pixie-led, though associated with Cornwall and Devon, were not confined to those areas, but came from all over the British Isles. The ostensible remedy, in its simplest form, was to turn a pocket or a piece of clothing inside out, but this method was sometimes known to fail. Pixies and other elves who led travelers and wanderers astray could be merely mischievous, echoing the behavior of Puck in *A Midsummer Night's Dream*, but they could also cause injury and even death as they trapped their victims in invisibility or led them toward bogs to be drowned. MacManus insists upon the truth of the tale of the Reverend Mr. Harris, the rector of his parish, being fairy-trapped on Midsummer's Day, 1916. On his way to visit a sick man on dangerous Midsummer Night, Harris walked through an enclosed field he had often used as a short cut, only to discover that the gate on one end, the stile on the other, and the path across the meadow had vanished. The fairies held him prisoner, lifting their spell only after a few hours had passed. Yeats comments that the field near the house of Biddy Early, a renowned fairy doctor, was famous for having people go astray in it "and wander about for hours in a twilight of the sense" (*Unpublished Prose* 2:61).[3]

Other, similar anecdotes were recorded all over England, records of an anarchic principle still present in the countryside, of the power of disruption still possible. The *Western Daily Mercury* of 6 June 1890, for example, carried a serious, non-ironic report of a man being pixie-led; folklorists retold the tale of a lad employed at farm near Dartmoor who heard (as did others) plaintive voices calling, "Jan Coo" and followed them, only to vanish on the moor.[4] To be pixie-led was to experience the "uncanny"; it was to be taken across the border between the civilized and the wilderness, to have the familiar become strange and the known become "other."

Being pixie-led was frequently mentioned in the fiction of the period, often for its embodiment of the fear of the uncanny, of a nature now perceived as alien or unfriendly. Thomas Hardy's Egdon Heath, for example, is believed to be full of pixies, and Mrs. Yeobright in *The Return of the Native* (1878) is warned not to lose her way home, for many have been misled on the heath (p. 26). Her death is caused, ironically, not by the pixies but by another metaphorically evil fairy, her daughter-in-law Eustacia Vye, thought to be a witch by several in the community and described by Hardy as "The Queen of Night" (p. 53), a fairy *femme fatale*. Hardy's Henchard, leaving Casterbridge, in *The Mayor of Casterbridge* (1886), passes a fairy circle or pixie ring, traditionally a place where humans are led astray or abducted, only to remember that it was there that his wife Susan stood when she bade him farewell after he had sold her (chapter 44). Sometimes fiction writers thought of the experience of being pixie-led as therapeutic or consciousness expanding, as a sort of reunion, however traumatic, with the magic still resident in nature. In J. M. Barrie's play *Dear Brutus* (1917), for example, being lost in Lob's mysterious wood (the puckian forest of *A Midsummer Night's Dream*) makes people come to terms with their lives.

In Algernon Blackwood's "May Day Eve" (1907), the experience is both destructive and redemptive as the "medical man," a sceptical scientist out to disprove the beliefs of his friend, a folklorist, learns about the supernatural the hard way. Traveling across the moors at twilight on a day he does not realize is May Day Eve, a time of fairy power, he is tormented by mysterious mists, buffeting winds, and visual and auditory hallucinations. He is tripped, plunged into prickly gorse, and turned around. The purpose is educative; he recognizes for the first time that there is something beyond the material and scientific, "that Nature . . . was instinct with a life differing from my own in degree rather than in kind" (p. 183). Only then is he ready for a face-to-face encounter with the "old, yet eternally young" (p. 186), free, powerful existences with the veiled eyes. In their presence, he feels mingled terror and delight—and great anxiety lest these powerful elementals expand his consciousness beyond what it can bear. When he is freed to race to his destination he discovers that on May Day Eve, "*They* [the elemental beings] have power over the minds of men, and can put glamour upon the imagination" (p. 194). What he has learned is obliterated, but feeling and belief remain. He is at last converted, willing to join with his folklorist-mystic friend in a quest for further knowledge. Another Blackwood tale, "Entrance and Exit" (1914), treats being pixie-led in different though equally multivalenced terms. In this story of a fairy wood and a man who disappeared into it some fifty years earlier, swept into some other place, "a hole in space" (p. 162), a priest is called upon to investigate the phenomenon. He too vanishes, although the inhabitants of a house near the wood hear him say, "pray for me." They follow his instructions, and three weeks later he reappears, pale and emaciated but "upon his face and in his eyes were traces of an astonishing radiance—a glory unlike anything ever seen" (p. 169). Unable or unwilling to tell them where he was, he merely comments that he was near but also elsewhere and otherwise—literally, displaced. However, the man he has gone to seek is never found.

In one sense, this experience of encountering the "other" could be seen as spiritually redemptive, as Hans Peter Duerr contends, a necessary going outside the boundaries that separate culture from nature to better understand the former upon returning to it.[5] More often—and this was truer to the tales told by the folk—the experience is one of lostness and terror. It is an encounter with a place of "No Exit" as in "Ancient Lights" (1914), a third Blackwood tale, in which a middle-aged Croyden surveyor's clerk, walking with his written instructions to a house on the Sussex weald, is cruelly trapped by fairies. He has come to see about a client's proposed destruction of a grove called Fairy Wood, and by disobeying a sign that says no trespassing, enters the dangerous world outside the bounds of culture. Like Mac-Manus's priest, he is trapped there. Pixie-led, lost, tormented, he learns that, as the sign now reads, "Trespassers will be persecuted" (*Best Ghost Stories*, p. 242). Gradually, as he hears footsteps, laughter, voices, and glimpses figures gliding by, he realizes that the "glade . . . [is] thick with moving life" (p. 244). It is life intent on punishing him for his intrusion, and when he falls, exhausted, he feels "a thousand tiny fingers lugging and pulling at his hands and neck and ankles" (p. 245). Ejected by the wood and its inhabitants, he reaches the sign again. Its message changed, it now announces "there *is* a short cut through the wood— . . . if you care [or dare] to take it" (p. 246).

To be pixie-led, though frightening, was, if one survived the experience, at least only a temporary state and hence one capable of being redressed. Moreover, it could be seen as a sort of crudely appropriate punishment for trespassing, for violating the fairy rights of property. But in general, the punishments the fairies administered, even to those who inadvertently offended them, far exceeded the crimes against them. A gatekeeper told Yeats and Lady Gregory of a family that made a great dinner to welcome their son back from school, but forgot to honor the fairies by leaving them food. The dinner went to waste, for the son fell off his horse and was killed. They were told of a girl who, for doubting the existence of the fairies, was severely beaten by them. In the West Riding, Gutch reported, a sceptical horsedealer was punished for his lack of belief by a fairy-sent severe rheumatism (p. 129). A plow-boy in Devon who broke a pixie's oven peel (a miniature version of a baker's shovel used for putting dough into an oven), saying that the elves would be unable to bake any bread, was, according to Lady Rosalind Northcote, immediately "set upon by invisible enemies and so severely pinched that he was forced to go home to bed, his bruises being so bad that he could not even open his eyes for days" (qtd. in Whitlock, p. 213). A mermaid of Galloway murdered the child of a pious woman who threw the mermaid's "chair" into her pool; one in Ayrshire killed another woman's child, adding the curse of barrenness to the woman who had angered her. A foolish young man who tried to steal a fairy flag was not only drowned in Dingle Bay but all his descendants—any man named Shea—were cursed with the same fate. As late as 1935, MacManus told of four children murdered by the fairies because their father, in extending his house, had inadvertently built over a fairy road. Only when, on the advice of a fairy doctor, the father pulled down the extension did his fifth child recover from a nearly fatal illness. The best thing to do, all agreed, was to avoid the fairies. Meeting them even in innocent encounters was dangerous; doing them injury or insult was bound to be damaging or deadly.

Less justly, to speak too freely to strangers, to tell them of yourself, to even give someone your name, could be to invite the malicious fairies in. These warnings were strongly voiced by collectors of Scottish as well as Irish lore. The fairies are stern monitors, cautioned Simpson, the author of *Folk Lore in Lowland Scotland*; they punish humans for being ungrateful or discontent—and they hear all. Again agreeing that the invisible world surrounded mortals, he cautioned against saying that a child could be healthier or crops could be better. He, too, noted the belief that fairies received the benefits of which humans were deprived, that they lived off human substance, stealing the nourishment out of mortal food, or the milk out of cattle, or the live child from its mother's arms. Their kine grew fat if human kine grew thin; their fields flourished if the fields of mortals withered. The parasitism suggested as characteristic of these fairies was also, according to some, a trait of all fairy tribes. It was not only out of necessity but also out of spite and mischief that they took what they wanted of human sustenance. In Scotland, one left them clear, clean water, not out of kindness but lest they drink one's blood. The trows or drows of Shetland were equally dangerous, said A. W. in an article on the "Fairy 'Folk-Lore' of Shetland." They punished mortals with disease for touching their property, stepping into their rings or venturing too near their fairy forts; they even punished humans for seeing them. In Ireland, Wales, Cornwall, and Scotland, fairies were literally thought to steal mortals' energy and eventually their lives.

Nature Personified

Obviously, some evil fairies were personifications of disruptive forces of nature, treacherous bodies of water transformed into malevolent river spirits, ferocious whirlwinds who became the slaugh, trees like MacDonald's alder or MacManus's demon thorns that trapped or tripped wayfarers. Female river spirits, like Peg Powler and Jenny Greenteeth, vampirishly thirsted for human victims. Peg, described by William Henderson as the local Lorelei, drowned and devoured people in the river Tees (p. 265). Jenny Greenteeth performed the same function in the streams of Lancashire. Some Victorian folklorists commonsensically explained these figures as bogies, manufactured by anxious parents to keep children from wandering too close to the dangerous waters, but others thought them survivals of ancient sacrificial practices.[6] Though mermaids were most often ambiguous, as amorphous in mind and behavior as in their half-human, half-fish bodies, some were seen as parasites or personified forces of a cruel nature. Charles Henry Poole, in his collection of Staffordshire lore, told of the vicious mermaid of Black Mere of Morridge near Leek. Alluring and destructive, she had killed many. When men attempted to drain her mere, she appeared and warned them that if water were taken she "would drown all Leek and Leek Firth" (p. 102). Mermaids of the Channel Islands and of Scotland were, like the classical sirens, deadly in their behavior to mortals. Whether young and lovely as in Sark or old and ugly, but endowed with beautiful voices as in Guernsey, they not only lured ships to the rocks and caused storms but also ate their victims when they drowned them (Benwell and Waugh, p. 159). Scotland, in particular, had vast numbers of dangerous water creatures haunting lochs, pools, and rivers. How dangerous they were, how much people retained belief in them is shown by the fact that, as late as 1928, an old Highland rhyming prayer still in use begged for protection "from every nymph and water wraith . . . from every siren hard pressing me" (Benwell and Waugh, p. 162).

The English nix or nixie was an equally dangerous version of the murderous siren "who allures the young fisher or hunter to seek her embraces in the wave that brings his death" (Kemble, p. 163). This sort of mermaid-siren, often painted in the 1890s, was beautifully captured both by John William Waterhouse in *The Siren* (c. 1890), with its central image of a beautiful though scaly-legged sea creature looking down with cool indifference at the drowning youth gripping her rock, and by Edward Burne-Jones in *The Depths of the Sea* (1887), where the exquisite mermaid's sinister smile of pleasure, her joy in the dead body of the drowned young sailor whom she holds, haunts the viewer's dreams (see figure 3.4).

The deadly water spirit took on a life of her own in fiction. She is richly alluded to in such works as George Eliot's *Middlemarch* (1871–72) and Edith Wharton's *Custom of the Country* (1913). Lovely but predatory Rosamond Vincy is repeatedly associated with water and with the enchantment of music; often described as a sylph and a nymph, she is identified with the sirens and their song. Twice labeled a mermaid, she is accused of having the shallow soul "of a waternixie" (p. 650); thus, she is depicted as a physically perfect and spiritually empty water nymph who parasitizes and helps diminish Lydgate.[7] Wharton's Ondine Spragg is rendered even more sinister (see chapter 3). Fiona Macleod's folkloric tales depict other such creatures. A wicked sea siren lures and destroys Mary Macleod's lover, Angus, in "The White Heron" (in *By Sundown Shores*, 1899). The Sea-witch of Earraid, described in "The Dark Nameless One," uses her sweet, young voice to summon her male victims to their doom.

F. Marion Crawford, in *Uncanny Tales* (1911), effectively uses the figure and the symbolism of the sirenlike water witch in a tale called "By the Waters of Paradise." Taught by Judith, his old Welsh nurse, about a beautiful but evil spirit clothed in white who periodically becomes "hungry," Lord Cairngorm, the protagonist of the tale, falls in love with a woman who physically resembles her. On the night before their wedding, as he and his beloved stroll over a bridge on his estate, the bridge breaks and the water claims his love. "You have fed the Woman of the Water," mutters old Judith (p. 280). In Algernon Blackwood's "The Glamour of the Snow" (1912), another tale of terror, the narrator is nearly destroyed by the power of nature in the form of a beautiful snow maiden. Captivating him with her beauty and silvery voice, drawing him down to smother and freeze, she is foiled only by his swift flight on skis as he hears behind him a pursuing demonic host. He is saved by encountering a religious procession; the snow maiden and her horde vanish at the sight of a priest bearing unction to a peasant. Joan of the Wad, a Cornish pixie according to Nora Hopper's poem "Joan O' the Wad: A Pisky Song" (first printed in *The Cornish Magazine* of 1882), is a nature spirit who disrupts the lives of her fellow creatures, ruining the fruit, hunting the owls, spoiling the milk, and frightening the country people, though she is most dangerous to young men's hearts.

Maurice Hewlett's fairies—those he insists he knows at first hand—are always the spirits of winds, trees, hills, and earth embodying themselves in humanoid forms, but they incorporate the amorality of post-Darwinian nature. His first encounter with one, described in full in *The Lore of Proserpine* (1913), demonstrated to him the essential cruelty of the elfin peoples, yet made him disinclined to judge them. Walking in the woods, he saw a fairy boy about his own age. The elf had a rabbit between his knees, and holding it by the throat, was throttling it the way "children squeeze a snap-dragon flower to make it open or shut its mouth" (p. 25). Although Hewlett saw that the fairy's "cruel fingers, as by habit, continued the torture, and that in some way he derived pleasure from the performance" (p. 25), he did not intervene. He recognized that the creature, not of the children of Adam, was simply following its alien nature, that it was not "outraging any law of its own being" (p. 26). Closer to animals in nature than to humans, Hewlett's fairies feel no compassion for suffering and no concern for the dead or dying of any species. They are, in human terms, cruel both to animals and to each other.

Un/Natural Cruelties

Fairy sadism, much like that described by Hewlett, is repeatedly depicted in Victorian painting. Richard (Dicky) Doyle's chubby, charming little elves, with their penchant for mischief, are, on closer examination, revealed as

5.1 Richard Doyle, "Triumphal March of the Elf-King," *In Fairyland* (1870).

compassionless and cruel. For example, in an illustration for his famous *In Fairyland* (1870), the "Triumphal march of the Elf King," the royal retinue of "Trolls, Kobolds, Nixies, Pixies, [and] Wood-Sprites" (pp. 10–11), are nonchalantly engaged in mistreating the birds, insects, and snails that serve as their mounts. One elf savagely kicks a beetle, another beats his snail on the horns to persuade it to move, a third, mature elf raises his fist to strike the bird on which he rides.[8] A later Doyle painting of *Elves Battling with Frogs*, ex-

hibited at the Grosvenor Gallery in 1885, centers on the gory death of a sol-
dier frog, "receiving full in his yellow stomach the thrust of a spear of
grass," as one critic noted (Engen, p. 143). Another Doyle painting depicts a
Hitchcockian battle between elves and crows.

   Victorian fairy painters seem almost obsessed with the cruelty of the
elfin peoples to their fellow natural creatures; they have apparently substituted this visual convention for the more forbidden one of fairy cruelty to
mortals, displacing evil onto more culturally approved forms. The hunting
and killing of an owl—a traditional fairy enemy—is a significant motif in

Sir Joseph Noel Paton's famous pair of paintings based on *A Midsummer Night's Dream*, *The Quarrel of Titania and Oberon* (1849) and *The Reconciliation of Titania and Oberon* (1847). Its appearance is no surprise in the former painting, for the work is filled with images of fairy malevolence as the rage of the royal pair erupts into and disrupts the world of nature. Around the painting's margins, just peripherally visible, are scenes of violence; in the upper right-hand corner, for example, five fairies pommel and poke a frightened owl as they fly nearby it or attempt to ride it. In the foreground, a weird froglike creature is tortured by a fairy orchestra blasting in its ears; to the left of this scene, fairies are beating a small frog to death. Less expectedly, the *Reconciliation* depicts in lurid detail the death of the owl, now lying in the foreground. While one elf, injured in the fray, lies partially beneath the bird, its claws in his side and his face distorted in pain, another fairy thrusts a lance into the fallen owl and a third raises a mushroom to pelt it with.

John Anster Fitzgerald's series of paintings on a group of fairies and a robin in its nest are almost studies in the stages of cruelty. Unsanctioned by the text of *A Midsummer Night's Dream*, and not ostensibly derived from a literary source, they answer the question "Who killed Cock-Robin?" by suggesting that the fairies did. In one painting, *Cock Robin Defending his Nest*, an initial response to a charming still life rich in Pre-Raphaelite detail (and rather like William "bird's egg" Hunt's) gives way to the recognition that a group of delicate and beautiful fairies—although there are a few of Fitzgerald's characteristic buglike goblins among them—are about to kill a robin and/or

5.2 Sir Joseph Noel Paton, *The Quarrel of Oberon and Titania*, oil (1849). Courtesy of National Galleries of Scotland, Edinburgh.

steal its eggs. In this study of fairy aggression, male and female fairies alike are armed with long lances made of thorns, and a gargoylelike goblin has already stolen one of the helpless bird's eggs. Another Fitzgerald painting (*The Chase of the White Mice*) depicts white mice pierced by the thorns used by fairies as stirrups. In the foreground of Huskisson's erotic *Midsummer Night's Fairies* (c. 1847), a group of elves with spears are battling an armored snail while, on the right, a fully armored elf attacks a fleeing spider. Thomas Heatherley's almost pornographic *Fairy Resting on a Mushroom* (c. 1860) is rendered more complex by the shadowy conflicts taking place within its borders. On the left side of the painting, one nearly transparent fairy spears another, while in the foreground three elves attempt to stop the onward progression of a large snail and its rider by stoning them and shooting them with bows and arrows. Even in such seemingly innocuous works as those of Edward Hopley and John George Naish, fairy cruelty to nature's creatures plays a considerable role. In Hopley's incongrously sweet *Puck and the Moth* (c. 1853), a cherubic flower-capped Puck prepares to spear a moth on his lance made of thorns. In Naish's seemingly saccharine *Midsummer Fairies* (c. 1856), an elf impales a harmless caterpillar on its lance and another beats its butterfly mount with a feather. Often, the fairy painters seem to conceptualize their fairies, no matter how elegantly or sensuously they depict them, as the naughty children who derive great joy from pulling off the wings of flies.

In a similar vein, M. R. James focuses on the playfully sadistic practices of the "little creatures" in his sole tale of the fairies, "After Dark in the Playing Field" (c. 1924). Here, in an incident similar to those depicted in Paton's

5.3 Sir Joseph Noel Paton, *The Reconciliation of Oberon and Titania*, oil (1847). Courtesy of National Galleries of Scotland, Edinburgh.

5.4 John Anster Fitzgerald, *Cock Robin Defending his Nest*, oil (c. 1858–68). Private Collection/Bridgeman Art Library International Ltd., London/New York.

paintings and Doyle's illustrations, the fairies torment an owl on Midsummer's Eve. "Four, small slim forms" (p. 347) pluck out a feather and carry off the bird while, to the sound of cruel laughter, they drop him in a pool. When midnight strikes, the owl takes to a tree and hides, while the nervous human narrator sneaks home. Brushed by multitudinous shapes he can feel but not see, he develops a fear of crowds and never again goes into the playing field after sundown. For the playing fields are not for human play and the players are the fairy hosts of the slaugh.

Moreover, fiction, folklore, and painting all depict fairies at war with each other, and internecine battles become symbolic of fairies' anarchical tendencies. Again, intrafairy violence and warfare are writ small but are everywhere present in the margins of major fairy paintings. In the foreground of Paton's *Quarrel*, two sensuous winged female sprites playfully attempt to drown an old male elf. Fairy "love play" in both this scene and the *Reconciliation* is strangely close to rape. Richard Dadd's brilliant, ominous *Contradiction: Oberon and Titania* (1854–58) is really a scene of guerilla warfare. In the bottom half of the picture, tiny, barely visible male and female fairies (the males in armor and the females winged) battle each other in an echo of the tension between their gigantic, Wagnerian king and queen. One grotesque archer attempts to shoot Titania, while hoards of little folk look on. Titania, oblivious to the threat, stands facing Oberon, her foot on the body of a tiny flower fairy she has trampled. Dadd's earlier illustration of the ballad "Robin Goodfellow" for *The Book of British Ballads* (1842) also superadds gratuitous cruelty to the text; an elf is impaled on the spikey lettering of the title; tiny,

5.5 Thomas Heatherley, *Fairy Resting on a Mushroom*, oil (c. 1860). Private Collection/ Bridgeman Art Library International, Ltd., London/New York.

5.6 Richard Dadd, *Contradiction: Oberon and Titania*, oil (1854—58). Collection of Lord Lloyd-Webber, England.

froglike creatures try to fight their way out of gigantic dew drops; foetal, goggle-eyed goblins peep menacingly out of margins. More surprisingly, in view of its ostensibly peaceful subject, Richard Doyle's *Enchanted Tree*, based on Shakespeare's *Tempest* is essentially a battle scene. Goblin bodies and weapons fall from the tall, slender palm; the trunk of the tree is being attacked by elves with axes; fairy archers shoot from under leaves at another group of elves flying by; the submerged body of a dead fairy drifts down the rivulet in the foreground.

There is relatively little direct depiction of fairies tormenting mortals in Victorian fairy painting, though it is occasionally suggested, as in Richard Doyle's watercolor of a version of the Cup of Aagerup legend called *Horseman and Gnomes*, in which a knight on horseback is surrounded and tormented by pixies, gnomes, and goblins. In general, the subject has been visually displaced, as if inappropriate for the eyes of the Victorian public. But in the margins of fairy paintings are miniatures of sadism and anarchy. Just as collectors and editors of fairy lore sometimes softened and prettified their tales for popular consumption, so fairy painters reduced cruelty in size and relegated it to the peripheries of paintings.

When fairies were not being overtly cruel or destructive to animals or each other, they were subverting or harassing human society in various ways. As dangerous as their indiscriminate, merciless devastation in the form of a host or slaugh was their seemingly random, invisible intervention in human affairs. As early as 1853, just after the Spiritualist craze for seances hit England, Edward Bulwer, later Lord Bulwer-Lytton, speculated that it was the fairies who caused the disconcerting raps and knocks at seances. In this year, he wrote to his son concerning what he believed to be the nature of the rappers at seances he had attended:

> They profess to be spirits of the dead, but I much doubt, supposing they are spirits at all, whether they are not rather brownies or fairies. They are never to be relied on for accurate answers, though sometimes they were wonderfully so, just like clairvoyants. (qtd. in Goldfarb and Goldfarb, p. 90)

As the interest in elementals—and their conflation with traditional folklore fairies—increased after the middle of the century, the spirits of the elements were held increasingly responsible for acts of mischief, deceit, and cruelty. They, not the honest spirits of dead relatives, were responsible for false answers and flying objects. Equally important, it was elementals or fairies who many thought created the poltergeist phenomena in which Victorians were so interested. Members of the Society for Psychical Research, formed in 1882, investigated a number of poltergeist outbreaks—that is, incidents in which these "noise spirits" moved objects, broke crockery, threw stones, and made general nuisances of themselves. Sir William Barrett, whose book, *Psychical Research* appeared in 1911, came to believe, as did Andrew Lang, in the genuineness of some of the phenomena (see Society for Psychical Research Proceedings, 25) Two cases in which he was involved persuaded Barrett that poltergeists did exist. In 1877, he investigated a poltergeist in an Irish farmer's cabin near Enniskillen, aided by "two sceptical scientific friends"; they were "all convinced that the phenomena could not be accounted for by any known agency" (p. 209). In 1910, in a town in County Wexford, he again encountered a case that convinced him "that it was practically impossible to attribute [such behavior] . . . to any other human being" (p. 209). He may not have considered the poltergeists fairies, as the local people did, but he did ascribe the phenomena he witnessed to some "supernormal" agencies. A poltergeist case of 1907 also aroused considerable interest and again connected the phenomenon with fairies. As Andrew Lang, the folklorist and psychic investigator, told the tale, a farmer's house in Northern Ireland was troubled with flying stones. The neighbors believed that fairies caused the problem, as the farmer had swept his chimney with a bough of holly, and the holly is "a gentle tree,"—that is, a tree dear to the fairies. Thus, he had offended them and the poltergeist phenomena was their revenge (Lang, "Fairies," *Encyclopedia Britannica*, 1911).[9]

Other believers, many Theosophists and some Rosicrucians, recorded as memorates their experiences with menacing elemental fairies. Bishop Leadbeater offered an account of his dangerous interaction with vicious elemental monsters. Violet Tweedale, a Spiritualist and medium, whose credentials involved introductions to the Queen as well as to Robert Browning, Mrs. Lynn Linton, Lord Leighton, and John Everett Millais, published an account of "An Austrian Adventure" with unpleasant elementals. Detained in Austria while traveling to meet her husband in Bavaria, she encountered "an elemental of a malignant type, and of grotesque form" (p. 206). Misshapen, froglike, yellow-eyed, it stared at her menacingly before gradually vanishing. The next night she was visited by a horde of equally grotesque but less threatening creatures. Insisting that what may read like "pure nonsense" is pure fact (p. 208), she argues that her consciousness was heightened by the extreme tension she was experiencing, thus enabling her to transcend the usual "veil of the flesh" (p. 209).[10]

More generally, it was probable, said Herbert Arnold, echoing Bulwer-Lytton and H. B. (Madame Helena Blavatsky, the co-founder of Theosophy) but citing "eminent astonomer" Camille Flammarion, that elementals were the causes of many disturbing or dangerous phenomena. Salamanders, for example, were responsible for mysterious fires as well as for such feats as fire-walking (p. 212). Yet, Arnold argued, elementals served functions more important than those of "tricksters," for they influenced human temperaments. Returning to the classical and medieval humoral theory in an attempt to forge a new psychology, Arnold believed in the power of elementals to determine personality. Gnomes, he indicates, predominate in melancholy persons, salamanders in the sanguine, undines in the phlegmatic, and sylphs in the giddy. Like Arnold, Franz Hartmann, a medical doctor writing on elementals in *The Occult Review* in 1911, believed salamanders were the cause of "otherwise unaccountable incendiarisms and conflagrations" (p. 28). In addition, he argues, they are partial causes of volcanic eruptions. Most important, they can possess someone, turning the person into a pyromaniac, either through a direct compulsion to set fires or through the psychic ability to will them (p. 29). Hartmann's comments constitute an interesting basis for quasi-scientific occult psychology. He does not claim that mischief is done without human cooperation, but that its perpetrators are weak-minded people who are unknowingly influenced by elementals.

Faceless in that they were usually heard and felt rather than seen and because they often functioned as a group, elementals were frequently perceived as forces and causes not yet understood but ultimately explicable. Repeated analogies compared them to recent discoveries such as radio waves (1888), X-rays (1895), and radioactivity (1896)—all of which appeared almost occult in impact and were difficult to explain in conventional scientific terms.[11] Significantly, both psychic researchers (many of whom were Spiritualists) and believers in the occult approached preternatural creatures through quantitative and mensurative techniques; in effect, they tried to weigh and measure the preternatural to give it the "reality" in which they so much desired to believe. Always torn between material and spiritual conceptions of life, they repeatedly tried to reconcile the two. The scientifically inclined rendered the spiritual in material terms. Even those inclined to mysticism used science or its terminology in their attempt to revive the magical interaction between mortals and their universe, to seek the lost animistic worldview of older ages. To members of both groups, anything, even the cruel or hideous, any act, even the anarchic or disruptive, was better than an empty universe.

Others, including some of the more traditional folklorists, added to the amalgam by unconsciously identifying the fairy hordes with the faceless mob; the elfin peoples' irrational, anarchic behavior could be seen as analogous to that of the *sans culottes* of Carlyle's French Revolution, the Communards of the Paris revolt, and the working-class rioters of Bloody Sunday. As Carlyle had compared the actions of the mob to those of witches and evil demons ("Instead of a Christian Sabbath . . . it shall be a Sorcerer's Sabbath; and Paris, gone rabid, [will] dance—with the Fiend for piper" [*French Revolution* 5:140])[12] so folklorists and middle-class respondents now equated the fairies with the demos.

For many, they were the demos turned demonic—snatching, plundering, killing, and abducting. When they were visually depicted, as in a few works by Richard Doyle and by his younger brother Charles, it was as a featureless, surging, shadowy mob. (See, for example, Richard Doyle's *Altar Cup of Aagerup* (1883), mentioned earlier, with its horde of trolls pursuing a man, or Charles Altamont Doyle's *Fantasy, with Elves, Horses and Figures* (1885), with its elfin masses cheering on the horsemen of apocalypse.) Even Bishop Leadbeater, usually sympathetic to them, described a mass of elementals who tested his courage as "shadowy and indistinctly seen . . . creatures like wreaths of mist or smoke, and yet somehow living and powerful" (*Perfume of Egypt*, p. 102), adding that they were "a vast army" that looked like a "gigantic antidiluvian mob—a hellish host" (p. 103).

Prisoners of the Gods

One of the "trooping" fairies' most ominous traits was their tendency to kidnap mortals for various but unsavory purposes, whether to serve as fairy nurses, midwives, servants, or lovers or in ways beyond the ken of mortals. To be "away" (or with the fairies), as the Irish called it, was closely connected to being mentally or physically ill or to being or appearing dead. Fairies took the good, handsome, and pious, said the experts; the able-bodied, especially good workers and good dancers; they took those whom others envied or praised without blessing; all became what Yeats refers to as "The Prisoners of the Gods" (*Unpublished Prose* 2:74). Young children were taken both because of the fairy difficulty in procreation and because they could serve their elfin masters longer. Women were especially vulnerable as brides or after childbirth, as they underwent periods of liminality or transition. If a recently married mortal woman was "taken," it might be because a man of the "others" desired her; if after childbirth, it might be to serve as a fairy nurse. Even Yeats, most sympathetic to fairy ways, had to admit that the elfin peoples lacked conscience and consistency and had "one most malicious habit" (*Mythologies*, p. 134)—that of kidnapping. One village alone had lost eighteen or nineteen young men and young girls in one year, he reported. There was not, he added "a place outside the big towns where they do not believe that the Fairies, the Tribes of the goddess Danu, are stealing their bodies and their souls . . . and always hearing all that they say" (*Unpublished Prose* 2:56).

That the fairies take what they want from mortals was emphasized by Yeats (as well as many others), and the "taking" becomes the theme of his poems "The Stolen Child" and "The Host of the Air," and of his play of 1894, *The Land of Heart's Desire*. While fairies seemingly prefer young and beautiful girls like the bride, Mary, in *Heart's Desire*, or handsome young men like Mr. Ormsby, in *The Celtic Twilight*, who was repeatedly abducted by a amorous female fay, one never quite knows who they will choose or when or why. Fairy motives are as ambiguous as fairy nature. In a chapter called "Kidnappers" in *The Celtic Twilight* (1893), Yeats retells endless anecdotes of the abducted. We hear of the Sligo woman who vanished from her garden to be found years later by her son in Glasgow, and of the young bride who was seen on the road (a sign that she had been taken "away") at the same time as she was found dead in her house. We learn of another woman stolen in her youth and returned seven years later without toes; participating in endless fairy dances, she had danced them off. We learn, too, of the dangers of being attractive and thus admired. More than one girl was abducted because men looking at her forgot to say, "God Bless You." They had "overlooked" her and hence exposed her to the fairies, who use human admiration as a sort of bridge to get to their victim (*Mythologies*, p. 274).

Among the Scots who believed that the fairies had to pay a tithe to the devil, many argued that they offered humans to him as substitute sacrifices. Sometimes, said others, the fairies merely took humans for sport; the trows or drows of Shetland were known to take people away out of malice, while even the milder, more generally benign tylwyth teg of Wales were inveterate kidnappers; their abductions were the basis of many tales. They (and they were generally female) entrapped young men by dancing; once a man entered their ring he vanished unless friends knew how to recover him. Fairies loved music as well as dancing; hence, musicians were prone to be abducted and the tale of Iolo ap Hugh, the great Welsh fiddler who was carried off (and whose music can be heard on Halloween), was endlessly repeated.

Sadly, even when rescued, a change of body or spirit usually accompanied the return to normal life by those who had been "away." Those who returned were often ghosts or ghostlike, in some accounts crumbling into dust, in others wasting away in sorrow for their loss of fairy bliss. In some way, they had been robbed of part of their humanity. In "The Cradles of Gold" (1896), Yeats told the story of Peter Hearne's wife, stolen to be nurse to the fairy king of Connaught's baby. In this tale (one of the relatively few in which the "taken" is restored), the emphasis is on the imperfection of the return. The rescued woman has come back from the other world with a "chill touch" and "a low voice" (*Unpublished Prose* 1:418); she has become queer, distraught, and pale. Compelled by a restless "desire to be far away" (*Unpublished Prose* 1:418), she goes out to the Lough on moonlit nights. For the most part, as a woman of the Burren hills announced, "Those that are away among them never come back, or if they do they are not the same as they were before" (*Unpublished Prose* 2:281). As in this tale, to be "away" might signify what twentieth-century medicine would label severe depression or even catatonia.

However, as a "spiritist," first a Theosophist, then a sort of nondenominational occultist, Yeats defined the state of being "away" as one in which the soul has left the body and gone with the fairies. Endlessly fascinated by the condition, Yeats explored the motif in such poems as "The Happy Townland" and "The Hosting of the Sidhe" and utilized it as the explanation for what happened to Cuchulain in his play, *The Only Jealousy of Emer*. Irish peasants, he explained, do not see, as he does, that the soul alone is taken; instead they think the whole person has been removed and, in some cases, a changeling substituted. In Yeats's view, at least, those taken, grew old in fairyland and were returned to this world (in old age) to receive the sacraments and die. Hence, many people really suffered two deaths: the first, a life serving the "others," the second, the actual death. Only the old died "natural" deaths and went to heaven, hell, or purgatory; the young were actually "elsewhere" (*Unpublished Prose* 2:101). Scottish belief was similar. In "The Hills of Ruel" (1901), for example, Fiona Macleod's narrator asks an old man why he does not think that his young son is dead, but has instead "followed the cruel/Honey-sweet folk of the Hills of Ruel" (*Works* 7:41). Because, says the father, citing one of the traditional reasons, he has seen his child after his ostensible burial, laughing and talking to a shadow, making love to this fairy with "wildmoss hair"—whom he then follows "over the hills and far away" (7:42). Frequently, however, being "taken" or "away" was used as a metaphor for being dead.[13]

Nevertheless, being "away" was also a way of describing physical and mental illness, and one could be both here and elsewhere simultaneously. To be "away" while physically present in this world meant that while pursuing ordinary tasks one was also in the power—and world—of the fairies. Among the symptoms of this condition were the dazed look and the vacant mind; fainting fits, trances, fatigue or languidity, even long and heavy sleeping, as well as any of the wasting diseases, were signs that one was away or soon to be "taken." Tuberculosis was popularly thought to be caused by fairy vampirism. As late as the 1980s, Patrick Logan, writing of his Irish childhood, describes himself as "foolhardy" for digging up a fairy mound; he and his two companions developed tuberculosis and all were certain that the fairies were the cause (p. 19). Even smallpox was connected to the fairies, as a tale of Cromarty (in Scotland) indicates. A wandering green lady, "of exquisite beauty and majestic carriage . . . was regarded as the Genius of the smallpox . . . who, when the disease was to terminate fatally, would be seen in the grey of the morning, or as the evening was passing into night, sitting by the bed-side of her victim" (Miller, *Scenes and Legends*, p. 70).

There were often preludes to the final "taking." To be fairy-kist could mean, as it does in Kipling's short story of the same name, that one was shell-shocked or traumatized;[14] the fairy's kiss could strike one dumb. Being elf-shot, or hit with an elf arrow, was yet another danger to humans as well as to their sheep and cattle. The wound inflicted by an elf arrow could result in excruciating pain or put one in a deathlike trance or cause apparent death. Epilepsy was, to many, clearly a result of the fairy stroke. The trows or drows of Shetland had a touch that paralyzed, according to A. W., author of "Fairy 'Folk-Lore' of Shetland." Possessing "great power and malignity," they were responsible for paralysis (they were thought to steal the affected limb and to substitute a log in its place) and for consumption (in which they took away the heart; p. 135.) They punished mortals with disease for touching their property, stepping into their rings, or venturing too near their fairy forts; they even punished human beings with illness for merely seeing them.

Frequently, the "touch" itself was serious; "you feel a sudden pain, and a swelling comes where you have felt the pain," said one informant (Yeats, *Unpublished Prose* 2:270). A spinning woman told Lady Gregory of how, twenty years earlier, a local girl had gotten the "touch." She made the mistake of telling her name to a red-haired woman who asked it and that night developed a pain in her thigh that had never left her. Not only could the "touch" suggest pinched nerves, phlebitus, or other uncomfortable conditions but it was sometimes a euphemism for stroke or for forms of catatonia. Even the wind could be dangerous, for it was a fairy vehicle. Its touch, like direct fairy touch, could bring psychic withdrawal and death. A fisherman told Yeats and Lady Gregory that he sent his son out to a neighboring village to get bread—foolishly, for he had heard a noise like thunder and a blast of wind passed by him. It was the host of the sidhe, who "travel like a cloud, or like a storm," as he should have known (Gregory, p. 226). The child came back insane, the guilty father noted; now in an asylum, he could only mumble that he had encountered some awful-looking people on the road at midnight (Gregory, p. 214).

Dalyell, writing of Scotland, tells of adults and children left at night at a certain well in Ross as a remedy for fairy stroke. All were suffering from declines ascribed to vampirish fairies abstracting their substance (pp. 338–39). Jeremiah Curtin states (in *Tales of the Fairies and of the Ghost World*, 1895) that he met two men injured by fairy strokes and attended the funeral of a third who had died of one. One of the men had fallen asleep near a fairy fort, received the stroke, and awoke to be crippled for life; the dead man had "interfered with the fort" (p. 4) and, in doing so, injured his hand, which caused his demise. Even more striking was Curtin's tale of Elizabeth Shea, wife of James Kivane, who died after getting the "fairy stroke" and became as malevolent as her supernatural abductors. Not truly dead, but "away," serving as a midwife to the fairies, she had asked for human rescue by her husband and the priest. When they decided not to try to free her (Shea had remarried), she used her powers to strike Shea's father blind, "touch" and thus kill her own child, make Shea's second wife seriously ill, and kill her successor's daughter.

Only Yeats saw the state of being "away" as something less than purely evil. Yet even he recognized its ambiguity and danger. Like "The Stolen Child," Yeats's poem "The Hosting of the Sidhe" contains the call to come "away." Implicit in the call, irresistible though it is, is the warning that if a mortal gazes on the beauty of the sidhe, a beauty described in "The Unappeasable Host" as greater than any that Christianity can provide, he loses "the deed of his hand," the ability to act, and the "hope of his heart" (*Poems*, p. 61), all human love and feeling. To most others, including Irish occultists like Vere Shortt, being taken was proof that the sidhe were almost always either passively or actively malignant to the human race. Solitary sidhe, like Dalua, the "fairy fool," whose "touch" drove one incurably mad, were really demons in disguise.[15]

To ordinary rural believers, being "away" and thus succumbing to mysterious disease or apparent death was a frightening demonstration of fairy power. To folklore theorists, however, it was not just a sign that curious superstitions were still alive but also proof of a theory of elfin origins. For the idea that fairies were kidnappers and bringers of illness and death was clearly linked to the concept that they were, themselves, the dead. Many folklorists noted resemblances between the behaviors of the two groups (see chapter 1). Fairies and ghosts were sometimes thought of as beings of one essence though of separate forms; both even shared the same tales. Folklorists noted that the dangerous slaugh, or fairy host, flying through the air or sailing in the wind, was composed of dead souls in some regions (the Western Isles of Scotland) and of malevolent fairies in others (Ireland). The endless reports—beginning with the Scottish witch trials of the seventeenth century—of seeing dead friends or relatives among the fairies, added to the support for this identification.[16]

So, too, did repeated retellings of such tales as "The Fairy Dwelling on Selena Moor." In this story from Cornwall, Mr. Noys, an elderly bachelor crossed the boundary between worlds by inadvertently entering a fairyland in the middle of the boggy moors. He was saved by a farmer's daughter who had been his sweetheart but who had died a few years earlier. She warned him not to touch her or any food or drink, and told him of her own fate: she was not dead, but had been first "pixie-led" and then "taken." (A changeling substituted for her later died and was buried in her stead.) At present, she told Noys, she was doomed to be a housekeeper to her fairy captors, among whom all was "illusion or acting and sham." "They have no hearts," she warned her former lover, "and but little sense or feeling" (Bottrell, p. 99). After seeing many who resembled dead acquaintances among the fairies, Noys escaped and returned to the mortal world. Yet like others who had been "away," he was changed, departing this life—whether for fairyland or true death—before the next harvest. Similar anecdotes, including one retold by Yeats in "The Host of the Air," were told of people from all over the British Isles.[17]

Significantly, the anxiety fairies caused, and the evil of which they were accused, came less from their identification with the dead than from, first, the fact that such an association gave them additional power (common belief suggests that the spirits of the dead are always stronger than those of the living); second, from the uncertainty of fairy behavior when the fays behaved like the dead; and, most important, from the consequences of this behavior for their dead-alive victims. With actual death, at least, came certainty; with abduction and apparent death came the possibility of a flawed resurrection and a resultant uncertainty about status. In the minds of the folk, for the most part, the possible return of the dead did not primarily constitute a consolation, but rather a nightmare, or so the tales of such events suggest. Such returns were perceived as anarchic, disruptions of both spiritual and social order.

One might argue that the fear of resurrection—of the reincarnated dead in imperfect form, and of the familial, economic, and social disruption that their reappearance caused—was greater than the fear of death itself. For death, often glamorized and sentimentalized by the Victorians, could be accepted. Moreover, it could be connected to religious faith, while the dead person's reappearance in material form suggested a transgression of the boundaries—a sort of cosmic disorder. The idea of a false death, the possibility of the reappearance of those presumed dead, bred social and cultural angst. What was the status of the second wife or the second family if a member of the first group reappeared? What of the vengeance heaped on the living by figures like Curtin's Elizabeth Shea? What of the cruelty caused by the jealous spirits who returned?

Portents of Death: Bean-nighs, Banshees, and Others

The identification of fairies with death and the dead was further strengthened by the existence of varieties of solitary fairies who were themselves symbols of impending death. Banshees, bean-nighs (or "washers of the dead"), and the Scottish cailleach were closely associated with premonitions of death—though not necessarily with causing one's demise—and all were women. Indeed, the face of death, like the face of evil, was often seen as female. The cailleach is described by Fiona Macleod/ William Sharp in a note to *The Dark Hour of Fergus* (1899) as "the green-clad Lady . . . the Siren of the Hill-Sides, to see whom portends death or disaster. When she is heard singing, that portends death soon for the hearer" (*Works* 4:95). In Scotland, too, a fairy creature known as the *cointach* or "keener" (because of her wailing), served the banshee function. Seen as a child or small woman, she looked, on closer contact, ancient or corpselike. Her Welsh equivalent was the equally hideous cyhiraeth. Old, withered, black-toothed, noteworthy for long, shriveled arms, she would appear at a crossroad or at a window, calling the victim's name. In a "blood-freezing shriek" (Rhys 2:453), she would announce the name of the wife, husband, or child who was to die. Still worse, if her wail was inarticulate, it meant the death of the hearer. The "hag of the dribble" was yet another Welsh equivalent; a hideous old woman who appeared in the mist or near water, her presence also signified death. Described to Wirt Sikes (pp. 83–84) as a horrible old crone, with long red hair, a face like chalk, and great tusklike teeth, she appeared only to old families, not to new Welsh stock.

The bean-nigh, or washing-woman, made famous to the reading public of the 1890s by Fiona Macleod's "The Washer at the Ford" (1896), was found all over the Celtic world, especially in Scotland, the Hebrides, Man, and Ireland. She, too, was a portent of death, for she washed the shrouds of those who were to die. Macleod, in her/his mystical tale, moralizes and spiritualizes the figure, perceiving her as a sort of Mary Magdalene who removes the stains of sin from the shrouds of those about to die and grieves for human mortality while she warns of fate. But the bean-nigh was usually depicted as old and ugly, rendered monstrous by breasts so long she could throw them over her shoulder. Reports indicated that she was most dangerous if she saw a mortal before being seen, for that empowered her. Like the banshee, her psychic sister, she could be merely neutral, a predictor of death, or else a malevolent demon who relishes its occurrence. In *The Secret Rose* (1897), Yeats tells of how English troopers saw the bean-nigh washing corpses at a Sligo river and how each man recognized his own features in those of the dead. He adds that the sight of the malevolent creature caused the frightened troopers to ride over the edge of a cliff to their destruction (*Mythologies*, p. 182). In Scotland, Hugh Miller reported on the demonic bean-nigh heard chuckling as she washed more then thirty shirts and smocks on a river stone. That evening, he told readers, the roof of a local church caved in, killing thirty-six parishioners (*Scenes and Legends*, p. 297).

But among the fairies who were death portents, the banshee took first place. Banshees, like mermaids, were ambiguous; some could be beautiful — sincere mourners of the person whose death they announced. But most were malevolent, hideous deathlike figures, usually assuming the form of grotesque old women and taking pleasure in the death. In his book devoted to banshees, Eliot O'Donnell noted the presence of a third variety, the truly demonic, whose response to impending doom was the satanic chuckle. One mid-nineteenth-century family of gentry in county Limerick, he wrote, had a banshee whose laughter was a sign of how much she hated the family. Her chuckle was heard not only when the heir to the family died but also when the young married daughter eloped and when the family was financially ruined. All Victorian commentators agreed that banshees were solitary fairies, seldom seen though often heard crying, wailing, or screaming, and following only those of the "old families" of Ireland, especially those with *O* or *Mac* in their names. They agreed, too, that one might shut one's door against a banshee, but not insult or harm her, for she could kill others as well as those whose death she came to proclaim. While a few described her as a great beauty, most perceived her as ugly and dead looking herself, as a white-haired old woman with a face pale as a corpse. Again, the face of death was female.

O'Donnell ends his book with a chapter on his "Own Experience with the Banshee," telling memorates in which he clearly believes. Proud of his family banshee, though she was of the malevolent variety, he tells of her announcement of his father's death, noting that he has sent materials and signed statements of verification to the Society for Psychical Research (who published his account in Autumn 1899). And he offers a description of the hideous creature seen by one of his sisters a few days before his father's murder: "Crowned with a mass of disordered tow-coloured hair, the skin tightly drawn over the bones like a mummy, it looked as if it had been buried for several months and then resurrected" (p. 237). Remarking on the eyes filled with glee at the thought of a tragedy among the O'Donnells, and the leering expression of the mouth, the sister testified: "It did not seem to her to be the face of anyone that had ever lived, but to belong to an entirely different species, and to be the creation of something wholly evil" (p. 237). Only much later did O'Donnell learn that another sister had also seen the family demon, this time before the death of his mother. Her description was similar:

> The head was neither man nor woman's; it was ages old; it might have been buried and dug up again, it was so skull-like and shrunken; its pallor was horrible, grey and mildewy; its hair was long. Its mouth leered, and its light and cruel eyes seem determined to hurt me to the utmost, with the terror it inspired. (p. 249)

The terror of the banshee here seems to lie in her zombielike qualities, in the fact that she looks like the dead reanimated rather than reborn, and in her crossing the threshold from the world of death to claim her new victim.

Oddly enough, Victorians made little use of the banshee motif in fiction; perhaps it was still too much believed, perhaps it was too localized, too identified with the Irish. Mrs. J. H. Riddell, did, however, tell a quintessential Banshee story in *The Banshee's Warning and Other Tales* (1894). In the tale from which the volume takes its name, a young surgeon (with an *O* in his name), Hertford O'Donnell, about to wed an heiress only for her money, hears "a low, sobbing, wailing cry" (p. 21) in his London rooms. A voice tells him to go quickly to Guys Hospital, at which he serves, and he does so, only to find that he has been summoned to try to save an injured child. He passes a barefoot, ugly old woman sitting on the steps of the hospital, but does not recognize her for what she is, and instead of performing the surgery that might save the child's life, he faints. The child dies and the doctor learns it is his own son, his illegitimate child by a poor woman he had loved but scorned to marry. In the course of the tale, Riddell tells other banshee incidents derived from Irish lore, but she softens the ending of her own tale, giving the heartless doctor a heart, a reconciliation with his parents, and a wedding with the mother of his dead son.

While the Irish partially focused on female fairies as portents of death, as banshees and bean-nighs, the Scots tended to emphasize the equation between wicked fairies and witches. In Scotland, famous for its witch trials and for the particularly grotesque and horrific nature of its supernaturals, the entire "unseelie court" was perceived as evil, as closely allied to witches in traits and powers. MacDougall (*Highland Fairy Legends*), argued that all fairies, when stripped of their veil of illusion, were really ugly and witchlike. Actually "old creatures," small and ill-favored, they used "glamour" to persuade us otherwise. Commentators noted that the barbaric traits of Scottish fairies probably meant that they were older in origin than those found in other sections of the British Isles, that their genesis was "savage" or pre-Aryan. But the fairy-witch equation was not limited to Scotland alone. Sidney Oldall Addy thought it characteristic of all of England, and East Anglia, in particular, kept its belief in the reality of witch and fairy craft, focusing on the deeds of a number of local old women throughout the nineteenth century.[18]

Like witches, fairies were thought of as servants or worshipers of Satan; or as really "just little devils, anyway." Both fairies and witches were boundary figures in Duerr's terms, capable of passing beyond the border between civilization and wilderness. Described as primarily female, both lived apart from the direct control of husbands and fathers and the indirect control of organized, patriarchal society. Banshees and bean-nighs might physically resemble the stereotypes of the wicked, old witch, but not all witches were perceived as ugly. Though the Brothers Grimm had popularized the image of the aged crone, folklore collectors in the British Isles seem more drawn to the solitary evil female spirits who appeared beautiful—to their blurring of the prevailing folklore assumption that the external revealed the internal. British folklorists were quick to note that the word *fay* (as in Morgan La Fay, the Arthurian sorceress) had meant both witch or enchantress and fairy. They remarked that it was often difficult to distinguish between a young female witch and a capricious fairy queen.[19] Both witches and fairies could suggest evil disguised as good; both had the same taboos and rituals used for protection against them; both were accused of the same unnatural crimes—of bringing disease and blight, of stealing and killing children, and of indulging in cannibalism. Moreover, they were similar in their traits: both favored the color red and were identified as wearing scarlet capes; both were thought of as riding horses at night or through the air; both were shape changers; both were enchanters. Both also loved to dance, and the orgiastic ring dancing at the witches' sabbath and the fairies' circle dances were seen as related.

More generally, some Victorian folklorists believed that witches and fairies were identical in their genesis, products of the same era, or so said such major figures as Clodd and Hartland. Creations of the Stone Age, both witches and fairies were derived from folk memories of the priestesses and medicine women who had once universally existed and still survived in savage and barbaric societies. Both were adept at herbal curing or killing; both knew the secret workings of nature. Gomme, that most scientific of folklorists, worked out an elaborate and ingenious explanation of the connections between witches and fairies in *Ethnology in Folklore* (1892). The difference between the two categories, he argued, was really that of point of view. Contending that "superstition" was the product of hostility between races—with each group ascribing special powers to the other—he argued that the early inhabitants of Britain (the non-Aryan aborigines) believed they had special powers and tried to spread this belief among their Aryan conquerors. Witchcraft, kept alive through the Druids and later through initiates, was a survival of aboriginal beliefs from aboriginal sources. Fairycraft (the belief in the power of fairies), on the other hand, was a survival of beliefs *about* aborigines from Aryan sources—that is, the conquerors' view of the supernatural powers of the conquered aborigines (p. 65). Witchcraft was pre-Aryan, while fairycraft was Aryan. Gomme's implication was that this second, Aryan system of belief was later in development, higher on the ladder of socio-religious evolution, and hence a product of a more evolved (and less barbaric) people.

The fear of and fascination with both witches and the evil fairies who resembled them was connected in part with the survival of religious belief; the devil and the demonic were very much alive in the Victorian world. To some, to not believe in the evil one and his subordinates was to not believe in God. As the Reverend Edmund Jones of the Tranch had earlier argued, although the fairies are alienated from God and have become his enemies, their very existence proves His, and they may serve Him by visiting mortals to predict death, by warning them of the future or by cautioning them against bad behavior (p. 34). To others the source of the fear was the form such religious belief could take; to even half-accept the reality of such diabolic creatures was dangerous. If they existed, they were an ancient, neglected race supplanted by civilization and Christianity and their evil might be seen as retribution on humans for having forsaken them. They were pagan and pre-Christian; to believe in them was to maintain a prohibited faith in the old gods.

Moreover, both witches and fairies were perceived primarily as groups of wild or uncontrolled women who were possessed of powers that had not been civilized or domesticated. These powers were symbolized by the wild, orgiastic dances both groups performed; dances that suggested the savage, sensual nature of the females who participated in them and, through them, lured innocent men to destruction.[20] That fairies and witches loved dance connected them in popular Victorian lore to sex-crazed women. Medically, the love of dancing was sometimes diagnosed as a form of hysteria; ethnologically, it was linked to savagery or barbarism, for, said medical doctors and the new anthropologists, rhythmic movement *is* primitive movement.[21] However, just as the greatest threat to society posed by mortal women was their yearning for self-assertion and their desire to dominate, so, too, witches and evil fairy females were notable for this trait. Female self-assertion was seen as essentially "devouring" to male power and control; it found symbolic embodiment in the image of the witchlike, ostensibly seductive but actually destructive female fairy who occasionally ate men's flesh and frequently drank men's blood.

The Victorians were not different from their predecessors and successors in finding a special horror in those creatures who indulged in anthropophagy or vampirism, as witches and witchlike fairies were accused of doing. But vampirism was particularly identified as a trait of a number of female fairies.[22] The Scottish glaistig was often vampiristic; in anecdotes re-iterated throughout the period, glaistigs were said to cut the throats of hunters and drink their blood. The least malicious of the species insisted on continual libations of milk (such offerings were still being made to them in the 1890s); otherwise they would kill or maim cattle and their human own-ers. Some insisted that it was necessary to keep all glaistigs, even those who appeared friendly, at arms length with a dirk. If permitted to come close, a glaistig might assume the attributes of the vampire and suck a man's veins dry. Glaistigs were also known to take the form of a man's beloved and vampirize him, absorbing his heart's blood.

Equally terrifying—because her beauty merely veiled her evil—was the nameless creature reported by both Gordon-Cumming (for the Heb-rides) and Hugh Miller. This destructive fairy, posing as a beautiful lady with a child in her arms, would ask a poor peasant woman to let her enter her cottage and warm her hands by the fire. In return for such kindness, the fairy would feed her goblin infant with the heart's blood of one of the peasant's mortal children, causing the mortal baby's death (Gordon-Cumming 1:143). In Hugh Miller's version, the fairy vampire is even more malevolent, for, dressed in green, she wanders from cottage to cottage wash-ing her imp in the blood of the youngest inmate, who would be found dead the next morning (*Scenes and Legends*, p. 70). In these accounts of an extreme version of parasitism, fairy fecundity—and female fairies were already per-ceived as threatening because of the gap between their enormous sexuality and their limited fertility—is seen as dependent upon human death.

The single most horrific fairy-vampire tale was also Scottish. Frequently retold, it concerned the Laird of Lorntie (in Forfarshire) who, returning from the hunt, heard a mermaid cry for help, saw her struggling in the water, attempted to rescue her, and was saved only by his servant's drag-ging him away. Enraged, he could barely accept the servant's warning that the ostensible mermaid was actually a vampire and her cry a ruse. Leaving, he heard her call out "in a voice of fiendish disappointment and ferocity":

'Lorntie, Lorntie,
Were it na your man
I had gart your heart's bluid
Skirl in my pan.'[23]

One can only speculate that perhaps the emphasis on the blood-thirsty female fairy, on her need for and consumption of the energy with which blood is connected, was linked to the recognition during the period of ane-mia as a disease to which women were especially prone, or to the increased awareness and discussion of the problems and effects of female menses. There were other reasons as well, and it is worth noting that the figures the collectors found most fascinating were the solitary, undomesticated, uncontrolled fairy females who went where they wished and when they wished, inverting all human laws of family and propriety. Parasites and anarchs, disrupters of marriage, their prey was almost always male.

The lhiannon-shee of Ireland and the Isle of Man, a figure that fascinated William Butler Yeats among others, is perhaps the most significant and widespread example. She simultaneously embodies the male fear of the female as dominating and anarchic and the widespread anxiety about women as parasites. Best known of the Manx fairies, she is ostensibly a fairy "follower" or "sweetheart"; but she is really a lamia or succubus, draining the life and energy of the man to whom she attaches herself. Andrew Lang argued for the universality of the figure, noting in *Folk Lore Record* ("Folk-Lore of France," p. 108) that this "belief in the deadly love of the spectral . . . woman" was a very primitive superstition, widespread enough to stretch from Ireland and Scotland to New Calidonia. In various guises she becomes a cliché of fin de siècle, decadent painting. She may be seen as as the naked *Kelpie* in the 1895 work of the Scottish painter, Thomas Millie Dow, or as the wistfully seductive water nymphs of Waterhouse's *Hylas and the Nymphs* (c. 1895), or as the mermaids of John William Whiteley's Royal Academy painting *A Sail* (1898), or as any of the dryads, oreads, mermaids, nixies, and russalkas that populate so many of the paintings of the era. A cultural icon, she inhabits the work of female painters as well as male ones; Isobel Gloag's lamia, for example, the central figure in *The Kiss of the Enchantress* (c. 1890), is another form of the lhiannon-shee, clearly in the process of sucking the life from the already emaciated knight she kisses. The lhiannon-shee's parasitism involved not only the sapping of a man's sexual and personal power but a subversion of his political and social role as well; under her spell he would gradually give up control and lose his ability to function as an authority.

On the Isle of Man (Walter Gill discussed the figure in detail in his second and third *Manx Scrapbooks*), the lhiannon-shee's manifestations connected her to the dead. There, she was seen as coming from the land of the dead and as invisible to all but the man she selected to seduce. His yielding to her would result in the death of both his body and his soul. In Ulster, she was also linked to death, for she was described as watching for the last person to leave a funeral. Should it be a young man, she would take the form of a beautiful woman and make him promise to meet her in the churchyard in a month. When he sealed the promise with a kiss, he sealed his doom, for her kiss sent "a fatal fire through his veins," and before the month was up, he died "the death of a raving lunatic" (*Second Manx Scrapbook*,

p. 239). Often too, Lady Wilde tells her readers, the evil spirit appears at Irish festivities and dances her male victim into fever and death (p. 84).

Victorian memorates of the lhiannon-shee abound, suggesting the pervasiveness of and interest in belief. Gill tells of the man who met a shee at a dance and could never shake her off again. He cites Roeder, another Manx folklorist, regarding a farmer who mistakenly thought he was being nocturnally visited and caressed by one of the women who worked on his farm and hence, in error, fired them all. It did him no good, however, and the shee sapped and destroyed him. He tells of old Harry Ballahane of Rushen Parish, who knew his fairy mistress so well (she had been with him for quite a while) that he would give her a sup of his porridge at dinner. Readers learn of one brazen lhiannon-shee who, in 1898, followed a farmer right into his house and was thought, by the man, to be his wife. Puzzled when she did not answer his questions, he asked his actual wife if she saw the fairy woman, at which, with a hideous grin, the shee walked through the door and vanished (*Second Manx Scrapbook*, pp. 355–57).[24]

Yet in some parts of Ireland, the lhiannon-shee was given compensatory traits and thought of as inspiring poets and musicians, even as she destroyed them. Denis Florence MacCarthy had poetically idealized her in a poem of 1851 called "The Lianhan Shee," published in the *Dublin University Magazine*, noting that her beauty prevented men from marrying mortal women, but that if her lover reciprocated her love, she would instruct him, rewarding him by teaching him music, healing, and the mysteries of fairydom. She would even leave him free after a number of years, MacCarthy optimistically argued.[25]

Yeats disagreed; it is clearly the lhiannon-shee's power as a vampire muse that is responsible for at least part of his obsession with her and that plays a prominent role in his description of the figure: "The Leanhaun Shee (fairy mistress)," he writes:

> seeks the love of men. . . . Her lovers waste away, for she lives on their life. Most of the Gaelic poets, down to quite recent times, have had a Leanhaun Shee, for she gives inspiration to her slaves. She is the Gaelic muse, this malignant fairy. Her lovers, the Gaelic poets, died young. She grew restless, and carried them away to other worlds, for death does not destroy her power." (*Unpublished Prose* 1:136)

Yeats may well have constructed Maude Gonne as his leanhaun-shee in life, but the figure of the soulless destructive beauty, as ineffable and implacable as desire, is as old as Irish mythology itself. The shee is the woman who enticed Connla the Bold with her apples, drawing him to Tir na Nog, the fairy who visited Angus Og in dream and played enchanting music to him until he forfeited his health and life in seeking her. In Yeats's mythological and folkloric poems and plays she is all of these, as well as Cleena of the Wave, who drives Owen Sullivan to madness; Niamh, who lures Oisin to the otherworld; the several incarnations of the Woman of the Sidhe, who dances at the Hawk's Well; and Fand or the Woman of the Sidhe, who seduces Cuchhulain and makes him come "away," in "The Only Jealousy of Emer." Seducing men in their sleep, alienating them from their mortal wives—she is like a succubus, and not unlike MacDonald's Lilith.

That the lhiannon-shee always desiccates and kills her victims, says Yeats, is certain. "Once a kiss is given, the man's doom is sealed. He wastes away and dies" (*Unpublished Prose* 1:75). But the manner of her victim's death is no more fearsome than her impact on his life, for she makes him sacrifice his human attachments and, in effect, drains his very humanity.

But even Yeats's merciless fairy was more benign than the lhiannon-shee described by William Carleton, the earlier Irish author and folklorist. In an unusual etiological tale ("The Lianhan Shee," c. 1850) based on folklore, he tells of a shee who, like a leech, fastened onto a woman, appearing as a protuberance behind her neck. Tormented, the woman offered great riches to anyone who would free her by becoming host to her parasite. Fearing the woman's "formidable power" (p. 430), the people of the community went for advice to their parish priest. Ironically, he was more frightened than they, for he knew the shee's host. She was his cast-off concubine, not dead as he thought her but mad and possessed by an evil spirit. In an account, which Carleton contends is true, the priest sacrifices himself, slashing his wrists (to avoid offering the shee his blood?) and burning himself to free the woman from her parasite. Thus, says Carleton, an unchaste female has come to be called a "Lianhan Shee," and "a priest's paramour," in particular, "is called Lianhan Shee an Sogarth" (p. 438).

The folklore icon of the lhiannon-shee syncretes both Celtic beliefs and the romantic image of "la belle dame sans merci." But the conception of her dreadful power, of her ability to both elude and torment her victim, to take complete dominion over her mortal lover and to destroy his feeling for all others, as well as his life, was not specific to Ireland or Man. In various forms, sometimes rendered nameless though not faceless, the figure was to be found all over England. To the literary minded she became identified with the perfect soulless beauty of the "glittering girl," the "fleur de mal," the "pale woman"—a transmuted form of the threatening new female of the 1890s. Visually, in various guises, she dominates the works of such '90s artists as Aubrey Beardsley and John William Waterhouse. She is always the woman "none can kiss and thrive," as Yeats describes her in "On Baile's Strand," the one who makes a man "follow with desire/Bodies that can never tire/ Or grow kind" and who makes mortal women's kisses feel like "hatred" (*Collected Plays*, p. 172).

Fictionalized, she appears in the works of figures as diverse as Laurence Housman, George MacDonald, Fiona Macleod, and George Fitzmaurice. In Laurence Housman's fairy tale for adults, "Blind Love" (1926), a king's refusal to consort with a lhiannon-shee, who, like a succubus, climbs into bed with him, results in a curse on his only daughter. George MacDonald's brilliant, terrifying Lilith, accurately rendered in terms of Scottish folklore, is another portrait of the shee. In *Lilith* (1895), she is a dream-composite figure: the blood-sucking night spirit or demon of the Talmud who preys on those who sleep alone and drinks the blood of children, and the fairy/witch succubus who seduces and desiccates men in their sleep. She has the fairy power to change her shape and metamorphoses into serpents, wild beasts, and a bat. Vampirishly sucking Vane's blood—nearly raping him—she is a glaistig or lhiannon-shee in her sexual aggressivity.

The same great beauty, shape-changing powers, and sexual malevolence mark the bhean-nimhir or serpent woman, of Fiona Macleod's tale, "By the Yellow Moonrock" (1899). The fate suffered by male victims of the "deadly love of the spectral woman" is depicted through the figure of Rory MacAlpine, a piper and the tale's handsome protagonist. In this almost paradigmatic version of the fairy-vampire stories proliferating around the end of the century, Rory sees, in dream, a bird settling on a meteor, called locally the yellow moonrock. The bird is suddenly transformed into a beautiful woman with white skin, long wavy hair, and dark mysterious pools of eyes, a supernatural figure who tells him that she is St. Bride of the Mantle. Though warned by an old wise-woman that what he has seen is no saint but a bhean-nimhir, a lamia who sucks a man's soul out through his lips and sends it and him "away," or who simply bites and kills him, Rory cannot resist her image. Totally obsessed, he goes to meet his love on St. Bride's night, knowing "it is that beauty that is my death" (p. 31). A witness reveals that he has heard Rory pleading with and wooing, singing and playing to an invisible woman. He watches the unfortunate piper dancing a mad reel with his invisible beloved, hears him scream, "let me go! Take your lips off my mouth!" (p. 34), and finally sees his dead body. Its lips are blue and swollen, and, in the hollow of his throat lies "a single drop of black blood" (p. 34). Some say Rory has been slain by the bite of an adder; most know the true reason for his death.

George Fitzmaurice's play *The Linnaun Shee* (1924), a dramatic fantasy, may be intended as a satire on Yeats's fairy and folk beliefs,[26] but it also contains a study of the psychological power of the shee and of the personal and social havoc that involvement with her causes. The story of Jamesie Kennelly, an ordinary farmer of North Kerry, who resumes his infatuation with the lhiannon-shee he rejected when he married his wife Hanora some thirty years earlier, it is the drama of a man obsessed. When the shee enters Jamesie's house, he alone perceives her as a beautiful young girl; to all others she appears as a "horrid wrinkled old hag" (1:51) with a cracked and grating voice. His love for the fairy, he reassures his wife, is not an earthly or a carnal one; the shee is a romantic ideal. In pursuit of this ideal, he becomes an outsider, rejected and despised, considered a fool for his dismissal of the "real" and the material. He is ready to relinquish everything, including his land and his wife, to gain his ideal love. Such perfect union (at least in fiction) can be gained only beyond death, but Jamesie is not granted such release. Instead, in a bitterly ironic comment on the quest for perfection, Jamesie is tortured and punished for his desires. Metamorphosing into a young and beautiful woman, the shee ignores her former lover who, being mortal, cannot rejuvenate himself. Instead she selects a new victim, a young man whom she entices from his fiancée. She will not even permit Jamesie to die of grief. Instead, she returns him to his family, ruined, incapable of feeling, and dead in spirit.

Jamesie's living death implies the psychologizing of the folklore motif, but the omnipresence of the lhiannon-shee and her sister fairies—their sucking of vitality and life, whether metaphorical or literal—suggests how widespread was the male Victorian fear of being devoured by the female. Perhaps, as Freud would have insisted, it was connected to a fear of and displacement of incest; perhaps it was a cultural embodiment of the infant's oral aggression directed to the nurturer's body—almost always a female body—and later distorted into the nurturer's primary characteristic and extended to all of her sex. Or, more generally, perhaps it was the response of the chiefly male folklorists to the less specific but broader threat they felt, the anxiety caused by the rise of the militant suffragettes and of the "New Woman" in all her forms. Perhaps it was the fear that these assertive or subversive creatures would weaken men and suck them dry. The pervasiveness of the anxiety is suggested by the large number of other female fairies who are also depicted as destroyers of human life and energy. If these creatures did not literally drink blood, they nevertheless drained the lives of their primarily male victims, destroying their vitality. Their weapon was their sexuality; their drive was to dominate and control.

Significantly, the deadly female fairy's male counterparts were also well known, but there are relatively few tales of demon lovers or male fairy-vampires recorded and analyzed in the great age of Victorian collecting. Bram Stoker's *Dracula* may have been the sensation of the book and drama worlds, but his male malevolence was not richly documented in English folklore.

By the end of the century, the growing misogyny identified in painting and literature[27] appears to have infected (or been infected by?) the folklore of the British Isles, or rather, the *folklorists*, who chose what to collect and emphasize. It seems fairly evident that male preoccupation with female control contributed to the retelling of so many tales of deadly supernatural women weakening and destroying their male partners. It seems equally evident that these tales often expressed anxiety about what might happen if men did not separate and domesticate female power and female sexuality. Perhaps the fear of an erosion of orthodox religious dogma and practice, of the diminuition of its support for patriarchy and authority, heightened the tension. Clearly though, growing female influence led to increasing emphasis on accounts of women's disruption of men's order, of their inversion of hierarchical authority and hence of society. As Barbara Leavy has suggested, "ancient fears of women or myths of feminine evil seem to rest at least in part on the anxiety that women will exercise an ever-present potential for wide-spread destruction of the social order" (p. 240).

While the fear of the mob—of the brutal force of demos—perhaps also intensified by anxieties about the loss of the respect for hierarchy and order that would result from a decline of religious faith and a weakening of religious institutions, found expression in images of an anarchic, destructive elfin horde, the fairy *femme fatale* reflected religious and cultural anxieties about female usurpation of power, as well as specifically male fantasies about destructive female sexuality. Whatever the specific causes, Victorian female fairies so often seem to embody a fusion of the erotic, the parasitic, and the anarchic that it is as if a voice within the culture had whispered, "give women power and they will revert to their natural inclinations and devour their men!" It is significant that, in an era when such threats were being felt in the religious, social, and political arenas, evil was so often clad in the external form of the faceless mob or endowed with the features of a deadly woman.

S I X

FAREWELL TO
THE FAIRIES

THE FAIRIES HAVE BEEN LEAVING England since the fourteenth century
—at least according to Chaucer's Wife of Bath—but despite their
perpetual farewells they had not completely vanished from Great Britain
by the 1920s, and, some argue, they have not yet left. The spreading of the
towns and the growing urbanization of former country people, the growth
of standardized education and the elevation of science, the widespread materialism, the power of official religion, whether Roman Catholicism in
Ireland, Presbyterianism in Scotland or Methodism in Wales, were all
among the factors blamed for their demise. Paradoxically, however, it was
their very prominence—their popularity especially after the turn of the
century—that seems to have hastened their ostensible departure.

Two less expected elements added to the apparent loss of the fairy faith.
First, the "Golden Age of Children's Literature" so ensconced the fairies in
the nursery that it virtually dislodged them from their places in adult literature and art. Second, the Cottingley fairy photographs and the subsequent publicity attendant on Arthur Conan Doyle's *The Coming of the Fairies*
(1922) hastened the process of their departure. In general, the tendency to
render the elfin peoples material and/or scientific inadvertently diminished
their importance.

By the 1880s, some commentators had begun to worry that the fairies and the faith in them were being contaminated by the media. Part of the blame was placed on the "moral influence" of the English press—the spreading of cheap and improving newspapers—part, on the fictionalizing of the fairies, their endless appearance and use in literature. While Francis Heath, writing on belief in the West of England in 1889, places the responsibility for the decline and departure of the fairies on the newspapers, George Laurence Gomme complains in *English Traditional Lore* (1885) that literature, "first, by mythologizing . . . and then by idealizing—has obscured the true meaning of the traditions" (p. vi).

Fairy Tales and Fairy Photographs

Ironically, children's literature was a partial though unintentional culprit. Many of the literary fairy tales designed for children altered, diminished, and trivialized their subjects. As the Golden Age of Children's Literature, beginning in the 1860s, burgeoned, literary fairy tales proliferated. A survey taken by the *Academy* (2 July 1898) of the ten most popular books for children listed five fairy tales or collections of them among the works. (Andrew Lang's colored "Fairy Books" and Mrs. Molesworth's tales joined the Alice books near the top of the list.) Lang himself commented in his introduction to *The Lilac Fairy Book* (1910) on the excess of authored fairy tales: "365 authors trying to write new ones are very tiresome. . . . These fairies try to be funny and fail, or they try to preach, and succeed" (p. xxiii).

This is not to suggest that many of the tales were not in themselves significant and splendid, imaginatively conceived yet authentic in feeling. George MacDonald, Mary de Morgan, Julia Horatia Ewing, Edith Nesbit, and Maria Louisa Molesworth created characters and situations that were both freshly original and consonant with the broader folklore tradition. In effect the tales *they* wrote helped keep the fairies and their lore from fading. Beyond this, much folklore material that twentieth-century readers (though not Victorian ones) might think esoteric was vitalized and preserved in childrens' fantasies.[1] Explanations of origins and comments on the realities underlying belief made their appearance in tales ostensibly for children.[2] Andrew Lang, for example, incorporates into "Princess Nobody" (1884) the folklore motif of the prohibited name as well as a brief comment on "primitive" peoples' taboo on the use of personal appellations: he interrupts the tale to announce that "some nations won't let a wife mention her husband's name" (qtd. in Zipes, p. 259). Kenneth Grahame, in "Snowbound" (1895), takes up the question of the actuality of fairies, but suggests the dilemma intellectual explanations could create. The narrator's sister, Charlotte, is badly out of sorts, for "she had been gently but firmly informed [by her governess] that no such things as fairies ever really existed."

" 'Do you mean to say it's all lies?' asked Charlotte bluntly" (p. 160). She is told that " 'these stories had their origin . . . in a mistaken anthropomorphism in the interpretation of nature. But though we are now too well-informed to fall into similar errors, there are still many beautiful lessons to be learned from these myths'"(pp. 160–61). Charlotte's rejoinder as she leaves the breakfast table defiant but depressed is very much to the point: " 'But how can you learn anything,' persisted Charlotte, 'from what doesn't exist?'"(p. 161). Though the narrator tries to protect Charlotte's fairy faith, telling her that "If a thing's in a book it *must* be true," we are told that "the Wee Folk were under a cloud: sceptical hints had embittered that chalice" (p. 162).

The underlying problem was less that many of the tales created for children were simple-minded, arch, and saccarine, or that they ignored, moralized or distorted folklore traditions, than that the enormous numbers and popularity of fairy books virtually overwhelmed the fairies. As the elfin peoples became staples of children's literature, the perception grew that they themselves were childish and that interest and belief in them befitted children only. Some of the tales promoted a false set of conventions, one that made the fairies tiny and harmless—moral guides for children or charming little pets—and a tradition of sentimentalization and idealization developed. In this literature, fairies were conflated with angels or further miniaturized into toys. In addition, fairies and witches were increasingly polarized; fairies grew purely good and sprouted wings, losing their demonic energy and power. In relegating them to the nursery, in creating a cult of fairy worship to replace or supplement conventional religion with something that would give children "religious" feelings (Avery, p. 84), writers reduced their import and significance.

In the first place, "tiny" fairies—with the possible exception of the early English portunes—were essentially literary rather than folkloric constructs. Used by Shakespeare (in descriptions rather than in the actual theater where fairies seem to have been played by children), they were further miniaturized in both the painting and the poetry of the seventeenth century. The little "putti" so popular in the Renaissance also had their impact on the visual imagination. Then, too, the human tendency to exaggerate intensified the problem: the fairies repeatedly described as "small"—the size of a three-year-old—became "tiny," or small enough to perch on a flower. Moreover, in both texts and illustrations, especially in books for children, the elfin peoples were increasingly depicted as small angels, specifically charged with guarding and teaching children. Fairies who had flown on their own power grew wings, an example of reverse logic ("since they fly, they must have wings") and as a parallel to the angelic hosts. As cultural seepage occurred, distinctions were blurred—after all, both groups were winged, both were guardians, both were supernatural and superior in power to mortals. The traditional analogy was indeed between fairies and angels, but it equated fairies with the fallen angels who had not chosen either Satan or God and hence had been thrust out of heaven.

In the second place, these once great powers were moralized and idealized, deprived of their ambiguity and capriciousness and often trivialized in literature designed for Victorian children. Lewis Carroll participated in both the sentimentalization and miniaturization of the fairies; his *Sylvie and Bruno* (1889) and *Sylvie and Bruno Concluded* (1893) are cases in point. Despite Carroll's significant preface to the second volume, with its essay on the states in which fairies may be seen, its fine distinctions between feeling "eerie" and being in a "trance" (p. xiii), his depictions of the supernatural within the books are saccarine and unpersuasive. Carroll's Bruno — who resembles a little girl rather than a little boy — speaks baby talk and is small enough to fit into a coffee cup. Sylvie, the loved and loving, may be a fairy-angel performing works of virtue, but she is vapid and devoid of energy. Though both fairies ostensibly metamorphose into children to reform a drunkard, do good deeds in a village, and bring the lovers together, there is nothing potent or mysterious about them. Carroll's moral orthodoxy and open didacticism destroy all sense of "glamour" in the books.

If Carroll's sentimentalizing and miniaturizing the elfin peoples contributed to reducing their impact, J. M. Barrie's *Peter Pan* helped to popularize them out of existence. Creating an early twentieth-century fairy cult for children, it made "keeping Tinkerbell alive by clapping" the tenet of a new religion. The idea of saving the fairies from extinction through belief is not at all alien to folklore, but in *Peter Pan* the transaction shifts the power entirely from the supernatural to mortals. Then, too, while some of Barrie's lore (especially the forgetfulness and capriciousness of Peter; see chapter 2) reverberates with power and truth, some of his invention is mawkish, especially when he deliberately equates fairies and children.

In the first version of *Peter Pan*, *The Little White Bird in Kensington Garden* (1902), Barrie establishes a series of analogies between fairies and babies, ironically rendering the former infantile. Babies are the genesis of fairies: "when the first baby laughed for the first time, his laugh broke into a million pieces and they all went skipping about. That was the beginning of fairies" (p. 160). No longer nature spirits or souls or guardians of the dead or even pagan gods diminished, fairies are now playmates of children, outgrown as children mature. "There are fairies wherever there are children" (p. 160), Barrie tells his readers, adding that like young children, the elfin peoples are ignorant, do nothing useful, and live in a world of make-believe. So tiny that they can camouflage themselves as flowers, their values and habits are those of the little ones with whom they are identified; for example, the youngest in a fairy family is the most important and fairy language is baby-talk, spoken chiefly by infants.[3]

In Barrie's quasi-Wordsworthian vision of childhood, a person loses the ability to fly or participate in fairy life because she or he is "no longer young and innocent" (p. 16). This concept, too, became a sacrosanct belief in the nursery fairy cult. In *Pinky and the Fairies* (1909), W. Graham Robertson's play, Pinkie is told that only children see fairies because the adult eye and mind rejects the reality of the elfin world. The problem lies in point of view; adults perceive a fairy dance, for instance, only as blowing leaves. The same argument, that for the most part only innocent children and young girls can directly witness fairy life, was to become an important one in arguing for the truth of the Cottingley fairy photographs.

Although Cottingley linked the fairies to the young and pure in heart, thus diminishing them to a phenomenon essentially for children, it also functioned in an inverse but equally reductionist way. Here, the photographing of the fairies—the literal visual depiction of the imaginary— rendered them trivial and foolish. The events on which the still-controversial fairy photographs taken at Cottingley (a place near Bradford in Yorkshire) were based occurred in the summer of 1917 to sixteen-year-old Elsie Wright and her ten-year-old cousin Frances Griffiths. Significantly, too, in 1917 the first and most popular of Rose Fyleman's poems, "Fairies," with its famous assertion, "There are fairies at the bottom of our garden" appeared in the 23 May issue of *Punch*. Perhaps coincidentally, the beginning of the poem, which Elsie admitted she knew, locates the supernatural creatures in a setting very similar to the one in which the girls photographed them.[4] The two girls who played in the glen above the Wright's cottage had spoken about meeting fairies there and, when teased by their parents about their "fantasy," Elsie had told her doubting father (a mechanic by trade, though employed as an electrician) that she would prove her point by photographing them. When developed, the pictures did indeed reveal "fairies," though nothing was made of the results until 1920 when Elsie's mother (a Spiritualist), attending a lecture, listened to a friend of Edward Gardner's being questioned about the existence of elfin creatures. This led her to give the photographs to Gardner's friend, who then sent them to Gardner, in part because Gardner (a Theosophist) was interested in spirit photography. Gardner, persuaded by the negatives he was sent that the pictures were not photographically doctored, had them sent to professional photographers for analysis. When the first of these found the pictures technically authentic, Gardner, contacting and consulting Sir Arthur Conan Doyle (who was then also working on a book on spirit photography), sent the photographs to Kodak, and the examiner for the firm agreed they had not been tampered with.[5] Only in 1920, three years after the pictures were taken, did Gardner (Doyle was about to go to Australia) go to Cottingley to seek positive testimony from the Wright family. There, he was impressed by Elsie's honesty and directness, and by the fact that the motives for "faking" the photographs, money and notoriety, could be ruled out. He asked for more evidence and arranged for the girls to take further photographs in "controlled" conditions—specifically on marked photographic plates so that the plates could not be substituted for others. He also decided that he had found in Frances, at least, indications of mediumistic powers. Thus, in August 1920, three more photographs were taken, though again the girls were left alone together so that the presence of adults would not disturb the fairies. Again tested, the photographs did not seem faked.

Doyle took the spotlight by writing an article on the reality of the photos for the *Strand* Magazine in 1920 (though Gardner was listed as co-author)[6] and publishing *The Coming of the Fairies* in 1922. He admitted that he, himself, had never seen a fairy, but noted that his own "truthful" children had told him that fairies exist. A third and last "test" was made in the summer of 1921, when Gardner returned to Cottingley bringing with him a friend, Geoffrey Hodson, whom he believed was clairvoyant, and the girls, now twenty and fourteen, were tested for their clairvoyance. In Gardner's words, "Mr. Hodson saw all they saw, and more" (*Fairies*, p. 36), though, this time, attempts to photograph the phenomena failed.

As a famous author, vice-president of the Marylebone Spiritualist Association, and an expert on psychic phenomena and especially "spirit photographs," Arthur Conan Doyle was an ideal contact for the less well known and somewhat suspect Gardner who was, after all, a Theosophist. Doyle's name and belief made the fairies famous; he was associated in the public mind with the quintessentially rational, supremely scientific, and essentially untrickable master sleuth, Sherlock Holmes—the man who knew everything. While, in the next few years Gardner scoured the British Isles interviewing people who claimed to have seen fairies or similar spirits first-hand, letters and memorates from all over the world poured into Doyle's hands. Meanwhile, Elsie and Frances, now adults, resisted the efforts of journalists and writers to make them confess to their deception. (They admitted pinning up cutout paper figures of fairies only in the 1980s when they were elderly ladies; however, even their final statements were ambiguous.)

Ironically, the photographs, the ostensible proof of the actual existence of the fairies, deprived the elfin peoples of their grandeur and status. In general terms, denuding the fairies of the invisibility that made them powerful and frightening diminished them. The theories that Gardner, Leadbeater, and Hodson formulated to explain the fairies' nature and function reduced them to the intelligence level of household pets and the size of insects. Specifically, the visual images that were offered—figures with the bobbed hair and makeup of the period—failed to satisfy the imaginations of most educated and sensitive viewers. (See also figure 1.3.) C. S. Lewis's comment is much to the point. When Doyle "claimed to have photographed a fairy, I did not, in fact, believe it: but the mere making of the claim—the approach of the fairy to within even that hailing distance of actuality—revealed to me at once that if the claim had succeeded it would have chilled rather than satisfied the desire which fairy literature had hith-

6.1 "Fairy Offering a Posy to Elsie," Cottingley photograph number 4.

erto aroused" (*The Pilgrim's Regress*, p. 9). Lewis's desire for verisimilitude not verity was echoed by many others, especially since in this case the images of the "truth" were found, even by believers, to be unsatisfactory.

While Doyle, Gardner, Leadbeater, Hodson, and others believed the testimony of the Cottingley photographs, others, including occultists and psychic researchers, could not accept them or the Doyle and Gardner theories. A rather embarrassed president of the Society for Psychical Research rejected the photographs as "obviously contrived," though he gently commented that children did have fantasies and it was natural that they would make figures representing them and than take snapshots (Society for Psychical Research, p. 59). The Folk-Lore Society, rendered uncomfortable (as was the Society for Psychical Research) by the enormous publicity the pictures were receiving, repeatedly refused to comment on them. Maurice Hewlett thought the pictures obvious fakes, as did H. Rider Haggard, while Arthur Machen used them to illustrate the fact that "there is no proposition, tale, or statement so monstrous that it will not find some true believers" (*Dog and Duck*, p. 49). He spelled out his objections in a second article titled "A Midsummer Night's Dream." Calling the Cottingley fairies the products of a "third-rate artistic conception" (*Dog and Duck*, p. 59), he argued that they are too conventional (resembling how one would dress children for a Christmas fairy play), too small (noting that the miniature fairy is a purely literary invention), and too inauthentic in terms of any strand of belief to be convincing. Fairies may well be MacRitchie's pre-Celtic aborigines, or the fearsome old gods and goddesses, or the elementals, or the lobs and Robin Goodfellows of the folk, but they are not, he concludes, the silly figures on the photographic plates (*Dog and Duck*, p. 65).

Interest in the Cottingley photographs was again revived, first in the 1970s, when the Folk-Lore Society, which had previously ignored them, labeled them "fakelore," and in the 1980s, when Elsie Wright, one of the original photographers, admitted that the photographs were fraudulent. James Randi, the magician, "debunked" them in *Flim-Flam* (1982), saying that by enhancing the photographs he found strings holding up the fairies. (His debunking appears to have been inaccurate, since Elsie said the girls used hat pins to put the fairy cutouts in place.) The sources of the specific images were found in illustrations to Alfred Noyes's poem "A Spell for a Fairy," in *Princess Mary's Gift Book*. Significantly, the poem provides instructions for the conjuring of fairies. But while Elsie may have admitted inventing the Cottingley fairies, Frances indicated (according to some interviewers) that she had actually seen them. Other people, including witnesses on an expedition to Cottingley called "Tinkerbell '86," reported having heard them. As Lynn Picknett, the group's leader, states:

> We heard two fairy bells and one of our members saw dark earth spirits scurrying along an old pathway. Another heard the sound of high fairy talk in a flower bed—in common with others, the capacity to see fairies in her childhood had given way to hearing them only in her adulthood. (p. 94)

The local forester, Ronnie Bennett, insisted that he, too, had seen fairies in the area. Before her death, Frances reaffirmed her fairy sightings, telling Joe Cooper that though she faked most of the photographs, the last of them was real.[7]

Thus for many, as I have indicated above, the fairies did not leave at all. Indeed, the very idea of the fairies' departure and of the fading of the fairy faith may be seen as an integral part of the fairy lore complex (Narváez, p. 3). The fairies—never quite believed in—are always leaving but never gone. Yet the threat of their imminent loss touched the Victorian and Edwardian temperamental affinity for the elegiac and nostalgic and led to the recording of numerous laments for (and the collection of numerous accounts of) their passing and to considerable discussion of the reasons for it.

"Fairies' Farewell": The Tradition

In the cities and towns, in the less isolated parts of Great Britain, the fairies' day was done by the late eighteenth century. Bishop Richard Corbet had, indeed, bid them good-bye in 1591, when he wrote "A Proper New Ballad: The Fairies' Farewell." But despite his famous line, "Farewell, rewards and fairies," later used by Kipling as the title of the second installment of his Puck tales, *Rewards and Fairies* (1910), they were not yet perceived as having left the British Isles. During the romantic period, Allan Cunningham had blamed their departure on the agricultural revolution, since they could not occupy ploughed land and their green hills had been planted with crops. But many other reasons were given as well.[8]

The departure of the fairies continued to be discussed and analyzed throughout the Victorian era. An old Lowland woman blamed it on all the preaching and Bible reading that was part of the Scottish religious revival. Early in this century, Lady Archibald Campbell met a Highland woman who, when asked, said dolefully, "the Shee are put past now. May be the gospel is too strong for them" ("The Men of Peace," p. 25). Many people, both ordinary folk and folklorists, blamed the demise of the fairy faith in Wales on the rise and rigor of Methodism and the changes in behavior it had wrought. Both Sidney Hartland and Wirt Sikes were told that the fairies simply could not bear Methodist preachers; Sikes's informant added that they also disliked teetotallers. Mary Lewes, on the other hand, charged that "standardised education and cheap newspapers" (*Queer Side of Things*, p. 112) were responsible for the departure of the fairies from Wales. In *Stranger Than Fiction* (1911), she comments that she had "only come across two people who had anything to say about the Tylwyth Teg, and they were not of the peasantry, but persons of antiquarian tastes. . . . I have never myself heard a single *first-hand* story about fairies," she continues, "and I fancy their disappearance from their old haunts dates very nearly from the time that Board Schools were established in Wales" (p. 160). Though she praises education, she regrets its destruction of the old lore, for "Romance and Glamour grow rare as the world grows older. . . . And the power to express them grows less" (p. 161). William Sharp, writing as Fiona Macleod in the 1890s, lamented that in Scotland "the Gentle People have no longer a life [in] common with our own. They have gone beyond grey unvisited hills. They dwell in far islands perhaps where the rains of Heaven and the foam of the sea guard their fading secrecies." Mortals can no longer find fairyland in this world, the author says, because *we* have altered. "There are new ways—the spirit has changed within us" (*Works* 5:287). One of Macleod's informants placed the blame on humans even more forthrightly. "They're not dead," Seumas Macleod reported, using the old euphemism *they* to apply to the elfin tribes. "They think *we* are. They do not change" (*Works* 5:263). Others, with equal sorrow, blamed materialism, urbanization, pollution, and technology.

But the fairies did not go out with a whimper; instead they staged numerous ceremonial departures, widely observed and noted. They seem to have abandoned Scotland first—some time around 1790—and there are, unaccountably, similar reports of their passing drawn from places far from each other. These reports, known to folklorists as "The Fairies' Farewell," were reiterated both in fiction and in folklore throughout the Victorian period. They are imbedded in Charlotte Brontë's *Shirley* (1849) and mentioned in *Jane Eyre* (the ten-year-old Jane believes that the fairies, for whom she has looked, are all gone out of England to a wilder, less populous place). The departure of the elfin tribes is the subject of Walter Besant and James Rice's "Titania's Farewell" (1876), forms the satiric backdrop to Andrew Lang and May Kendall's *'That Very Mab'* (1885), and is the substance of one of the best known tales in Kipling's *Puck of Pook's Hill* (1906). It plays a powerful role, as well, in Lord Dunsany's "The Kith of the Elf-Folk" and in Algernon Blackwood's "When Pan was Dead," and it constitutes a major motif in the works of Irish writers such as Nora Hopper.

The best known folkloristic "farewell" account was that of Hugh Miller, the famous geologist-collector, printed in *Old Red Sandstone* (1841) as a note to chapter 11 and set in Cromarty in about 1790. Miller speaks of a Sunday morning when all were in church except for a herdboy and his sister, who at noon (a favorite fairy time) saw a procession of horses and riders climbing out of a ravine:

> The horses were shaggy, diminuitive things . . . the riders stunted, misgrown, ugly creatures, attired in antique jerkins of plaid, long grey cloaks and little red caps from under which their long uncombed locks shot out over their cheeks and foreheads.

Finally, overcoming his amazement at the strangeness of the long cavalcade, the boy asked its last rider:

> "What are ye, little mannie? And where are ye going?" . . . "Not of the race of Adam," said the creature, turning for a moment in his saddle.
> "The People of Peace shall never more be seen in Scotland." (p. 122)

In Allan Cunningham's account, set in Nithsdale and supposed to have occurred in the same year, the time of day is sunset and the fairies appear more like children than dwarfs. Also in ceremonial procession, they enter a green hill, while "one, taller than the rest, ran before them and seemed to enter the hill, and again appeared at its summit" (Cunningham as Cromek, *Remains*, pp. 122–23). The action was repeated three times and then all the fairies vanished. Those who beheld the scene memorialized it as "The Farewell o' the Fairies to the Burrow Hill" (p. 123).

Another Scottish farewell occurred in the 1790s. Recorded in *Scottish Fairy and Folk Tales* by Sir George Douglas as "The Gloaming Bucht," the incident was recounted by an old shepherd named Robbie Oliver. It was ostensibly witnessed by Peter Oliver, his father, also a shepherd of the Border territory. Not knowing that the fairies were getting ready to leave, Peter encountered a little creature clad in green; "raisin' a queer unyirthly cry, 'Hae ye seen Hewie Milburn?'" it asked. The creature was

> nae bigger than a three-year auld lassie, but feat an' tight, lith o' limb, as ony grown woman, an' its face was the downright perfection o' beauty, only there was something wild an' unyirthly in it e'en that couldna be lookit at, faur less describit. (p. 193)

It kept crying for its companion, Hewie Milburn, until, threatened by an evil servant, it fled. The anecdote promptly spawned a poem by James Telfer, schoolmaster in Liddesdale (1800–1862) called "The Fairy's Song" and beginning:

> O where is tiny Hew?
> And where is little Len?
> And where is bonnie Lu,
>   And Menie of the Glen?
> And where's the place of rest—
>   The ever changing hame?
> Is it the gowan's breast,
>   Or 'neath the bells of faem? (p. 139)

At the end of this "farewell," the fairy speaker provides additional material on the future of the displaced Scottish elves, announcing that the band will now fly to the "shadowy side" of the moon to find a home away from mortals (p. 140).

In Ireland, those who believed the fairies had actually departed (and many did not) disagreed about the exact time and circumstances. Some placed it on the night of the "Big Wind" in 1839. One old man told a folklorist that the elfin peoples had left Ulster—if not all of Ireland—in 1852; a woman who was their friend had been told by them that they were to battle with the fairy host of Connaught. They warned her that if they were defeated the stream would run red. One morning, after a night of strange noises in the air, the stream did run red, and, the story goes, no more fairies were seen in Ulster (Andrews, p. 81). Ulster people also blamed the departure of the elfin races on the outcome of a great battle between the Irish and Scottish fairies. Again, the mark of defeat and the sign of the departure of the Irish force (in this version they, like their nation, would be carried away into slavery for a thousand years) was to be the reddened water of a stream, while lights on all the forths would indicate the night of the battle (Andrews, pp. 80–81).

Orkney, too, provided a tale of the disappearance of the evil local fairies called trows. Children no longer need to be afraid to go out after dark because "all the trows are drowned." According to this account, the Orcadian trows—known for their malice—decided to move their homesite. They were to travel on a straw rope stretched across a large and deep sound. When the great troop of "flitting" fairies reached the middle of this frail bridge, it collapsed and, like many Orkney sailors, the trows were overwhelmed by the stormy sea. The one surviving trow, the so-called Dwarf of Hoy, who had already leapt across the sound to secure the rope bridge at its other end, committed suicide, determined not to survive his friends. In another version of the tale, he stopped for a minute to lament the passing of his race in rhyme (see Fergusson, pp. 134−35).

And so the reports abound, some more dramatic than others, some general explanations, others accounts of the disappearances of local fairy groups. Wirt Sikes was told, repeatedly, that the last Welsh fairyland had been located in Craig y Ddinas, a rugged crag pitted by caves and crevices near Glamorganshire, now deserted. William Bottrell, the collector of Cornish lore, told of the taunting and subsequent departure of the local fairies from the "Eastern Green" (2nd series, pp. 93−94).

And the passing of the fairies became a popular motif in poetry and fiction as writers ranging from Walter Besant to Lord Dunsany utilized the reasons for the elfin migration to indict the society they left behind. Sometimes their departure was seen as a bitter result of the triumph of Christianity, sometimes as the loss of respect for the "old ways." For Nora Hopper and for Algernon Blackwood, it was both.

Hopper, the Irish poet whom William Butler Yeats found so worthy of praise, contributed her "farewell to the fairies" to a collection of tales and poems called *Ballads in Prose* (1894). Her poem "The Wind Among the Reeds" is one of the loveliest (and most Keatsian) of the fairy elegies, though it is clear that she does not believe the sidhe have really left:

Mavrone, Mavrone! the wind among the reeds
It calls and cries, and will not let me be;
And all its cry is of forgotten deeds
When men were loved of all the Daoine-sidhe.

O Shee that have forgotten how to love,
And Shee that have forgotten how to hate
Asleep 'neath quicken boughs that no winds move,
Come back to us ere yet it be too late.

Pipe to us once again, lest we forget
What piping means, till all the Silver Spears
Be wild with gusty music such as met
Carolan once, amid the dusty years.

Dance in your ring again: the yellow weeds
You used to ride so far, mount as of old—
Play hide and seek with winds among the reeds,
And pay your score again with fairy gold. (p. 79)

Hopper almost made a career of lamenting fairy departures. She commemorates the "last of the race" in a poem called "The Lament of the Last Leprechan," with its refrain reiterating the "grief" of the solitary elfin shoemaker, and in another called "The Fairy Fiddler," in which the isolated fairy complains that he is the last of his tribe: "None of my fairy kinsmen/Make music with me now:/ Alone the raths I wonder/ Or ride the whitethorn bough" (p. 91). But her most culturally significant tale, "Daluan," suggests that the shee are the old gods and the culprit is the Christian faith.

Encountered by an ordinary mortal, Daluan, a strangely magical Irishman, vanishes in a cloud of dust as the two men walk to Galway. Years later, the man returns to the same place to find a group of mourners keening "Daluan is dead. Da Mort is King" (p. 101). Only then does he learn that on this Halloween night he has witnessed the passing of an era. *Da Luan* is the Erse word for "Monday", *Da Mort* (with its pun on death) for "Tuesday." What he has seen is the Irish version of the death knell of paganism. Instead of the mysterious cry that arose when Jesus was born, "Pan is Dead, the Great God Pan is Dead," he has heard the Irish version of the lament. Yet another tale, "When Pan Was Dead" (1914) by Algernon Blackwood, recounts the sad fate of the last of the "woodlings"—brown-skinned, long-haired tree fairies—who in her loneliness tries to persuade the nuns of a convent to be her companions and failing, sinks into the earth as a mandrake. Again, the subtext is the departure of the old gods, as it is in John Duncan's wistfully elegant study of the seaward procession of the Scottish fays, *The Riders of the Sidhe* (1911). In none of these examples is the triumph of Christianity over paganism, a victory over the life and beauty of nature, applauded.

6.2 John Duncan, *The Riders of the Sidhe*, tempera (1911). Courtesy of Dundee Arts and Heritage, McManus Galleries.

A number of folklorists and collectors joined in blaming the demise of the fairies on institutionalized and orthodox religion. Angus MacLeod of Harris (in an account given to Alexander Carmichael in 1877 and translated as an entry in Evans-Wentz) blames the church for the dispersion of the elfin tribes—in a vehemently anticlerical tone. It is the clerics with their disputations about denominations and churches, "who have put the cross round the heads and the entanglements round the feet of the people" (qtd. in Evans-Wentz, p. 167), he protests; his implication is that only the fairy faith can heal the people's wounds. MacLeod's argument is echoed by others, including Lady Archibald Campbell. A believer in the occult, member of the Society for Psychical Research, wife of the folklore collector of *Waifs and Strays*, Sir Archibald Campbell, as well as an author in her own right, she speaks, in an article on "Faerie Scotland" in the *Occult Review* (1909), of "the tyranny of the priest in Ireland and the tyranny of the Calvinist fanatic in Scotland" (p. 25). A neo-pagan herself, she accuses orthodox religion of causing "a blight on the vision of our people . . . of preventing them from knowing the only wisdom" (p. 25), that of the fairies. However, both nationalism and optimism persuade her that the blight can only be temporary. "If the element of faery is within us," she proclaims, "the vision of the Celt can be bleared, but not extinguished" (p. 25). More hopeful than Angus MacLeod, she believes in "progress," arguing that with the decline of ignorance and of the fear of witchcraft, psychic powers and vision will increase. As human nature evolves, it will increasingly accept the fairies and their world.

In one of the best-known contributions to the genre of the fairies' farewell, Rudyard Kipling's tale of "Dymchurch Flit" in *Puck of Pooks Hill* (1906), the cause of the fairies' departure is the triumph of Calvinism and its puritan values. In this remarkable piece of imaginary history, Puck tells Old Hobden, the Bee Boy (Hobden's retarded son), and Una and Dan, why and how all the fairies but he left England. The Reformation and its attendant bloodshed, the Pharisees' recognition that "Merry England's done with an' we're reckoned among the Images" (p. 188)—the Idols to be destroyed—led them first to flock to Romney Marsh and then to seek human aid to flee to France. Needing a boat and a crew to sail them across running water, they requested the help of a poor widow, a "wise woman," with two sons, one born blind and the other rendered dumb through an accident. Her generosity in lending her sons to sail the boat of exodus enabled the fairies to "flit," and restored the marsh and its people to health. (Because of their vast numbers and distress at leaving, the fairies, like Oberon and Titania in Shakespeare's *Midsummer Night's Dream*, had disordered nature, causing fires, fevers, and animal plagues.) After taking the fairies across the channel, the wise-woman's sons returned, but not cured or healed—for that would have been "unnatural" as well as inconvenient for the fairies who wished their secrets kept. The fairies did, however, leave the family a special

6.3 Arthur Rackham, illustration for Rudyard Kipling, *Puck of Pook's Hill*, 1906.
'"Go!' she says. 'Go with my Leave an' Goodwill."' (frontispiece.)

gift. There would always be a child who would have preternaturally sharp
senses but who would be, like the Bee Boy, a "natural." The Pharisees' gift is
the village simpleton, says Kipling, offering his audience an etiological legend. Arthur Rackham's illustration of the tale enriches its impact, depicting
—in a reversal of the traditional Noah's ark procession—the elfin peoples
of all varieties, ranging from grotesques to pretty female fairies, making
ready to depart forever.

While "Dymchurch Flit" focuses more on the departure itself than on its
causes, "Titania's Farewell," Walter Besant and James Rice's little-known
novella of 1876, provides a litany of explanations for the fairies' decision to
leave England. Besant and Rice's elfin peoples suffer less from the pressures
of puritan morality and institutionalized religion than from the decline of
belief in general. As the narrative imitates in form the stately ceremonial
procession of departure, Oberon and Titania enunciate—and others repeat
—the underlying cause: the decline of belief. "We live by faith of man," says

Oberon. "Tell me, my children, if any faith remains" (p. 20). When he is answered by silence, he must sadly decide that "it is time to be gone" (p. 20).

As representatives of the fairy peoples speak, the reasons for departure are amplified. The goblin troop reluctantly chooses to leave an England that has forgotten it. Like the army of empire, it expresses both its patriotic love of country and its sense of racial superiority to the inhabitants of the new realm it will colonize. But though "there is no land like the land of the English" (p. 21), and though the goblin army cannot "love . . . the black man so well as the Saxon" (p. 22), it has no choice but to depart.

The political situation in Europe becomes a motive when Titania, who does not wish to go to the islands of the Indian Ocean, wonders why (since their origins are Teutonic) the fairies cannot go to Germany. "It is all Prussia," Oberon tells her. "We love not iron heels and martial despotism" (p. 28). Prussian militarism has made Germany a place fit only for ghosts, witches, and spectres, inappropriate for fairy peoples who "love the lands of liberty" (p. 28).

For the gnomes, depicted as miners, the problem is the scientific temper of the age. Their "dusky king" (p. 41) announces that although the gnomes continue to "work at the mines for men. . . .Geology takes everything to its own credit" (p. 42). Men will be sorry, he remarks, when without gnomes, "coals get scarcer" (pp. 41–42). Ariel adds that the rational and scientific temper has even destroyed childhood. Children have become creatures of utility:[9] "They are little chemists now, and little philosophers; little linguists, little scorners and scoffers at what they cannot understand" (p. 116). Puck, too, has been demoralized by the rationalism of the age; belief in him has been overturned by "natural" explanations of his powers.[10] Even when he pixie-leads two men returning from a lecture on "the debasing influence of old superstitions" (p. 102), his existence and the reality of the men's experiences are denied.

And so it goes, as Besant and Rice pile up reason after reason—economic, cultural, and social—for the fairies' farewell. Titania complains that the problem of the "two nations" has not been solved: "the rich in this country grow ever richer, and the poor poorer! The struggle for life is harder, the temptations are greater, selfishness and greed increase: luxury grows more and more . . . and the sweet contentment is wholly gone" (p. 112). She laments the failure of art; the human child she nurtured to be a "poet of the people" (p. 112) has indeed become a "mighty poet," but of the wrong sort. He sings "to his own learned kind" of "mighty problems of the brain" and has become "a poet of the town, not of the forest" (p. 113).

But most destructive to elfin life is the wanton ruining of the earth: the pollution caused by careless industrialization. Puck sounds like William Morris when he says:

the smoke of the factories poison us; there are hardly any forests where we can lurk; no rivers but are foul with refuse; hardly any commons but are enclosed by the Lord of the Manor. They've stolen great slices of Epping Forest, and wanted to build over Hampstead Heath; and on the sea-shore are the Coast-guard." (p. 115)

Thus, the fairies decide to emigrate, to leave behind a sterile kingdom of riches without content and power without greatness. They will not return till "England be merry England again, and . . . [the people] return to their good old belief" (p. 145). But they are not without hope, for they await a reaction against factualism, utility, and false progress that will permit them to return once more.

Andrew Lang and May Kendall's[11] satiric novel of 1885, '*That Very Mab*,' though less conservative and Carlylean in its critique of English society, is ultimately more pessimistic about the fate of the fairies; here, too, the primary cause of the elfin departure is a false idea of progress. In this satire sprinkled with allusions to Victorian anthropology and comparative folklore, the fairies are described as having first left England "when the Puritans arose" (as in Kipling's account), but as migrating not to France but to a sacred island near Samoa. There, they interbred with Polynesian fairy folk and Mab's court now includes "strange brown fairies of the Southern Ocean" (p. 3). However, the fairies must again relocate, for the missionaries have invaded, bringing settlers and the British flag. In an ironic comment on colonialism, Lang and Kendall note how when beautiful (and naked) Polynesian woman come to greet the missionaries with flowers and fruits, the horrified clergymen avert their eyes and make the women put on "bonnets and boots, and cotton gowns and pocket-hankerchiefs." As "the men in black coats" explain that "unless they wore these things, and did and refrained from many matters, they would be punished dreadfully after they were dead" (p. 8), the Germans arrive; battling the British for possession of the colony, they kill the women in their new cotton gowns. Thus Mab, loathing both the missionaries and the killing, comes back to England to investigate the possibility of elfin resettlement. She finds her former homeland polluted, crass, and unbelieving. Even the insects, now rendered scientific by Sir John Lubbock in the "International Scientific Series," no longer hold the fairy faith. Queen Mab is informed by the Queen Bee that she is "merely an outgrowth of the anthropomorphic tendency" (p. 17). Birds are the fairies' only allies.

But more important, the England to which Mab returns is a place of ecological destruction, bizzare religious sects, and a pervasive tension between anarchy and philistinism. An owl, her guide, announces that the English are still worshipers of nature. Yet they foul their world, and the owl can only wonder if the picnic litter humans leave—their corks, and paper bags, and cigar butts—are ritual offerings to the nature goddess. Those who believe in fairies in this unfortunate new world are mainly eccentric occultists—"persons who believe in Faith-healing and Esoteric Buddhism, and Thought-reading, and Arbitration, and Phonetic Spelling" and can thus "believe in anything" (p. 22).

Mistaken for a butterfly and caught by a philosopher, Mab is worshiped by his child, who instinctively invents a religious ritual and names her Dala. (In an amusing moment of self-satire, Lang has the child's philosophical father locate the origins of religion in butterfly worship.) Functioning as the traditional satiric visitor from another world or country, Mab quickly learns why England is unfit for fairies. London is dangerous; she must avoid the smoke, the labyrinth of wires, and the anarchists who carry dynamite in small black bags. She learns that what she sees as "British Polynesians going to a war-dance" (p. 114) is actually a Salvation Army marching band. She is most upset by her visit to an exhibition of machinery; the triumph of technology has resulted in weapons of destruction, including torpedos. And she dislikes the social Darwinism of the country; she cannot accept successful manufacturers as examples of "survival of the fittest."

Fleeing the absurdities of the city, she returns to the country and the home of the philosopher. His child has become robust and ignorant (in preparation for attending Eton); he has forgotten his fairy faith and now throws stones at her. Thus, Mab chooses to again depart, for "the Philistines had made of the island she once loved well a wilderness wherein no fairy might henceforth furl its wings" (p. 212). Instead, she and her people will move to the remote Admiralty Islands. She recognizes "that only among the heathen, in some obscure corner of Oceania . . . will she still [be] permitted to linger on till that lagging island too receives its chrism of intellect and is caught up into the van of time" (p. 214). There, only temporarily secure, "too tangible by far for a higher Pantheism" (p. 214), she will await that hour "when she will be ultimately reduced by scientific theologians to a symbol of some deeper verity (the conception of men who can cope with abstract truth)" (p. 213).

Thus did Victorian writers of fiction utilize the fairies' farewell as social critique.[12] Some, like Kipling, or Besant and Rice, used it to express their yearning for the return of "Merry England"; others, like Lang and Kendall, as a comment on imperial expansion. But both conservatives and radicals saw the demise of the fairies as the outcome of false values and ideas of progress.

Other Victorian commentators, however, argued that the fairies had diminished in numbers rather than actually departed. Some folklorists declared that increased sophistication among the peasantry now prevented believers from expressing their belief. If the fairies were always leaving (though never gone), they were always fewer than they had been in the past. Charles Hardwick in 1872 remarked that forty years earlier, the fairies called feeorin in Lancashire, the county about which he wrote, had been "as plentiful as blackberries" (p. 126), but were now greatly reduced in numbers.[13] Wirt Sikes noted in writing British Goblins that belief in fairies was still present in Wales, but that it was always placed by his informants in districts other than their own or in the generation just before their own.[14]

Jeremiah Curtin (in *Tales of the Fairies and of the Ghost World*), writing at the end of the century, remarked that many Irish would no longer confess that they believed in fairies. When he was a boy, nine out of ten people spoke of their fairy faith; now only one in ten would admit it. He notes, however, that it is remarkable to find a society that contains even 10 percent professed believers. Those who will not confess their faith, he remarks, are "timid believers . . . men without the courage of their convictions" (p. 2).[15] He agrees with Nora Hopper that "there are pishogues and sheogues in Ireland yet, for all the mills in Belfast and Armagh" (*Ballads in Prose*, p. 103). Belief has simply gone underground.

Variations on "Farewell":
Science and Transformation

The reasons given for the fairies' leaving or diminution were, as I have already indicated, numerous. Additional factors—things such as electrification, which caused change in ordinary lives—played in as well.[16] All altered the pattern of rural life, discouraging night visits with close neighbors and the telling of local tales. In this sense, the industrial revolution and the technology that had vitalized the fairy races also forced them to migrate to greener pastures. The Victorians did not cease to wonder, though it is true that the factories with their astonishing machines became new fairy palaces (not always in the ironic way in which they are used by Dickens in *Hard Times*), and true that people wondered at new miracles of science, instead of the old ones of fairy faith. Sabine Baring-Gould, for example, sadly comments that in his lifetime

> belief in the existence of pixies, elves, gnomes, has melted away; and in its place a door has been opened, disclosing to our astonished eyes a whole bacterial world, swarming with microbes, living, making love, fighting. . . . Titania and Robin Goodfellow have been replaced by the Schizophyta and the Baccilli. (*Early Reminiscences*, p. 20)[17]

Perhaps predictably, while some made the departure of the fairies a symbolic center in the lament for the passing of the good old ways, others sought to incorporate the fairies into new rational and scientific modes of thought.

Long before the attempts to authenticate the Cottingley fairy photos, members of the Society for Psychical Research had been investigating related supernatural phenomena including fairylike poltergeists. Many outside the society applauded the scientific verification of such creatures, the rendering of them factual; some viewed the enterprise with mixed emotions. Commenting in the *Dublin University Magazine* in 1879 on W. F. Barrett's essay on poltergeists, "The Demons of Derrygonelly," the editor praises the factuality—the believability—of the account but suggests a certain ambivalence about its broader ramifications:

> What a change in the last twenty years! The weird legends of our childhood are vanishing; their superstitious glamour, which we are both glad and sorry to lose, is being replaced by the conscientiously gathered minutiae of the scientific investigators. . . . This scientific age is realistic in its ghost stories. Mr. Wallace catches a small sprite at work in a hinged slate; Mr. Crookes photographs one by the electric light. . . . When the haunts of the "Krakens" of the supernatural are found, science will have some fun and we may expect some good stories." (p. 696)

While some did not applaud, finding scientific thought an adversary to the fairy faith, others, like this editor, tried to reconcile the two.

Algernon Blackwood, for example, blames the foolishly scientific mind (in *A Prisoner in Fairyland,* 1913) for not recognizing that the two views "ought to run in harness" as "opposite interpretations of the universe" (p. 59). For, without belief, without the fairy faith, "all the tenderness seems leaking out of life" (p. 59). Sabine Baring-Gould agrees, regretting the loss of his own belief in the elfin peoples as well as the world's.[18] Less tolerantly, Lady Archibald Campbell suggests that a foolish preoccupation with other planets has prevented scientists from seeing what is right before their eyes:

> We wait for a system of signs and signals that shall enable us to correspond with Mars. Yet Mars is further off than the enchanted hills, the canals sound dull compared to the green and purple Hills of Peace where among the Riders of the Shee the boundless deer and roe pass on immortal in twos and twos." ("The Men of Peace," p. 39)

Although some in the human community tried to reconcile the fairies with science and technology,[19] most recognized that, at least according to tradition, elves and fairies do not like or live in technologically advanced and urbanized environments. Only occasionally were they seen in or near urban centers. F. Hindes Groome, chronicler of gypsy lore, tells of a gypsy boy's encounter with the fairies at the Edinburgh Electrical Exhibition of 1890. The boy "saw two dear little teeny people," and promptly stoned them, only to be cautioned by a policeman, "Don't, they're fairies" ("Influence of Gypsies," p. 301). But the "teeny people" promptly vanished. As a character remarks in Graham Robertson's *Pinkie and the Fairies,* the elfin peoples don't like town and never enter it; the "Horns of Elfland, all are drowned/By the motors' hoots" (p. 27). Nora Hopper, commemorating "Joan O' the Wad," queen of the pixies,[20] notes that while Joan, a fairy *femme fatale,* has deserted her native countryside and been lured to "the deep-walled town" (p. 361), she may herself be destroyed there: "A live flame caged and in dusk shut down" (p. 362).

Lord Dunsany's tale "The Kith of the Elf-Folk" (1908) perhaps best encapsulates the traumas of the elfin peoples as they faced the modern scientific and industrial world. In this ironic version of Hans Christian Andersen's "The Little Mermaid," a "Wild Thing" ("somewhat human in appearance, only all brown of skin and barely two feet high," *Sword of Welleron*, p. 24) chooses to leave the marshes of East Anglia and enter human civilization. Drawn to the music and ritual of the cathedral, she willingly gives up fairy immortality and uninterrupted joy to gain an imitation soul—one she must find a mortal to take from her should she change her mind. She is transformed to a young, beautiful woman, helped first by a farm couple who think her a lost gypsy and then by the dean of the cathedral, who names her Mary Jane Rush. When, moved by the preaching of a young curate, she naively tells him that she loves him, she is sent away to "a great manufacturing city of the Midlands, where work had been found for her in a cloth factory" (p. 33). Rejected by the religious community, she is now placed in a soul-destroying industrial town.

Here, in a factory world where all is made by machinery but without beauty, the world against which John Ruskin and William Morris protested, she is forced to work a twelve-hour day. Her job is to tend the mechanical thread maker that has displaced the human hands of skilled workers—to pick up the ends of threads broken by the machine and then to reinsert them. She cannot survive in this murky, gray urban world of stench and noise and aniline dye: "All here was ugly; even the green wool as it whirled round and round was neither the green of the grass nor yet the green of the rushes, but a sorry muddy green that befitted a sullen city under a murky sky" (*Sword of Welleron*, p. 34). Thus she decides to offer her soul to a human recipient and return to the marshes. But she can find no taker in the factory town, for "all the poor have souls. It is all they have" (p. 35). Although she is finally freed by her power to sing (her song of lamentation is heard by an impressario; she becomes an opera singer, and finds in the only member of the audience unmoved by her music a recipient for her soul), the emphasis is on the impossibility of life in the modern human world. What use is it, Dunsany implies in a brilliant inversion of the biblical aphorism, if one loses the world to gain a soul?

For the sophisticated—and for the many nationalists among the Celts—the fairy faith was something worth preserving. For some, including writers of fiction like Dunsany, the neopaganism it implied was liberating; to believe or half-believe in fairies was, by the turn of the century, an expression of revolt against complex urbanized society, so tightly conscious of its manners and morals. Moreover, such a faith was a response to the conflict between society's demand for respectability and conformity and the forces of demonic energy that lie beneath the surface of human nature. Conservatives and radicals alike could find in such belief a cogent criticism of the age. For most it was an oblique form of social protest, implying as it did a rebellion against statistics and measuring, a liberation from the ordinary quantifications of logic.

For ordinary folk in the less urbanized parts of the British Isles, belief in fairies was even more important. As Gramsci says, folklore and folk belief constitutes "a religion of the people which functions in opposition to 'official' conceptions of the world" (pp. 188–89)—those of the intelligentsia, the church, and the state. In the British Isles it contested the hegemony of orthodox, organized religion; it gave the people an alternative belief and a private system of knowledge. In Wales, for example (said Hugh Evans in *The Gorse Glen*), the fairy faith was an aid to cultural survival. The ordinary Welsh of the nineteenth century were a persecuted underclass who spoke the Welsh tongue and were often dissenters. Their landlords, on the other hand, spoke English and the established church filled with pro-landlord, English-speaking parsons had little contact with and sympathy for them. Not only the Welsh sustained themselves through fairy faith in various forms. Rural peoples all over the British Isles found in it a separate belief and private knowledge—something they did not have to share with oppressors or repressors, whether represented by the church, the government, or standardized education. For the Irish it remained "a secret kingdom," while fairies themselves were made into a kind of peasant nobility.

Perhaps this will to believe explains the fact that fairy sightings, especially of such species as mermaids, did not radically decline toward the end of the nineteenth century and the turn of the twentieth. Numerous memorates, testimonies of belief, punctuate the pages of journals such as *Light* and *The Occult Review*, many by clergymen or by people described as "sober, thrifty, unimaginative" (J.H.C., p. 197). The Deerness Mermaid, who appeared in Newark Bay for two or three summers during the 1890s, was supposedly seen by hundreds of sightseers. She was still being sighted in the 1920s. As late as 1959, in county Mayo, the fairies could still cause the rerouting of a public road (see the *Daily Mail*, 23 April 1959). Twenty-five laborers went on strike rather than destroy a fairy palace in the proposed route and, after consultation, the community changed the direction of the road.

Many were persuaded that the trows did not leave Orkney and the Shetland Isles at all. One of the most convincing of the memorates states that a man named W. E. Thorner of Luton, not identified as an occultist, witnessed them in the 1940s. Stationed on Hoy (the island where the last of the trows, the Dwarf of Hoy, ostensibly committed suicide) during World War II, he had been struggling along a cliff in the middle of the high winds so typical of the islands. As he looked down in the mist to retain his footing he was amazed to see that he "had the company of what appeared to be a dozen or more 'wild men' dancing about, to and fro. . . . These creatures were small in stature, but they did not have long noses nor did they appear kindly in demeanour. They possessed round faces, sallow in complexion, with long, dark bedraggled hair." Their dance was so wild that the speaker thought he "was a witness to some ritual dance of a tribe of primitive men" (Marwick, *Orkney and Shetland*, p. 38).

Another touching memorate, this time from the Scottish Isle of Skye, testifies to an abiding faith in the continuance of fairy life:

> Late in the nineteenth century a secret was entrusted to a small boy and his sister by an old couple who lived at Torrin, in Skye. The old folk had guarded it until the last moment when the husband was bedfast and the wife very frail, though still afoot. One summer evening she beckoned to the children and, without a word, led them away from her cottage over a range of low green hillocks towards the setting sun. . . . Just at sunset they reached the farthest hillock where the grass parted and . . . the fairy people came out. (Aitken, p. 135)

The children went home in silence, not comparing notes till the next morning, and then agreeing as to what they both had seen. The boy grew up to become a minister of the Church of Scotland and—feeling compelled to record his experience—put the incident on record in 1967.

The existence of numerous memorates such as these suggests that traditional belief has not been utterly destroyed. However, the relatively new hypotheses spawned by the Cottingley fairy photographs have received far more publicity. Interpreted by Theosophists and other believers, the fairy photographs have supperadded a "biological-psychical" theory of fairy existence to the older ideas. Adherents to this theory are somewhat numerous, though often regarded as eccentrics. Air Marshall Dowding, for example, recorded his experiences with the elfin peoples after World War II in *The Dark Star* (1951), a record of his posthumous conversations with those killed in the war. Echoing the Theosophist argument of Gardner and Hodson, the "naturalist" seers, he argues that "were it not for the work of Nature-spirits of various kinds, the vegetable kingdom would not exist, and without the vegetable there would be no animal or human kingdoms" (pp. 36–37). He agrees, too, with their basic description of fairies: in their normal state they are formless "blobs" of light, but they may at times appear humanoid. He even asserts their view of fairy evolution—fairies are not human but on their own line of development—while disagreeing with Leadbeater and others who argue that fairies evolved from the avian species. He finds it unlikely that "warm-blooded creatures, who have developed to the stage of sexual and mother-love with capacity for thought, and elementary reasoning powers, should undergo a process of apparent retrogression" (p. 39). In his eyes, fairy life is lower than bird life.

Visiting Slieve Inish, Dowding speculates about gnomes while expressing concern about their power. Since they can "possess" and control human beings, he believes them dangerous. Linking demonic influence and medicine, he also believes that gnome influence is responsible for the abundance of "demented and simple-minded people" (p. 233) in the area. Likening possession by gnomes to "sexual perversion on another plane" (p. 233), he protests that it is not right that two different lines of evolution meet, and he predicts that a struggle for control will ensue. He fears that the area will become "a battlefield between gnomes, fairies and man" (p. 234).

At the Bottom of the Garden

Similar statements about similar forms of fairy life, many influenced by the statements of Gardner and Hodson, have been recorded in other parts of the British Isles, most spectacularly in northern Scotland. "Biological-psychical" fairies are responsible for the "Magic of Findhorn" (in the 1975 book of the same name by Paul Hawken), that mystical commune in northern Scotland "where the elemental world of plants and animals co-operate with fairies, elves, and gnomes in creating a land where nothing is impossible and legends are reborn" (p. 1). Here, their effect is said to have helped create a beautiful garden at a latitude farther north than Moscow and Alaska and allowed mortal gardeners to grow forty-two-pound cabbages and sixty-pound broccoli, as well as sixty-five varieties of vegetables and twenty-one kinds of fruit in arid, cold, and sandy soil.

The miracle of Findhorn, much publicized in the 1970s, is ascribed to Peter and Eileen Caddy, but it was others in their commune who directly interacted with various devas and fairies. Indeed, contact with the fairies or nature spirits, the actual builders and makers of specific plants—and their overlord, Pan, the great force of universal energy—was first made by "Roc," Robert Ogilivie Crombie, in 1966. A later meeting with Pan, this time on the sacred isle of Iona, led to what the commune describes as a "sort of reconciliation between the Nature kingdom and man" (p. 138), despite man's cruel ransacking and destroying of the natural world. Through Pan, Roc could see the elfin peoples: "myriads of beings—elementals, nymphs, dryads, fauns, elves, gnomes, fairies—far too numerous to catalogue . . . [who] varied in size from tiny beings a fraction of an inch in height . . . to beautiful elfin creatures three or four feet tall" (p. 139).

Another Findhornian, Dorothy Maclean, received a spiritual message telling her "to cooperate in the garden by thinking about the Nature Spirits . . . [including] the spirits of the clouds, of rain, of the separate vegetables" (p. 112). Her basically Theosophical orientation led her to communicate with both a great "landscape angel," the overlord of the whole geographical area, and the individual "beings of light" or devas who are archetypal thoughts and energies and the essences and forms of given species. Each specific deva taught her about its species; through these angelic designers, she learned, for instance, how to grow tomatoes in a cold climate. As each new species of plant entered the garden, Dorothy's role was to welcome it by contacting its individual guardian. Thus, specialized and benevolent fairies made the Findhorn garden grow.

The Findhornians' explanation of the appearance and function of these nature fairies is again in accord with Conan Doyle's, Gardener's, and Hodson's theories. In their essential state fairies are "light bodies"—nebulous vortices of colored light of different sizes and intensities; however, they can assume many "thought forms" and appear personified in various supernatural guises.[21] Their primary functions are as agents of growth.

However, as members of the commune recognized, the fairies were increasingly angered by human disregard for ecology and the environment. An encounter in a ruined fairy glen with warrior elves revealed their rage and issued in an ecological warning for human beings. An elf king voiced the fairies' reasons for their enmity to humans and threatened mortals with another, more serious fairy farewell; "You upset the balance of nature, destroy the animals, turn land to desert, cut and burn the large trees, maim the landscape, blasting great wounds in the hills and mountains, slashing the living earth so that it will not heal" (p. 151), began the accusation. It ended with a threat: the fairies are immortal; mortals cannot destroy them, but they, warned the elf king, can easily destroy the human race, by making the "vital force in all that grows . . . cease" (p. 153). Despite elfin cooperation in the Findhorn garden (where the gardeners have even left a "wild area" as a sanctuary for the fairies), the deep interspecies rift has not been healed. The elfin peoples have withdrawn from many farms and gardens and now mainly haunt the wilds. Their total absence, their ultimate farewell to humans could—we are reminded—end us.

Other recent accounts, like Dora van Gelder's *The Real World of Fairies* (ostensibly written in the 1920s but not published until 1977), present less menacing creatures but preach much the same ecological message.[22] Polluting the air and ravaging the water and soil of the earth will lead both to the destruction of the fairies and the diminution of human well-being. Dame Branwen, herself a supernatural, offers a more powerful version of the same ecological warning to Morgan Spider, queen of the Welsh fairies, in "Visitors to a Castle" (1977), one of Sylvia Townsend Warner's brilliant fictional studies of fairy lore.[23] In this tale set in the 1890s, Warner's fairies predict their own demise. Dame Branwen's vision is one of elfin diminuition and extinction caused by pollution and the hostile environment of the modern world. "I saw trees blighted and grass burned brown and birds falling out of the sky. . . . I saw," she reports, "the last fairy dying like a scorched insect" (*Kingdom of Elfin*, p. 102).

But the "biological-psychic" strand of fairy faith with its admonitions about ecology is only one, though perhaps the best known, among many beliefs. Some contemporary believers, like Janet and Colin Bord in *The Secret Country* (1978), place fairies in other paranormal theoretical structures. They connect the tribes of elfin with the ley lines, mysterious paths that overlie magnetic currents that flow through the earth. The Bords suggest, for example, that widespread beliefs in fairy paths are actually degenerated folk memories of the actual leys, and that the reason fairies are attracted to ancient sites of all kinds is because the sites themselves were built on leys. Others, including Lynn Picknett and Joe Cooper, connect the fairies to the concept of the Cosmic Joker. Fairies as fertility figures play a role in the revival of Wicca and in the new and often feminist perpetuation of the worship of the great Earth Mother. Recently, another tribe of elfins has been implicated in the strange rings, swirls, and patterns mysteriously appearing in the summer grain fields of the British Isles.

While the more traditional fairies show signs of continuing life in Ireland and Scotland—at least according to a recent collection of lore by distinguished folklorists edited by Peter Narváez (*The Good People*, 1991)[24]—new and different elfin species are continually being invented or discovered. The gremlins (who cause trouble in aviation) are among the products of the twentieth century; stemming from the perceptions of World War II Royal Air Force pilots, they are blamed for otherwise inexplicable airplane failures and crashes. Fairies, like mortals, have been touched by new technologies: now when they speak, their voices sound like tape recordings played at too fast a speed. Believers are already speculating that the recent mysterious computer viruses are new, submicroscopic species of the elfin world.

Meanwhile, science fiction has transmuted fairies to the small green men from outer space. As Edmund Little suggests in *The Fantasts* (1984), the world of faerie industrialized and rendered technological becomes the realm of science fiction: "The machine replaces magic, technical jargon the spell or incantation, and the wizard acquires a labcoat to be called a scientist" (p. 8). Moreover, the adult fantasies so popular in the 1980s and '90s (some scientifically based and future-oriented, others closer to "pure" fantasy) serve in ways similar to those of the fairy tales we read as children. They, too, provide symbols for the starved imagination and create a unifying mythos for our time; they, too, provide remedies for tired postmoderns, weary of realism, and can function as vehicles for social protest or as quasi-religious reassurances of a peopled universe.

Equally significant, contemporary UFOlogists argue that the fairies really *are* the little green men—alien creatures from outer space who have come to join us. The connections between fairies and aliens are made explicit in such works as Whitley Strieber's memorate, *Communion* (1987). Unfortunately, his encounters with these intruders in his psyche are primarily occasions of terror. While he cannot tell his readers exactly what the creatures are, he repeatedly sees them as analogous to grotesque fairies. Too small to be human, about three and a half feet tall (the height most witnesses assign to fairies) and smaller boned and lighter than children, they have the fairy power of glamour and can give the fairy stroke. They often carry little lights, like the fairy lights or stones that glow in traditional folklore. They move rapidly and appear to vanish, though Strieber can hear their tiny, scampering feet. Their workers, characterized by a sort of hive mentality, are reminiscent, even to their blue garments, of kobolds,

6.4 A New Age fairy, book jacket for Whitley Strieber, *Communion* (London: Arrow Books, 1988).

the dwarflike miners of folklore. The creatures' high-pitched whistling voices and rapid alien speech all add to their fairylike effect.

In addition, their leaders, larger in size and marked by huge almond-shaped eyes, use wands to read minds and to cause terror or "panic." And their queen is a sort of fairy *femme fatale*, though contact with her is more of a rape than a seduction. Streiber is even taken to a strange round room in an incident that reminds him of the abductions of Connla and others. And, he speculates, these creatures may very well be from earth itself.

Strieber suggests that the ancientness of fairy lore indicates that the creatures with whom he has unwillingly communed have been with humans for more than the forty or fifty years since they took on their present appearance. Alternatively, he wonders if they are true aliens simply masquerading as creatures from our folklore. Perhaps, he speculates (borrowing from Theosophy), they are the "thought forms" of our era, emerging from our unconscious minds and taking actual shape to haunt us. Perhaps, on the other hand, they are an actual species, now utilizing unidentified flying objects because they too "have enjoyed their own technological revolution" (p. 110).

Whatever they are, "Something is out there, and it wants in" (p. 242). Streiber's book ends on an uncertain note:

Maybe there really is another species living upon this earth, the fairies, the gnomes, the sylphs, vampires, goblins, who attach to reality along a different line than we do, but who know and love us as we do the wild things of the woods . . . who, perhaps, are trying to save us from ourselves, or whose lives are inextricably linked to our own. (p. 248)

But he cannot affirm this speculation, either. All he knows is that "they" —whatever their identity and purpose—are here and must be investigated.

Thus, as the fairies continue to metamorphose in the time-honored fashion, assuming new forms or varying their old shapes, they retain their power to fascinate. They have made the fortunes of popular writers like Colin Wilson who, in a series of best-sellers of the 1980s (*Mysteries, The Occult, The Supernatural*), has argued that the spirits (and the fairies) are potent and omnipresent. They have made the best-seller list in books like Nancy Arrowsmith's *A Field Guide to the Fairies* (1977) and in variations on it like Wil Huygen's *Gnomes* (1977). They have figured in contemporary fantasy, in the romances of J. R. R. Tolkien and the many works derived from them, in the fantasies for adolescents of Jane Yolen and Ursula LeGuin, in the strange imaginative stories of Sylvia Townsend Warner and the tales of Tanith Lee, as well as in the haunting novels and short stories of Angela Carter.[25]

John Robertson, the eminent folklorist, reports that, when he was a child an old woman told him "the fairies only left . . . when folk stopped seekin' them" (qtd. in Marwick, *An Orkney Anthology*, p. 279). She did not mean, he says, that feeling lonely or neglected they had gone elsewhere but that the actual fading of belief signaled their extinction. Revitalized, transmitted as part of our cultural legacy from our Victorian forebears, the fairies are still with us and so, too, is our fascination with them. In a postmodern world that does not speak of "the reality" but of "realities," the need remains to half-believe another race just might live side by side with mortals. Perhaps we do not wish to be alone. Thus, the "hidden people," strange and secret, always leaving us yet never gone, have simply used their everlasting "glamour" to transform themselves once more.

NOTES

Introduction

1. Michael R. Booth lists and briefly describes some of the spectacular pantomimes (pp. 74–89) and the glittering Victorian theatrical representations of Shakespeare's so-called fairy plays—*A Midsummer Night's Dream* and *The Tempest*. It is worth noting that both plays spawned fairy illustrations as well as fairy paintings. *The Tempest* was illustrated by Birkett Foster and Gustave Doré in 1860; by R. A. Bell in 1901; Walter Crane in 1902, and Edmund Dulac in 1908. *A Midsummer Night's Dream* was illustrated by J. Moyr Smith in 1892, Bell in 1895, and Arthur Rackham in 1908 (p. 38).

2. See, for example, the fairy pottery of Daisy Makieg-Jones in the Victoria and Albert Museum.

3. Eliot even refers to a "favorite red volume" from which Mary's sister Letty has taught her elders the story (p. 641). Interestingly, Eliot changes Taylor's softened ending—in which Rumplestiltskin must use two hands to pull out his foot (once the queen has discovered his name)—back to the more brutal German original in which the dwarf is unable to retrieve his leg and thus tears himself apart.

4. Coleridge's "Christabel," Keats's "La Belle Dame sans Merci" (discussed in the text), and Shelley's "Queen Mab" were among the poems often cited by Victorian folklorists. But there were others, now forgotten, that were almost as popular. Thomas Hood contributed many works, including "Queen Mab"; Tom Moore's popular Irish melodies included a number based on Irish lore; Felicia Hemans wrote several fairy lyrics including the "Fairies' Recall," "Fairy Favours," "Water Lilies," and "Fairy Song"; L. E. L. (Letitia Elizabeth Landon) contributed "The Fairy Queen

Sleeping," "Fairies on the Sea-Shore," and "Fantasies." Scott's *Minstrelsy of the Scottish Border* may have been the most popular collection of all.

5. The passage continues: "The stories that were invented concerning this people, passing through the mouths of so many ignorant relators, would soon acquire all the degrees of the marvelous, of which they were susceptible. Thus the dwarfs soon became . . . the forgers of enchanted armour. . . . They were possessed of caverns, full of treasure entirely at their own disposal" (Mallet 2:42).

6. For more on supernatural dwarfs, see chapter 4. Like the White Lady, Fenella is a composite figure derived from the traits of various supernatural creatures. Scott offers both natural and supernatural interpretations of her character and behavior, in effect allowing his readers to choose which to believe; Fenella, however, is barely plausible either as a woman or a fairy.

7. Cunningham ascribed one of his fairy poems, "We Were Sisters, We Were Seven," to an old peasant woman, another more important one, "The Mermaid of Galloway," to one Jean Walker, a young girl from the area. "We Were Sisters . . ." is a fake fragment, notable for using "Billi Blin," the Scottish brownie (and John Milton's "lubber fiend") as its *deus ex machina*. "The Mermaid . . .," anthologized and reprinted throughout the century, amply borrows from "Sir Patrick Spens" but effectively utilizes folk belief. Cunningham's mermaid, singing, combing her golden hair, and luring and destroying a handsome young bridegroom (identified in Cunningham's notes as one William Maxswell, Esquire, of Cowehill) is authentic in lacking a specific motive for her act. Her murder of her victim is ingenious: she knots his hair in elflocks and binds a lock of her own hair around his brow, simultaneously enchanting, burning, and throttling him before she bears him out to sea. His reappearance as an apparition, cold and wet, to his rightful bride is particularly effective and may well be the source of the similar, strange ending of William Morris's mysterious poem, "The Blue Closet" (1858).

8. Both the story and the poem are major sources of J. M. Barrie's play *Mary Rose* (1920). Mary Rose's first disappearance is when she is eleven and she, too, is found under a tree and can give no account of what has happened. A popular novel of 1870 called *Kilmeny* by William Black uses the poem as the subject of a painting, and suggests how popular the poem still was by allusions to it. Jane Brown, however, in Hogg's incident (one he clearly believes), has a peculiar trait, probably inherited from Ralph of Coggeshall's "green children." Hogg tells us that "her skin had acquired a bluish cast," which gradually went away. He also tells another anecdote of an old man, Walter Dagleish, for whom Hogg's father helped to search. He too returned after twenty days, believing that he had been gone for years. Unlike Jane, who lived to a ripe old age, Dagleish ate human food, fainted, and died a few weeks later, without speaking intelligibly (2:32n).

9. It is worth noting that, while the romantics were deeply interested in fairies, they were even more preoccupied with "larger," more cosmic forces—Wordsworthian "powers," Shelleyian *anima mundis*, deities of every nation and denomination. The nineteenth-century conflict between two views of reality, the material and the spiritual, was still in its youth. Moreover, the romantics were not quite as threatened as the Victorians were to be by the thought that—human presence excepted—the universe might be totally empty.

10. Among these works are *Oberon; or The Charmed Horn* (1826); *The Gnome King; An Elfin Freak* (1819); and *Oberon, or Huon de Bordeaux: A Mask in 5 Acts*, by William Sotheby (1802), really a translation of the original. Most important was *Oberon: A Romantic and Fairy Opera in Three Acts*, by J. R. Planche (1826) with its music by Weber.

11. Thomas Carlyle, for example, translated one of E. T. A. Hoffmann's most famous (and important) tales, "Der goldnes Topf" ("The Golden Flowerpot") and

Thackeray translated another ("The History of Krakatuk"). Other Victorians, including Major Alexander Ewing and J. T. Bealby, translated other of the Hoffmann tales as well as some of those of Novalis, Tieck, and Brentano. The influence of German romantic literary fairy tales on such figures as George MacDonald is considerable.

12. Among the major fairy paintings derived from *A Midsummer Night's Dream* (many others are discussed later in this book) are David Scott, *Puck Fleeing Before the Dawn* (1837); Richard Dadd's *Puck*; Robert Huskisson's *The Midsummer Night's Fairies*, Sir Joseph Noel Paton's late canvas, *Oberon watching a Mermaid* (1883); Edwin Landseer's *Titania and Bottom*; and John Simmons' oil paintings and watercolors of Titania, standing, sleeping, resting, sitting.

Tempest paintings include Joseph Severn's two versions of *Ariel* (riding a bat), John Everett Millais's famous Pre-Raphaelite *Ariel* (1849), and John Anster Fitzgerald's less well-known version. There is also David Scott's *Ariel and Caliban*. Other scenes ostensibly but less directly derived from *The Tempest* include Dadd's *Come unto these Yellow Sands*, and Richard Doyle's *The Enchanted Tree*.

13. Another *Titania and the Fairies* was commissioned by Lord Egremont with his family as its subjects. The Titania here is not as seductive as Lady Hamilton who is, perhaps, a source of Fuseli's fairy courtesan image.

14. His portrait of *Perdita* (1875–76) from *The Winter's Tale* introduces fairies, not because the old shepherd in the previous scene mentions "fairy gold" or because the fairies participate in Perdita's fate (Tate, p. 60) but because she sits dreaming. Hence Queen Mab, the bringer of dreams, rests near her and fairy creatures hover protectively over her. A painting of *Mamillius in Charge of a Lady of the Court* (1875–76), derived from the same play, "invents" in a similar way. Here, the child's promise to tell a tale of "sprites and goblins" (II,1) is visually rendered while its setting is moved outdoors from a wintery room in Leontes' palace to a summery, fairy-filled world of nature.

15. Among his other important Shakespearean fairy paintings are *Cobweb* from *A Midsummer Night's Dream*, again a portrait of Queen Mab leading her ape-faced incubus (the figure from the *Nightmare*) on a chain, while Cobweb stands holding a feather broom and Puck flies overhead; a later addition to the *Midsummer Night's Dream* paintings (1793–94) called *Oberon Squeezes the Flower on Titania's Eyelids*; yet another of the awakening, *Titania Awakes, Surrounded by Attendant Fairies, Clinging Rapturously to Bottom, Still Wearing the Ass's Head*, a *Tempest* drawing of "Ariel Driving in Trinculo, Stephano and Caliban," and the interesting *Queen Katherine's Dream* from *Henry VIII*, which Fuseli also peoples with fairy forms.

16. See the Tate Gallery's Fuseli catalogue, pp. 61–63, and Philpotts, *Fairy Paintings*, p. 14, for these interpretations.

17. How much Sir Joseph Noel Paton borrowed from Fuseli becomes obvious when one places the parallel Paton paintings *The Quarrel of Oberon and Titania* and *The Reconciliation*, side by side with Fuseli's works.

18. In addition to the important *The Shepherd's Dream* from *Paradise Lost* designed for the Milton Gallery, Fuseli painted an almost equally famous *Faery Mab* (1793) eating her junkets, derived from "L'Allegro," and a splendid Lubber Fiend, also from "L'Allegro," to be compared with Blake's *Goblin*. He executed a series of paintings for *Oberon*, including *Scherasmin and Huon Flee from Oberon*, *Titania Shows Amanda her New-born Son in the Grotto*, and *Titania Finds the Magic Ring on the Beach* (1804–5). And he did an *Undine* series, quite late (in 1821), including *Undine Comes to the Fisherman's Hut*, *Undine Displeased Leaves the Fisherman's Hut*, *Kühleborn startles Bertalda*, and *The Ghost of Undine Emerging from the Well*.

19. Belinda's neck, encircled by a thin red thread that shows vividly against her remarkable pallor, adds to the deathlike quality, as does the presence of the owl— symbol of sleep and death— in the right-hand corner of the painting.

20. Among the private fantasies are, of course, the various versions of *The Nightmare*, with its incubus and mare; another non-Shakespearean oil, misnamed *Titania's Dream*, in which fairies watch a sleeping woman; an interesting early pencil and watercolor drawing of *The Changeling* (1780) (see chapter 2) filled with figures derived from folklore; and the visionary *Ladies of Hastings*, inexplicable except that one has a sense that the male figure in the dunes is looking up at supernatural beings, perhaps elementals, who—despite their calm—are members of the fairy rout, or Herodias or Diana's rout, bringers of storm or evil.

21. Though Blake's fairy poems were virtually unknown during his lifetime, his fairy paintings were, at least, accessible. In Blake's poems "The Fairy," "A fairy skipd upon my knee," and in *Europe*, whose fairy serves as muse and dictates the poem, elfin creatures are associated with the natural or the creative joys. In the poems "William Bond" and "Long John Brown," from the Pickering manuscript, they are associated with sexual pleasure and, in the last-mentioned poem, used as euphemisms for sexual parts. Fairies are also present in Blake's *Milton* and in *The Song of Los*. For a specific and useful study of Blake's use of supernatural figures, see John Adlard's *The Sports of Cruelty*.

22. See also *Oberon and Titania Reclining (on a Lily)* in *The Song of Los*; and *Il Penseroso*. See also the illustrations to *Night Thoughts*, where fairies appear to be symbols of time and of poetic clichés.

23. Romantics also deeply influenced Victorian book illustration. The master in this area was George Cruikshank, who dominated Victorian fairy illustration for several decades. He illustrated most of the important texts the Victorians used, adding his witty and sometimes grotesque figures to Croker's *Fairy Legends*, Keightley's *Fairy Mythology*, and the first English edition of the Grimms' tales, Edgar Taylor's *German Popular Tales* (1823). His brilliant etchings of minute creatures and richly detailed accounts of their activities, as well as his personal knowledge of folklore, influenced many who came after him (especially Richard Doyle). Few Victorian fairy illustrators were untouched by his work. He also published his own *Fairy Library* (1853—64) and rewrote popular tales like "Cinderella" to preach abstinence from alcohol and, in general, to moralize folklore.

Chapter 1

1. Thoms wrote a column on folklore for *The Athenaeum* under the pseudonym of Ambrose Merton.

2. For Æ, see Eglinton, pp. 15—16; for Sharp, see Tuohy, p. 147. See also Kennedy, p. 114; Lady Gregory, *Visions and Beliefs*, I:15; Lady Wilde, p. 259; for Hyde, see Evans-Wentz, p. 25.

3. For two slightly different versions of the account, see Baring-Gould, *Early Reminiscences*, pp. 18—19, and *A Book of Folk-Lore*, pp. 198—200.

4. See, for example, Charles C. Smith's, "Fairies at Ilkley Wells," pp. 229—31. It is an account of fairies seen earlier at the "Wells" or thermal baths by one William Butterfield, described as "honest, truthful, and steady." See also such accounts as a "Tale of Anglesey," a report on the fairies of East Yorkshire who were seen dancing by an informant, p. 132. More predictably, such later publications as *Light* (the Spiritualist newspaper) and *The Occult Review* regularly published mediumistic or firsthand or, at least, "believed" accounts of fairy sightings.

5. For a recent account of the "luck," see Marjorie Rowling, *The Folk Lore of the Lake District*, pp. 86—89; for an earlier account of this popular legend, see Scott, *Minstrelsy*, p. 322.

6. For a summary of currently held views on fairies as the dead, see K. M. Briggs,

Fairies in Tradition and Literature, pp. 141–42. There are, in addition, other reasons for this belief related by Victorian folklorists. Briggs is right in suggesting that in the north of England and the Scottish Lowlands the belief in fairies as the dead predominates (p. 149), but the idea is found all over the British Isles and the fairies are often linked to specific groups of the dead. In Wales, the tylwyth teg are thought of as the souls of Druids, for example, and on the Isle of Man, as those who perished in Noah's flood. The pixies of Cornwall were thought of as souls of the region's prehistoric inhabitants; as the souls got older, they became smaller and would eventually vanish.

Moreover, certain types of fairies had specific associations with the dead; Irish banshees, with their function as premonitory apparitions and their wailing for the dead, are the best known variety, but there are others as well. Significantly, first Evans-Wentz and later Lewis Spence argue that the fairies are a special category of the dead in a different sense—that is, they are "the spirits of the departed who awaited rebirth or reincarnation." Spence believes that the worship of the fairies as the dead lasted until quite late historically and that the fairies were worshiped at tumuli.

7. This is not to argue that folklorists and proto-anthropologists did not speculate on social evolution long before Darwin. The idea of a progression from savagery to civilization is present or implied in eighteenth-century thought and probably earlier, as is the idea that different races develop at different speeds.

8. Interestingly, Tylor took a euhemerist or "realist" position on fairy origins, believing "that some of the myths of giants and dwarfs are connected with traditions of real indigenous or hostile tribes" (1:385). He commented that, although it was difficult to determine how far preternatural creatures in folklore derived from "elves, or gnomes, or such like nature-spirits" and how far from "human beings in [their] mythic aspect," it was "impossible not to recognize the element derived from the aborigines" (1:385–86) of a given land.

9. Some folklorists were quite explicit about the importance of their studies to the welfare of the empire. E. S. Hartland, the president of the Folk-Lore Society, for example, announces in *Mythology and Folktales* (1900) that "to govern a subject people properly, it is necessary to understand them." To teach savage people "higher religion and a higher morality, to impose upon barbarians the laws of a higher civilization, you must first penetrate their modes of thought" (pp. 14–15); he suggests that the best way of doing this is by knowing their folklore.

10. Andrews even described these builders of the raths and souterrains of Ireland. Allied to the modern Lapps, they "rode on ponies, were good musicians, could spin and weave, and grind corn. The tradition would point to their being red-haired" (p. 12).

11. I have taken the liberty of appropriating the title of the article by Sir Harry Johnston, K.C.B., in the *Pall Mall Magazine* 26 (Jan–April 1902). The article itself is cited in chapter 4.

12. This clipping from the vertical file of the Conan Doyle Collection of the Toronto Metropolitan Library is identified only by its headline: "British Columbia: Fairies are bright blue in the hop fields and silvery green elsewhere." It is, however, from about 1923, and from a Canadian newspaper.

Chapter 2

An earlier form of this chapter, called "The Child That Went with the Fairies," was given as a paper at the CUNY Graduate Center Conference on Victorian Popular Culture in 1989. It thus predates the useful articles in Narváez's *The Good People* of 1991. However, valuable material from both Susan Schoon Eberly and Joyce Underwood Munro's articles has been added to it. I am indebted to both.

1. My reading of folklore published during the period reveals hundreds of tales of those abducted, whether for a year and a day, seven years, or a lifetime, included in the category of changeling tales. There are additional, numerous tales of "The Fairy Midwife," "Fairy Nurse" or "Fairy Ointment"—that is, tales of mortal women temporarily abducted or lured to fairyland to help fairy women deliver their off-spring. Contrary to popular belief, all varieties of these tales were found not only in Wales, Ireland, Cornwall, and the Scottish Highlands—the Celtic "pockets" of the British Isles—but also all over England itself.

2. I have been unable to find Luther's original text, ostensibly but not actually in his *Table Talk*, and quoted by Southey, by Benjamin Thorpe in *Northern Mythology*, by William Henderson, by Canon J. A. MacCulloch, ad nauseam.

3. In 1989, Henry Glassie reported on a changeling narrative told to him by a friend of his, Peter Flanagan, of Ballymenone, Northern Ireland, who insisted that he had seen the changeling in question. "He described him as strangely and almost impossibly thin, very long feet, very long, thin legs, as though he weighed nothing at all. And he had a very strange appearance of being enormously ancient, despite the fact that he wasn't. That is, he was a man of perhaps thirty years old who would have looked like he was ninety-five. And he sat in the fire, literally in the fire right next to the fire, and played with the stuff in the fire"(p. 520). Glassie's point is that Peter, an intelligent, educated, twentieth-century man, still believes in the reality of changelings and insists that he has seen one.

4. This interesting but mysterious anecdote is quoted by K. M. Briggs in her ar-ticle on "Fairies" for the *Encyclopedia of Occultism and Parapsychology* (1:308).

5. The *Cork Examiner*, which covered the trial and story in detail from 25 March to 30 March 1895, and from which I have taken most of my material, headlined it "The Tipperary Horror." E. F. Benson, on the other hand, describing the sensational tale for *The Nineteenth Century* in June 1895, labeled his piece "The Recent 'Witch-Burning' at Clonmel" (pp. 1053–1059).

6. This statement—with slight variations—is repeated throughout the trial by various witnesses. It is reported in the *Cork Examiner* of 27 March 1895, p. 7; 28 March, p. 5; 30 March, p. 5, and in the *Irish Times* of 27 March 1895, p. 5.

7. T. Gwynn Jones, the Welsh folklorist, provided a list of how the Welsh "got rid" of changelings in his *Welsh Folklore and Folk-Custom* (1930). The same methods, with local variations, were used throughout the British Isles: "to leave them without at-tention, to be cruel to them, to throw bits of iron at them; to place salt on a shovel, making the sign of the Cross over it, to open the window and hold the shovel over the fire until the salt was baked, or to bathe the infant in a solution of foxglove. Wizards were consulted in the matter, and these methods seem to have been sug-gested by them" (p. 69). Jones ends with a statement supporting his belief in the medical causation of changelingism and relevant to my argument later in this chapter, saying "One shudders at the thought of what the poor *cretin* had to suffer" (p. 69).

8. Rarely, however, does one read of incidents in which the abnormal child or altered woman becomes an accepted replacement and is reintegrated into the com-munity.

9. Among the works and figures relevant to my argument but not discussed in its body are Ainsworth's changeling in *The Tower of London* (1840), Pearl in Hawthorne's *The Scarlet Letter* (1850), and those who, in effect, descend from her, including Pru-dence, the accuser of Lois, in Elizabeth Gaskell's tale of the Salem witch trials, "Lois the Witch" (1859). A few of the numerous accounts of fairy kidnappings will be found in other chapters, especially chapter 5, while William Butler Yeats's early play *The Land of Heart's Desire* is also examined in chapter 5.

10. Earlier than Kipling, Wirt Sikes (*British Goblins*) had attacked the "creed of ignorance as regards changelings" (p. 57), commented on the barbaric tests to which they were subjected, and noted that many of their ostensible traits had to do with their treatment. Their voracious appetites, for example, were probably due to their not being fed in the first place. In Wales, at least, Sikes commented, a suspected changeling was "given an exceedingly frugal meal" (p. 58) to help banish it.

11. For Anster's "Fairy Child" (pp. 48–49) and Lover's "Fairy Boy" (p. 68), see Duffy, *The Ballad Poetry of Ireland*.

12. Yeats is truly preoccupied with fairy abductions, dealing with the theft of a bride in "The Host of the Air" and again in his play *The Land of Heart's Desire,* dealing with a whole set of kidnappings in his chapter on them in *Mythologies,* and examining them as a folklorist in a long essay called "Away," reprinted in his *Unpublished Prose.*

13. The most interesting twentieth-century tale utilizing the changeling motif is Sylvia Townshend Warner's "The One and the Other" in *Kingdoms of Elfin* (1978). Warner's brilliant understanding and use of folklore leads to irony in this story of two changed children. When the mortal child is expelled from fairyland because of his aging, it is the changeling who, in the name of scientific curiousity, heartlessly kills and anatomizes him.

14. The painting was begun in December 1861, resumed in September 1865, and finished in April 1867. It is presently at the Glasgow Art Gallery, Kelvingrove.

15. The fairies of the Isle of Man were especially known as abductors. Numerous tales exist in Manx folklore of men whose wives are taken and who are too cowardly or indifferent to get them back. The trows of Orkney were also particularly interested in young women. A recent folklorist (Marwick) notes that their eagerness for females is because they can only beget male children. One group of them, says Mrs. Saxby (quoted in Marwick, *Folklore of Orkney*), abducts and marries human wives, "and as soon as the baby-Trow is born the mother dies" (p. 34). Interestingly, George MacDonald knows and uses this motif in his first Curdie book, *The Princess and the Goblin* (1872).

16. In *Mary Rose*, J. M. Barrie's play of 1920, derived in part from Hogg's "Kilmeny" (see Introduction), Mary Rose is twice abducted by the fairies, once at the age of eleven, when she vanishes for twenty days after sitting under a fairy rowan tree on an isle in the Outer Hebrides, again when she returns there on her honeymoon. Her "otherness" takes the form of her inability to mature, her slowness in physical aging, and a certain mysterious, "elusive" unearthly quality about her.

17. Occultist though he was, Evans-Wentz was also psychological in his approach; he commented that although parents often thought the suspected changeling had altered in appearance, the real transformation was "a change in personality, as recognized by psychologists" (p. 250).

18. In *The Celtic Heritage*, Alwyn and Brinley Rees suggest that the changeling exoricism rituals are derived from pre-Christian baptismal rites whereby the human child was ritually exposed or expelled to separate it from being possessed by its mysterious other selves (p. 243). The suggestion here is that the "changeling [is] the personification of the other-worldly side of the human child's nature" (p. 253).

19. Twentieth-century folklorists have asked why the replacement offered to mortals was generally ancient and infirm. Was it, asks Hannah Aitken in *A Forgotten Heritage* (p. 4), because fairy mothers, who had difficulty in childbearing, were unwilling to part with their infants? Was it because fairies, like some actual tribes, expelled their useless citizens? Or did it come, as Aitken finds most probable, from a belief in reincarnation? If the original fairies were the spirits of the dead lingering near their former home, the wizened changeling might represent an ancestral spirit seeking reentry into the community.

20. I am indebted to Susan Schoon Eberly, "Fairies and the Folklore of Disability: Changelings, Hybrids, and the Solitary Fairy," in Narváez (pp. 227–50), for useful medical and psychological materials on the changeling phenomenon.

21. Monro, "The Invisible Made Visible: The Fairy Changeling as a Folk Articulation of Failure to Thrive in Infants and Children," in Narváez (pp. 251–83). Monro's argument, that changeling narratives really display children in unhappy or single-parent homes, does not pay sufficient attention to the physical transformations noted in the tradition. She does, however, comment accurately that folk tradition saw in these wretched, emaciated children what it took medicine much longer to see.

22. Von Sydow, one of the authorities cited by Yeats, believed that rickets, which at its onset appears to turn a healthy child suddenly into a deformed cripple, was often the culprit (quoted in Peter Alderson Smith, p. 142).

23. The failure of the changeling to grow, a motif common to the folklore figure, is interestingly illustrated by a Welsh anecdote retold in T. Gwynn Jones's *Welsh Folklore*: A child stolen in infancy by the fairies, managed to escape when he was twenty-one and returned to his home as a handsome young man. "He found the fairy was still of infant size, crying day and night" (p. 69). Using an unusual form of exorcism, he put a bridle around the changeling's head and used a whip on its body. The creature assumed the form of a horse and galloped away.

24. Peter Pan is a case in point. He is identified in the earliest version of the fantasy, *The Little White Bird in Kensington Garden* (1902), as half-bird, half-human. Though only one week old, he is ancient in knowledge yet incapable of growth or change. Like a senile old man or the ancient imp often used as a changeling, he is devoid of memory and of a sense of human time. His egoism and lack of humanity are increasingly depicted, and by the time of *When Wendy Grew Up* (1907), an epilogue to the play *Peter Pan* (1904), he can threaten to murder Wendy's child and does not even remember Hook. "I forget them after I kill them," he tells Wendy (*Wendy*, p. 26). Increasingly depicted as heartless and anarchic, he partakes less of Pan than of the Lord of Death—a borderland creature whose realm is appropriately the netherland.

25. I am indebted to Stephen Jay Gould's "Dr. Down's Syndrome" in *The Panda's Thumb*, pp. 133–39, for the discussion of Down's "Observations on an Ethnic Classification of Idiots." Dr. Down was medical superintendant of an asylum for idiots in Surrey when he published his observations, and his other examples of racial reversion are worth noting. At the bottom of his list, representing the most degenerate types, are "several well-marked examples of the Ethiopian variety . . . specimens of white negroes, although of European descent." Slightly higher are idiots who "arrange themselves around the Malay variety," while above them are those "who with shortened foreheads, prominent cheeks, deep-set eyes, and slightly apish noses" (p. 137) resemble the aboriginal Indians of America. Mongolian idiots are, ironically, at the top of his hierarchy, closer in their adulthood to white, Caucasian children than are the other categories.

26. In the same passage, Darwin states his agreement with Maudsley's statement that the bestiality of some of the insane stems from their "brute nature" (qtd. in *Expression of the Emotions*, p. 244)—that is, the lower animal nature within them.

27. Ultimately, Besant argues that nurture triumphs over heredity; the real failure in humanizing Humphrey lies with Lady Woodruffe, who has not loved and cannot love her changeling child. She becomes a metaphoric rendering of the selfish mother in the famous judgment of Solomon.

Chapter 3

An earlier version of this chapter was presented at The English Graduate Union of Columbia University and edited by Nina Auerbach for *Woman and Nation* (Fall 1987). I am also indebted to Auerbach's study of mermaids in *Woman and the Demon* (Cambridge, Mass.: Harvard University Press, 1982).

1. For more information on fairies in ballet, see Ivor Guest, *The Romantic Ballet in England.*

2. In *Swan Lake*, first performed in 1877, but made popular in 1895, the libretto functions to exonerate both the fairy queen and her mortal lover. Prince Siegfried, who goes to hunt swans, only to see them metamorphose into beautiful maidens, is tricked by the evil enchanter into believing Odile (the "Black Swan") is Odette, and hence into betraying his oath of fidelity to the latter. Odette, who has earlier fled from and been wooed by the prince, is condemned to retain her swan form or accept the advances of the sorcerer. As she flings herself into the lake in an act of suicide, but one true to love, she is followed by Siegfried. In an apotheosis (not always performed) the swan maidens and the audience see the lovers united in the world beyond death.

3. Among the many versions of the tale popular among victorians were those in Baring-Gould's *Curious Myths of the Middle Ages* (Second Series, p. 206); in Keightley's *Fairy Mythology* (he retells five tales); in Sike's *British Goblins*, pp. 38—40; in Kennedy's *Legendary Fictions of the Irish Celts*, p. 280; in J. F. Campbell's *Popular Tales of the West Highlands* 3:400; and in Burne's, *Shropshire Folk-Lore*, pp. 59—62. Slightly later retellings include those in Archibald Campbell's *Waifs and Strays* and in Lady Gregory's *Kiltartan Wonder Book*, as "The Man that Served the Sea" (pp. 174—75) and as "Beswaragal" (pp. 156—61). The tale is retold or alluded to in just about every volume published on the folklore of the Hebrides during the period.

4. This profile of fairy brides is a composite portrait derived from the tales told by the folklorists discussed in this chapter (whose works will be cited as they are mentioned), the author's own observations (based on the reading of nineteenth-century folklore volumes), and some of the opinions of Katharine Briggs. See, for example, her entries in *A Dictionary of Fairies* for "Fairy Brides" (pp. 135—37), "Seal Maidens" (pp. 349—50), and "Swan Maidens" (pp. 386—87).

5. Goethe's Melusina is the tiny, delicate fairy bride of one of his literary fairy tales.

6. I have cited the William Archer translation, known to the Victorians (in *The Chief European Dramatists*, ed. Brander Matthews). While Archer's translation calls Nora an "elf," Otto Reinert, in his translation in *An Introduction to Literature*, ed. Sylvan Barnet et al., 7th ed. (Boston: Little Brown, 1981), substitutes "elfmaid" (p. 851); and Peter Watts's Nora, in *Plays: The League of Youth, A Doll's House, The Lady From the Sea* is a "fairy" who will "dance on a moonbeam" (p. 187). The implications of the line remain the same.

7. Perhaps it is significant that the other major female folklorist, Charlotte Sophia Burne, writing on *Shropshire Folk-Lore*, is among those who relate various versions of the tale, including the story of Wild Edric and his elfin bride who leaves him for "reproaching her" about the existence of her sisters and for mentioning the enchanted house and dance in which they met (pp. 57—58), but declines to analyze the tale.

8. With the exception of Marion Rolfe Cox (whose major work was on Cinderella), Charlotte Burne (see note 7) and Alice Bertha Gomme, most of the folklore theorists were male; hence my use of masculine pronouns. The women folklorists tended to collect and comment upon rather than theorize materials.

9. For one of the early primary studies of this matter, see Elizabeth Fee, "The Sexual Politics of Victorian Social Anthropology," *Clio's Consciousness Raised*, pp. 86—102.

10. I am indebted to Fee's analysis of the arguments of the social anthropologists (pp. 90–100), as well as to the primary sources and to George W. Stocking, *Victorian Anthropology*, pp. 167–68, for his discussion of "primitive promiscuity." Stocking criticizes Fee's contention that the Victorian anthropologists defended patriarchy for ulterior motives. Motives aside, the point is (as Stocking himself notes) that social scientists accepted "the culturally pervasive view of women's nature" (p. 206). Later in his important book, he indicates that many of the concepts I find so significant in Victorian folklore theory—marriage by capture, primitive promiscuity, and matriarchy—were "largely a fantasy of the Victorian male anthropological imagination" (p. 315).

11. See John F. McLennan, *Primitive Marriage:* passim, but especially pp. 154–77, 54–55, 92, 247–48.

12. For Lubbock, see Fee, p. 100.

13. See Spencer, *The Principles of Sociology* 1:682–84, 711–12, 734.

14. Tom Peete Cross argues in *Modern Philology*, pp. 585–646, that in Celtic lore fairy brides were originally animals, that they later became supernatural women in animal forms, and, finally, that fairies' power really resides in their clothing.

15. See Alfred Nutt and Joseph Jacobs's critique of the theory in "Mr. Stuart-Glennie on the Origins of Matriarchy," *Folk-Lore* 2 (1891): 367–72.

16. David Thomson comments in his *People of the Sea* that, despite the popularity of the legend and the ballad of the great male selkie of Skuleskerry, most seal-human marriages were between mortal men and seal women and that it is this form of the legend that is found all over the western and northern Isles (p. 47).

17. Barbara Fass Leavy's useful book was not available until after all but the final draft of this chapter was completed. I am nevertheless indebted to her for several insights.

18. Devoting much space to the question in *The Science of Fairy Tales*, Hartland remarks on the dominance of one idea, that "of a man wedding a supernatural maiden and [being] unable to retain her" (p. 298). Canon J. A. MacCulloch, a follower of Hartland, agreed that tales of swan maidens partially originated in tales or myths of beast marriages. These tales were merged with stories of human women captured by men who stole their clothing. He argued that, in primitive societies, clothes both symbolized and protected human sexuality. He speculated that "savage" women were cautioned against letting men steal their garments—an act equivalent to letting males gain sexual mastery over them. See MacCulloch, *The Childhood of Fiction*, p. 364.

19. According to Norman Page (*Thomas Hardy*, p. 62), Hardy had been reading Edward Westermarck's *History of Human Marriage*. Page comments on first-cousin marriages, but more to my point is Hardy's knowledge of the other marriage theories evidenced by the following passage in the novel:

> [Gillingham] "But if people did as you want to do, [that is, let Sue simply elope with Jude without a formal divorce] there'd be a general domestic disintegration. The family would no longer be the social unit."
> [Phillotson] "And yet, I don't see why the woman and the children should not be the unit without the man."
> [Gillingham] "By the Lord Harry!—Matriarchy! . . . Does *she* say all this too?" (pp. 183–84)

20. I am endebted to Carl Ray Woodring for the suggestion that Venus and Apollo are chosen by Hardy as identifiable by his readers but, equally possibly, to serve as Sue's own bridge from the world of faerie to Victorian Hellenism. It is worth noting as well that Jude sees Sue's alien nature as both that of another order

of being and as that of another order of civilization. He says, at one point "you seem . . . to be one of the women of some grand old civilization . . . rather than a denizen of a mere Christian country" (p. 214).

21. English divorce law was itself ticklish. Before 1857, divorce, under ecclesiastical jurisdiction, provided only for separation and prohibited remarriage. The Matrimonial Causes Act of 1857 created one new Divorce Court and did permit absolute divorce; however, by permitting the husband to divorce for adultery alone, while requiring the wife to prove adultery plus an additional offense such as cruelty, desertion, incest or bigamy, it enshrined the double standard. Costs remained prohibitively high, denying all but the rich the right to divorce and the double standard remained intact until the next revision of the law in 1923. For full information on this, see Lawrence Stone, *Road to Divorce: England 1530–1987*. See also critiques of Stone on specific issues, including Hammerton. Hammerton points out that contrary to popular opinion, a review of court cases reveals that "upper class men were as likely as those lower in the social scale to strike their wives with pokers and similar weapons, throw them downstairs, beat them during pregnancy . . . etc." (p. 276).

22. The Maintenance Acts did affect the poor and lower middle classes since they allowed battered or deserted wives to obtain temporary maintenance orders from local magistrates (Stone, p. 386).

23. Stone, for example, suggests that the first real reform of the divorce laws was not that of 1923 but of 1937.

24. Lewes, a believer, makes much of the fairy bride's instruction of her youngest son in *The Queer Side of Things*. She incorporates into her retelling the information that when the fairy's youngest son came to the lake's edge to mourn her, she would rise up, talk to him, and teach him to gather flowers and herbs to be used in healing. But Lewes's interpretation of the tale is unusual in several respects. She sees the story as one of the oldest Welsh tales, as combining Druidical beliefs with the mystical idea "that happiness derived from the fairy-plane is independent of events, but cannot survive any discordant emotion, whether the emotion be justified from the human point of view or no" (p. 129). She notes that the fairy bride who cannot differentiate between joy and woe (when others experience it) is first developing "a shadowy soul" (p. 129) through her marriage with a mortal; yet, while the bride is incapable of sympathy beyond the personal limit, she can and does feel "mother-love for her youngest son, the first and oldest of unselfish instincts" (p. 129).

25. Leavy and others before her speculate that Melusina's prohibition against being seen is connected with her menstrual cycle. Interestingly, the Victorian version of Melusina is a particularly tamed one. Gwendolen Harleth in George Eliot's *Daniel Deronda* is the most obvious example and, despite her serpentine beauty and allure, she is more victim than victimizer.

26. See, however, Oscar Wilde's fairy tale for adults, "The Fisherman and His Soul" as a direct comment on Andersen. Inverting the tradition that elementals, including undines and mermaids, seek human lovers in order to gain souls and the chance of salvation, Wilde makes his fisherman discard his soul and renounce the claims of society, religion, and commerce—all for love. The fisherman's reward is union with his fairy bride, though he must die to attain it.

27. Interestingly, and perhaps not coincidentally, Hewlett was a important witness before the Divorce Commission of 1909; he was in favor of permitting freer and easier divorce.

28. "Mrs. Jorkens," in Lord Dunsay's *The Travels of Mr. Joseph Jorkens*, is a highly comic treatment of the mermaid-bride motif. It becomes an ironic comment on his earlier mystical and sentimental romance. Here, Jorkens picks up, chats and flirts

with a mermaid "on view" in a tank in an Aden hotel who reminds him of a barmaid he once knew. Enchanted by the mystery of her eyes and unaware of the triviality of her mind, he steals her from the hotel and marries her. He soon ceases to find her fascinating—her sole interest is in local gossip—and her manners begin to disturb him. He begins to find her uncivilized in preferring her fish live as well as raw and in snapping at both her food and gulls. Deluding himself into thinking that his theft of her bothers his conscience, he decides to take her back to the hotel and captivity. When, at the beach, he tells her his intentions, she slips back into the sea. His last sight of her, ironically, a surprise to him, is her flinging the wedding ring he has given her into the ocean (pp. 143–69).

The recent film *Splash* takes a more romantic view of a mermaid-mortal union, but the couple can be united only when the mortal male leaps into the ocean and joins the mermaid's world. The final scene of the film may be, as Leavy says, a parodic version of the end of *Swan Lake* (p. 278).

29. The recent film *The Secret of Roan Innish* (*roan* means "seal") plays on the idea of the returned offspring of a vanished selkie bride; it is based on a children's story of the early 1930s.

30. For more information on "informal" divorce, see Menefee, *Wives for Sale*.

31. For a recent treatment of this theme, see Tanith Lee's fantasy tale, "Because Our Skins are Finer," in *Dreams of Dark and Light*.

32. Among the most interesting of the recent fairy brides is Favvers, Angela Carter's magical fairy bird-woman in *Nights at the Circus*.

Chapter 4

1. Much of the material I have used here was first cited in a book from the Victorian period that suggests the cultural fascination with dwarfs; Edward J. Wood, *Giants and Dwarfs*.

2. He is described as being covered with black hair and naked except for leaves and moss; though he could speak, he spoke rarely. (qtd. in Eberly, p. 243, from Osgood MacKenzie, *One Hundred Years in the Highlands*).

3. The anonymous author of the article in *All the Year Round* focuses on the evil dwarfs of German legend, noting that the triumph of the Reformation pushed dwarfs, gnomes, and elves from Germany. Luther's voice, like the crowing of a cock, forced them to leave. But, he adds, no sooner did they depart than adepts of the occult tried to recreate them. He ends with an anecdote about the kobolds, the teutonic gnomes Luther considered demonic, and with a tale supposedly told by Luther attesting to their reality ("Dwarfs and Elves," pp. 66–67).

4. Moreover, dwarfs, Hall notes, had been assimilated with fairies of other types and origins by the end of the sixteenth century. The Oberon of Shakespeare's *Midsummer Night's Dream* is none other than Elberick, king of the germanic supernatural dwarfs or dark elfs (Hall, p. 57). Other Victorian commentators, including E. B. Tylor (1:385), saw them as nature spirits, probably suggested by their mythical genesis from the earth as well as the earth- and verdure-colored garb in which they were usually dressed. Others including Jacob Grimm and Frazer thought them the souls of the dead, an idea fortified by the Victorian "new" ethnologists who found similar beliefs among the "primitive" peoples they were examining.

5. By 1922 and Walter de la Mare's *Memoirs of a Midget*, a novel told from the midget's (Miss Midgetina) point of view, some attitudes had begun to change. But the perfect Midgetina is still initially repelled by Mr. Anon, the dark, sallow, hunchbacked achondroplastic dwarf who loves her, and she chooses to love instead the full-size *femme fatale*, Fanny Bowswater, who treats her with contempt and cruelty.

6. Meg Mullach, one of the few females was described as a diminuitive brownie-like creature, "a little hairy creature, like a child . . . but by the blessing of God and reformation from popery and more pure preaching of the gospel, she is almost now invisible," remarks the informant (qtd. in Dalyell, p. 541).

7. If Ruskin's dwarfs in *The King of the Golden River* (1850) seem less malignant than usual it is, in part, because there are no women in the tale. Traditional, though heavily based on the *märchen* figures of the Brothers Grimm, as is Ruskin's tale itself, they have been turned into moral agents. Their sexuality has been totally repressed.

8. Thomas and others note that the dwarf as a character in fairy tales is seldom a benevolent figure and consider the Seven Dwarves of "Snow White" an anomaly.

9. Trows were described as dwarfed old men, ugly, hairy, and long-nosed, who were inveterate thieves and kidnappers. Although in one incident they snatched a bridegroom, returning him seven years later, unrecognizable and covered with hair (in token of his having become primitive like themselves), most of their victims were young women. They kidnapped human wives, but could only beget male children on them and the mortal mother was said to die at the birth of the baby trow.

Brownies, hobs, and lobs (interchangable names) were all seen as "small, wizened and shaggy, clad in rags or naked; grotesque in appearance, they often lacked noses or separate toes and fingers" (Briggs, *Dictionary*, p. 38). The Welsh boggart, bwbach, or bwca was a more sinister form of brownie, less a household helper and more "a terrifying phantom" according to Wirt Sikes (p. 32). Sikes adds that coblynau who haunt the mines and quarries of Wales, like the German kobolds, correspond to "the cabalistic gnomes" and are "always given the form of dwarfs in the popular fancy" (p. 24).

Cluricane, luricane, and leprecaun may all be names derived from *lubberkin*, a word for "goblin" or "fiend." The image of them as charming and amusing derives from a work of fiction, James Stephens's *The Crock of Gold* (1912). Victorian folklorists saw them as "ugly, stunted creatures," disliked even by the fairies for whom they made shoes. McAnally, in *Irish Wonders*, derived them from fathers who were evil spirits and mothers who were degenerate fairies (pp. 149–50); modern commentators note that their iron tools connect them to dwarves rather than fairies who cannot abide iron.

Far darrigs and larrigs were dwarfs associated with blood and terror; like them, too, were the Lowland red caps, whose red hats were dyed in the blood of the travelers they had slain.

10. Kipling's Puck is repeatedly described as having "bare, hairy feet," and in *Rewards and Fairies*, his "brown,square, hairy foot" (p. 5) is again mentioned.

11. One of the miners, discussing the goblins' appearance, comments that "such must have been the primordial condition of humanity." He believes, in Lamarckian fashion, "that education and handicraft had developed both toes and fingers" (p. 65).

12. Interestingly, Tyson's proof of the nonexistence of the pygmies was republished as *A Philosophical Essay Concerning the Pygmies of the Ancients* in 1894 with a long introduction by Bertram C. A. Windle updating the controversy and proving Tyson wrong. (See Windle's "Introduction" in Tyson).

13. De Quatrefages, the respected nineteenth-century French anthropologist, hypothosized that all Pygmies—typically located in hot, humid, tropical areas—were of the same race. His view was dominant until 1963.

14. Darwin himself further muddied the waters by suggesting in the conclusion to *The Descent of Man* (1870) that he would as soon claim descent from "a heroic little monkey" or an "old baboon" who saves his "young comrade" as from a savage who

tortures his enemies, practices infanticide and human sacrifice, treats his wives like slaves, "knows no decency and is haunted by the grossest superstitions" (p. 619). He clearly considered the instincts of the higher animals superior to the behavior of the "savage" races that ostensibly descended from them. Thus, without specifically mentioning the Pygmies, he too may be seen as suggesting their inferiority.

15. See Stocking's helpful *Victorian Anthropology*, pp. 24–26, on this issue. He remarks that phrenology bequeathed a faith in the biological basis of human capacity to physical anthropology. It also, of course, rendered many phrenological assumptions "scientific" and hence even "liberal" ethnologists and folklorists were caught by its spell—or at least its terminology. It seemed so absolute in its calculations.

16. Sabine Baring-Gould, Sir John Rhys, David MacRitchie, and others used the cephalic index to ascertain the racial sources of folklore.

17. Grogan's comments about the so-called apelike men he encountered reveal much about how racism rendered some groups subhuman:

"I observed some ape-like creatures leering at me from behind banana palms, and with considerable difficulty my Ruanda guide induced one of them to be inspected,' he begins. 'The stamp of the beast was so strong on them that I should place them lower in the human scale that any other natives I have seen in Africa. . . . Their face, body, and limbs are covered with wiry hair, and the hand of the long powerful arms, the slight stoop of the trunk, and the hunted, vacant expression of the face made up a *tout ensemble* that was a terrible pictorial proof of Darwinism." (p. 173)

18. Compare Stanley's picture to the image of the "dwarfs" in figure 4.4.

19. He tells of the charms, for example, of the Pygmy "handmaiden" of his traveling companion, Dr. Thomas Parks, whose skill in foraging probably helped the doctor survive. Stanley's first description of a female Pygmy "specimen" is especially telling: "She measured thirty-three inches in height, and was a perfectly formed young woman of about seventeen, of a glistening and smooth sleekness of body. Her figure was that of a miniature coloured lady, not wanting in a certain grace, and her face was very prepossessing. . . . Absolutely nude, the little demoiselle was quite possessed, as though she were accustomed to be admired, and really enjoyed inspection" (1:198). Yet Stanley's depiction of the Queen reveals his underlying ambivalence about Pygmy women. Although we are shown a pretty and delicate face, our attention is focused on gargantuan breasts that connect her to the mammalian and subhuman.

20. Other interesting examples include the negroid dwarfs of "The Kiss of Judas" and of "Enter Herodias" (from *Salome*). There is even an Asiatic dwarf—a Mongol fighting a Caucasian dwarf—in *The Toilet of Helen*, an illustration for "Under the Hill." (See also the illustration for Juvenal in the *Yellow Book* IV.) Moreover, Beardsley's fusion of fetal and dwarf creatures as in *Enter Herodias*, the *Bon Mot* vignettes, Lucian, and *The Kiss of Judas*, suggests his own version of ontogeny recapitulating phylogeny. Just thumbing through *The Early Work of Aubrey Beardsley* and *The Later Work of Aubrey Beardsley* reveals further examples and makes plain that Beardsley's Pierrot midgets are yet another species, quite distinct from his fetal and dwarf figures.

21. Though, like the Infanta, he is derived from the Velázquez painting, Haliburton and MacRitchie would see the distorted dwarf in Wilde's tale as one of their Spanish Akkas.

22. In the Shetland Islands, Beddoe located short, thickset, dark peoples whom he thought were probably Finns and aboriginals, while he suggested that Cornwall held the darkest people in England, hence the most primitive. Significantly, Bed-

does found more "dark" people in the working class than in the upper classes (p. 270) and more dolichocephalics (longheads) than brachycephalics (round heads), thus linking the working class of England to the more primitive "lower races."

23. In this paper, MacRitchie characterized these "lower races" as "anthropoid rather than human" (p. 10). He also connected Africans in general with the popular myth of the wicked children of Ham. His disciple, Andrews, added another link to the chain by noting that in medieval tradition, at least, Ham was also the father of "wee-bodies" or pygmies, as well as of "every other deformed shape that human beings wear" (p. 32).

24. Even Victorian scientists who prided themselves on their liberal and enlightened views like Arthur Mitchell, whose *Lectures on Archaeology* of 1878 were quite influential, feared that racial atavism and degneration were the facts of life—that savages might well become more savage (*The Past in the Present*, p. 228).

25. The Eloi are described as "perhaps four feet tall" and beautiful and graceful, as fair as "Dresden china" (p. 17). In form and behavior, complete with delicate little voices, they are "fairy" midgets.

26. Burrows did once see an albino Pygmy and noted its rarity and extremely grotesque appearance (p. 194).

27. The brutish, bestial Gomangani cannibals are depicted as the natural enemies of the great apes, who are described as more attractive and more human than the cannibals, even in their dancing. Tarzan, described as "a child, or a primeval man, which is the same thing" (*The Return of Tarzan*, p. 129), is torn between his nature (as John Clayton, Lord Greystoke) and his nurture by the apes. Nurture almost wins when, seeing Jane, he comes close to raping her.

28. There is a suggestion of polygenesis in the statement that the children born of Huns and Gothic thralls either favor their fathers or are born as "naturals" or idiots. There is implicit racism in the fact that the Huns value most those thralls who are whitest.

29. Doyle's fantasy becomes a compendium of popularized scientific lore when Professor Challenger, his protagonist, and Summerlee, the other scientist in the party, debate contemporary issues. When the two men meet a group of cannibals, they stop to argue about whether they are of the mongolian type (p. 75). They even examine the cranial capacity and facial angle (p. 166) of the dwarfs and midgets, deciding that the ape-men are the earlier species. When Malone is chased by one of the monsters, Challenger asks him if he has noticed whether it can cross its thumb over its palm.

The most interesting aspect of the science in the fantasy is Challenger's forced self-recognition. The professor, himself a near-dwarf, "a stunted Hercules," becomes Gulliver confronting the Yahoos when he must recognize how similar his body is to that of an old ape-man chief. The resemblance ceases only at the cranium, the measurable site of Challenger's giant intellect as: "the sloping forehead and low, curved skull of the ape-man were in sharp contrast to the broad brow and magnificent cranium of the European" (p. 160). Significantly, Challenger is embarrassed and disgusted at the resemblance, asking his colleagues to forget what they have seen—and eager to promote the extermination of the dwarfs.

30. One of the protagonists, Dyson, expresses his relief at their failure to rescue the girl. "You saw the appearance of those things that gathered thick and writhed in the Bowl" [a natural amphitheatre in the hills], he tells his friend Vaughan. "You may be sure that what lay bound in the midst of them was no longer fit for earth" (p. 46). In Machen's cultural myth, the young woman's miscegenation with the little goblin men—no matter how unwilling—renders her unfit for life.

Machen returned to his mongoloid dwarfs yet again in "Out of the Earth"

(1920). Rising from the dunes near the sea: "horrible little stunted creatures with old men's faces, with bloated faces . . . with leering eyes" (p. 57) they are identified as absolute evil, rejoicing in evil times.

Chapter 5

1. Yeats, for example, argued that fairies needed human beings to provide phys-ical force. "Being but shadows," he says, "they can do little without the aid of mor-tals" (*Unpublished Prose* 2:268 – 69); thus, they bring away mortals to do their work. Lady Gregory also suggests that physical power is what the Irish fairies need from humans. In the preface to *Visions*, she notes that "the strength of a human body is needed by the shadows, it may be in their fighting, and certainly in their hurling to win the goal. Young men are taken for this" (p. 10). In effect, as Yeats later made ex-plicit, humans provide the brawn while fairies provide the brain, thus leading to an antagonistic but somewhat dependant relationship between the two groups (*Mem-oirs*, p. 166).

2. Interestingly, MacManus specifically identifies the alder as one of the species favored and haunted by fairies.

3. Yeats never did write the "big book on the commonwealth of faery" he had planned; however, he did write six major articles on the subject for various period-icals. They are collected in *The Unpublished Prose of William Butler Yeats*, Volume 2. The articles consisted of:

"The Tribes of Danu" (*The New Review*, November 1897)
"The Prisoners of the Gods" (*Nineteenth Century*, January 1898)
"The Broken Gates of Death" (*Fortnightly Review*, April 1898)
"Ireland Betwitched" (*Contemporary Review*, September 1899)
"Irish Witch Doctors" (*Fortnightly Review*, September 1900)
"Away" (*Fortnightly Review*, April 1902)

A number of his other articles and reviews of the 1890s, also included in the two vol-umes of *Unpublished Prose*, contain additional valuable comments on folklore and folk belief.

4. When the boy whose name was Jan chose to follow the voices and vanished, the voices ceased (Whitlock, p. 34).

5. See Hans Peter Duerr, *Deamtime: Concerning the Boundary Between Wilderness and Civ-ilization*, passim, but especially pp. 42 – 43.

6. E. B. Tylor explained the connection by suggesting in *Primitive Culture* that rivers may appear to be alive. Moving, flowing, changing, they seem to have the traits of living beings.

7. *Nixie* as a word for a female water elf or water nymph (from Germanic and Scandinavian sources) came into English in about 1816. Rosamond's constant con-nections to supernatural water creatures reverberate throughout the novel. Nymphs are undines, and she is called nymph or nymphlike on pp. 94, 112, and 352. She is identified as a mermaid on p. 437 and again as "an accomplished mermaid" re-plete with a comb, mirror, and song on p. 583. She is described as one of the sirens on p. 299, and as a "water-lily" (p. 346). Her music is also repeatedly connected with watery enchantment. She plays tunes like "sea-breezes" (p. 456); her music soothes like oars on a lake (p. 655). She sings, "Flow on thou shining river" (p. 116), and when she is displeased her voice is like "cold water drops" (p. 659).

8. The creatures fight back, however, and an illustration of the "lingerers"—those late for the Triumphal Progress—shows an elfin rider thrown by his bird, and several recalitrant and balking snails; elfin cruelty is not always unpunished.

9. The comments on the poltergeist phenomenon of Walter Yeeling Evans-Wentz, in a newspaper article quoted in *Light* 33 (1913): 9, best summarize the views of many educated believers. Evans-Wentz is persuaded that much if not all of the poltergeist activity that psychical researchers report is "due directly to the mischievous little fairies . . . which medieval mystics called elementals. . . . I can only suggest," he concludes, "that the phenomena attributed by the Celtic peoples to invisible or fairy agency are in most cases identical with the phenomena attributed to the agency of spirits amongst ourselves" (p. 9).

10. She argues in *Ghosts I have Seen* (1920) that "at ordinary times the veil of the flesh seems denser and the consciousness much less acute" (p. 209). Tweedale comments that elementals may be good or evil in nature and impact and that they may be "artifical spirits"—that is, "thought-forms" as well as nature spirits.

11. Jonathan Rose indicates this in the *Edwardian Temperament* (p. 4). Rose notes that to such members of the SPR as Balfour, Lodge, and Sir William Crookes, the existence of radio waves, for example, suggested that mental telepathy, extrasensory perception, and clairvoyance were worth investigating. X-rays, for instance, proved that (although materialist science had earlier thought otherwise) bodies could act upon each other at a distance (see Rose, pp. 6–8).

12. Carlyle's mob as a "living deluge, plunging headlong . . . billowing uncontrollable . . . in a hot frenzy of triumph" that results in "all outward, all inward things fallen into one general wreck of madness!" (*French Revolution* 7:164) sounds remarkably like the slaugh. Descriptions of working-class groups by much less metaphorical and dramatic authors bear out my contention. A writer for the staid *Times* of 14 November 1887 described the rioters in Trafalgar Square as a vicious mob of "hounds" and "howling roughs," "debased" and "ranting," and motivated by "simple love of disorder" and "hope of plunder" (qtd. in Thompson, *William Morris*, p. 491).

13. How one knew if one's relative or loved one was dead or had been taken, and thus might be rescued, was a matter of some debate. However, if one saw the deceased again either in dream, trance, or reality, it was a sure sign that he or she was with the fairies. Anna MacManus, as Ethna Carbery, published a number of poems on those abducted by the elfin peoples. Many are accounts by female narrators of the male lovers they have lost. As in her best-known verse, "In Tir-na'n-Og," the mortal beloved sees her lover in dream and vision while he, forgetting earth and her, "wanders in a happy dream thro' scented golden hours" and woos "a fairy love" (p. 6).

14. The story, published in *Limits and Renewals* (1932), alludes to and gains much of its impetus from a Victorian fairy tale by Juliana Horatia Ewing.

15. Interestingly, Dalua, the "fairy fool," who in folklore is one of the most sinister male representatives of fairy evil, is treated as an attractive and romantic figure in Victorian fiction and commentary. Thus, male evil is diminished or glamorized. Yeats merely mentions Dalua while Fiona Macleod/William Sharp depicts him in both a poem and a tale (each called "Dalua") as a handsome, dark-haired man who roams the mountains and wastes, playing wonderful melodies on his pipes—thus, as a type of the artist. In Sharp's hands, Dalua's touch brings poetic inspiration and his voice is a summons to divine madness.

16. Some folklorists also argued that the fairies, if not the actual dead, were their guards and keepers; in effect, that they served as "threshold guardians" watching the gate to the other world. Occult believers and theorists have often considered them a special subcategory of the dead: those awaiting reincarnation (see chapter 1).

17. I am using the popular version told in William Bottrell, *Traditions and Hearthside Stories of West Cornwell* (Second Series), pp. 94–102—a version used by Robert Hunt and K. M. Briggs, among others. In "The Host of the Air," based on a Gaelic ballad, poet and singer O'Driscoll is saved from eating fairy food by Bridget, his bride, already

"taken" by the elves. Yeats's note to the poem indicates that in the original ballad O'Driscoll returns home to find keeners bewailing the death of his wife.

18. See Addy's comments in *Folk Tales and Superstitions*, pp. 70 – 71. See also the chapter on witches (pp. 147 – 60) in Porter.

19. Visually, fairy painters could capitalize on the similarity. If one did not know the folk tale (from Keightley) on which Richard Doyle's paintings of *The Altar Cup of Aagerup* are based, for example, it would be difficult to differentiate between the beautiful long-haired, young witch in Doyle's paintings and the many female fairies he depicts in his other works.

20. The anarchic, destructive impulses that fairies (and witches) can be seen to represent were often depicted in images of wild, orgiastic dance. For example, the folktale, "Kate Crackernuts" (the English version of the Grimms' "Twelve Dancing Princesses") depicts its clever female hero as rescuing her prince from female fairies who are literally dancing him to death. Joseph Jacobs's version of this tale (in *English Fairy Tales*, pp. 207 – 11) makes much of the deadly effect of a dance in the fairy mound; the prince is enervated and incapable of action; he is slowly dying on his feet until rescued by Kate. Maurice Hewlett, in *The Lore of Proserpine*, describes the erotic, almost insane nature of female fairy dancing, even suggesting elfin lesbianism, in an account of a ritual circle dance he "witnessed" on Parliament Hill. Fairy painters endlessly depicted fairy dances, in part for commercial reasons, as these diminuitive, nude or semi-nude figures provided voyeuristic pleasure without offending the Victorian sense of decency, but it seems evident that they, too, found something culturally compelling about such materials. See, for example, Daniel Maclise's *Faun and the Fairies*, Richard Dadd's famous *Come unto these Yellow Sands*, and Joseph Noel Paton's *Reconciliation of Titania and Oberon*, for just a few examples.

21. On hysteria, see Showalter, pp. 129 – 34; for views of dancing connecting women and "savages," see Dijkstra, pp. 243 – 45.

22. Cannibalism in all forms seems to permeate almost all folklore as a basic embodiment of evil and always inspires horror. Yet relatively few fairies catalogued by Victorian collectors indulged directly in it; anthropophagy was usually restricted to giants and ogres. When it was associated with fairies, as with the fir darig of Ireland (described several times by Yeats), who make a man turn the spit on which they are roasting a corpse and warn him that they will devour him if he burns it, or with the red caps, who dye their caps in human blood after they have slaughtered their victims, the cannibals were depicted as dwarflike male figures.

23. The version I use here comes from Robert Chambers, *Popular Rhymes of Scotland* (1826), but other versions bear the identical message.

24. "White Ladies" or "White Women," especially prominent on the Isle of Man, shared many of the lhiannon-shee's traits without her gift of inspiration. They, too, attached themselves to men and drained their bodies and souls. Gill reports that one grabbed a man by the arm, leaving him with the marks of her fingers—"dark imprints on the biceps"—that remained with him until his death. Another man suffered both the disfiguring marks and a sudden aging; his meeting with a White Lady cost him ten years of life. (*Second Manx Scrapbook*, p. 358). Other memorates like these support the argument that nocturnal encounters—whether specified as sexual or not—with these female supernaturals result in the male loss of force and vitality, often followed by death.

25. In a long note to the poem he describes her as the "tutelary spirit of all persons called to ministrations of truth and beauty" (p. 416), whether in action or in art. Other tellers of Irish lore suggested that one could be freed from the shee by setting her on a replacement host. They added to her positive traits the fact that she

could bring her host wealth, though her gift must be given to and could only be used by someone other than the host.

26. This argument is made by Jochen Achilles (p. 155, n.9) and I am indebted in general to Achilles's reading of this play. Austin Clarke's introduction to the plays (Fitzmaurice, *Dramatic Fantasies*), also contains Clarke's statement that Fitzmaurice told him he was satirizing Yeats "and his cult of the fairies" (p. x).

27. See the illustrations in Dijkstra's *Idols of Perversity*, especially pp. 235–71.

Chapter 6

1. For example, George MacDonald, whose knowledge of Scottish lore and belief was formidable, deals in just one of his tales, "The Golden Key," with the fairies' dislike of dirt and their punishment of slovenly housekeepers, with the differences between time in fairyland and on earth (in the former, three earthly years pass in what seems an instant), and with the lore of elementals so important to Victorian Spiritualists and Theosophists (including the relative antiquity of the spirits of water, earth, air, and fire). Mark Lemon's "Tinykins Transformed" and Mary De Morgan's tales are equally laden with authentic lore: Tinykins is a Sunday child and hence can see fairies: bees are elfin messengers; land fairies cannot cross running water; foxgloves (with their powerful digitalis) are fairy bells and fairy medicine. When Tinykins is transformed into various animals, he appears to ordinary mortals to be "away," a state repeatedly discussed by folklore theorists. In De Morgan's "Wanderings of Arasman," the evil fairies are identified as the "dark elves" of Scandinavian legend, while in "Through the Fire," all the major figures except the protagonist are elementals. Questions of the size of fairies and of their tribes and species, as well as of elfin relations with gypsies (supposedly traditional enemies), occur throughout Jean Ingelow's "Mopsa and the Fairies," while elementals, especially evil gnomes, play dominant roles in Ford Madox Ford's "Brown Owl." (See Auerbach and Knoepflmacher; and Zipes for these tales.)

2. For a more extended discussion of the use of fairy lore in Victorian children's literature, see my critical review, "When Rumplestiltskin Ruled: Victorian Fairy Tales," pp. 327–36.

3. They are responsible for the naughtiness of infants; Barrie also indicates that their life span is very short, rather like that of insects. For another more sinister connection between babies and fairies, see Charles Altamont Doyle's drawing, "The Fairy's Whisper" (in *Charles Doyle's Fairyland*), with its image of a small adult fairy floating above the head of a large mischievously smiling infant. Its caption reads: "any body who has nursed a baby as I have, will recognize this smile I think." It is also important to remember that Charles, a believer in the reality of fairies, was the father of Arthur Conan Doyle.

4. Rose Fyleman's poem, "Fairies," reprinted in the *Rose Fyleman Fairy Book*, opens with lines that may have inspired the girls' hoax:

There are fairies at the bottom of our garden!
    It's not so very, very far away;
You pass the gardener's shed and you just keep straight
      ahead—
    I do so hope they've really come to stay.
There's a little wood, with moss in it and beetles,
    And a little stream that quietly runs through;
You wouldn't think they'd dare to come merry-
      making there—
          Well, they do. (p. 1)

5. While agreeing that the photos were single-exposure shots and not montages, Kodak would not issue a certificate of authenticity.

6. It was first published under the sensational title, "An Epoch-Making Event—Fairies Photographed." Doyle was not, as he makes clear, either the principal investigator of the photographs or an on-site observer of the phenomena. But he did believe in the "simplicity and integrity" of the girls, even printing a letter from Frances written in 1917 to a friend of hers in South Africa in which she matter of factly notes that she is enclosing a photo of herself "with some fairies up the beck" ("The Cottingley Fairies: An Epilogue, *Strand*, February 1923). His "scientific" explanation of the phenomenon was that fairies were usually outside the normal limits of human visual and color spectra, but that they could appear when states of consciousness were altered by the weather—especially on hot, still days. He also speculated that the fairies were "thought-forms" conjured up by and projected by the imaginations of the seers (*Coming of the Fairies*, p. 39), but was later convinced that the girls, natural mediums, had actually seen rather than mentally created the fairies. In this interpretation he agreed with Gardner who also saw the girls as mediumistic, materializing the fairies in the way that mediums materialize spirits through ectoplasm. That the spirits were materialized would also explain why they had the stance and style of women of the 1920s! Both Doyle and Gardner, however, agreed that one cannot materialize what is not there in the first place.

7. Elsie admitted the pictures were fakes, but Frances was always ambiguous in discussing their fraudulence. After her mother's death Frances's daughter affirmed that her mother had seen fairies throughout her life. Their last visitation had been when her mother was in the kitchen washing dishes during World War II (Cooper, p. 143).

8. See Cunningham's comments in the Introduction. Hartland specifically blames Howel Harries's Methodism in Wales for the lack of English märchen. He says this kind of Evangelical Protestantism crushed what it considered false doctrine.

9. In effect the fear expressed first by Lamb, Coleridge, and Wordsworth, and later by Dickens and Ruskin, that children deprived of imaginative literature, especially fairy tales, would become little utilitarians has proved prophetic.

10. For example, his "pinches" are now considered fleabites; his tidying up is attributed to the farmer's change of habits and his messing up to the servants' laziness.

11. May Kendall, who went on to become a poet as well as a feminist and social activist, was in her early twenties when she collaborated on this little-known satirical novel with Lang, who already had a distinguished reputation.

12. Others simply use the motif for its own sake. "The Defeat of Time" in Ernest Rhys's *Fairy Gold* (1907) is another attempt to explain why the fairies have said farewell to England. This tale for children deals with Time's attempt to drive Titania and her people into extinction. They are rescued, albeit temporarily, by the ghost of Shakespeare. See also Thomas Hood's poem, "The Plea of the Midsummer Fairies."

13. But as if to contradict his own statement, he next quotes the account of a Mr. Wilkinson, a man no more superstitious than most, on his recent sight of "a real dwarf or fairie" (p. 127).

14. Charlotte Burne, in collecting *Shropshire Folklore* in the 1880s, was at first tempted to report that there were no fairies left, that all traces of them had vanished. She learned, however, that although they had not been seen in many years, their fairy music, with all its enchantment, still remained (p. 4).

15. Curtin goes on to state that belief is still alive, however. The common assumption made by both Celtic commentators and English ones is that Celts have always had and always will have what Macleod describes as "a more fraternal com-

munion with the secret powers of the World" (5:189). Michael Wood, for example, in a tale called "The Piper of Elfhame," in *The Theosophical Review* 31: 306–13, explores the ability to believe in fairies as a racial and ethnic inheritance. Using the old clichéd opposition between the stolid Anglo-Saxon and the imaginative Celt, he suggests that the Englishman could be in fairyland or Elfhame without even recognizing it for what it is. The natural mysticism of the Celtic peoples is the basis for W. Y. Evans-Wentz's important book.

16. The impact of such elements as rural electrification, with its outside and inside lights and night lights, wider roads, improved transportation, and the development of radio, cinema, and television cannot be overlooked.

17. In 1913, Baring-Gould is more convinced that since all the apparitions were "due to the effect of a hot sun on the head," they were hallucinations. His answer to the question of why we all see such similar beings is that hallucinations are never "originally conceived; they are reproductions of representations either previously seen or conceived from descriptions given by others." He is almost certain he and his wife saw imps because their nurses had described them and that his son, having read the Grimms tales illustrated, remembered them. But in 1922, whether because of the Cottingley fairy photos, the temper of the times, or his nostalgia for belief he questions his own answer (*Book of Folk-Lore*, p. 200).

18. See Baring-Gould's *Early Reminiscences*, pp. 20–22.

19. Even frankly mortal theatrical fairies became increasingly technological. Gilbert and Sullivan's *Iolanthe*, when performed in 1882, strove for its magic through the wonders of late Victorian technology. The fairies wore batteries on their backs concealed by their hair; they switched on electric lights on their foreheads. In the finale, all the mortals turned into fairies and sprouted mechanical wings.

20. A fortune was made in the 1930s by selling images of Joan; brass amulets wrought in the shape of a female fairy and dipped in a Cornish fairy well before they were sold, were supposed to bring good luck.

21. To work with the denser forces and counterparts of the plants, they assume etheric bodies. These are thought-forms produced by folklore tales and the human imagination. Clarifying why there are so many species of preternaturals and so many different accounts of them, Roc explains that an elemental "can put on any of these thought forms and than appear personified as that particular being . . . elf, gnome, faun, fairy, and so on" (Hawken, p. 143).

22. Van Gelder, who often replicates Leadbeater, provides records of her sightings of various classes of fairies. Her individual descriptions may differ from those of others, but the underlying principles are the same: there are fairies for the four elements and subspecies of each; fairies range from the miniscule to the gigantic and from the reasonably intelligent to the mindless. Her book, too, assumes an elegiac tone as an epilogue speaks of the effects of pollution on the elfin tribes. They are fewer, less joyous, and less energetic, she warns. Mortals are in danger of losing both the fairies and their own well-being.

23. In another tale written for, but not included in the collection, Warner writes of the fairies' destruction by technology and their own greed. In one of the tales in *One Thing Leading to Another*, called "Narrative of Events Preceding the Death of Queen Ermine" (pp. 148–60), the fairies of the Pennines decide to invest in an iron mine in their district; one fairy even joins the mine's board of directors. Though the meadows are defaced and the smelting furnaces glare and stink, though the mine entirely destroys the once decent life of the mortal village, the fairies choose not to notice. When the mine floods, however, most of the fairies are drowned and their kingdom destroyed.

24. In "Fairylore from the Midlands of Ireland," Patricia Lysaght notes that even

among the anglicized Irish the belief survives that places have special power because fairies are still present in them. Margaret Bennet writes that in Balquhidder, a Presbyterian community in the Highlands famous as the birthplace of the fairy scholar Reverend Kirk, lore is still present. Others comment on Rathlin Island, Orkney, and Shetland as places where the fairy faith survives (see Narváez, authors cited). There are still reports of mermaid sightings near the Orkney and Shetland Islands and off the coast of the Isle of Man, though no one has, to my knowledge, yet collected the reward offered by the Manx for the collection of a mer-specimen.

25. See also recent novels like Steve Szilagyi's *Photographing Fairies* of 1992, a book derived in part from the Cottingley incident.

WORKS CITED

Primary Sources

A. E. [George William Russell]. *The Candle of Vision*. London: Macmillan, 1919.

A. W. "Fairy 'Folk-Lore' of Shetland." *Antiquarian Magazine* 1 (Jan.–June 1882): 135–37.

Addy, Sidney Oldall. *Folk Tales and Superstitions*. 1898. Reprinted, London: E.P. Publishing, 1973.

———. *Household Tales and Traditional Remains*. London: Nutt, 1895.

Aitken, Hannah, ed. *A Forgotten Heritage: Original Folktales of Lowland Scotland*. Totowa, N.J.: Rowman and Littlefield, 1973.

Allen, Grant. "Who Were the Fairies?" *Cornhill Magazine* 43 (1881): 335–48.

Andrews, Elizabeth. *Ulster Folklore*. London: Elliot Stock, 1913.

Arnold, Herbert. "The Elementals." *Occult Review* 18 (July–Dec. 1913): 208–13.

Atkinson, Rev. J. C. *Forty Years in a Moorland Parish: Reminiscences and Researches in Danby in Cleveland*. London: Macmillan, 1891.

Bachofen, J. J. *Myth, Religion, and Mother Right: Selected Writings of J. J. Bachofen*. Trans. Ralph Manheim. Bollingen Series. Princeton, N.J.: Princeton University Press, 1973.

Balfour, Mrs. M. C. "Legends of the Lincolnshire Cars." *Folk-Lore* 2, pt.1 (1889): 145–65; pt. 2: 257–85.

Baring-Gould, Sabine. *A Book of Folk-Lore*. London: W. Collins, 1913.

———. *Curious Myths of the Middle Ages*. London: Rivingtons, 1866. Second Series, London: Rivingtons, 1868.

235

———. *Early Reminiscences: 1834–64*. New York: Dutton, 1922.

Beddoe, John. *Races of Britain: A Contribution to the Anthropology of Western Europe*. London: Trubner, 1885.

Benson, E. F. "The Recent 'Witch-Burning' at Clonmel." *Nineteenth Century* 37 (Jan.–June 1895): 1053–59.

Blavatsky, H[elena]. P. *Isis Unveiled: A Master-Key to the Mysteries of Ancient and Modern Science and Theology*. Vol. 1, *Science*. 1877. Reprinted, Los Angeles: Theosophy Company, 1982.

Bottrell, William. *Traditions and Hearthside Stories of West Cornwall*. Cornwall, Penzance: privately printed, 1870. Second Series, Penzance: Beare and Son (privately printed), 1873.

Bray, Anna Eliza. *A Description of the Part of Devonshire Bordering on the Tamar and the Tavy; its Natural History, Manners, Customs, Superstitions, . . .etc.* 3 vols. London: John Murray, 1836.

———. *A Peer at the Pixies or Legends of the West*. London: Grant, 1854.

Briggs, Katharine M. *The Anatomy of Puck: An Examination of Beliefs Among Shakespeare's Contemporaries*. London: Routledge, 1959.

———. *A Dictionary of Fairies: Hobgoblins, Brownies, Bogies and Other Supernatural Creatures.* Harmondsworth: Penguin, 1977.

———. *The Fairies in English Tradition and Literature*. Chicago: University of Chicago Press, 1967.

———. "Fairies." *Encyclopedia of Occultism and Parapsychology*, 2nd ed. 3 vols. Detroit: Gale, 1984.

———. "Fairies." *Man, Myth, and Magic: an Illustrated Encyclopedia of the Supernatural*. Vol. 2. New York: Marshall Cavendish, 1970.

———. *The Vanishing People: A Study of Traditional Fairy Beliefs*. London: B. T. Batsford, 1978.

Briggs, Katharine, and Ruth L. Tongue, eds. *Folktales of England*. Chicago: University of Chicago Press, 1965.

Britten, James. "Irish Folk-Tales." *Folk-Lore Journal* 2 (1884): 193–97.

Buchan, John. *The African Colony: Studies in the Reconstruction*. Edinburgh: Blackwood, 1903.

Burne, Charlotte Sophia. *Shropshire Folk-Lore*. London: Trubner, 1883.

"Burning of the Woman Cleary." *Irish Times*, Thursday, 28 March 1895. n.p.

Burrows, Guy. *The Land of the Pygmies*. Intro. H. M. Stanley. London: C. Arthur Pearson, 1898.

Byrne, Patrick F. *Tales of the Banshee*. Cork: Mercier, 1987.

Campbell, Archibald. *Waifs and Strays of Celtic Tradition*. Argylshire series, no. 1–5. London: David Nutt, 1889–95.

Campbell, Lady Archibald. "Faerie Ireland." *Occult Review* 6 (1907): 259–74.

———. " 'The Men of Peace': Faerie Scotland." *Occult Review* 9 (1909): 25–39.

Campbell, J. F. *Popular Tales of the West Highlands*. New ed. 4 vols. 1893. Reprinted, London: Wildwood House, 1984.

Campbell, John Gregorson. *Superstitions of the Highlands and Islands of Scotland*. Glascow: James MacLehose, 1900.

———. *Witchcraft and Second Sight in the Highlands and Islands of Scotland*. Glasgow: James MacLehose, 1902.

Carleton, William. *Traits and Stories of the Irish Peasantry*. New ed. London: William Tegg, n.d.

Carlyle, Thomas. *The French Revolution: A History*. New York: Modern Library, n.d.

Carmichael, Alexander. *Carmina Gadelica: Hymns and Incantations . . . Orally Collected in the Highlands and Islands of Scotland*. 5 vols. 1900. Reprinted, Edinburgh: Oliver and Boyd, 1928.

Chambers, Robert. *Popular Rhymes of Scotland, with illustrations, Chiefly Collected from Oral Sources*. Edinburgh: W. Hunter, 1826.

Clodd, Edward. *Tom Tit Tot: An Essay on Savage Philosophy in Folk-Tale*. London: Duckworth, 1898.

"Cottingley Fairy Photographs Vertical File." Conan Doyle Collection. Toronto Metropolitan Library.

County Folk-Lore: Gloucestershire, Suffolk, Leicestershire, and Rutland. The Folk-Lore Society. London: David Nutt, 1895.

Cox, George W. *An Introduction to the Comparative Science of Mythology and Folklore*. London: C.K. Paul, 1881.

Cox, Marian Roalfe. *An Introduction to Folk-Lore*. London: Nutt, 1895.

Croker, T[homas]. Crofton. *Fairy Legends and Traditions of the South of Ireland*. 3 vols. Ed T. Wright. London: William Tegg, 1825–28.

Cromek, R. H. [Allan Cunningham]. *Remains of Nithsdale and Galloway Song: With Historical and Traditional Notes relative to the Manners and Customs of the Peasantry*. 1810. Reprinted, Paisley: Alexander Gardner, 1880.

Cross, Tom Peete. "Celtic Elements in the Lays of Lanval and Graelent." *Modern Philology* 12 (1915): 585–646.

Crossley-Holland, Kevin, ed. *Folk Tales of the British Isles*. New York: Pantheon, 1985.

Cunningham, Allan. *Traditional Tales of the English and Scottish Peasantry*. London: George Routledge and Sons, 1887.

Curtin, Jeremiah. *Tales of the Fairies and of the Ghost World: Collected from Oral Tradition in South West Munster*. London: David Nutt, 1895.

———. *Myths and Folk-Lore of Ireland*. Boston: Little, Brown, 1889.

Cuthbert, Arthur A. *The Life and World-Work of Thomas Lake Harris: Written from Direct Personal Knowledge*. Glasgow: C.W. Pearce, 1909.

Dalyell, John Graham. *The Darker Superstitions of Scotland*. Glasgow: Richard Griffen, 1835.

Danaher, Kevin. *Folktales of the Irish Countryside*. Cork: Mercier, 1967.

Darwin, Charles. *The Descent of Man and Selection in Relation to Sex*. In *The Origin of Species by Means of Natural Selection; or, The Preservation of Favored Races in the Struggle for Life* and *The Descent of Man and Selection in Relation to Sex*. New York: Modern Library, 1936.

———. *The Expression of the Emotions in Man and Animals*. 1872. New York: Philosophical Library, 1955.

Dasent, George Webbe. *Popular Tales from the Norse*. Edinburgh: Edmonston and Douglas, 1859.

De Kay, Charles. "Women in Early Ireland," *Century Illustrated Monthly Magazine* 38, new series 16 (1889):433–42.

Deane, Tony, and Tony Shaw. *The Folklore of Cornwall*. The Folklore of the British Isles, series ed. Venetia J. Newall. Totowa, N.J.: Rowman and Littlefield, 1975.

Dorson, Richard M., ed. *Peasant Customs and Savage Myths: Selections from the British Folklorists*. 2 vols. London: Routledge and Kegan Paul, 1968.

Douglas, George, ed. "The Glooming Bucht." *Scottish Fairy and Folk Tales*. London: Scott, 1893.

Dowding, Chief Marshal Lord. *The Dark Star*. London: Museum Press, 1951.

Doyle, Sir Arthur Conan. *The Coming of the Fairies*. London: Hodder and Stoughton, 1922.

———. "The Cottingley Fairies: An Epilogue." *Strand*, February 1923.

———. *The Edge of the Unknown*. London: John Murray, 1930.

Doyle, Richard. *In Fairyland: A Series of Pictures from the Elf-World*. London: Michael Joseph/Webb & Bower, n.d.

Dublin University Magazine 90 (1879): 696. Editorial note on W. F. Barrett's "The Demons of Derrigonelly."

"Dwarfs and Elves, On." *All the Year Round,* new series, 29 (1882): 64−67.

Dyer, T. F. Thiselton. *The Folk-Lore of Plants.* London: Chatto and Windus, 1889.

Edmondston, Eliza. *Sketches and Tales of the Shetland Islands.* Edinburgh: Sutherland and Knox, 1856.

Engels, Frederick. *The Origin of the Family, Private Property and the State.* Ed. Eleanor Burke Leacock. London: Lawrence and Wishart, 1972.

Evans, Arthur J. "The Rollright Stones and Their Folk-Lore." *Folk-Lore* 6 (1895): 6−51.

Evans, Hugh. *The Gorse Glen.* Trans. E. Morgan Humphreys. Liverpool: Brython, 1948.

Evans-Wentz, W[alter]. Y[eeling]. *The Fairy-Faith in Celtic Countries.* 1911. Reprinted, n.p. University Books, 1966.

"Evidence of Mrs. Burke's Daughter." *Irish Times,* 28 March 1895, n.p.

"Extraordinary Case in Tipperary." *Cork Examiner,* 27 March 1995, p. 7.

"Extraordinary Case in Tipperary." *Irish Times,* 27 March 1895, p. 5.

"Fairy Legends of the County Donegal." *All the Year Round* 28 (1882): 461−69.

"Fairies in New Ross." *Illustrated Magazine of Art* (1853): 131.

Farrer, James Anson. *Primitive Manners and Customs.* London: Chatto and Windus, 1879.

Fenton, I. D. "Where The Fairies Hide." *Once a Week,* 10 February 1866, pp. 151−54.

Fergusson, R. Menzies. *Rambling Sketches in the Far North, and Orcadian Musings.* London: Simpkin, Marshall, 1883.

Findhorn Community, *The Findhorn Garden.* London: Wildwood House, 1975.

Gardner, Edward L. *Fairies: The Cottingley Photographs and their Sequels.* London: Theo-sophical Publishing House, 1945.

Gill, W. Walter. *Second Manx Scrapbook.* London: Arrowsmith, 1932.

———. *Third Manx Scrapbook.* London: Arrowsmith, 1963.

Glassie, Henry. *Passing the Time in Ballymenone: Culture and History of an Ulster Community.* Philadelphia: University of Pennsylvania Press, 1982.

Gomme, George Laurence. *English Traditional Lore.* London: Stock, 1885.

———. *Ethnology in Folklore.* London: Trubner, 1892.

Gordon-Cumming, Constance F. *From the Hebrides to the Himalayas: A Sketch of Eighteen Months' Wanderings in Western Isles and Eastern Highlands.* 2 vols. Vol. 1. London: Sampson, Low, 1876.

Gregor, Rev. Walter. "Stories of Fairies from Scotland." *Folk-Lore Journal* 1 (1883): 25−27, 55−58.

Gregory, Lady Augusta. *The Kiltartan Wonder Book.* New York: Dutton, 1911.

———. *Visions and Beliefs in the West of Ireland.* 2 vols. New York: Putnam, 1920.

Grogan, Ewart S. "Through Africa From the Cape to Cairo." *Geographical Journal: Including the Proceedings of the Royal Geographical Society* 16 (July−Dec. 1900): 164−83.

Groome, Francis Hindes. *Gypsy Folk-Tales.* London: Hurst and Blackett, 1899.

———. *In Gypsy Tents.* Edinburgh: Nimmo, 1880.

———. "The Influence of the Gypsies on the Superstitions of the English Folk." *International Folk-Lore Congress, 1891: Papers and Transactions.* Ed. Joseph Jacobs and Alfred Nutt. London: David Nutt, 1892.

Gutch, Eliza. *Examples of Printed Folk-Lore Concerning the North Riding of Yorkshire, York and the Ainsty.* London: David Nutt, 1901.

Haggard, Sir H. Rider. *The Days of My Life: An Autobiography.* Ed. C. J. Longman. 2 vols. London: Longmans, Green, 1926.

Haliburton, R[obert]. G[rant]. *Dwarf Survivals and Traditions as to Pygmy Races.* London: n.p. 1895.

———. *The Dwarfs of Mount Atlas.* London: Alexander and Shepheard, 1891.

————. *"The Holy Land of Punt": Racial Dwarfs in the Atlas and the Pyrenees.* London: Alexander and Shepheard, 1893.

————. *How a Race of Pgymies was Found in North Africa and Spain.* Toronto: privately printed, Arbuthnot Bros., 1897.

Hall, Frederic T. *The Pedigree of the Devil.* London: Trubner, 1883.

Hall, Mrs. S. C. [Anna Maria]. *Tales of Irish Life and Character.* Edinburgh: Foulis, 1909.

Hardinge-Britten, Emma. "Nature Spirits and Elementals." *Light* 1 (3 Dec. 1881): 382.

Hardwick, Charles. *Traditions, Superstitions, and Folk-Lore: (Chiefly Lancashire and the North of England).* Manchester: Ireland, 1872.

Hartland, Edwin Sidney. *Mythology and Folktales: Their Relation and Interpretation.* London: David Nutt, 1900.

————. *The Science of Fairy Tales: An Inquiry into Fairy Mythology.* London: Scott, 1891.

Hartmann, Franz. "Some Remarks about the Spirits of Nature." *Occult Review* 14, pt. 2 (July—Dec. 1911): 316—22.

Hawken, Paul. *The Magic of Findhorn.* New York: Harper and Row, 1975.

Hazlitt, W. C. *Fairy Tales, Legends and Romances Illustrating Shakespeare and Other Early English Writers: To which are prefixed. . .1. On Pygmies   2.On Fairies by Joseph Ritson.* London: Kerslake, 1875.

Henderson, William. *Notes on the Folk Lore of the Northern Counties of England and the Borders.* 1866. Reprinted, Yorkshire: EP Publishing Limited, 1973.

Hewlett, Maurice. *The Lore of Proserpine.* New York: Charles Scribner's Sons, 1913.

————. "On Fairies." *English Review*, March 1911, pp. 643—48.

Hinde, Sidney Langford. *The Fall of the Congo Arabs.* 1897. Reprinted, New York: Negro Universities Press, n.d.

Hodson, Geoffrey. *Fairies at Work and at Play.* Wheaton, Ill.: Theosophical Publishing House, 1982.

Howells, W[illiam]. *Cambrian Superstitions comprising Ghosts, Omens, Witchcraft, Traditions, &c.* London: Longman, 1831.

Hull, Eleanor. *Folklore of the British Isles.* London: Methuen, 1928.

Hunt, Leigh. "Fairies." *Leigh Hunt's London Journal*, 1 October 1834, pp. 209—11; continued 15 October 1834, pp. 231—32.

Hunt, Robert. *Popular Romances of the West of England; or, The Drolls, Traditions, and Superstitions of Old Cornwall.* First and Second Series. 2 vols. London: J.C. Hotten, 1865.

J. H. C. "Chaucer's Canterbury Tales." *Notes and Queries*, 4th series, 2 (July—Dec. 1868): 197.

Jacobs, Joseph. "Childe Rowland." *Folk-Lore* 2 (1891): 182—97.

————, ed. *English Fairy Tales.* 3rd ed. New York: Putnam, [1898].

Jacobs, Joseph, and Alfred Nutt, eds. *The International Folk-Lore Congress, 1891. Papers and Transactions.* London: David Nutt, 1892.

Johnston, Sir Harry. "The Pygmies and Ape-like Men of the Uganda Borderland." *Pall Mall Magazine* 26 (Jan.—April 1902): 173—84.

Jones, Edmund of the Tranch. *A Relation of Apparitions of Spirits in the County of Monmouth, and the Principality of Wales. . . by the late Rev. Edmund Jones of the Tranch.* Newport, Monmouthshire: E. Lewis, 1813.

Jones, T[homas]. Gwynn. *Welsh Folklore and Folk-Custom.* Cambridge: D.S. Brewer, 1979.

Jones-Baker, Doris. *The Folklore of Hertfordshire.* The Folklore of the British Isles, series ed. Venetia J. Newall. Totowa, N.J.: Rowman and Littlefield, 1977.

Keightley, Thomas. *The Fairy Mythology: Illustrative of the Romance and Superstition of Various Countries.* 2 vols. London: Whittaker, Treacher, 1833. Rev. ed., 1850. Reprinted, New York: AMS, 1968.

Kemble, John Mitchell. *The Saxons in England: A History of the English Commonwealth till the Period of the Norman Conquest.* 2 vols. London: Longman, 1849.

Kennedy, Patrick. *Legendary Fictions of the Irish Celts*. London: Macmillan, 1866.

Kinahan, G. H. "Notes on Irish Folk-Lore." *Folk-Lore Record* 4 (1881): 96–125.

Kirk, Robert. *The Secret Commonwealth of Elves, Fauns and Fairies: A Study in Folklore and Psychical Research*. Ed. Andrew Lang. London: Nutt, 1893.

Lang, Andrew. "Fairies." *Encyclopedia Britannica*, 11th ed., 1911.

———. "The Folk-Lore of France." *Folk-Lore Record* 1 (1878): 99–117.

———. Introduction, *The International Folk-Lore Congress, 1891. Papers and Transactions*. London: David Nutt, 1892.

———. *My Own Fairy Book (Prince Prigio, Gold of Fairnilee)*. New York: Caldwell, n.d.

———. Introduction to *Grimm's Household Tales with the Author's Notes*. Trans. Margaret Hunt. London: George Bell, 1884.

———., ed. *The Blue Fairy Book*. New York: A.L. Burt, 1899.

———., ed. *The Lilac Fairy Book*. New York: A.L. Burt, 1910.

LeFanu, W. R. *Seventy Years of Irish Life: Being Anecdotes and Reminiscences*. London: Edward Arnold, 1928.

Leadbeater, Charles W. *The Astral Plane: Its Scenery, Inhabitants and Phenomena*. London: Theosophical Publishing Society, 1895.

———. *The Hidden Side of Things*. Adjar, India: Theosophical Publishing House, 1974.

Leather, Ella M. *The Folk-Lore of Herefordshire, Collected From Oral and Printed Sources*. Hereford: Jakeman and Carver, 1912.

"Legend of the Rollright Stones." *Folk-Lore Record* 2, 3 (1879): 165–193.

Leslie, Robert Murray. "Pygmy or Pigmy." *Encyclopedia Britannica*, 11th ed., 1911.

Lewes, Mary. *The Queer Side of Things*. London: Selwyn and Blount, 1923.

———. *Stranger Than Fiction (Being Tales from the Byways of Ghosts and Folk-Lore)*. London: Rider, 1911.

Light: A Journal of Psychical, Occult, and Mystical Research 1 (1881): passim; and 33 (1913).

Lloyd, A[lbert]. B. *In Dwarf Land and Cannibal Country: A Record of Travel and Discovery in Central Africa*. London: T. Fisher Unwin, 1900.

L. M. C. "Folk-lore of the County Donegal." *Cornhill Magazine* 35 (1877): 172–81.

Logan, Patrick. *The Old Gods: The Facts about Irish Fairies*. Belfast: Appletree, 1981.

Lover, Samuel. *Legends and Stories of Ireland*. Dublin: Wakeman, 1832.

Lysaght, Patricia. *The Banshee: The Irish Supernatural Death-Messenger*. Dublin: Glendale Press, 1986.

———. "Irish Banshee Traditions: A Preliminary Survey." *Béaloideas* 42–44 (1974–76): 94–119.

Macaulay, Thomas Babington. *History of England From the Accession of James II*. 5 vols. Philadelphia: E.H. Butler, 1856–61.

MacCulloch, J[ohn]. A[rnott]. "Changelings." *Encyclopedia of Religion and Ethics*. Vol 3. New York: Scribner's, 1911.

———. *The Childhood of Fiction: A Study of Folk Tales and Primitive Thought*. London: John Murray, 1905.

———. "Fairy." *Encyclopedia of Religion and Ethics*. Vol. 5. Edinburgh: T. and T. Clark, 1912.

MacDougall, James. *Highland Fairy Legends: Collected from Oral Tradition by Rev. James MacDougall*. Ed. Rev. George Calder. 1910. Reprinted, Totowa, N.J.: Rowman and Littlefield, 1978.

MacGregor, Alasdair Alpin. *The Peat-Fire Flame*. London: 1937.

Macgregor, Alexander. *Highland Superstitions connected with the Druids, Fairies, Sacred Wells and Lochs. . .[and] Highland Customs and Beliefs*. Stirling: Mackay, 1901.

Machen, Arthur. *Dog and Duck*. New York: Knopf, 1924.

———. *Dreads and Drolls*. New York: Alfred A. Knopf, 1926.

———. *Things Near and Far*. London: Martin Secker, 1923. Vol. 9 in *The Caerleon Edition of the Works of Arthur Machen*.

Mackinlay, James M. *Folklore of Scottish Lochs and Springs*. Glasgow: William Hodge, 1893.

MacManus, D. A. *The Middle Kingdom: The Faerie World of Ireland*. Gerrards Cross, Bucks.: n.p., 1973.

MacRitchie, David. *Fians, Fairies, and Picts*. London: Kegan Paul, 1893.

———. "Hints of Evolution in Tradition." Paper given before the British Association (Section of Anthropology), Glasgow, Scotland, 18 September 1901.

———. "The Historical Aspect of Folk-Lore." *Transactions of the International Folk-Lore Congress*. London: D. Nutt, 1892. 103–12.

———. *The Testimony of Tradition*. London: Kegan Paul, 1890.

Mallet, Paul Henri. *Northern Antiquities; or An Historical Account of the Manners, Customs, Religion and Laws . . . of the Ancient Scandinavians*. 2 vols. Trans. Bishop [Thomas] Percy. London: H. G. Bohn, 1847.

Marwick, Ernest W. *The Folklore of Orkney and Shetland*. Totowa, N.J.: Rowman and Littlefield, 1975.

———. *An Orkney Anthology: The Selected Works of Ernest Walker Markwick*. Vol. 1. Ed. John D. M. Robertson. Edinburgh: Scottish Academic Press, 1991.

McAnally, D. R. *Irish Wonders: The Ghosts, Giants, Pookas, Demons, Leprechawns, Banshees, Fairies, Witches, Widows, Old Maids, and other Marvels of the Emerald Isle*. Boston: Houghton, Mifflin, 1888.

McClintock, Letitia. "Folklore of the County Donegal—The Fairies." *Dublin University Magazine* 89 (1877): 241–49.

McLennan, John F. *Primitive Marriage: An Inquiry into the Origin of the Form of Capture in Marriage Ceremonies*. Edinburgh: Black, 1865.

McNeill, F. Marian. *The Silver Bough: Scottish Folk-Lore and Folk-Belief*. Vol. 1. Edinburgh: Canongate, 1989.

Merton, Ambrose [William John Thoms]. "Superstitions and Beliefs." *Athenaeum*, nu. 983, 29 August 1846, p. 55.

Miller, Hugh. *The Old Red Sandstone or New Walks in an Old Field*. 17th ed. Edinburgh: William Nimmo, 1873.

———. *Scenes and Legends of the North of Scotland or, the Traditional History of Cromarty*. 2nd ed. London: Johnstone and Hunter, 1850.

Mitchell, Arthur. *The Past in the Present: What Is Civilization?* Edinburgh: D. Douglas, 1880.

Montfaucon de Villars, Abbe N. de. *Comte de Gabalis* (1670). Trans. Lotus Dudley. New York: Macoy, 1922.

Morley, Henry. *Memoirs of Bartholomew Fair*. Rev. ed. London: Chatto and Windus, 1880.

"Negro Nileland and Uganda." *Quarterly Review* 194 (July 1901): 1–32.

Norway, Arthur H. *Highways and Byeways in Devon and Cornwall*. London: Macmillan, 1911.

Nutt, Alfred. "Monsieur Sebillot's Scheme for the Collection and Classification of Folk-Lore." *Folk-Lore Record* 3, pt. 2 (1881): 195–200.

Nutt, Alfred, and Joseph Jacobs. "Mr. Stuart-Glennie on the Origins of Matriarchy." *Folk-Lore* 2 (1891): 367–72.

Nutt, Alfred, and Kuno Meyer. *The Voyage of Bran, with an Essay upon the Irish Vision of the Happy Otherworld and the Celtic Doctrine of Re-Birth*. 2 vols. London: David Nutt, 1895.

O Giollain, Diarmuid. "The Leipreachan and Fairies, Dwarfs and the Household Familiar: A Comparative Study." *Béaloideas* 52 (1984): 75–150.

O'Donnell, Eliot. *The Banshee*. London: Sands, n.d. (c. 1917).

O'Sullivan, Sean, ed. *Folktales of Ireland*. Chicago: University of Chicago Press, 1966.

Ormonde, H. "A Chat About Fairies." *Cassells Family Magazine* (1891): 691–93.

Palmer, Kingsley. *The Folklore of Somerset*. Folklore of the British Isles, series ed. Venetia J. Newall. Totowa, N.J.: Rowman and Littlefield, 1976.

Poole, Charles Henry. *The Customs, Superstitions, and Legends of the County of Stafford*. London: Rowney, 1875.

Porter, Enid. *The Folklore of East Anglia.* Folklore of the British Isles, series ed. Venetia J. Newall. Totowa, N.J.: Rowman and Littlefield, 1967.

"Prisoners Before the Magistrates." *Cork Examiner,* 27 March 1895, p. 8+.

Raven, Jon. *The Folklore of Staffordshire.* Folklore of the British Isles, series ed. Venetia J. Newall. Totowa, N.J.: Rowman and Littlefield, 1978.

Rhys, John. *Celtic Folklore: Welsh and Manx.* 2 vols. 1901. Reprinted, London: Wildwood House, 1980.

———. "Manx Folk-lore and Superstitions." *Folk-Lore,* 2 (1891): 284–313.

———. "Welsh Fairies." *Nineteenth Century* 30 (1891): 564–74.

Robertson, R. Macdonald. *Selected Highlands Folktales.* London: David and Charles, 1961.

Robertson, W. Graham. *Life Was Worth Living.* New York: Harper and Bros., n.d.

Roby, John. *Traditions of Lancashire.* 2 vols. London: George Routledge and Sons, 1882.

Rolleston, T. W. *Myths and Legends of the Celtic Race.* London: Constable, 1985.

Rowling, Marjorie. *The Folklore of the Lake District.* Folklore of the British Isles, series ed. Venetia J. Newall. Totowa, N.J.: Rowman and Littlefield, 1976.

Sands, J. "Curious Superstitions in Tiree." *Celtic Magazine* 8 (1883): 252–55.

Scott, Cyril. *The Boy Who Saw True.* London: P. Nevill, 1953.

Scott, Michael. *Irish Folk and Fairy Tales.* 3 vols. London: Sphere, 1984.

Scott, Mina H. "Islay Beliefs." *Occult Review* 16 (1912): 358–63.

Scott, Sir Walter. *Letters on Demonology and Witchcraft, Adressed to J. G. Lockhart, Esq.* 1830. Reprinted, New York: Ace, 1970.

———. *Minstrelsy of the Scottish Border.* Ed. T. F. Henderson. 2 vols. Edinburgh: Oliver and Boyd, 1932.

Shortt, Vere D. "Fairy Faith in Ireland." *Occult Review* 18 (1913): 70–78.

"Shocking Affair in Co. Tipperary: Body of the Missing Woman found Burned and Buried." *Cork Examiner,* 25 March 1895, p. 1.

"Sketches of Superstitions: The Fairies of British Superstition." *Chambers Edinburgh Journal,* 18 April 1840, pp. 103–4.

Sikes, Wirt. *British Goblins: Welsh Folk-Lore, Fairy Mythology, Legends and Traditions.* Boston: Osgood, 1881.

Simpson, Eve Blantyre. *Folk Lore in Lowland Scotland.* London: Dent, 1908.

Simpson, Jacqueline. *The Folklore of the Welsh Border.* Folklore of the British Isles, series ed. Venetia J. Newall. Totowa, N.J.: Rowman and Littlefield, 1976.

Smith, Charles C. "Fairies at Ilkley Wells." *Folk-Lore Record* 1 (1878): 229–31.

Society for Psychical Research. *Proceedings* 25 (1911): passim., especially presidential address, Andrew Lang; and W. F. Barrett, "Poltergeists, Old and New," pp. 377–412.

"South Tipperary Horror." *Cork Examiner,* 26 March 1895, p. 3.

Southey, Robert. "'Home Tours'—Mrs. Bray's 'Letters on Devonshire.'" *Quarterly Review* 59 (1836): 275–320.

Spencer, Herbert. *The Principles of Sociology.* 2 vols. 3rd ed. New York: Appleton, 1915.

Stanley, Henry M[orton]. *In Darkest Africa, or the Quest Rescue and Retreat of Emin, Governor of Equatoria.* 2 vols. London: Sampson Low, 1890.

Stevenson, Robert Louis. *The Essays of Robert Louis Stevenson: A Selection.* London: Macdonald, 1950.

Strieber, Whitley. *Communion: A True Story, Encounters with the Unknown.* London: Arrow, 1987.

"Tale of Anglesey." *Notes and Queries,* 4th series, n. 9 (Jan.–June 1872): 132.

Thorpe, Benjamin. *Yule-Tide Stories: A Collection of Scandinavian and North German Tales and Traditions, from the Swedish, Danish, and German.* London: Bohn, 1853.

"Tipperary Horror" and "Fairy Doctor and Others." *Cork Examiner,* 29 March 1895, pp. 5–6.

"Tipperary Horror" and "A Visit to the Scene." *Cork Examiner,* 28 March 1895, p. 5+.

"Tipperary Horror: The Last Chapter." *Cork Examiner*, 30 March 1895, p. 5.

Tweedale, Violet. *Ghosts I Have Seen and Other Psychic Experiences.* 2nd ed. London: Herbert Jenkins, 1920.

Tylor, Edward Burnett. *The Origins of Culture* (originally published as chapters 1–10 of *Primitive Culture*, 1871). New York: Harper and Row, 1958.

―――. *Religion in Primitive Culture* (originally published as chapters 11–19 of *Primitive Culture*, 1871) New York: Harper and Row, 1958.

Tyson, Edward. *A Philosophical Essay Concerning the Pygmies of the Ancients.* Ed. Bertram C. A. Windle. 1894. Reprinted, Freeport, N.Y.: Books for Libraries, 1972.

Van Gelder, Dora. *The Real World of Fairies.* Wheaton, Ill.: Theosophical Publishing House, 1977.

Vize, Maunsell. "Some Adventures With Fairies." *Occult Review* 36 (1922): 375–86.

Waldron, George. *The History and Description of the Isle of Man.* London: Bickerton, 1744.

Westermarck, Edward Alexander. *The History of Human Marriage.* 5th ed. 2 vols. London: Macmillan, 1921.

Whitlock, Ralph. *The Folklore of Devon.* Folklore of the British Isles, series ed. Venetia J. Newall. Totowa, N.J.: Rowman and Littlefield, 1977.

Wilde, Lady [Speranza]. *Ancient Legends, Mystic Charms and Superstitions of Ireland.* Boston: Ticknor, 1888.

Wilde, [Sir] W[illiam]. R. *Irish Popular Superstitions.* 1852. Reprinted, Dublin: Irish Academic Press, 1979.

"Witch-Burning Superstition." *Cork Examiner*, 29 March 1895, p. 6.

Wood, Edward J. *Giants and Dwarfs.* London: Richard Bentley, 1868.

Wood-Martin, W. G. *Traces of the Elder Faiths of Ireland: A Folklore Sketch.* 2 vols. London: Longmans, 1902.

Yearsley, Macleod. *The Folklore of Fairy-Tale.* London: Watts, 1924.

Yeats, William Butler. *Memoirs.* Ed. Denis Donoghue. New York: Macmillan, 1973.

―――. *Mythologies: The Celtic Twilight, The Secret Rose, Stories of Red Hanrahan, Rosa Alchemica, etc.* New York: Collier Books, 1959.

―――. *Unpublished Prose by W. B. Yeats.* 2 vols. Ed. John P. Frayne and Colton Johnson. New York: Columbia University Press, 1976.

―――, ed. *Irish Fairy and Folk Tales* (1899). Reprinted, New York: Barnes & Noble, 1993.

"You Can't Believe in Fairies: Famous British Photos Unmasked as Phonies After 66 Years." *Toronto Star*, 19 March 1983, p. A3.

Literary and Visual Sources

Allderidge, Patricia. *The Late Richard Dadd: 1817–1886.* London: Tate Gallery, 1974.

―――. *Richard Dadd.* London: Academy, 1974.

Allingham, William. *Long Ballads and Stories.* London: Bell, 1877.

Andersen, Hans Christian. *The Complete Fairy Tales and Stories.* Trans. Erik Christian Haugaard. New York: Doubleday Anchor, 1974.

Auerbach, Nina, and U. C. Knoepflmacher, eds. *Forbidden Journeys: Fairy Tales and Fantasies by Victorian Women Writers.* Chicago: University of Chicago Press, 1992.

Barrie, J. M. *The Little White Bird: Or Adventures in Kensington Garden* in *The Novels, Tales, and Sketches of J. M. Barrie.* Vol. 11. New York: Scribners, 1927.

―――. *Peter Pan.* New York: Signet, 1984.

―――. *Peter Pan: A Fantasy in Five Acts.* New York: Samuel French, n.d.

―――. *The Plays of J. M. Barrie: Dear Brutus, Mary Rose: A Play in Three Acts.* New York: Scribner's, 1938.

―――. *When Wendy Grew Up: An Afterthought.* New York: Dutton, 1958.

Beardsley, Aubrey. *The Early Work of Aubrey Beardsley*. New York: Dover, 1967.

———. *The Later Work of Aubrey Beardsley*. New York: Da Capo Press, 1967.

Besant, (Sir) Walter. *The Changeling*. London: Chatto and Windus, 1899.

Besant, Walter, and James Rice. *The Case of Mr. Lucraft and Other Tales*. London: Sampson Low, 1876.

Black, William. *Kilmeny*. 3 vols. London: Sampson Low, 1870.

Blackwood, Algernon. *Best Ghost Stories of Algernon Blackwood*. Ed. E. F. Bleiler. New York: Dover, 1973.

———. *Pan's Garden*. London: Macmillan, 1912.

———. *A Prisoner in Fairyland (The Book that 'Uncle Paul' Wrote)*. London: Macmillan, 1913.

———. *Selected Tales of Algernon Blackwood*. London: John Baker, 1964.

———. *Ten Minute Stories*. 1914. Reprinted, Short Story Reprint Series. Freeport, N.Y.: Books for Libraries, 1969.

Blake, William. *The Poetry and Prose of William Blake*. Ed. David V. Erdman and Harold Bloom. Garden City, N.Y.: Doubleday, 1965.

Brontë, Charlotte. *Jane Eyre*. Ed. Richard J. Dunn. Norton Critical Edition. New York: W.W. Norton, 1971.

———. *Shirley*. New York: Eagle Books, n.d.

Brontë, Emily. *Wuthering Heights: Text, Sources, Criticism*. Ed. Thomas C. Moser. New York: Harcourt, Brace, 1962.

Buchan, John. *The Watcher by the Threshold and Other Tales*. Edinburgh: William Blackwood, 1902.

Burroughs, E[dgar]. R[ice]. *The Return of Tarzan*. New York: Balantine Books, 1990.

———. *Tarzan and the Jewels of Opar*. New York: Random House, Balantine Books, 1963.

———. *Tarzan of the Apes*. New York: Ballantine Books, 1990.

Carroll, Lewis. *Sylvie and Bruno*. London: Macmillan, 1889.

———. *Sylvie and Bruno (Concluded)*. London: Macmillan, 1893.

Carter, Angela. *The Bloody Chamber and Other Stories*. London: Penguin, 1979.

———. *Nights at the Circus*. London: Penguin, 1985.

Cott, Jonathan, ed. *Beyond the Looking Glass: Extraordinary Works of Fairy Tale and Fantasy*. Intro., Leslie Fiedler. Woodstock, N.Y.: Overlook Press, 1973.

Craik, Dinah Muloch. *Olive*. London: Chapman and Hall, 1850.

Crawford, F. Marion. *Uncanny Tales*. London: T. Fisher Unwin, 1911.

De la Mare, Walter. *The Collected Tales of Walter de la Mare*. New York: Knopf, 1950.

———. *Crossings: A Fairy Play*. London: Faber and Faber, 1923.

———. *Memoirs of a Midget*. New York: Knopf, 1924.

De la Motte Fouqué, Baron Friedrich Heinrich Karl. *Undine*. London: Simpkin and Marshall, 1818.

Dickens, Charles. *Bleak House*. Ed. Norman Page. Harmondsworth, England: Penguin Classic, 1985.

———. *Dombey and Son*. Ed. Edgar Johnson. New York: Dell, 1963.

———. *Hard Times*. Ed. David Craig. Harmondsworth, England: Penguin Classics, 1969.

———. *The Old Curiosity Shop*. Ed. Angus Easson. Harmondsworth, England: Penguin, 1972.

———. *The Pickwick Papers*. New York: Bantam, 1983.

Doyle, Sir Arthur Conan. *The Lost World*. London: J. Murray, 1912.

———. *The Sign of Four*. London: Spencer Blackett, 1890.

Doyle, Charles. Exhibition of Drawings and Studies, "The Humourous and The Terrible," 31 Jan.–13 Feb. 1924. London: Bond Street Galleries, 1924. (Catalogue)

Doyle, Richard. *Richard Doyle and his Family*. Exhibition Catalogue. Victoria and Albert Museum, 1983–84.

Duffy, Sir Charles Gavan, ed. *The Ballad Poetry of Ireland*. 1869. Delmar, N.Y.: Scholars' Facsimiles and Reprints, 1973.

Dunsany, Lord. *A Dreamer's Tales*. London: George Allen, 1910.

————. *The King of Elfland's Daughter*. New York: Putnam, 1924.

————. *The Sword of Welleron and Other Tales of Enchantment*. New York: Devin-Adair, 1954.

————. *The Travel Tales of Mr. Joseph Jorkens*. London: Putnam, 1931.

Eliot, George. *Middlemarch*. Ed. Rosemary Ashton. New York: Penguin Books, 1994.

Engen, Rodney. *Richard Doyle*. Stroud, Glos.: Catalpa Press, 1983.

Fitzmaurice, George. *The Plays of George Fitzmaurice*. Vol. 1. *Dramatic Fantasies*. Ed. Austin Clarke. Dublin: Dolmen Press, 1967. Vol. 2. *Folk Plays*. Ed. Howard K. Slaughter. Dublin: Dolmen Press, 1969.

Fyleman, Rose. *The Rose Fyleman Fairy Book*. New York: Doran, 1923.

Gaskell, Elizabeth. *Mrs. Gaskell's Tales of Mystery and Horror*. Ed. Michael Ashley. London: Victor Gollancz, 1978.

German Literary Fairy Tales. Ed. Frank G. Ryder and Robert M. Browning. German Library, vol 30. New York: Continuum, 1983.

Gilbert, W. S. *Iolanthe or The Peer and the Peri*. In *Complete Plays of Gilbert and Sullivan*. New York: Modern Library, 1936, pp. 237–88.

Grahame, Kenneth. *The Golden Age*. London: Elkin Mathews and John Lane, 1895.

————. *Pagan Papers*. London: Elkin Mathews and John Lane, 1894.

Haggard, H. Rider. *Ayesha: The Return of She*. London: Macdonald, 1965.

————. *The Best Short Stories of Rider Haggard*. Ed. Peter Hainig. London: Michael Joseph, 1981.

————. *She: A History of Adventure*. Harmondsworth, England: Penguin, 1982.

Hambourg, Doria. *Richard Doyle: His Life and Work*. New York: Pelegrini and Cudahy, 1948.

Hardy, Thomas. *Jude the Obscure*. Ed. Irving Howe. Boston: Houghton Mifflin, 1965.

————. *The Mayor of Casterbridge*. London: Penguin, 1978.

————. *The Return of the Native*. Ed. James Gindin. Norton Critical Edition. New York: W.W. Norton, 1969.

Hearn, Michael Patrick, ed. *The Victorian Fairy Tale Book*. New York: Pantheon, 1988.

Herodotus. *The Histories*. Trans. Aubrey de Sélincourt. London: Penguin, 1954.

Hogg, James. *The Works of the Ettrick Shepherd*. Vol. 1. *Tales and Sketches*. Vol. 2. *Poems*. Reprinted, New York: AMS Press, 1973.

Homer. *The Iliad*. Trans. E. V. Rieu. London: Penguin, 1950.

Hopper, Nora. *Ballads in Prose*. London: John Lane, 1894.

————. "Joan O' the Wad: A Pisky Song." *Cornish Magazine* 2 (1882): 361–62.

Housman, Laurence. *The Kind and the Foolish: Short Tales of Myth, Magic, and Miracle*. London: Jonathan Cape, 1952.

Ibsen, Henrik. *A Doll's House*. Trans. William Archer. In *The Chief European Dramatists*, ed. Brander Matthews. Cambridge, Mass.: Houghton Mifflin, 1916.

————. *A Doll's House*. Trans. Rolf Fjelde. In *Four Major Plays*, vol. 1. New York: Signet, 1965.

————. *A Doll's House*. Trans. Peter Watts. In *Plays: The League of Youth, A Doll's House, The Lady From the Sea*. Harmondsworth, England: Penguin, 1965.

————. *The Lady from the Sea*. Trans. Michael Meyer. London: Rupert Hart-Davis, 1960.

James, Montague Rhodes. *The Collected Ghost Stories of M. R. James*. New York: Longmans, Green, 1931.

Johnson, Diana L. *Fantastic Illustration and Design in Britain, 1850–1930*. Exhibition catalogue. Museum of Art, Rhode Island School of Design, 1979.

Kipling, Rudyard. *Limits and Renewals*. New York: Scribner's, 1932.

————. *Puck of Pook's Hill*. Ed. Sarah Wintle. Harmondsworth, England: Penguin, 1987.

————. *Rewards and Fairies*. London: Pan, 1975.

————. *Wee Willie Winkie, and Other Stories*. Allahabad: A. H. Wheeler, 1890.

Lang, Andrew, and May Kendall. *'That Very Mab.'* London: Longmans, Green, 1885.

Leadbeater, C. W. *The Perfume of Egypt and Other Weird Stories*. Madras: Theosophist Office, 1911.

Lee, Tanith. *Dreams of Dark and Light*. Sauk City, Wisconsin: Arkham House, c. 1986.

————. *Red as Blood or Tales from the Sisters Grimmer*. New York: Daw, 1983.

Lee, Vernon. *The Snake Lady and Other Stories*. Ed. Horace Gregory. New York: Grove, 1954.

LeFanu, J[oseph]. S[heridan]. *Ghost Stories and Mysteries*. Ed. E. F. Bleiler. New York: Dover, 1975.

Lytton, Edward Bulwer. *A Strange Story*. Boston, Estes and Lauriat, 1892.

————. *Zanoni*. Boston: Little, Brown, 1897.

Maas, Jeremy. *Victorian Painters*. New York: Abbeville Press, 1984.

MacCarthy, Denis Florence. "The Lianhan Shee." *Dublin University Magazine* 38 (1851): 416–19.

MacDonald, George. *The Complete Fairy Tales of George MacDonald*. New York: Schocken Books, 1977.

————. *The Gifts of the Child Christ: Fairytales and Stories for the Childlike*. Ed. Glenn Edward Sadler. 2 vols. Grand Rapids, Mich.: William B. Eerdmans, 1973.

————. *Phantastes* and *Lilith*. London: Victor Gollancz, 1962.

————. *The Princess and Curdie*. New York: Puffin, 1966.

————. *The Princess and the Goblin*. New York: Puffin, 1964.

Machen, Arthur. *The Strange World of Arthur Machen*. Ed. Arno Eckberg. The Classics of Mystery, vol. 6. New York: Juniper Press, n.d.

Macleod, Fiona [William Sharp]. *"Pharais"* and *"The Mountain Lovers."* New York: Duffield, 1914.

————. *The Sin Eater and Other Tales and Episodes*. New York: Duffield, 1907.

————. *The Washer of the Ford and Other Legendary Moralities*. Edinburgh: Patrick Geddes, 1896.

————. *The Works of "Fiona Macleod."* 7 vols. London: Heinemann, 1912.

MacManus, Anna [Ethna Carbery]. *The Passionate Hearts*. Dublin: M. H. Gill, 1903.

Mew, Charlotte. *Collected Poems of Charlotte Mew*. London: Duckworth, 1953.

Mitford, Bertram. *The Weird of Deadly Hollow: A Tale of the Cape Colony*. London: n.p., 1899.

Monro, Neil. *The Lost Pibroch and Other Sheiling Stories*. Edinburgh: Blackwood, 1896.

Morris, William. *The Earthly Paradise*. Ed. May Morris. Reprinted, New York: Russell and Russell, 1966. Vols. 3–6 of *Collected Works of William Morris*.

————. *The Roots of the Mountains*. Ed. May Morris. Reprinted, New York: Russell and Russell, 1966. Vol. 15 of *Collected Works of William Morris*.

————. *The Wood Beyond the World*. Ed. May Morris. Reprinted, New York: Russell and Russell, 1966. Vol. 17 of *Collected Works of William Morris*.

Murray, Amelia Jane. *A Regency Lady's Faery Bower*. London: Collins, 1985.

Paton, Sir Joseph Noel. *Poems by a Painter*. Edinburgh: William Blackwood, 1861.

————. *Spindrift*. Edinburgh: Blackwood, 1867.

Philpotts, Beatrice. *Fairy Paintings*. London: Ash and Grant, 1978.

————. *Mermaids*. New York: Ballantine Books, 1980.

Rhys, Ernest. *Fairy Gold: A Book of Old English Fairy Tales*. London: Dent, 1907.

Riddell, J. H. *The Banshee's Warning and Other Tales*. 2nd ed. London: Remington, 1894.

Robertson, W. Graham. *Pinkie and the Fairies*. London: Heinemann, 1909.

Rossetti, Christina. "Goblin Market." *Norton Anthology of English Literature*, 6th ed. Ed. Myer Abrams et al. Vol 2. New York: W. W. Norton, 1993, pp. 1479–90.

Scott, Sir Walter. *The Black Dwarf*. Ed. Andrew Lang. Boston: Dana Estes, 1893.

———. *The Monastery*. Cambridge, Mass.: Jenson Society, 1907. Vol.10 in *Works of Sir Walter Scott*.

———. *Peveril of the Peak*. Edinburgh: James Ballantyne, 1824. Vols. 20–22 in *Complete Works of Sir Walter Scott*.

———. *The Pirate*. Edinburgh: James Ballantyne, 1824. Vols. 23–25 in *Complete Works of Sir Walter Scott*.

Sotheby, William. *Oberon, or Huon de Bordeaux: A Mask in Five Acts*. London: Codell, 1802.

Spofford, Harriet Prescott. *The Amber Gods and Other Stories*. Ed. Alfred Bendixen. New Brunswick, N.J.: Rutgers University Press, 1989.

Stephens, James. *The Crock of Gold*. New York: Macmillan, 1924.

Stevenson, Robert Louis. *The Strange Case of Dr. Jeykll and Mr. Hyde and Other Stories*. New York: Putnam, n.d.

Szilagyi, Steve. *Photographing Fairies*. New York: Ballantine, 1992.

Tate Gallery. *Henry Fuseli: 1741–1825*. London: Tate Gallery, 1975.

Waite, A. E., ed. *Elfin Music: An Anthology of English Fairy Poetry*. London: W. Scott, 1888.

Wark, Robert R. *Charles Doyle's Fairyland*. San Marino, Calif.: Huntington Library, 1980.

Warner, Sylvia Townsend. *Kingdoms of Elfin*. New York: Delta, 1978.

———. *One Thing Leading to Another and Other Stories*. Ed. Susanna Pinney. London: Chatto and Windus, 1984.

Wells, H. G. *The Sea Lady: A Tissue of Moonshine*. London: Methuen, 1902.

———. *The Time Machine* and *The Island of Dr. Moreau*. In *The Complete Science Fiction Treasury of H. G. Wells*. New York: Avenal Books, 1978.

———. "Mr. Skelmersdale in Fairyland." *Twelve Stories and a Dream*. London: Macmillan, 1903, pp. 103–27.

Wharton, Edith. *The Custom of the Country*. New York: Charles Scribner's Sons, 1913.

Wilde, Oscar. *The Happy Prince: The Complete Fairy Stories of Oscar Wilde*. London: Duckworth, 1970.

Wood, Michael. "The Piper of Elfhame." *Theosophical Review* 31 (Sept. 1902–Feb.1903): 306–13.

———. *The Willow Weaver and Seven Other Tales*. London: Dent, 1915.

Yeats, William Butler. *Collected Plays of William Butler Yeats*. New ed. New York: Macmillan, 1953.

———. *Poems, A New Edition*. Ed. Richard J. Finneran. New York: Macmillan, 1983.

Zipes, Jack, ed. *Victorian Fairy Tales: The Revolt of the Fairies and Elves*. New York: Metheun, 1987.

Secondary Sources

Achilles, Jochen. "George Fitzmaurice's Dramatic Fantasies: Wicked Old Children in a Disenchanting Land." *Irish University Review* 19: 148–63.

Adlard, John. *The Sports of Cruelty: Fairies, Folk-Songs, Charms and Other Country Matters in the Work of William Blake*. London: Woolf, 1972.

Altick, Richard. *The Shows of London*. Cambridge, Mass.: Belknap Press, 1978.

Arrowsmith, Nancy. *A Field Guide to the Little People*. New York: Hill and Wang, 1977.

Avery, Gillian. *Childhood's Pattern: A Study of the Heroes and Heroines of Children's Fiction: 1770–1950*. London: Hodder and Stoughton, 1975.

Baker, Michael. *The Doyle Diary: The Last Great Conan Doyle Mystery. . .* London: Paddington Press, 1978.

Benwell, Gwen, and Arthur Waugh. *The Sea Enchantress: The Tale of the Mermaid and her Kin*. London: Hutchinson, 1961.

Bolt, Christine. *Victorian Attitudes to Race*. London: Routledge and Kegan Paul, 1971.

Booth, Michael R. *Victorian Spectacular Theatre: 1850–1910*. London: Routledge, 1982.

Bord, Janet, and Colin Bord. *The Secret Country*. London: Paladin, Granada, 1978.

Bottigheimer, Ruth B. *Grimms' Bad Girls and Bold Boys: the Moral and Social Vision of the Tales*. New Haven, Conn.: Yale University Press, 1987.

———. "The Face of Evil." *Fabula* 29, 3–4 (1988): 326–41.

Bradford, Phillips Verner, and Harvey Blume. *Ota: The Pygmy in the Zoo*. New York: St. Martin's, 1992.

Briggs, Julia. *Night Visitors: The Rise and Fall of the English Ghost*. London: Faber, 1977.

Carpenter, Humphrey. *Secret Gardens: A Study of the Golden Age of Children's Literature*. Boston: Houghton Mifflin, 1985.

Cooper, Joe. *The Case of the Cottingley Fairies*. London: Robert Hale, 1990.

Dance, Peter. *Animal Fakes and Frauds*. Maidenhead, Berkshire: Sampson Low, 1976.

Dijkstra, Bram. *Idols of Perversity: Fantasies of Feminine Evil in Fin-de-Siècle Culture*. New York: Oxford University Press, 1986.

Dorson, Richard M. *The British Folklorists: A History*. Chicago: University of Chicago Press, 1968.

Douglas, Mary. *Purity and Danger: An Analysis of the Concepts of Pollution and Taboo*. London: Ark, 1966.

Duerr, Hans Peter. *Dreamtime: Concerning the Boundary between Wilderness and Civilization*. Trans. Felicitas Goodman. Oxford: Basil Blackwell, 1985.

Duffy, Maureen. *The Erotic World of Faery*. New York: Avon, 1972.

Eberly, Susan Schoon. "Fairies and the Folklore of Disability: Changelings, Hybrids, and the Solitary Fairy." In *The Good People: New Folklore Essays*. Ed. Peter Narváez, pp. 227–50. New York: Garland, 1991.

Eglinton, John. *A Memoir of Æ*. London: Macmillan, 1937.

Fee, Elizabeth. "The Sexual Politics of Victorian Social Anthropology." In *Clio's Consciousness Raised: New Prospectives on History of Women*. Ed. Mary S. Hartman and Lois Barner, pp. 86–102. New York: Harper, 1974.

Fiedler, Leslie. *Freaks: Myths and Images of the Secret Self*. New York: Simon and Schuster, 1978.

Frye, Northrop. *Fearful Symmetry: A Study of William Blake*. Princeton, N.J.: Princeton University Press, 1969.

Gilchrist, Alexander. *Life of William Blake Pictor Ignotus: With Selections from his Poems and Other Writings*. Vol. 1. London: Cambridge, 1863.

Goldfarb, Russell M., and Clare R. Goldfarb. *Spiritualism and Nineteenth-Century Letters*. Rutherford, N.J.: Associated University Presses, 1978.

Gould, Stephen Jay. *The Mismeasure of Man*. London: Penguin, 1981.

———. *The Panda's Thumb: More Reflections in Natural History*. London: Penguin, 1980.

Gramsci, Antonio. *Selections from Cultural Writings*. Ed. David Forgacs and Geoffrey Nowell-Smith. Trans. William Boelhower. Cambridge, Mass.: Harvard University Press, 1985.

Green, Roger Lancelyn. *Andrew Lang: A Critical Biography*. Leicester: E. Ward, 1946.

Guest, Ivor. *The Romantic Ballet in England: Its Development, Fulfilment and Decline*. London: Pitman, 1972.

Hammerton, A. James. "Victorian Marriage and the Law of Matrimonial Cruelty." *Victorian Studies* 33, 2 (1990): 269–92.

Haynes, Renee. *The Society for Psychical Research 1882–1982: A History*. London: Macdonald, 1982.

Heuvelmans, Bernard. *On the Track of Unknown Animals*. Trans. Richard Garnett. London: Rubert Hart-Davis, 1958.

Hirsch, Edward. "Yeats's Apocalyptic Horsemen." *Irish Renaissance Annual*, 3. Ed. Dennis Jackson. Newark, Del.: University of Delaware Press, 1982.

Hutchins, Jane. *Discovering Mermaids and Sea Monsters*. Tring, Herts.: Shire Pub., 1968.

Huygen, Wil. *Gnomes*. New York: Abrams, 1977.

Joseph, Gerhard. "Change and the Changeling in *Dombey and Son*." *Dickens Studies Annual* 18 (1989): 179–96.

Kotzin, Michael G. *Dickens and the Fairy Tale*. Bowling Green, Ohio: Bowling Green University Popular Press, 1972.

———. "The Fairy Tale in England, 1800–1870." *Studies in English Literature* 4, 1 (Summer 1970): 130–54.

Kucich, John. *Excess and Restraint in the Novels of Charles Dickens*. Athens, Ga.: University of Georgia Press, 1981.

Leavy, Barbara Fass. *In Search of the Swan Maidens: A Narrative on Folklore and Gender*. New York: New York University Press, 1994.

Lees-Milne, James. *Ancestral Voices*. London: Chatto and Windus, 1975.

Levy, Anita. *Other Women: The Writing of Class, Race, and Gender, 1832–1898*. Princeton, N.J.: Princeton University Press, 1991.

Lewis, C. S. *The Pilgrim's Regress: An Allegorical Apology for Christianity, Reason and Romanticism*. 3rd ed. London: Bles, 1943.

———. *Surprised by Joy: The Shape of My Early Life*. New York: Harcourt, Brace, 1955.

Little, Edmund. *The Fantasts: Studies in J.R.R. Tolkien, Lewis Carroll, Mervyn Peake, Nikolay Gogol and Kenneth Grahame*. Amersham, U.K.: Avebury, 1984.

MacDougall, Hugh A. *Racial Myth in English History: Trojans, Teutons, and Anglo-Saxons*. Montreal, Canada: Harvest House, 1982.

Maitland, Edward. *Anna Kingsford: Her Life, Letters, Diary, and Work*. 2 vols. London: Redway, 1896.

Menefee, Samuel Pyeatt. *Wives for Sale: An Ethnographic Study of British Popular Divorce*. Oxford: Basil Blackwell, 1981.

Munro, Joyce Underwood. "The Invisible Made Visible: The Fairy Changeling as a Folk Articulation of Failure to Thrive in Infants and Children." In *The Good People*. Ed. Peter Narváez, pp. 251–83. New York: Garland, 1991.

Narváez, Peter, ed. *The Good People: New Folklore Essays*. Garland Reference Library of the Humanities, Vol. 1376. New York: Garland, 1991.

Oppenheim, Janet. *The Other World: Spiritualism and Psychical Research in England, 1850–1914*. Cambridge: Cambridge University Press, 1985.

Packer, Alison, et al., *Fairies in Legend and the Arts*. London: Cameron and Tayleur, 1980.

Page, Norman. *Thomas Hardy*. London: Routledge and Kegan Paul, 1977.

Parsons, Coleman O. *Witchcraft and Demonology in Scott's Fiction*. Edinburgh: Oliver and Bouyd, 1964.

Picknett, Lynn. *Flights of Fancy? 100 Years of Paranormal Experiences*. London: Ward Lock, 1987.

Randi, James. *Flim-Flam: Psychics, ESP, Unicorns and other Delusions*. Buffalo, N.Y.: Prometheus Books, 1982.

Rees, Alwyn, and Brinley Rees. *Celtic Heritage: Ancient Tradition in Ireland and Wales*. London: Thames and Hudson, 1961.

Reidar, Th. Christiansen. "Some Notes on the Fairies and the Fairy Faith." In *Hereditas: Essays and Studies Presented to Professor Seamus O' Duilearga*. Ed. Bo Almquist et al., pp. 95–111. Dublin: Folklore of Ireland Society, 1975.

Richards, Thomas. *The Imperial Archive: Knowledge and the Fantasy of Empire*. London: Verso, 1993.

Rose, Jonathan. *The Edwardian Temperament: 1895–1919*. Athens, Ohio: Ohio University Press, 1986.

Russell, Cynthia Eagle. *Sexual Science: The Victorian Construction of Womanhood*. Cambridge, Mass.: Harvard University Press, 1989.

Sanderson, S. F. "The Cottingley Fairy Photographs: A Re-Appraisal of the Evidence." *Folklore* 84 (Summer 1973): 89–103.

Showalter, Elaine. *The Female Malady: Women, Madness, and English Culture, 1830–1980*. New York: Penguin, 1987.

Silver, Carole. "When Rumplestiltskin Ruled: Victorian Fairy Tales." *Victorian Literature and Culture* 22 (1995): 227–36.

Smith, Paul. "The Cottingley Fairies: The End of a Legend." In *The Good People*. Ed. Peter Narváez, pp. 371–406. New York: Garland, 1991.

Smith, Peter Alderson. *W. B. Yeats and the Tribes of Danu: Three Views of Ireland's Fairies*. Gerards Cross, Bucks.: Colin Smythe, 1987.

Spence, Lewis. *British Fairy Origins*. London: Watts, 1946.

———. *The Fairy Tradition in Britain*. London: Rider, 1948.

———. *The History and Origins of Druidism*. 1949. Reprinted, London: Aquarian Press, 1971.

———. *The Magic Arts in Celtic Britain*. London: Rider, 1945.

———. *The Minor Traditions of British Mythology*. 1948. Reprinted, New York: Arno, 1979.

Stewart, Susan. *On Longing: Narratives of the Miniature, the Gigantic, the Souvenir, the Collection*. Baltimore: Johns Hopkins University Press, 1984.

Stocking, George. W. *Victorian Anthropology*. New York: Free Press, 1987.

Stone, Lawrence. *Road to Divorce: England 1530–1987*. London: Oxford University Press, 1990.

Street, Brian V. *The Savage in Literature: Representations of 'Primitive' Society in English Fiction 1858–1920*. London: Routledge, 1975.

Temple, Jean. *Blue Ghost: A Study of Lafcadio Hearn*. New York: Haskell House, 1974.

Thomas, Joyce Augusta. *Inside the Wolf's Belly: Aspects of the Fairy Tale*. Sheffield, England: Sheffield Academic Press, 1989.

Thompson. E. P. *William Morris: Romantic to Revolutionary*. London: Merlin, 1977.

Thomson, David. *The People of the Sea: A Journey in Search of the Seal Legend*. London: Barrie and Rockliff, 1965.

Tuohy, Frank. *Yeats*. New York: Macmillan, 1976.

Twitchell, James B. *The Living Dead: A Study of the Vampire in Romantic Literature*. Durham, N.C.: Duke University Press, 1981.

Zipes, Jack. *Breaking the Magic Spell: Radical Theories of Folk and Fairy Tales*. New York: Methuen, 1984.

INDEX